HORACE

HORACE

A NEW INTERPRETATION

BY

ARCHIBALD Y. *oung* CAMPBELL, M.A.

PROFESSOR OF GREEK IN THE UNIVERSITY OF LIVERPOOL
FORMERLY FELLOW AND LECTURER OF ST. JOHN'S COLLEGE, CAMBRIDGE

liberius si
dixero quid, si forte iocosius, hoc mihi iuris
cum venia dabis: instituebat Horatius hoc me

["If some things I have said are too bold, and others too
jocular, you must allow me at least one excuse—the precedent
of my author himself."—Horace, *Satires* I. iv. 103-5, adapted]

GREENWOOD PRESS, PUBLISHERS
WESTPORT, CONNECTICUT

Originally published in 1924
by Methuen & Co., Ltd., London

First Greenwood Reprinting 1970

Library of Congress Catalogue Card Number 70-109714

SBN 8371-4204-0

Printed in the United States of America

PREFACE

I HAVE to thank three old Cambridge friends, Mr. F. M. Cornford and Mr. D. S. Robertson of Trinity, and Mr. R. Hackforth of Sidney Sussex, for reading parts of this book in manuscript and helping me with criticism. My chief debt, however, is to my colleague, Professor Slater, who has most kindly read and criticised the entire work in proof.

Chapter II. is perhaps stiff reading, and although indispensable to my *thesis*, may be omitted without serious detriment to the understanding of the remaining chapters. The Conspectus, on the other hand, is designed solely as an aid to the reader in following the argument.

CONTENTS

PART I

GENERAL

PART II

PARTICULAR

CONSPECTUS

PART I

GENERAL

CHAPTER I

A CLASSIC AS SEEN BY ROMANTICS

The fountain of Bandusia and its apparently gratuitous pollution—Other and stranger odes—Horatian Habits that puzzle the modern reader—Landor's marginal anathemas — Romanticism generally votes against the Odes — Reason : the Romantic's preference for superficial attractions to the true beauty of form—The XVIIIth Century no true Classic Age, Romantic rather—Its failure to grasp the real point of the Horatian Ode—The so-called " Romantic " Revival is properly much more a Classic Revival—Its new understanding of Form in Lyric—But its poets were prejudiced against Horace as an XVIIIth Century idol ; and XIXth Century perpetuates rather their romantic qualities ; result, Horace's Odes still unappreciated, their fundamental merits unrecognised—Enemies of the Odes among scholars proper—Tyrrell—*Per contra*, Sellar—Contemporary literary spirit dead against Horace—Poetry in the ancient world has a totally different function and position—True appreciation of Horace impossible until that is understood ; therefore object of following chapter will be, radically to revise our conception of Poetry in the light of the Ancient view . . . . *page*

CHAPTER II

THE FUNCTION OF POETRY IN THE ANCIENT WORLD

Poetry, nowadays treated as parasit   upon life, was regarded by the early Greeks as having a function, *viz.*, the spiritual education of the community. This, *the Classical*, conception of it, is right (I.) historically, (II.) theoretically.

Latin literature mainly reproduces Greek forms, but had one native " cycle,"
abortive yet distinguishable : (i) crude lyric, (ii) the fescennines, and early
dramatic satura (iii) (A *and* B) the satura of Ennius—" Roman satire " proper,
i.e., from Lucilius on, has roots in both (ii) and (iii), and accordingly is largely
sophistical, yet still retains to a fair extent a politico-moral function .   *page* 50
Thus through Roman satire the old politico-moral function of Poetry is to a fair
extent restored to Classical Literature, after having lapsed in the Greek
Decadence—How this affects Horace both in his Satires and in his other
work   .   .   .   .   *page* 53

II. (pp. 54-5).
A summary and dogmatic defence of the Classical, or religious-moral, conception
of Poetry—But the Poet does *not* " teach " ; he trains .   .   .   *page* 54

CHAPTER III

HORACE'S OWN THEORY AND PRACTICE OF POETRY

Of the ancient, or classical, conception of Poetry, as defined and illustrated in
the preceding chapter, the most all-round and complete exponent is Horace. He
voices the religious-moral view of Poetry in (i) his statements on the Theory of
Poetry, and (ii) his accounts of Poetic Origins ; and, consistently, he is faithful to
it in (iii) his own poetic practice   .   .   .   .   .   .   *page* 56
i. The Horatian THEORY OF POETRY. The vocation of Poet is a high one ; he has
    a function in the community ; a spiritual and moral function ; a *kind of* a
    priesthood, a priesthood " of the Muses "—*i.e.*, he is dedicated not to this or
    that god, but to the purely *literary* service of gods and heroes in general. He
    is dedicated, also, to the moral education of his fellow-men .   .   *page* 58
ii. Horace on POETIC ORIGINS. Discussion of *Epist.*, II. i. 139-60. Reference
    to other passages   .   .   .   .   *page* 65
iii. Horace in his POETIC PRACTICE. In his mature work—*Odes* and *Epistles*—he
    speaks as " priest of the Muses " and Mentor of his fellow-countrymen. [The
    Epodes and *Satires* show at least the *de*structive or " exorcising " aspect of
    the same function.]   .   .   .   .   *page* 67
As " priest of the Muses," he celebrates gods and heroes. The gods he celebrates
are mostly Greek, the Olympians ; but he celebrates these as a national and
moral poet, because (*a*) they had to a great extent become *national* Roman
gods, (*b*) they traditionally represented the *moral* order. He also celebrates
some strictly *national* Italian deities. His main " hero " is Augustus. In his
serious poems he employs a sacerdotal and oracular style, derived to a large
extent from Pindar.   Formally, his poems are practically all either (1) Hymns,
(2) Prayers, or (3) Injunctions or " Sermons "   .   .   .   *page* 69
In his capacity of Mentor, he is chiefly to be seen in this last-mentioned category ;
these " admonitory addresses " comprise the great majority of the *Odes*, and
the *Epistles* generally   .   .   .   .   *page* 74
The endeavour after an oracular and arresting manner explains many features of
the *Odes*, *e.g.*, the deliberate abruptness and tendency to sudden transitions ;
instances (I. iv and vii) considered, and further explained in light of the particular
" admonitory " purpose in view.   This last is often a key to disconcerting
contrasts between end and beginning of numerous odes.   Further examination
deferred to chapter on the *Odes* (ch. VII.)   .   .   .   .   *page* 76

CHAPTER IV

LIFE AND WORK

Born 65 B.C. at Venusia—History of that town—His father—To school in Rome—
To the University of Athens—The war—Return to Rome—Patronage of
Maecenas—His enlightened conception of Reconstruction—Journey to
Brundisium, and the frogs—*Epodes*—*Satires*, I.—The Sabine farm—Before
Actium—At Actium—Publication of *Satires*, II.—Habits about this time
page 82

PART II

PARTICULAR

CHAPTER V

EXPERIMENT : THE EPODES

CHAPTER VI

FEELING AFTER FORM: THE SATIRES

CHAPTER VII

COMPOSITION: THE ODES

HORACE

CHAPTER VIII

Compromise: The Ars Poetica and Epistles

HORACE

CHAPTER I

A CLASSIC AS SEEN BY ROMANTICS

Non dices hodie, quorsum haec tam putida tendant ?
—HORACE, *Satires* II. vii. 21.

Te flagrantis atrox hora Caniculae
Nescit tangere, tu frigus amabile
    Fessis vomere tauris
      Praebes et pecori vago.
Fies nobilium tu quoque fontium,
Me dicente cavis impositam ilicem
    Saxis, unde loquaces
      Lymphae desiliunt tuae.

THESE words have bewitched generations of readers into thinking *O fons Bandusiae* a good poem. It is perhaps small wonder, for they are very beautiful ; beautiful in the simplicity of the picture they call up, beautiful in their suggestions of rest and coolness and relief from thirst, beautiful, too, no less in their skilful alliteration, with its crisp and ringing dentals (especially in the former stanza) varied by a judicious distribution of liquids and that PVF series which so much attracted Stevenson.[1] The lyric of which they form the second half is famous ; and it is indeed interesting ; but a successful poem it is not. It has one absolutely fatal flaw. Most of us would probably have seen this, if we could have come upon it for the first time free from prejudice and in circumstances which made imagination sharp. Suppose it actually *were* the dog-days ; that you were tired and hot and thirsty, and no drink available ; but, suppose, at the same time, that you had a pocket Horace ; in the search for *some*

[1] *Essays in the Art of Writing,* pp. 34, 39.

I

refreshment, you might naturally turn to that. *Tale tuum carmen*, says a shepherd in one of Virgil's Eclogues,[1]

> Tale tuum carmen nobis, divine poeta,
> Quale sopor fessis in gramine, quale per aestum
> Dulcis aquae saliente sitim restinguere rivo ;

and any purely beautiful poem might be expected to serve you as in some measure a restorative ; but if your eye then chanced to fall on the beginning of this very ode, it would seem welcome not alone as poetry but as poetry on an appropriate theme. " O fountain of Bandusia, more glittering than glass, worthy of sweet wine, not without flowers "—so far, all well. But now what follows ? " To-morrow thou shalt be presented with a kid, whose brow, now swelling with his sprouting horns, gives promise of his loves and battles. Vain promise ! for he shall "—to-morrow, that is—" stain thy cool waters with his red blood—he, the offspring of the wanton flock."

Who wants a drink out of the fountain of Bandusia after that ?

You would return your Horace to your pocket, and bear up again as best you could.

Such an impression might be still more forcibly borne in upon you, if the book you happened to be carrying were not a Horace, but Mr. Duff's *Silva Latina*. In that admirable and delightful school-book this very poem finds itself (by mere accident I should imagine) placed next to a passage from the third *Georgic* [2] where the subject is a cattle plague. Virgil's theme is a diseased ox, but out of it he has made fine poetry. Horace has contrived to be disgusting even about a healthy kid ; for surely that " lascivi suboles gregis "—call it a conventional periphrasis [3] as you will—surely that amazing effort of *curiosa infelicitas*, coming where it does, only increases the brutality.[4]

---

[1] *Ecl.*, v. 45-7. [2] 515-30.

[3] Like *olentis uxores mariti* for she-goats in Carm., I. xvii. 7.

[4] This would be inevitably discovered by an attempt to make a verse translation of the piece. I find from an old school magazine that I once encountered this very problem, with the following result :—

> He dreams to-day of loves and fights ;
> To-morrow his hot blood shall stain
> Your fountainful of cool delights,
> And he shall never skip again.

I had evidently decided that the best resort was to face it out and modernise it ; but this is hardly translating !

The lines that follow this are beautiful, as I have said ; but it is no use. What pleasure, what even purely æsthetic pleasure, can we take in the imagined draughts of these same weary sheep and cattle, or how can we suppose *they* relish it, when we have been told that what they will to-morrow be imbibing is the *blood*—the *warm* [1] blood—of their pastoral fellow-creature ? No, *that* fountain is quite effectually polluted ; at such a Helicon the poet may lead his Pegasus to water, certainly, but he will hardly make him drink.[2]

The fact is, it is not always easy for us moderns to admire Horace. Our criticisms may be in the right in this instance ; [3] but even then, it still remains for us to account for his having done such a thing. In the great majority, however, of those poems or passages which are at first sight similarly [4] perplexing, we may be—I may as well explain at once that I believe we shall be—in the wrong, in presuming to give an adverse verdict, at all events until we have understood what *kind* of poem he means to write ; always a very different kind from anything with which we are now familiar. Fully to realise his poetic standpoint and to see his various poetic purposes is an undertaking which is literary and not scholastic, which has, indeed, often been withheld from the highest scholars, and which demands, for perfection's sake at least, not only an intimate knowledge of the poet's works themselves but of the whole preceding course of classical literature. Nothing so ambitious, it should at once be said, is intended to be attempted here ; but simply a re-examination of the whole series of Horace's works from a somewhat new standpoint—a much newer standpoint for this age than for the poet's own—undertaken in the conviction, not indeed that his poetic instinct is infallible, but assuredly that he is one of the world's first poets,

[1] Implied in *gelidos*, as *rubro*, after the Horatian manner, suggests the cleanness of the spring.

[2] After writing this passage, I came by accident on a poem which expresses the same view, Hartley Coleridge's clever pointed and pleasing " Bandusian Spring."

[3] For explanation of this poem see Ch. III., pp. 70-1 ; and for my final criticism, Ch. VII., pp. 211-12.

[4] In this book I am not at all concerned with verbal difficulties as such. For explanation of these the reader is referred to commentaries. The best modern English editions are those of Gow and Wickham.

and that at his best we must accord to him the poet's crowning epithet with all that it implies ; we must acknowledge that, in his highest moments, he can be sublime.

In the meantime, and at a first glance, what is one to make of *Odes*, III. xvii. for instance ? But before I quote it, let me take a slight English lyric of the same length, selected for no better reason than that it is one of the acknowledged master-pieces of a writer with a severely classic style and tone—and of a writer who, as we shall see, has left us some very curious criticisms upon Horace :—

> Mother, I cannot mind my wheel ;
> My fingers ache, my lips are dry :
> O, if you felt the pain I feel !
> But O, who ever felt as I ?
>
> No longer could I doubt him true—
> All other men may use deceit ;
> He always said my eyes were blue,
> And often swore my lips were sweet. (LANDOR.)

Two things we can feel immediately about that lyric ; it has point, and it sounds poetical. By " point," I mean what I may perhaps call the *pathetic humour* by which the deserted girl is shewn to be so unsophisticated, that she feels as a new thing in the whole history of suffering a situation which every reader knows to be one of literature's most ancient common-places ; and so guileless that she has surrendered to the very simplest arts of flattery, while treasuring its every time-worn phrase.

Now turn, not indeed in expectation of any comparable jewel, but in hope of something that may appear to be at least an exercise in the same branch of literary art—now turn, I say, to this :—

Odes, III. xvii.   Addressed to Aelius Lamia.

" Aelius, whose nobility is from ancient Lamus—(since it was from him, so we are told, that the Lamias of old days took their name, and the whole race of their children's children whose memory lives in archives ; yes, the founder to whom you trace your origin is he who is said to have been the first who ruled the city of Formiae and the Liris where it swims on the shores of Marica—even so far spread his realm)—to-morrow, a storm descending from the East will strew the forest with a carpet of leaves and the shore with useless sea-weed, unless my soothsayer deceives me—the old crow who prophesies rain. Whilst you may, house

your wood in the dry. To-morrow you will be treating your genius
with wine and a two months' porker, with your household freed from
their tasks."

From the ancestry of Aelius Lamia to dry faggots and a
sucking pig ! What is the *point ?* and where is the *poetry ?*
Not, why do people think it a good poem ?—perhaps they don't ;
but why was it written even ? [1]

And even if we rule out the obviously queer poems, we shall
still hear complaints about the poet's curiously disconcerting
habits. Probably the characteristic of Horace's style which
presents the greatest difficulty, at least to his more conscientious
readers, is his use, alike in Odes and Satires and Epistles, of
sudden transitions. His tangential velocity appears to be quite
unconscionable. He will pursue a subject steadily for some
twenty lines, and then in a moment he will seem to be talking
about something which has almost no connection with it.
Mr. Stephen Gwynn, M.P., novelist, litterateur, and Irishman,
once edited and annotated Horace in a little book which remains
at least interesting from its unlikeness to other works of the
kind, and because it shows us how this most " classic " of poets
can appear to an intelligent and talented but unacademic
reader. On this subject he refers to *Ars Poetica*, 242, *series
iuncturaque pollet*, " it is sequence and connection that counts "
—and he complains that although this is Horace's own advice
to poets, no poet ever more conspicuously neglected it. That
must obviously be unlikely, and as a matter of fact I believe
it to be entirely wrong. Mr. Gwynn has expected him from
this to make his sequence of thought obvious and his connections of sentence smooth ; what Horace means is almost nearer
to the opposite ; that a telling, a forcible, juxtaposition will
establish its own connection.[2] *Some* of the abrupt transitions
are perhaps due to slight carelessness of writing or laxity of
thought, but they are the exceptions, and even so they are only
to be found in the Satires ; there is certainly not a single instance in the Epistles or the Odes. For the rest, they are

[1] The solution appears in Ch. IV., p. 114, and cf. Ch. VII., p. 221.

[2] Authorities are divided as to whether Horace is there referring to
diction or to *subject*. Personally, I wish he were referring to the latter,
but I am bound to say that on the whole I think the arguments for the
former have it.

without a doubt deliberate, and, once you have caught the trick of Horace, always effective and not seldom powerful ; all of which I hope in due course to explain.

Of a somewhat similar nature is another frequent source of youthful perplexity ; for if a poet's mind should be inconsequent, we could hardly expect his poems to be anything but formless. Towards the end of the first Satire of the first Book, after a lengthy digression, Horace recalls himself to the subject of the opening lines with the remark *illuc unde abii redeo ;* and if this were his invariable practice, his occasional excursions might seem pardonable and even desirable. But what astonishes the beginner is the fact that, in his odes especially, he is often to be found, some stanza or stanzas before the finish, embarking on an irrelevancy from which he never returns. He opens with great *éclat,* mounting the high horse, and seems to challenge our admiration of his skill ; there follow one or two impressive prancings and curvettings, certainly ; but what is that, if in the upshot his Pegasus has run away with him ? We are left, in plain language, with the uncomfortable suspicion that he does not much care what he sings about ; that an ode of Horace is about no particular subject, or, worse still, has no particular shape. This impression I have so far been describing sympathetically, to give more force to my assurance when I say that no impression possibly could be more false. The distinguishing feature of the odes of Horace is their form. They are constructed more carefully, more skilfully, and more often perfectly, than perhaps any other poems that were ever written. They all have a unity,[1] but it is not the sort of unity that the English reader is accustomed to expect. The English [2] lyric has for the most part one theme, and one theme only ; on that it rings incessant changes. I suppose this is due mainly to the influence of ballad-poetry and folk-song. At any rate from Dunbar's *Lament for the Makers* right down to

---

[1] Horace himself insists on organic unity as the supreme necessity for a poem, in *Ars Poetica,* 1-37 ; see esp. 23. In view of this fact, it is really extraordinary that so many critics of the Odes have taken it for granted that these poems were not even *meant* to have unity.

[2] I mean of course the characteristic English lyric ; naturally my principle does not apply to poems written under Horatian or similar (*e.g.,* Pindaric) influence.

Swinburne's *Dolores* or *The Forsaken Garden*, this is the rule ;
the poet develops his theme and exhausts its possibilities,
ending in the same mood as he began. To Horace that would
have seemed not unity but monotony. We, for our parts,
read an Horatian ode expecting something like a circle ; gradually it dawns upon us that this poet's path is a parabola, and
we watch him glide off towards minus infinity with a feeling
that we have been betrayed. There seems no limit to the gulf
of thought or mood which may exist between the end of one
of his poems and its commencement. He will begin by telling
us how perilous an ambition it is to copy Pindar, and end by
a specification of the bull-calf which he is going to sacrifice
in honour of Cæsar's home-coming—on its brow a white spot
shaped like the crescent moon when she is three days old—
cetera fulvus are his last words " all the rest of it is to be of a
reddish colour." He will begin with a snowscape, and end
with a picture of a *demimondaine* giggling roguishly in a street
corner ; he will begin with a country scene, and end with a
description of a free fight between a jealous lover and his
mistress at a Bacchanalian revel. He will begin by cursing
the nameless wretch who planted a tree that nearly fell upon
him, and end by imagining how Orion in the lower world is
so charmed by the singing of Alcaeus that he forgets to hunt.
He will begin with the praises of his own poetry, and end with
a panegyric on the character of a friend. He will begin with
Hercules, and end with the consulship of a certain Plancus.
Of the very ode in which he prays that his beloved Tibur may
be the retreat of his old age, he devotes the second half to the
praises of Tarentum, and declares that to him it " smiles "
more than all other corners of the earth. He will begin by
saying that he has given up love-making, and end by indicating
that he is in love. Worse still, he will write an ode whose real
theme is Lalage, and wind it up by bundling together the names
of a few other beauties, and then remarking that if a certain boy
called Gyges were to be dressed up like a girl, a chorus of girls
itself would not detect him.

From all this it follows that we ought not to be at all surprised if we should find some readers of Horace boldly declaring
that many of his poems would be positively improved by the
removal of the concluding stanza or stanzas. A fresh and

remarkable instance of this very criticism has just recently
come within my knowledge. A pocket Horace originally
owned by Walter Savage Landor, and by him afterwards
presented to Robert Browning,[1] contains a number of marginal comments on the Odes in Landor's own writing ; judgments, most of them, on the purely poetical aspects, whether
in whole or part, of those Odes which happened particularly
to attract or irritate him. As criticisms of one fellow-craftsman
by another, they have an interest and value quite different
from that of scholastic annotations ; and they are nothing if
not sweeping. As Landor was born in January 1775, and this
edition published in 1829, he must have been 54 at least when
he recorded them, so that they are to be taken as expressing
his mature opinions.[2] Sometimes he writes " beautiful ode "
or " very beautiful ode "—" very pleasant ode "—" good "
—or by a cross at the beginning demonstrably indicates
approval. Just twice or thrice he dismisses one *in toto*,
with " sad stuff " or " miserable ode." But perhaps the
most interesting or at least amusing comments are those
in which he corrects the elder poet. Over and over again a
couplet, or a stanza, or as many as four stanzas in succession, are condemned outright as " poor " or " vile," " what
trash," " stuff "—or he will run his pen straight through
them and write " dele." Often his remark is simply " better
without," and as I have already hinted, this stigma is several
times affixed to the last stanza, occasionally with a perversity
that is quite astounding. A lyric may be intended to close·
with something happily unexpected or otherwise arresting,
and Landor in his practice at any rate could understand that
when he cared. The example of his poetry which I have
already cited (p. 4) is a case in point. If someone were to

---

[1] It is now in the private possession of the Director of the Fitzwilliam
Museum, Mr. Sidney C. Cockerell, who most kindly lent it me and allowed
me free use of it for the purposes of this book. It is edited by J. C.
Zennius and dated 1829.

[2] Mr. Cockerell thinks they may belong to his old age. They are not,
however, substantially in disagreement with his published opinions on
Horace, for which see *Imag. Conversns.* Asinius Pollio and Licinius
Calvus, 1st Conversn. (1st publ. 1855). Asinius Pollio and Licinius
Calvus, 2nd Conversn. (1st publ. 1855). Virgilius and Horatius (1st
publ. 1861).

complain that the last couplet spoils it, on the ground that it seems trivial after the poignancy of the first stanza, he would be treating Landor no worse than Landor has occasionally treated Horace. If someone else were to delete it for the reason that the evidence here adduced by the young woman does not substantiate the theory above advanced as to the young man's sentiments, he would be doing for the text of Landor no less service than some of Horace's editors have done for his.

Now, by these marginal remarks of Landor's hangs a tale. For their significance is much wider than might at first sight appear ; through them speaks, not only Landor on Horace, but Romanticism on the Classics. And there we have an issue which, besides having been, as everybody knows, fought out at the commencement of our present literary era, namely, in the end of the eighteenth century and the beginning of the nineteenth, had been fought out many times—more often than is suspected—in the history not only of English but of European literature before that ; an issue which, moreover, though everybody seems to be resting comfortably in the reflection that with Wordsworth's Preface to his *Lyrical Ballads* of 1798 it was decided for good and all (as everybody always has imagined for an indefinite period after each alternate victory), is, it may be safely affirmed, not settled yet, and will in some form or other come to the fore again in the next period of healthy literary activity, which always requires some atmosphere of contest to provide the more immediate and external sorts of stimulus. In the meantime, it may be worth while briefly to retrace this minor trail of it.

It is to be noted, in the first place, that all these complaints of Landor's are directed against the Odes.[1] In the matter of exciting likes or dislikes, the three or four different classes into which Horace's writings are divisible have from the very outset [2] had somewhat different histories. Roughly it may be said, if

---

[1] In Mr. Cockerell's copy there are no remarks of a literary-critical nature on the rest of Horace.

[2] *Epist.*, II. ii. 58-60 :—

> Denique non omnes eadem mirantur amantque ;
> Carmine tu gaudes, hic delectatur iambis,
> Ille Bioneis sermonibus et sale nigro.

for the moment we exclude the faithful, that his lyric style has appealed to one party and his familiar to another. " Horace," said Gruppe, " is Horace only in his Odes ; " " the real Horace," said Lehrs, " is never found in his Odes." [1] But the point I wish to make here is that the vote of what are called " romantic " periods has regularly been given against the lyrics ; and, further, that each age or generation has only understood or appreciated them according as it really deserves the term " classical." In 1280 A.D. Hugo of Trimberg recorded his opinion that the Satires and Epistles are the important part of Horace's work ; the Odes are " of less practical value." And that is a faithful reflection of the preference of the Middle Ages as a whole.[2] Petrarch, who heralds the revival of learning and classicism, also in this matter restores the balance. By the time of Shakespeare, the Italian appreciation of Horace had got so far as not only to admire, but imitate, the Odes, and it is perhaps noteworthy that this was accompanied by imitations of Pindar, as indicating an interest in the formal ode as such.[3] Meanwhile the *Ars Poetica*, which in this connection tends, I fancy, to share fortunes with the Odes rather than with its sister epistles, as appealing especially to those who are interested in the principles, theoretical and practical, of poetic composition, had been exploited by Vida and paraphrased by Robortelli, two early pilots of its destined eighteenth-century ascendancy. In England, the Elizabethan age naturally turned to Horace's Odes as to other classical sources in the search for literary stimulus to its own originality ; and Campion [4] caught twice or thrice just something of the true Horace—not merely his faculty for shaping a poem out of consecutive moralisings, but his use of the occasion as a *point de départ* for that purpose. But the first modern poems that can truly be called Horatian, in the sense that they are not imitative merely, whether of superficial or of fundamental

---

[1] These *dicta* are contrasted by Tyrrell, *Latin Poetry*, p. 185.

[2] " Out of 1289 scattered quotations from Horace in the Middle Ages, exactly 250 (or less than one-fifth) are from the lyrics and as many as 1039 from the hexameters."—Sandys, *Hist. Class. Schol.*, i. 637, referring to Moore's *Studies in Dante*, i. 201, which, however, depends on Manitius, *Horaz im Mittelalter* (1893).

[3] Sandys, *op. cit.*, ii. 281-2.   [4] See Appendix.

features, but that their resemblance in point of form is also the expression of a kindred vital poetic force, that their urgency of tone is the outcome of a similar conception of the poetic calling, and that their pervading personality is the reflection of a not less ingrained if less attractive but sublimer egotism, are I believe to be seen in the sonnets of Milton. In this sense, these still remain perhaps the most Horatian, certainly the best Horatian, poems in the language ; and if they have not the Latin's boldness of abrupt transition or variety of ingredients, that is partly because of their spatial circumscription, partly because no later poet has even attempted to follow Horace in these two respects.

In comparison with these, even so careful and serious a piece of work as Marvell's *Horatian Ode upon Cromwell's return from Ireland* is merely an imitation, an elaborate and earnest exercise ; yet it is noteworthy for our present purpose as shewing already a full understanding of just that aspect of the Odes which the romantic as such does not see, their structure. It is, indeed, thoroughly Horatian in idea ; in the occasion, and the poetic uses that is put to ; in the marshalled procession of subjects including a short forceful sketch of a great occasion ; and in the attempt, at least, to maintain consistently a lofty moral tone. In fact it has every constituent of an ode of Horace except one ; it lacks his power. It is too *cold* to be really noble ; it has not the thrill which is conveyed by the Roman's incomparably superior word-music ; with the result that, in spite of all that has just been claimed for it above, it falls as far short of Horace as Cromwell's work and character are merely negative beside the constructive genius of Augustus.[1]

But English classicism quickly degenerated under French influence into that mere reproduction of accidental details or at best of surface qualities, and fashionable affectation of what were rightly or wrongly imagined to be the rules of the ancients, which remained the dominant characteristics of the succeeding century. That century represents of course the high-water mark both of the cult of Horace generally, and of his Odes in particular ; but neither in poetry nor in criticism has it anything

---

[1] I think a poem of Marvell's that has really more of the genuine spirit of Horace is " To his Coy Mistress," which rings true just as the Cromwell ode does not; but of course it has not the Horatian compactness.

to show which is really akin to his work in spirit, that is to say which has equal artistic originality, independence of judgment, or condensation of expression, or which is "loaded" as his is " in every rift " with the rich " ore " of individual experience; and in the result it has done by now less good than harm to the poet's reputation in England, by making admirers and enemies alike envisage him instinctively through eighteenth-century spectacles. It can be no disparagement to the scholastic genius of Bentley, which has done more for the text of Horace than is even yet recognised in what might be called the " vulgate "of to-day, to say that he too made such strictures on passages of the Odes as remain to convict him of limitations in poetic instinct which relate him to his age. For that age, while it exalted the Odes, did not really understand them. And the reason is that it was not properly, whatever the critics may say, an age of classicism.

What is a stucco porch, leading to nothing, and with a decent proportion of its columns tastefully decapitated, standing in a verdant grove which remains private property ? Classic ? No ; because instead of being functional and original (the two main principles of all classic art) it is imitative and idle. Romantic ? Yes ; not in the best sense, certainly, but still, so far as its merits go (and I admit I should at first be thrilled to see it), undoubtedly romantic. By the same token is the eighteenth century romantic, at any rate up to a point ; it certainly is not in the best sense of the term classical. Characteristic in this respect are its ideas of drama. Nothing in English yet written can stand a moment's comparison, for essential kinship to Greek Tragedy, with Milton's *Samson Agonistes*, unless it be his *Comus*, which is even more allied thereto at least on one side, as representing the conversion into an art-form of a social or communal ceremony. The period that began with the Restoration saw the introduction and growth of ideas of drama that are primarily French, and only Latin in so far as the French writers and critics had been under Latin influences, while how far they are from being Greek at all may be gathered (for example) from Racine's observations on the *Ajax* of Sophocles.[1] It is the same in lyric poetry ;

---

[1] Briefly, he regarded it as a static drama ; *i.e.*, he did not perceive the action at all ; and accordingly entirely missed the point.

they saw and wrote what they thought was classical, but the deeper and more truly characteristic qualities of classic art were a closed book to them. How Greek and how Latin, in essentials and superficials alike, is the first deliberately classic ode in English, Ben Jonson's on the death of Sir Henry Morison ; [1] how like Horace in the abrupt transition which begins the second stanza, how like Pindar in the splendidly effective *enjambement* of " Ben — Jonson," how like both in tone and process. Compared with it, how frigid, how stilted, how painfully obvious in their attempts at effect, but in particular how monotonous, are those two vulgarly pretentious and grossly overrated efforts of Dryden, " For St. Cecilia's Day " and " Alexander's Feast," marking as they do the transition to the succeeding century. Of that century the typical " Pindaric " ode may be seen in Gray's poem on the Progress of Poesy ; a strange title for a work in which the poesy, unlike Pindar's, makes no progress ; a title as inappropriate as is the label " Pindaric " to a poem which lacks not only an occasion, but more than half of the more or less regular constituents of Pindar's own odes, and which from beginning to end is far too *general*. Yes, this is a romantic poem ; romantic in the sense in which the Romantic movement is still operative among the poets of to-day ; every superficial detail which in the writer's own age is fashionably or popularly admired is here worked in, but no new organic unity is created from them, in other words there is no true poetic art ; though Gray at least, unlike the moderns, has the subordinate art of verse. Similarly with the Horatian model ; in the poets from the Restoration up to (but not including) the age of Wordsworth will be found many a time the Horatian echo and occasionally the Horatian touch, never, I think, the Horatian method or the Horatian range.[2] Except, indeed, once, and that is in Cowper's *Boadicea ;* there and there only are to be seen, not only the spirited and patriotic

---

[1] The reader will find it in *The Oxford Book of English Verse*, No. 194.

[2] This holds good even in the field of satire, where Horace is *less* methodical. Wickham has well remarked that " when Pope ' imitates Horace ' he copies and even improves upon the wit of individual lines and passages, but he misses always much of the play, the delicacy, the inner unity of thought, and he puts Horace to very un-Horatian purposes."

tone, but the plunge *in medias res* with the opening lines, the indirect conveyance of the main lesson of the poem by representing it as reported, the climax in a quotation ; and the harmony and compactness.[1]

The so-called Romantic age, on the other hand, although of course a romantic reaction in a certain sense, was in a more important sense classical. Wordsworth and Keats took up English literature again where it had been left by Milton, whom the former invoked to reappear and save his country, and the latter—though in one strikingly simple and self-illustrating sentence he put his finger whether consciously or not upon the main flaw in the style of *Paradise Lost* [2]—admired, absorbed, and in *Hyperion* followed. The great thing that these two poets did—a thing which even Shelley [3] did not do, while Byron is in this matter [4] merely eighteenth-century—was that they restored Form to the English lyric. In the sonnets of Wordsworth and the sonnets and odes of Keats there is progress ; and it is an ordered progress, with a particular end in view. There is variety, yet concentration. Subjects may be introduced which the reader would not have foreseen from the title ; and he cannot foretell with what apparently minor detail or ostensibly digressive simile, on what light relief or fresh vista, the poet may suddenly leave off ; [5] as a result, there is a *climax*. It would be idle to pretend that these two great and original poets were indebted for such features of their art to any direct influence from the odes of Horace. Wordsworth

---

[1] Cf. Sir A. Quiller Couch, *Studies in Literature*, I. 68 : " of all our poets the one who, but for a stroke of madness, would have become our English Horace, was William Cowper."

[2] " I have given up *Hyperion*—there were too many Miltonic inversions in it—Miltonic verse cannot be written but in an artful, or rather, artist's humour. I wish to give myself up to other sensations. *English ought to be kept up.*"

[3] Shelley demonstrated anew that poetry could be, as it had been in Greece, intellectual and humanist and yet passionate ; but in his poetical technique he is, it seems to me, romantic.

[4] As also, later, Mrs. Browning, who even in her maturity remained, to a greater extent than has been recognised, a follower of Byron.

[5] To give only one example from many which the reader will readily supply for himself, what eighteenth-century poet, indeed how very few poets in any age, would have begun their imagination's voyage at Homer and ended it upon a peak in Darien ?

indeed admired him ;[1] though the entry " Horace, influence of, on Keats " in Sir Sidney Colvin's *Life* of the latter poet will lead the curious inquirer to even less than he might have expected. But when Wordsworth took up the Miltonic sonnet, it immediately bore out the truth so finely uttered in his own valedictory address to the River Duddon :—

> Still glides the Stream, and shall for ever glide ;
> *The Form remains, the Function never dies.*

The inextinguishable fire of Greek art, παντέχνου πυρὸς σέλας, blazed up again immediately from its last receptacle. The best poets of this period, Shelley as well as Keats and Wordsworth, reverted in their most characteristic work to the old and original " Function " of poetry, which it had had for the ancients and for Milton ; the prophetic.[2] They all teach ; their hope is to redeem. And in doing so they almost inevitably—some less than others, Shelley on the whole least, revert to or half-unconsciously revive the classic style and " Form." Shelley in his most Shelleian [3] lyrics is essentially a singer, an ἀοιδός ; he takes a theme and intensifies it as no one else could do. Keats and Wordsworth are, by comparison in this respect, ποιηταί ; they construct ; they dispose their matter tellingly ; *series iuncturaque pollet.* They vary their tone ; " Great God ! " cries Wordsworth suddenly, and ends a sonnet with the opposite side of the antithesis from that on which he began.[4]

But neither the " Romantic " Revival nor the nineteenth century were more than partially classical. For the Romantics *were* romantics, after all, and though it was the romantic spirit that inspired Wordsworth and Coleridge to rebellion against the age that had preceded them, and made Keats and Shelley thrill to the glories of Greek literature and art, it was also the romantic spirit that was responsible for the defects or failures of these poets and their contemporaries, both in art

---

[1] Direct Horatian influence is traceable in Wordsworth ; perhap the best example is the ode *To Lycoris*, a " carpe diem " admonition to a friend, *apropos* of the season of Spring.

[2] " I will be thy priest "—Keats, Ode to Psyche ; and see that poem generally.

[3] *E.g., Ode to a Skylark, The Cloud.*

[4] It is Horatian to do so, cf. pp. 224-7.

and criticism. The century which they ushered in was to produce, indeed, in Tennyson a poet at least more Virgilian in style and method than any English predecessor, and in Arnold one who drew classic influences both from his masters Keats and Wordsworth and from the fountain head, and wrote in his noble and beautiful ode on the burial of Dean Stanley a poem more genuinely Pindaric in conception and outline than anything in the language yet. But a period of classical influence in the proper sense of these two terms, a period of poetry classic in spirit rather than in letter, in method and not in mannerism, is a phenomenon which it is to be hoped our literature may one day see, but which it has assuredly not seen yet; and the fact remains that even the nineteenth century, despite its great advances of scholarship, is in the main tradition of its original poetry far less classical than romantic, and increasingly so as it proceeds. Tennyson and Arnold in the respects above mentioned stand out as exceptions; but Tennyson lacked power, and Arnold energy.

Consistently therewith, the nineteenth century did not much appreciate the *Odes*, any more than had the Romantic revivalists. " Not much "—for its literary attitude is here, as in general, anomalous, rather half-and-half. In the world of scholarship,[1] this century was to see far more progress than any preceding one in the interpretation of the sequence and proportion of thought in these poems, but it was also to produce the editors who have understood these features least. Tennyson and Arnold, again, wrote the two most Horatian of all deliberate echoes of the Odes, the laureate's *To F. D. Maurice* being far the more variously coloured and better packed, but the school-inspector's " Horatian Echo " the nearer to the originals in a sort of poignancy. Yet such effusions are at the best mere exercises, not properly poems at all; and there is little [2] else, if anything, in these poets recalling or resembling Horace, and very little, if anything at all, in the other poets of the century.[3] And Tennyson has left it on record that his school experience of Horace resulted in such a dislike of that

---

[1] See p. 22.

[2] Tennyson's *Diary* is not Horatian in thought or feeling, but his short ode to Milton ends quite in Horace's manner.

[3] Excluding Mr. Austin Dobson, who is eighteenth-century all round.

author as he never quite succeeded in recovering from. Unfortunately this has happened only too often. It was the same with Swinburne. As for the public of the present day, and even the majority of the academic world, their prevailing taste might be said to set in almost any direction rather than towards Horace's Odes.

To return, then, to Landor, it may now be seen that his work and preferences alike are thoroughly characteristic of the ninety years out of two different centuries spanned by his generally rather turbid life and reflected by his usually somewhat turbid style, in being both classic and romantic, but on the whole more romantic than classic. As a lyric poet, however, he is perhaps the only other contemporary who is with Keats and Wordsworth. " Of Clementina " is a very eighteenth-century piece—at first sight ; yet that sudden surprise-ending—he may not have been conscious of it, but it was Horace who taught him that. Probably the most effective retort, however, to his adverse comments on the *Odes*, would be to point to his own ode addressed to his friend J. Ablett, which is not only Horatian in tone but in variety ; it has the excursions, the ostensible but deceptive [1] desultoriness, and the noble and beautiful two final stanzas form a conclusion of a quiet and generalising sort that we feel Horace at any rate, if he could see it, would not have the inconsistency to carp at. It was mainly the classic in Landor that wrote those perfect, and in addition beautiful, short poems ; it was the romantic in him, wholly, that moved him to his repeated disparagements of Virgil,[2] and to those captious strictures on the Odes of

---

[1] Except that Landor's desultoriness is much less " deceptive " ; for, truth to tell, a detailed comparison of structure would work out strongly in favour of Horace. Landor's poem is nowhere near so well-knit either in thought or metre.

[2] Note that, like a true romantic, he makes an exception (though qualified) in favour of the 4th book of the *Aeneid*. But he called it as a whole the most mis-shapen of epics ; the description of Winter in the 3rd *Georgic* is stigmatised by several speakers in *Imaginary Conversations*, as are also the 4th *Eclogue* and the episode of Orpheus and Eurydice. Elsewhere, it is true, he has praise for special passages, and for the versification in general. It has, however, been remarked (*e.g.* Walker, *Literature of the Victorian Era*, p. 1031), that Landor's literary criticism generally has a tendency to " carping peevishness."

Horace. These two Latin poets had been the idols of the
period from Dryden to the didactic successors of Thomson.
As the gods of a conquered people, they were inevitably given
relatively low places in the revised hierarchy. The verdict
was against them before their case was heard, so that their
merits were never given a decent consideration even. They
were left for a Byron to take leave of heartily,[1] for the critical-
minded to pick holes in,[2] and for the creative-minded like
Keats and Shelley more or less to ignore. Here again it is, as
we can now see clearly, in his capacity as a pioneer of the Romantic movement in Europe that Goethe condemns the Odes.

The second point to notice about these criticisms of Landor's
is that so many of them are directed against the *subject-matter*
of the censured passages. He objects, it is clear, to what he
unreflectingly supposes to be idle digressions or stark irrele-
vances. That too is romantic. " Poetry," said Keats, in this
as in so much else a classic in principle, " should be . . . a
thing which enters into one's soul and does not startle or amaze
it with itself, but with its *subject;* " italics mine. Matthew
Arnold, too, in that most remarkable preface to his 1853
volume, proved himself in theory as in practice Keats's truest
or perhaps only [3] successor, by insisting on the fundamental
importance for the poet of a sound choice of *subject;* by which
he did not mean the raw material merely, but the poet's idea in
selecting this or that raw material, in one word his *conception.*
In nothing does the romantic more surely and more uncon-

----

[1] " Then farewell Horace whom I hated so." So the line is usually
quoted. But its context gives it a very different complexion, and is
worth quoting more fully here, for the neatness and precision with which
it voices the whole complaint of many a modern against Horace :—

> Then farewell Horace ; whom I hated so
> Not for thy faults, but mine ; it is a curse
> To understand, not feel, thy lyric flow ;
> To comprehend, but never love, thy verse.
>   —*Childe Harold,* IV. lxxvii.

[2] " If you take from Virgil his diction and metre, what do you leave
him ? "—Coleridge, *Table Talk.*

[3] Tennyson is rightly reckoned a *disciple* of Keats, but that is a very
different thing.

sciously betray himself, at this day or at any other, than in a
total failure, not so much to grasp this principle, as to realise
that there is or can be any such principle to be grasped. And
the result is not merely that he does not appreciate the structure, that he complains of chaos where there is really order ;
rather he does not feel the life, and therefore cannot understand the function of each member of the organism. The point
of his own work lies in the treatment, in the detail, in this or
that effective epithet, phrase, or " touch " ; whereas in the
classic product it lies far less in such matters (sometimes, it
may be, almost not at all) than in the consecutive dispersal of
subject-matter ; once more, " it is *the series* that is effective."
What the romantic aims at achieving by a still more striking
adjective or a heightened description, but all in the same key,
the classic achieves by an unexpected modulation into a fresh
topic ; to complain of irrelevance is merely to betray one's
insensibility of the subtle relation, which of course cannot be
absolutely proclaimed and shouted by the poet, or it must
lose its point and charm. These complaints of Landor's on
the *Odes* are quite consistent with the attitude he takes up in
his published criticisms of Horace's chief contemporary ; upon
which criticisms some pertinent general remarks are made
by Dr. Elizabeth Nitchie in her *Virgil and the English Poets*.[1]
" He regards all three, *Eclogues*, *Georgics*, and *Aeneid*, as pieces
of literary workmanship, and criticises them as such." . . .
" There is no word of the *Eclogues* as the first evidence of a new
tradition in Latin poetry, or of the *Aeneid* as a great national
poem. He does not seem to have had even the realisation that
Dante had of the universal significance of the great Roman
epic. He is more like the mediæval rhetoricians and gram-
marians, with their tendency to pick out individual passages
for consideration." Exactly.

Finally, it is noteworthy that his comments often amount
to an accusation of bad taste. This count is, indeed, closely
connected with the preceding. It means, in most cases, that
he is judging a word or phrase either without regard to the real
purpose of the whole piece, or in ignorance of its own implication. As he does not see what is behind the poem, so he fails
to detect what is " between the lines "

[1] Columbia University Press, 1919.

So far we have been considering poets and literary critics.
But among scholars too there have been several who have had
just the same sort of perplexities about the *Odes*. The best-
known instance is that of Peerlkamp who in 1834 brought out
an edition of them in which he italicised as spurious no small
proportion of the entire text![1] His reason being that it was
not good enough ; for Peerlkamp professed, indeed, to be an
immense admirer of Horace ; but it was of a very *a priori*
Horace ; and the fact remains that what is ordinarily denoted
by the term " Horace's Odes " appeared to Peerlkamp to be
a shocking hash. His disciple Gruppe reproduced both sides
of his atrocious paradox, his other disciple Lehrs preferred the
consistency of holding a poor opinion of the *Odes*. But of
course for English readers the main exponent of the case
against the *Odes* is the late Professor Tyrrell, both in the chapter
in his *Latin Poetry* and in the later articles contributed to the
Nineteenth Century. The first-mentioned is a readable and
amusing piece of devil's advocacy, not without one or two
hard knocks, but pig-headed, sometimes unduly repetitive, and
here and there quite unconscionable, as for example when the
Odes are compared to the effusions of that wretchedest of
jinglers, T. Moore, in the matter of " subservience of expression
to metre ; " or when in criticising the fourteenth epode with
reference to its treatment of Phryne,[2] he complains that the
poet " seems to have forgotten all about her before he finished
the epode," though the last word but one of the poem is—
Phryne !
  Tyrrell, indeed, is remarkable even among the enemies of
Horace for his irreconcilability ; he is one of the very few
(excluding the many voiceless) who remain hostile to him in
all three of his phases. And it must be acknowledged that
if the *Odes* present, on examination, a number of features that

[1] It is remarkable that Landor's anathemas frequently agree with
Peerlkamp's ; *e.g.*, on I. i. *fin.*, ii. 5-12, 17-20, iii. 15-20, xii. 40 (*circ.*), xx.
5 ; II. xi. 21-4 ; III. xxvii. generally.
  [2] For Tyrrell's actual objection see his *Latin Poetry*, p. 204 ; it arises
from his apparent ignorance of an extremely common (and amply recognised) Horatian practice of *compressed antithesis* ; *i.e.* by calling
Phryne a freed-woman and a wanton the poet implies that Maecenas'
wife is unexceptionable on both these counts.

are calculated to make them appear (at first) forbidding to the modern general reader, to say the same of the *Satires* and *Epistles* might not seem to require so much as an examination. For at least we know what we mean by a lyric, and we try to write them, whereas both the other two are now felt to be obsolete even as literary forms. Satires exist indeed in English verse, but they are mere imitations, academic exercises ; poetical epistles have been penned, even by a Keats and a Shelley, but most of them are comparatively seldom read. Moreover, of the habits of the poet which surprise us in the *Odes*, some of the most remarkable reappear in his other works. Abrupt transitions, for example ; one of the oldest sorts of stumbling-block in Horace, as we can see from the manuscript tradition and the testimony of the scholiast Porphyrion ; it appears that early critics were at times driven to regard these as the beginnings of fresh poems, and a single piece was by some thus split into two not only at *Epodes*, ii. 23, ix. 27 ; *Odes*, I. vii. 15, III. iii. 17 and xxiv. 25, but also at *Epist.*, I. xv. 26 ; while the *Satires*, as being naturally the most desultory of Horace's writings, show a still larger number of such real or apparent changes of subject. Abrupt beginnings and abrupt endings, making many pieces give the impression that they are chance cross-sections of Horace's mind, samples taken deliberately at random, barometrical records of his spiritual atmosphere from any one moment for a given number of minutes—this also is just as much a feature of satires and epistles as of odes. The *Satires*, certainly, have seldom if ever been adopted as the favourite form in which the reader cared to take his Horace. The *Epistles*, however, often have been ; they have appealed strongly and still do,[1] to many who either respectfully forbear, or do not forbear even, from criticising the *Odes*. Especially, of course, those of the first book ; in regard to which it is note-worthy, for example, that Tyrrell himself can do nothing more than ignore them (with the exception of the fourteenth) entirely. Goethe extended his already mentioned animus to the *Ars Poetica*, of which he said that no two people would think alike of it, and no single person for ten years together.

Within the scholastic world, indeed, the nineteenth century

[1] Among distinguished living English Latinists I know of at least two.

did (it is perhaps hardly necessary to say) an immense amount
for the elucidation of Horace. In textual criticism and explanation and illustration it contributed far more than the
preceding two together, if we except Bentley. In general interpretation, in tracing the sequence of thought and estab-
lishing the relevance of censured words or passages (and of
course occasionally the spuriousness of others), the growth of a
school who approached these authors primarily from a literary
standpoint—represented by such commentators as Orelli,
Ritter, Dillenburger, and their English follower Wickham,
later again by Kiessling and in this country Gow—to say
nothing of the valuable contributions made to the study of
particular odes by distinguished non-specialists from Mommsen
to Warde Fowler—all this resulted in an understanding of
Horace's work that may be said hardly to have been approached
before. Nor was literary criticism itself all on Tyrrell's side ;
far from it ; the solid, sound, compact, judicious, and altogether
admirable essay of Sellar, even if it does not (and I am far from
sure) make this present work superfluous, may perhaps help to
justify my so copiously widening the issue, as to seem at times,
it may be, to be using Horace as a mere drumstick.

But the fact remains, that Horace's audience in the last
half century or so, if " fit," has been distinctly " few." The
active literary world has neither cared to read him much, nor
to be influenced by him at all. Indeed it is obvious that the
whole present tendency is in the opposite direction. Great
as is the diversity of our new poets, they hold perhaps at least
one article of faith in common, and that is, that he who is
dignified is damned. All strive after effect, and show it ; all
use this or that of many desperate devices ; to be obscure,
discordant, slangy, to use words in anything but their natural
meaning, to be strident, maundering, affected, abject, prosy,
merely feeble-minded or stark raving mad—these things, in
their search after new spheres of conquest, the majority of them
count no shame ; but majesty they will not attempt ; they
one and all despise it. Modern reviewers for the most part
do not slate ; but when they are by way of doing so, the one
word " pompous " provides an absolutely sure extinguisher.
Now Horace knew just as well as any present-day aspirant that
if a poet deliberately aims at grandeur he risks turgidity and

bathos. *Pindarum quisquis studet æmulari*—whoever strives to equal Pindar is like Icarus who set out to fly with waxen wings, and the only notoriety that he will come by is to be proverbial for his fall.[1] The difference is that Horace distinguished between success and failure, between the sublime and the ridiculous, and the writers of these days do not. For them the mere attempt at an elevated style of writing is absurd. Their aim is above all things, realism ; and no aim could be more laudable if sincerely and large-mindedly pursued ; but strange as it may appear in an age of heroism in daily action, the heroic is shunned in literature as if it were almost synonymous with the unreal and the false. To put the same distinction in a narrower form, no one, in verse or prose I fancy, now uses *Rhetoric ;* it is not merely a lost art, but a discredited one. For Horace, rhetoric was at least one mode of poetry, to be used not constantly but as occasion served ; and that, we may remember, is what it was for Shakespeare.

When Tyrrell wrote that " no reader of the Odes, however careless, can have failed to notice the extraordinary difficulty of discovering in them anything like a connected train of thought," he added that " one may safely say that hitherto there has been no even moderately successful attempt to meet this difficulty." That, in 1895, was a gross exaggeration. At the same time, there is perhaps more to be said in the way of attempting to remove this difficulty ; or in any case, such understanding as has already been arrived at is still very far from general. These were the considerations that prompted the writing, some years ago, of an essay which became the nucleus of the present book. But if any new light however faint is to be thrown on so well worn a problem in these late days, it will be necessary to re-investigate the question from its fundamentals ; and indeed some of the strictures we have already noticed are hardly to be answered satisfactorily by any shorter course. It will be necessary, in fact, not only to extend our examination to the entire body of Horace's work, which is, after all, ultimately homogeneous to a remarkable degree, but radically to revise our whole conception of poetry. Antiquity's

---

[1] Cf. also *Ars Poetica*, 27, *professus grandia turget.*

idea of the poet's function was totally dissimilar to ours. In brief, the modern world regards the poet as a dilettante ; there are many doubtless, who would not own to such a view, but bring them to the practical test, and their actions and their attitude are at once seen to be instinctively based upon it. In the ancient world—in the Greek world before the decadence, and the Græco-Roman world of Augustan Rome—the poet had a definite place in the life of the community. We may think, if we are so minded, that the ancient view was wrong ; but even then we shall have to understand it before we can properly appreciate those of the Greek and Latin poets—and they happen to be those which have been, and still are even now, recognised as the best—who accepted the position that had been immemorially assigned to their profession. And no one accepted it more completely than Horace did. Take him at his own valuation of the poetic office ; interpret him on his own principles ; and it will be seen that despite the grumblings above alluded to, what Suetonius said of him is true ; on the whole, obscurity is the last fault that can be attributed to him ; *quo vitio minime tenebatur.*

APPENDIX

"THE HORATIAN MODEL IN ENGLISH VERSE "

THE bulk of my first chapter had already been written when a lecture with the above title was published by Prof. Sir A. Quiller Couch in his *Studies in Literature*, Vol. I. After reading it I revised my own pages which touch briefly on the same subject, and made a number of modifications as the result of hints taken from his lecture. In particular, I am indebted to it for my reference to Campion ; but I think that of the three poems referred to by Sir Arthur the only one that is Horatian in *method* is " Rose-cheek'd Laura " ; that is certainly very like some of the slighter odes, and shows that, as I have maintained, Horace's strictly poetic qualities came nearer to being appreciated in the Elizabethan and Miltonic period than at any time since. It is a beautiful piece in its quiet way ; but personally I can never take much interest in an English lyric which is rhymeless. I am glad to see the Professor insisting on the importance, in a sense the supreme importance, of Horace's metrical achievement, and quote him on that subject in a later chapter ; and therefore I am all the more surprised at his final suggestion, that the

secret of Horace might possibly be captured by the experiment of
" delicate metres divorced from rhyme." The *reason* of the importance
of Horace's metrical art is that by means of it he makes his verse *sing ;*
and English lyric verse without rhyme *cannot* sing. If that sounds
too dogmatic, I merely remark that in four centuries no one has
succeeded in making it do so; the choruses in *Samson Agonistes* are
docked blank verse (with rhymes occasionally), and are unique in
other ways. Horace—and of our finest lyric poems the same holds
true—does something supremely difficult in such a way that it looks
as if it had been supremely easy ; the man who writes rhymeless
verse in English does something absurdly easy in such a way that
from its awkwardness or heaviness it looks as if it had been difficult,
and gives the average reader a vague feeling that it ought to be regarded with some respect.

I am very glad to find Sir Arthur reasserting the seriousness of Horace
(which has so little pomposity or solemnity that it has often been quite
unrecognised) and to be able to refer to him as supporting (p. 67) my
contention that English poetry has never yet " captured the whole of
Horace's secret." " We can compass the Horatian manner ; we can
compass the Horatian phrase." . . . " But what of his metrical secret ? "
True, we have not yet invented anything even analogous to Horace's
metres. I think myself, however, that the main deficiency is something
more fundamental than that. Horace has only one eye on his literal
meaning ; his real aim is a certain single *effect*, dependent on a series
of suggestions which are " between the lines." (It is very simple really
—to see, not to do—however it may sound complicated.) The English
lyric, in general, has no between-lines element at all. Its aim is sweetness and not harmony. That is what Milton and Wordsworth and Keats
reacted against.

Of Landor, Sir Arthur (going further than I do) writes : " Landor
has all the classical sense of form, and his best I dare almost aver to be
as good as Horace :

> Tanagra ! think not I forget
> Thy beautifully storied streets !

But he is heir rather to the Greek anthologists than to Augustan Rome."

CHAPTER II

THE FUNCTION OF POETRY IN THE ANCIENT
WORLD [1]

Philosophari est mihi necesse, at paucis, nam omnino haut placet.
—ENNIUS.

W ITH just some notable exceptions,[2] literary criticism
is in a poor way nowadays. This might seem to be
due, in part at any rate, to the fact that contemporary
literature itself is poor. But indeed, it does not follow ; the
great critical ages have as a rule followed the creative, not
synchronised with them. The real trouble is the almost total
absence of anything that can properly be called a principle.
Some even of our ablest writers succeed only by a series of
suggestive or sometimes wonderful *aperçus*.

There are two reasons for this perhaps. In the first place,
the eighteenth century is held up before us as an awful warning
against the practice of criticism on principle. And certainly
the age that followed, the age of Coleridge, Lamb and Hazlitt,
is one for which we can hardly feel too grateful. But the eighteenth century did not criticise on principle, it criticised by rule.

[1] In case some readers may feel that the views expressed in this
chapter are more dogmatic than is warranted by the arguments adduced
or evidence cited, I should like to say that the chapter was originally
more than three times its present length and was entitled " A New Theory
of Poetry "—the new theory being a rehabilitation of the ancient one.
The present chapter represents an attempt to reduce to proportions
more consistent with the size of the book, a statement of views indispensable to the proper understanding of the book both as a whole and
in its parts. The original chapter may possibly appear later as an
independent treatise, properly documented.

[2] The greatest is Mr. A. C. Bradley, whose *Shakespearian Tragedy* is
surely the most remarkable example ever seen of the illuminating application of sound æsthetic principles to the interpretation of literature.

Its rules were always arbitrary, even when they were not absurd ; and it has hardly a better right to be called " critical " than it has to be declared an age of " classicism." On both these counts it went for superficials absolutely. It was formal and it was French.

In the second place, we are still vaguely but considerably under the influence of the *l'art pour l'art* theory that was started by the *Parnassiens* about the middle of last century. " Art for art's sake " is of course a doctrine that may be true or false according to what one means by it. The phrase that has probably done most to give us foolish notions is the everlasting phrase " fine art." [1] In so far as that means anything that is intrinsically and fundamentally distinguishable from an applied art, it is little better than a contradiction in terms. Any art must have a practical end ; it must be an art of doing something. It must aim, of course, at beauty ; but beauty apart from its effect is meaningless, it is a mere abstraction, a concept for philosophers. And in any case, what is functionless cannot be beautiful ; even the mid-Victorian drawing-room might have taught us that. Where there is not at least some question of the adaptation of means to ends, beauty has nothing to subsist upon.[2]

Nothing at all events could well be more unlike the general attitude of the ancients themselves to their own poetry than any such romantic notions—if indeed they are romantic in anything but the historic sense. Ancient literary criticism, in the scholastic ages, was in some respects perverse enough ; but it had at least this great asset of method, that as its name of " Rhetoric " itself implies, it regarded the art of literature as a fundamentally practical one, whose object throughout was to *persuade*. But in truth its object is something better and more deep than that. This is to conceive of literature as appealing to the reason ultimately ; to think of the poet as of a person with a thesis to maintain ; it is a view derived entirely from the standpoint of the fifth-century sophists, the fathers of

---

[1] A conception due, in the last resort, to Aristotle ; so at least Butcher, *Aristotle's Theory of Poetry and Fine Art*, p. 115.

[2] " Utility is an element of Beauty," said Dürer (*Engravings of Dürer*, by Lionel Cust, p. 81). Of many other references which might be given, one rather peculiarly interesting one is Hirn, *Origins of Art*, p. 184.

scientific literary criticism.[1] Sounder and more understanding
was the popular view which held the field before the sophists
won it. Up to the age of Aristophanes, and including him and
those who shared his views, poets and public alike regarded
the function of the poet as being essentially that of the *teacher*
of society. The "*locus classicus*" is *Frogs* 1008-1088. There
Aeschylus is represented as saying (and his wire-puller is obviously speaking through him) that the relation of the poet to
the adult public is analogous to that between a master and a
class of boys. Even Euripides, the intellectual, though he
is made to put " cleverness " first, declares the poet's claim
to honour to be founded on the fact that he " admonishes,
and makes men better in the cities." Clearly no other basis of
discussion was conceivable ; [2] in the imaginary contest between
those two tragedians, opposite as are their poetic characters,
this view of poetry remains throughout the common ground.
That it had been the traditional Greek view hitherto is shewn
by lines 1030 to 1036 in the same context, where the several
departments of the four great patriarchal poet-teachers,
Orpheus, Musaeus, Hesiod, and Homer, are in turn briefly
specified. That it was the comedian's own view is further
shewn by the many passages [3] in which he applies it even to
his own branch of the poetic art, a branch of which we for our
parts are not accustomed to think as being *imprimis* edifying.
But perhaps the most striking testimony to the deep-seatedness
of this idea in the Greek mind is to be found in the various
passages in the dialogues of the next great Greek author (and
of course particularly in the *Republic*) where he directs himself
to the criticism of the poets. With the perversity, with the
brilliant stupidity, with the astonishingly keen-sighted colour-
blindness, of these criticisms we are not here concerned ; exactly
how the poet teaches, how he exercises and purifies the emotions,
Plato either could not or would not see, but then neither did

---

[1] One of the queerest surprises of ancient criticism for the modern
student is to find writers like Thucydides or Sophocles treated as a kind
of orators, and classified accordingly.

[2] The weight tests that follow are subordinate, see 1056-1061. The
whole passage, 1008-1088, should be carefully considered ; it is most
illuminating.

[3] For some of these see Butcher, *Aristotle's Theory*, etc., p. 218.

Aristophanes, really,[1] nor the popular Greek view before him ; it was Aristotle with his κάθαρσις theory of tragedy who was the first to glimpse this truth. What is important is that, despite their obvious differences of temperament and of mind, the comedian and the philosopher are here at one, and both are against the Sophists ; they are concerned for the moral influence of literature, while the Sophists care only about its immediate practical effectiveness.

It is commonly [2] said that this conception of the function of poetry as being morally educative continued to exist in the Greek world ; and passages from Strabo and Plutarch are cited in support of such a statement. This hardly represents what happened. Rather that conception, after the days of Plato and Aristophanes, lapsed as completely as did the production of the sort of literature that had justified it. What these passages from Strabo and Plutarch do tend to show is that it revived again. But I believe the really vital forces inspiring this revival to have been, not Greek, but Roman.[3]
Nec vera virtus, cum semel excidit, Curat reponi deterioribus.

If there is such a thing as *Theory* of Poetry at all, I believe [4] this the ancient theory, though it may require in the light of modern thought a more accurate statement or a more scientific exposition, to be substantially the right one ; as against, that is to say, the current theory (implicit or expressed) of

[1] *E.g.*, the mission of Homer is regarded in just the same curiously practical-didactic light at *Frogs* 1035-1036 as it is in Plato's *Ion*.

[2] *E.g.*, Jebb, *Growth and Influence of Classical Greek Poetry*, p. 257, " But the older conception held its ground, and often reappears in the later Greek literature."—Butcher, *Aristotle's Theory*, etc., p. 217. " This remarkable passage (= Strabo, 1, 2, 3, and 5) accurately reflects the sentiment which persisted to a late time in Greece," etc.

[3] The Greeks got it from the Romans ; Strabo from the spirit of the Augustan age ; similarly, I think, so-called " Longinus " later (1st cent. A.D.), with his " ὕψος μεγαλοφροσύνης ἀπήχημα." Cf. Rhys Roberts's edition, p. 11, *fin.*, and Introd. generally.

[4] Cf. footnote to title of this chapter.

" art for art's sake." I shall attempt very briefly to give my reasons for this belief in a later part of the present chapter. In the meantime, the ancient view itself will be better understood, and its relation to the work of Horace, both generally and in respect of the various literary " Forms " which he adopted, will become apparent, if we consider very summarily the origin and evolution of classical poetry [1] in the light of this ancient conception of the function of the poetic art.

ORIGIN OF CLASSICAL POETRY

So far as we can learn anything about it, the origin of Classical Poetry is such as to bear out entirely the prevailing modern theory of the origin of Art in general. It is now rapidly becoming almost a commonplace that Art, as a social phenomenon, is a development of primitive ritual.[2] In the cases, for example, of Dancing, Music, Sculpture, Painting, and the special form of Poetry called Drama, such an origin has been abundantly established. But the extent to which a similar origin may be found for Poetry itself in general has not been nearly so much emphasised ; probably because its beginnings are more obscure. What evidence there is, however, points in just the same direction.[3] The first poets were a kind of priests. They were the

[1] Or " pure " literature, which in its first stage is always in the form of poetry, though later, of course, a certain amount of prose is also included.

[2] See *e.g.*, (i) Archæology :—Miss Harrison, *Ancient Art and Ritual* (1913), and Themis (1912). E. A. Gardner, *Religion and Art in Ancient Greece* (1910). Grosse, *Die Anfänge der Kunst* (1894), American translation in Chicago Anthropological Series, 1897. French translation, 1902. (ii) Aesthetics and Psychology :—Hirn, *The Origins of Art : a Psychological and Sociological Inquiry* (1900). Guyau, *L'Art au point de vue Sociologique* (5th ed. 1901). Lange, *Das Wesen der Kunst* (1901). Müller-Freienfels, *Psychologie der Kunst* (1912).

But altogether, the best introduction for the ordinary reader is Baldwin Brown's *The Fine Arts* (Murray, 1902).

[3] The most recent work on the subject, Gummere's *The Beginnings of Poetry* (1901), is more concerned with the sociological treatment of folk-poetry than with literature as such. Other modern books are :— Brunétière, *Evolution of Species in Literature ;* Letourneau, *L'Evolution Littéraire dans les diverses races humaines* (Paris, 1894) ; Posnett, *Comparative Literature* (1886). But the original credit for the discovery

spiritual teachers of the community. It is in the *Vedas* of ancient India, and particularly in the *Rig-Veda*, that we find at once the most copious and the purest example of original poetic literature.[1] The *Rig-Veda* (about 1200 B.C., that is to say some centuries, in any case, before the Homeric poems) is a collection of over a thousand lyrics. They are almost all hymns to gods, intended to be sung on occasions of sacrifice. They are not mere ritual formulæ, but literature ; they have similes, they have " style." They were composed by priests, and transmitted orally through the priestly families. Their tone is not merely ceremonial but moral ; " sin in the *Rig-Veda* means the transgression of the divine laws which govern the universe." [2] The didactic function of poetry is already seen in their title, which practically means " verse-knowledge " ; that is to say, they are designed to preserve by means of rhythmic phrases, for an age unacquainted with writing, the sum total of spiritual wisdom. Hieratic or religious poems of a similar kind also form some of the most ancient elements in Babylonian and in Egyptian literature, and are to be seen again some five or six centuries later in a sacred literature which reproduces some of the *Rig-Veda's* mythological and ceremonial features, the *Gathas* of the Persian Zendavesta. The Hebrew Psalms (to which the *Rig-Veda* has been compared) offer another case in point.

Neither in Greek nor in Latin literature have we, perhaps, anything strictly parallel to these. But that is simply because Greek literature, and then under its influence Latin, became in course of time so secular that the early ritual poetry was out-poeticised and so swamped. What evidence there is makes it clear enough that the prehistoric Greeks and Romans used verse, in just the same way, for sacerdotal or ritual purposes.[3]

that the ultimate source of literature is the primitive festal rite is due to Dr. John Brown, whose *History of the Rise and Progress of Poetry through its Several Species* (Newcastle, 1764) was noticed with approval by Percy (Reliques, Note B to Introductory Essay). See *e.g.*, pp. 126-8 of Brown's book for a surprisingly modern idea.

[1] For an account of these see Prof. Rapson's *Ancient India* (1914), ch. 3. [2] Rapson, *op. cit.*, p. 48.

[3] See Jebb, *Greek Literature* (small primer), ch. 1, § 18 (which still, I think, holds true) and § 22 ; Murray, *Greek Literature*, pp. 62-3 ; Wight Duff, *A Literary History of Rome*, pp. 76-9, and note especially his quotation (77 n. 1) from Lamarre, *Hist. Litt. Lat.*, i. 49, one of the passages where the *raison d'être* of poetry is well explained.

In the case of Latin we have indeed some fragmentary remains in the native Saturnian metre ; a few scraps from hymns sung by the Salii or dancing priests of Mars, litanies which were transmitted orally, and, like the Vedas, eventually became practically unintelligible not merely to the ordinary Roman of Horace's time [1] but even to the Salii themselves,[2] though modern scholarship has made something out of one of them ; and the short litany to the same god sung by the religious brotherhood who "beat the bounds" of the City. The "Fescennine" verses, too, on which more will be said presently,[3] and which it is probable were also originally in Saturnians, undoubtedly present one instance of that impromptu licentious banter which is a regular feature of a certain type of harvest festival. Oracles again, must have been given from the earliest times in this native metre ; otherwise the response [4] brought from Delphi in 398 B.C. would presumably have been translated literally into prose.

We see, then, that the religious-moral theory of poetry held by the ancients is justified so far at least as origins are concerned. But that in itself, though far from unimportant, remains to some degree rather an academic justification. What matters far more from every point of view, what matters far more for a proper understanding of the *monumentum aere perennius* which was Horace's life-work, is that in the *fully developed* Greek poetry, and its Latin derivative, the function of the poet remains fundamentally similar. We shall therefore now briefly review in outline the whole history—or *evolution* is perhaps the more significant term—of classical poetry from Homer to Augustan times. With poetry must be considered,[5] as literature becomes more civilised, that small proportion of prose which is in the nature of " pure " literature.

The Evolution of Classical Literature

The process above referred to,[6] by which poetry springs from hymns, literary song from ritual song, did not, of course,

---

[1] *Epist.*, II. i. 86-7.   [2] Quintilian, I. vi. 40.
[3] Pp. 51-3.   [4] Livy, V. xvi.
[5] As above explained, p. 30, n. 1.
[6] To be explained more fully later, p. 34.

take place once for all in the history of man. We have already spoken of several distinct occasions. It must now be remarked further, that even within the single field of Greek literature, that process took place more than once. In some literatures it does occur once only. Latin poetry, for example, is in its entire " classical " period a *derivative* literature, and only in one department, the *satura*, can it show an indigenous root extending back through the " Fescennine " to a native ritual. But Greek poetry is a very different matter ; in this respect it resembles rather the famous banyan-tree. At intervals in the course of its history it re-roots itself in the native soil of literature,[1] *viz.*, the rite or festal ceremony, and from this return to earth derives, like an Antaeus, fresh vigour for its succeeding effort. Thus Epic—to give one instance now for clearness— Epic, effete in Ionia, amalgamates with a native Attic festal rite and results at length in Aeschylus. Such junctions are— or here at least will be regarded as—literary *origins*, no matter how demonstrable it may be that the literary factor in them, like the ritual factor, has a long previous history ; for even on the same principle do we speak of the banyan's " roots."

It follows at once that Greek literature can be divided, from this standpoint, into several successive periods, or, as I prefer for my immediate purposes to call them, " cycles," [2] and that Latin literature should supply us with one such cycle. If we compare these cycles—I reckon four altogether in Greek and Latin literature [3]—with one another, we shall find, I believe, that their outlines present a general resemblance ; that they each consist of a series of *phases*. For a perfect example of a cycle, complete in all its phases and without bothersome excrescences, we should probably search all existing literatures in

---

[1] This point is well put, though from a slightly different " angle," in Mahaffy's *History of Greek Literature*, I. pp. 4, 5.

[2] Friendly critics of my original " Chapter II." objected to my calling these periods " cycles," on the ground that a cycle ought to return to what it began in. But so mine do ; if the reader will but think of the banyan-tree as literature, and the soil as ritual, he will see what I mean. Epic influence coming to bear on early Attic tragedy is an instance of the " return " ; thereupon an old cycle ends and a new one commences.

[3] But I believe the principle of the " cycle " to operate to a greater or less degree in all literatures.

3

vain ; I therefore, to explain my meaning, will narrate briefly what happened to the inhabitants of a certain Literary Utopia.

The Literary "Cycle" and the Successive "Phases" of which it Consists

For many centuries these Utopians had no literature at all. But they had a regular form of religious rite, a mimetic dance combined with words sung to music. They had two great fixed festivals, and a large number of smaller ones, in every year ; each festival had a different ceremony from every other, but within each ceremony the words and music, and to a lesser degree the dancing, were at first traditional and invariable. In course of time, however, a certain amount of blending took place, as formulæ from one rite were incorporated into another. This gave the priests, who had the direction of all such ceremonies, their chance ; editing once forced upon them, they very gradually took to composing. Thus in the course of generations the language of each rite became elastic ; the cult-epithet was often varied, and so became an *epitheton ornans ;* instead of the formula appeared the phrase ; until at length arose a priest who was by accident a born poet, and became famous (as ministers do in Scotland) for the originality of his addresses to the Supreme Being. Ritual had become art ; by a pious fraud long afterwards unsuspected, the litany had transformed itself into the lyric. This was—for these Utopians—the *Origin* of Poetry.

In rivalry or emulation of the priest-poet aforementioned, a large and flourishing school of lyric poets presently arose. Before very long, public interest in their work was such that the words of their poems became detached from the original performance and by consequence neither sung nor danced to but *recited* simply ; and these spoken poems circulated freely, at first by word of mouth and later in manuscript. In the course of some three centuries this poetry became more and more secularised with increasing rapidity ; while still retaining traces of its origin in the style, which was either formal and solemn, or playfully pretended to be so, and in the form, in respect of which it was divisible into three classes, the Hymn, the Prayer, and the Injunction or Sermon (this last a descendant of their primitive Oracles). This was *the first phase* of their literary history, and is represented by their LYRIC.

Towards the latter part of this phase, a poet already famed for his lyrics made a further innovation. It must be understood that alongside the new *spoken* poetry, the old choral dances had, in their poeticised form, continued. But this poet, instead of making his choir sing all together, divided them into groups which held dialogue with one another in song (accompanied of course by appropriate gesture or " dance ") ; or sometimes a single individual would sing in dialogue with a group. Poetry intended for recitation *only* was now also a familiar institution ; and so the next step was a similar distribution of *recited* poetry (and ultimately of prose) between several persons. Thus was invented Drama, which itself in turn, like Lyric, became detached from the performance, and circulated in manuscript and (as these Utopians became more civilised) in printed books. This was *the second phase*, and is represented by their DRAMA.

The third and last phase is distinguished principally by its fundamental difference from *both* the preceding. To understand this difference, we must go back once more to the original rite. That rite, in all its varieties, had had a function, namely, to put the soul of the participant at rest regarding his relation with the gods of the community. In the literary works of the first and second phases this function had been substantially preserved. The lyrics and the dramas of this race had for their object, to put the soul of the reader or spectator at rest, not indeed in respect of his relation to " the gods," for by this time many of these Utopians did not believe in the old gods ; but in respect of his relation to the spiritual world in general. They aimed at putting the soul of the reader or spectator at rest with itself, and with the souls of the other Utopians, and with the soul of the community. The authors of these works did not inquire if this was worth doing ; it seemed self-evident.

The poets, by consequence, were held in honour, and the rewards of poetic office attracted charlatans. There now began to appear an enormous multitude of literary works, some verse, some prose, which, so far from being, like lyric and drama, the direct expression of emotions, and therefore appealing directly to the emotion of the recipient, were merely *about* things—" about it and about "—and appealed only to the intelligence. These works had neither function nor form ; though they might have purpose and they might have shape. The old lyrics had occasionally contained short stories, illustrating the power or beneficence of the god concerned ; now appeared stories for the story's sake, to while away periods of idleness. Those who in this age were born poets made the best of such opportunity as was offered them, and, debarred from lyric and drama, wrote stories in poetry, and thus invented Epic. But the enormous majority of the stories were simply Novels. Here and there, even in Epic and Novel, appeared a writer who in the two preceding epochs would have been not only a poet but a great poet, and who therefore succeeded to a considerable extent in making mere *narrative*—mere consecutive information supplied *apropos* of nothing by a single individual—appeal, indirectly of course but still appreciably, to the emotions, and thus act (within limits) as a moral stimulus. One such writer, for example, conceived his works as tragedies, and then turned them into narrative to obtain a living. But Epics and Novels of true artistic-moral value were very very few—even among the Utopians. The enormous mass were " realistic," that is to say they aimed fundamentally at giving information, like a photograph, not at producing an effect, like a picture ; they were speech, not action. This, in a word, was the single characteristic which entitles the works of this period to be classed together, in spite of the multiplicity of their varieties ; in spite, too, of the fact that the practitioners in each department considered their own department to constitute in itself a whole branch of Literature and to be fundamentally distinct from many another which the present classification (at which they would have been extremely indignant) groups with it. The playwrights, for example—since stage performances continued, and indeed increased enormously —spoke of themselves as the successors (and thought of themselves as the superiors) of the great dramatists of the preceding era ; but their works were in fact totally different from those in aim, being of three classes—(i) dialogues with a thesis to maintain, *e.g.*, " that virtue is always rewarded " (moral apologue disguised as drama), or " that virtue is never rewarded " (satire disguised as drama) ; these often began well enough, with action as in a drama proper, but sooner or later, as the abstract interest inevitably superseded the concrete, the life went out of the action ; this type therefore might be labelled *Abortive* Drama : (ii) realistic " slices from life," exactly like the novels above described except in being arranged for (actual or supposed) stage-performance ; a class conveniently termed *Mime :* (iii) a compound of i and ii.

Other types must be briefly alluded to. The imparting of information or opinion being now regarded as the one aim of a self-respecting writer, the ablest brains, both of authors and readers, finding Epic and Novel inadequate or distasteful, turned to History, Philosophy, and Science. The earliest works in these fields were just early enough to be influenced to a greater or less extent by the great " functional " literature of the preceding epoch. The first historians were half concerned to give an accurate account of facts, but half to produce an impressive moral effect ; their writings were partly modelled upon Tragedy. The first Philosophers, having arrived at their various theories through conversation, found it convenient to expound them in dialogue form ; these Dialogues, also, but to a much less extent, were modelled upon Tragedy ; in the result, however, their chief resemblance was to the " abortive dramas " above described, indeed not unnaturally several extant works (in Utopian) seem to be on the borderline between these two. Scientific works, it is strange to think, sprang (among these Utopians), somewhat indirectly, from Comedy ! In the preceding epoch, experts had been distrusted, and a stock type of Fool in the old comedies had been a Learned Doctor—sometimes Wizard—who delivered a long lecture or dissertation ; in *Late* Comedy this part rapidly extended at the expense of the comedy proper, which it eventually extinguished. Thus arose the *Textbook*, the only form of book which was ultimately to flourish among these Utopians at all ; it might be about anything, from house-flies to literary criticism.

That, then, is " the third phase " ; represented by two main literary classes, one an old literary *form* deteriorated, the other a new " form," though only by courtesy called a " form " at all ; these are :—A. *Abortive Drama*, with Philosophic Dialogue, Mime, etc. B. *Narrative*, including Epic and Novel.

Such was the stage reached by our Utopian civilisation when their country was suddenly invaded by the Barbarians, and subdued. For centuries thereafter there was no literature at all. But the Barbarians also had their primitive ritual, their choral song-and-dance ; and the chance discovery by a Barbarian priest of an early Utopian semi-religious lyric caused the good man to have a " wild surmise," and became the occasion (through his adapting it for a Barbarian religious service) of the commencement of a new literary cycle, which proceeded, in its turn, very much as above.

I have now explained what I mean by the literary " cycle " and its three " phases." These last correspond, in one aspect, to the three great main literary forms as generally recognised— Lyric, Dramatic, Epic. But whereas Epic is generally regarded as the most primitive, I regard it as the most sophisticated. We must now very summarily examine the actually existing cycles of Ancient Classical Literature. We shall then see what Horace had behind him ; and so, as this book proceeds, we shall, it is hoped, understand something about his choice of literary forms.

Application of the " Theory of Cycles " to the Evolution of Classical Literature

Now that we pass from the consideration of the purely theoretic cycle to various cycles that have actually existed, we must begin by noting three important points :—

(i) The cycles as they appear in actual literary history are often not complete ; *e.g.*, the second phase may drop out altogether, the first leading directly to the third.

(ii) Although the literary types which appear in the third phase, as contrasted with those of the first and second, are non-functional and therefore artistically debased, still, the genius of individual writers can often produce in them results so brilliant in details (*e.g.*, wit, style), that a particular good novel, for example, may turn out superior to a particular poor lyric. *Ceteris paribus*, however, it is Lyric and Drama that attain the greatest heights.

(iii) The literary types which appear in the third phase, although not, strictly, *functional*, can be, and in the ancient

world almost invariably were, *tendencious ;* they cannot like
Lyric and Drama make the reader feel moral emotions, but they
can, appealing to the reason, " point a moral." [1]

(iv) Cycles may chronologically overlap ; an old cycle may
continue in some localities long after a new one has begun in
others.

THE FIRST CYCLE IN GREEK LITERATURE

It is now a commonplace that the Homeric poems, so far
from being the primitive productions they were once thought
to be, represent a highly advanced stage both of society and
of the poetic art.[2] For pre-Homeric poetic history we have,
unfortunately, only the most meagre evidence. It is generally
agreed, however, that the cradle of pre-Homeric poetry was
the (then Thracian) Pieria ; and that the poetry was hieratic,
being associated with the cult of the Muses, with which it seems
to have travelled from Pieria to Mount Helicon in Boeotia.
How did a type of poem so secular as the *Iliad* or *Odyssey* develop
out of primitive hieratic verse ?   Briefly,[3] more or less thus :—

Pre-literary period—*Ritual*-hymns, addressed to the Muses,
or to Zeus or Apollo, the two great gods with whom the cult
of the Muses became early associated.   Also, doubtless, oracles.
Then—

First Phase—*Poetic* hymns of the same sort as those just
described.   For a late example which, however, represents this
stratum, see Hesiod, *Works and Days*, 1-9.   Then, as epithets
like ᾿Αργειφόντης or εἰραφιώτης come to be expanded into narrative,[4] the hymn grows a new member, which gradually increases
at the expense of the original stock, until the latter is left
simply as a more or less perfunctory invocation prefixed to
the " lay."   Again, for a late representative, see the type of
" Homeric Hymn " of which ii-v are good examples.   The next
stage is reached when the lay, according to the process of general
secularisation which is an almost universal feature of Greek

---

[1] The distinction here made seems to me, I must say, of absolutely
immense importance for literary criticism ; not that I suppose its importance to be limited to that.

[2] See *e.g.*, Murray, *Rise of the Greek Epic*, 92, and generally.

[3] For a full account see Croiset, *Hist. Litt. Grecque*, Vol. I., ch. i.

[4] Cf. *Hom. Hymn*, ix. 2-3 ; Virgil, *Aeneid*, viii., 293-5.

literature, concerns itself with the adventures not of a god but of a hero ; and it is noteworthy that even in this stage the invocation to a god is still retained. Thus did Demodocus in the *Odyssey* " begin from a god " his lay of the wooden horse ; detached preludes of a similarly conventional kind are the majority of the Homeric Hymns. In due course—the " second phase " being entirely absent from this first cycle—we reach the *Third Phase,* in which the Story is everything, the invocation (to the Muses) practically nothing. This phase is represented by the Homeric Epic and its following, no matter what may be the right view as to the precise relation between Epic and Lay.

But while we have thus summarily traced the development of the hymn, we have said nothing more about the oracle. That, by contrast, is addressed to a mortal, and gives him a warning in deliberately mysterious language. Corresponding to this ritual form, and ultimately (as I think) originating from it, we find a type of poem which has little if any vogue in modern civilisation, but had a distinct place in ancient life and presents a long evolution in ancient literature. That is the earnest personal exhortation, most often in the form of lyric, and therefore in the first phase. No survivors from the First Cycle have come down to us, but we shall meet with plenty in the Second. The First Cycle does, however, give us one remarkable example of a type of poem, one of the many " adulterate " types which arise in the *third* phase, in which we see what happens to this *personal ode* (as we may here call it) when it survives to be transformed under Epic influences. The example is Hesiod's *Works and Days,* and the type is one which we shall meet again in the " third phases " of later Cycles.

The name of Hesiod has probably not often been coupled with that of Horace, yet here is the first appearance in classical literature of a class of poem which it was reserved for Horace to make peculiarly his own. There is, indeed, one poem of Horace's which is on one side at least in direct descent from the *Works and Days* itself, and that is the *Ars Poetica.* The one poet is concerned with farming and the other with an even more arduous art or chancier occupation ; but the later work belongs quite distinctly to the class strictly called *Didactic,* of which Hesiod is the father. But if Hesiod had lived in " the first phase," this poem would have been a lyric ; and that is not a merely idle remark ; the *Works and Days*, strikingly different as it is from the remainder of the Hesiodic corpus, has an artistic structure, and one of a kind that reminds us of the many lyrical examples of this class of poem. Its myth of Prometheus and the ages of mankind, for example, is no mere digression like the stories embedded in Epics, but an integral part of the work, designed, as with Pindar, to illustrate and enforce the immediate lesson. The *Works and Days*, in fact, is something of an Epistle, and such a piece as Horace's *Epist.*, I. ii. is not without points of resemblance to it. But the Horatian admonitory address was not derived direct from Hesiod ; we shall find its prototype in the succeeding poetic Cycle.

The Second Cycle in Greek Literature

This cycle is complete ; the fullest and clearest in all literature, just as its products are the finest.

Its pre-literary background is, of course, the ritual mimetic chant, as it survived wherever Epic influence had not yet penetrated ; *e.g.*, in Attica. It is the spread of epic literature that gives the initial fertilisation to this cycle. The early elegiac of Callinus and Tyrtaeus is a blend of the old epic style with the new spirit of native lyric. Sappho and Alcaeus are under Homeric influence.

The Cycle consists of :—

I. *First Phase.* Lyric, in the largest sense, including not only pure lyric, or *melic* as the Greeks themselves originally called it, but also the types often referred to by moderns as " semi-lyrical," *viz.*, Elegiac and Iambic.

As the parent ritual had two forms, a serious and a sportive, so has its literary offspring two forms. The serious, comprising *pure* lyric, extends from Terpander to Pindar ; it also includes Elegiac. The sacerdotal tone, and even the religious form, are strikingly maintained ; the poems profess [1] to be either Hymns or Prayers addressed to the gods, or Exhortations, Oracular Injunctions, " sermons," earnest personal appeals, and the like, addressed to mortals. The importance of this will be seen when we come to consider Horace's *Odes*.

The other, the sportive type of ceremony, gave rise to the

[1] Cf. p. 34 *fin.*

class of poetry called Iambic, of which the founder was Archilochus. Its origin is one which it will be worth our while to glance at here, not only because in this case both rite and *genre* are unfamiliar to the modern world, but partly because Horace imitated Archilochus, and partly because of a similar phenomenon in Italian life which constitutes another of Horace's main literary antecedents.

The sportive type of religious ritual was evidently a widespread feature of prehistoric life both in the Greek world and in the Italian.[1] It presents variations, naturally, according to the different localities in which it can be traced ; but on the whole, the main characteristics of it are as follows. First and foremost, *licence* in a general sense is the spirit of the hour, the licence appropriate to holiday. Anybody may abuse anybody ; the abuse, no matter how violent, is understood to be playful ; women mock men, men bandy railleries among one another, slaves take liberties with their masters. A good deal of this banter is naturally of a ribald kind. At one time it may be a Spring festival, and phallic ceremonies are in progress to promote fertility, while phallic language is in any case a countercharm against the evil eye ; at another time it will be Harvesthome, everyone is in good spirits and nobody will take offence at anything. But even that licence is to some extent regularised, and formalised ; and few traits of this type of ritual are so universal in the surviving developments of it as an *alternation* of the abuse between two persons or sets of persons.

Such ceremonies are naturally (from the two occasions above indicated) connected with vegetation-gods. In Greece the cults of the vegetation gods Dionysus and Demeter became united, particularly (near the beginning of the sixth century) at Eleusis in Attica, where their " mysteries " were celebrated ; and at the revel in honour of the wine-god a congenial atmosphere, despite a perhaps too boisterous reception, was found for the spirit of Jest as represented in Iambe, whose pleasantries had first brought a smile to the face of the Corn-goddess in her mourning for her lost daughter.[2] The name is evidently

---

[1] On the general radical unity of art-forms in the Greek and Latin worlds (and the difference of their development), Mommsen, *Roman History*, I. 35-6 (English tr.) is good.

[2] *Hom. Hymn*, ii. 202-5.

only a personification of the verse-form ; but proves its early association with the Demeter-cult ; for the " Homeric Hymn " which tells this story is older than the Eleusinian admission of Dionysus, and is assigned to the seventh century. Presumably, then, satirical exchanges of the well-attested type above described were regularly held in honour of this goddess, and for these iambic verse was specially employed.[1] Consistently with this, when the iambic first appears in literature, it is used for lampoons in which scurrility occasionally passed into obscenity. The author of these is Archilochus, and unpromising as this description of them may sound, he was undoubtedly a great writer. So far as purely literary style is concerned, it is he and not Terpander who begins the new era. All poets before him had been under the influence of Homer's style. With him and after him, though the Homeric influence on vocabulary and diction continues as in fact it always did, the Homeric style is gone for ever. The revolution he made was of the same kind as was our own Romantic Revival. Poetic style before him had been *proper ;* even Homer is proper ; but Archilochus is never that. His is the style that succeeds by an apparent scorn of style ; he seems to take no thought how he shall say a thing ; he writes from the heart, fiercely, tersely, and disdainfully. Even his obscenity, which, it should be realised, was an innovation in literature, and one not altogether destined to lapse, is but a part of his heroic impudence. The whole lyric movement, the early simple and the late ornate, owes its general style to him ; not only Alcaeus and Sappho their force and purity, but Simonides his seemingly spontaneous inevitability, and Pindar his abruptness and impressionism. Archilochus is the first literary free-lance. " In my spear is kneaded bread, in my spear is wine of Ismarus," would have been a stumbling block or foolishness to Homer.

II. *Second Phase.* DRAMA, again in the largest sense, including both Tragedy and Comedy. Greek Tragedy is obviously an extremely composite product ; but all that it is necessary to insist on here is, first, that on the literary side it arises out of the Dithyramb or hymn to Dionysus, in other words it is an offshoot from the " First Phase "—from a particular type of

---

[1] With the iambic naturally goes the trochaic measure, the trochee being simply the inversion of the iambus.

Lyric ; and secondly that, on the social side, the rite on which it is founded is (despite the inherence of a ribald strain, eventually regularised as Satyr-drama) fundamentally of the solemn and serious variety. From the gross and boisterous type of rite, that is from the phallic ceremonies alluded to by Aristotle, developed Comedy. It will be noted that according to these principles Comedy appears as just what Aristotle said it was—the successor of Iambic.

Now Greek Tragedy and Comedy, it will be well to realise before we pass in due course to the third phase of this cycle, were both extremely " functional," far more so than any preceding Greek literature ; and the nature of the function corresponds in both to the ritual from which they were evolved. " To justify the ways of God to man " to enable men " to glorify God and to enjoy him " if not for ever at least during the ceremony and as long afterwards as can be provided for—that is the prime object of the priest as such, and the religious service, the Mystery play, unlike the mere sermon, achieves that object not indirectly but directly ; not by demonstration, but by action. That too is the fundamental purpose of Greek Tragedy as seen in Aeschylus or Sophocles.[1] The situation at the end is always seen to be one which the gods had in view from the beginning, and which they have brought about by supernatural intervention at critical points, however much their actions may have been resented by the suffering heroes or heroines. Mr Mackail and M. Allègre, among others, have both emphasised the element of the *marvellous* in Sophocles. It is quite true ; the Philoctetes for example has every right to be called a Mystery play, and its whole point would have been stultified if it had not ended with the intervention of the now deified Heracles. But what is perhaps not so obvious, certainly not so familiar to modern ideas, but of the very first importance for a true understanding of classical literature, is that Comedy too regarded itself as having a salutary social

---

[1] The plays of Euripides are not functional, or those of them which preserve the functional structure are not true to it. A common modern view is that many of them were written to support a thesis, *i.e.*, they are tracts. I think they are each a variety entertainment, of a peculiarly Greek, and therefore intellectual, kind ; a series of sophistic scenarios. For more on Euripides see p. 47.

function ; and this is true in varying degrees of Comedy's literary cognates. At its highest, Comedy was even moral ; as is explicitly claimed by Aristophanes in *Ach.* 500 το γὰρ δίκαιον οἶδε καὶ τρυγῳδία ; [1] and it is from the same standpoint that Horace asks *ridentem dicere verum quid vetat ?* In a general way, however, the function of Comedy may be said to be the exposure of social pests, whether persons or tendencies. It is here especially that we can see its affinity, as alleged by Aristotle, to the earlier iambic poetry, and also, as emphasised by Horace,[2] to its successor the *Satura* of Latin literature, a form, as will be seen,[3] so closely allied in origin to the Greek iambic type. For despite the " sublimation " of the iambic trimeter by Tragedy, it had begun for satirical purposes and it continued to be used for such ; as for example (in its "lame " form) by Herondas. Scurrilous associations continued to cling to the very name of the metre till Horace's own day.[4] Abuse, if directed on the right objects, has a high value in the estimation of the primitive community. Obscenity itself is an antidote to the evil eye. *Expose* the devil and he will flee from you ; this is the principle that, in the original story,[5] underlies the declamatory outburst of Apollonius in Keats's *Lamia*, and is seen at work in the immediate vanishing of the witch ; this is why Macbeth, confronted with the ghost of Banquo, tells it to its face that it is only a wretched shade. Exorcism—that, in one word, is the function of Comedy. One type of poet invokes a good spirit in the grand style ; another assails the evil spirit with derision. The latter method has its uses ; according to Horace at least—or one mood of Horace—it is the more effective ; *ridiculum acri fortius et melius magnas plerumque secat res*, he says in *Sat.*, I. x. 14-15.

III. *Third Phase.* As the literary form of the First Phase had been Lyric, and of the Second, Drama, so the Third is associated with the one remaining major literary form, the Narrative. But it is not only co-extensive with that form, as in the case of the two preceding phases.

---

[1] For didactics in Sicilian Comedy see my chapter on the Satires, pp. 149-50 and 177. [2] *Sat.*, I. iv. 1-7.

[3] P. 53. [4] *Odes*, I. xvi. 2-3.

[5] Philostratus, *De Vit. Apoll.* IV., referred to by Burton in the passage from the *Anatomy of Melancholy* which Keats appended to his poem.

The distinctive work of the Third Phase is that all the literary works which represent it are, by contrast with those of the preceding two, *non*-functional. It is thus the parent not only of Narrative, but of the other two non-functional literary forms, " Abortive Drama " and Scientific (or semi-scientific) Textbook. In other words, whereas both of the first two Phases had been Poetic, the third phase is Sophistic. This last word, if it may be adopted as the designation of what is after all a single literary category (I shrink from using " form " of what I regard as non-functional) although (as Aristotle would say) the name for it does not as yet exist—this term *Sophistic* is at once the most comprehensive and the most appropriate to retain in contrast with the already accepted designation of the more familiar categories *Lyric* and *Dramatic*. It is the singer, the poet, that composes lyrics and tragedies ; but it is the man who *knows* (or is believed to know) that tells a story or compiles a treatise ; it is the Highbrow who writes Abortive Drama.

As a consequence the works of this phase tend (though not necessarily or exclusively) to be written in Prose rather than Verse.

It is a further sign of the essential similarity of all the " Sophistic " types of literature, that works belonging to this Third Phase cannot infrequently be classified alternatively under one or another of such types, or else described as a sort of fusion of them. Herodotus and Thucydides, for example ; are they " Science " ? " ἱστορίη " began as it has ended, in " research " ; for the Ionians it was research *par excellence*. Or are they " Narrative " ? or a blend of both ? The last description will best suit Herodotus ; but neither is Thucydides, with all his caution and veracity, a mere " scientific historian " in the modern sense. And then again, while obviously not " abortive " drama, their works present, both of them, an unmistakable dramatic structure. They might indeed be regarded, and have in fact (particularly in recent times) been treated, as a sort of *transferred* drama ; nay more, it is undeniable that both works have, and were meant to have, a definite moral function similar to that of Tragedy. But while recognising their moral sublimity, we cannot, I think, on that account regard them as *fully* functional and relate them to the

Second Phase ; the reason being that it is not *free* drama that we find in them ; their object is primarily to state and interpret *facts*, that is, their works are fundamentally " sophistic."

The only other author of the first magnitude in this phase is Euripides. His works, which are either " enigmatical " or merely bad, according as one may or may not believe them to possess each a certain single significance however difficult of decipherment, present a problem too complicated to be even touched on here. I regard them quite definitely as " Abortive Drama," but must leave my detailed diagnosis of them for another work. In the meantime, I do not expect that anyone will be inclined to quarrel with me for saying that they have not any direct moral function, as have the tragedies of Aeschylus and Sophocles, nor indirect as have the histories of Herodotus and Thucydides. In all these authors, power that is moral, whether of Man or Nature, is represented as in itself glorious and always ultimately triumphant ; power that is immoral is brought low. In Euripides what is moral is not glorious, what is base or vile is dwelt on with gusto or perverted tenderness.[1] And I do not think that anyone will dispute the statement that where the method of Aeschylus and Sophocles had been poetic, that of Euripides is " Sophistic."

An author who has considerable affinity with Euripides is Plato ; but for him, as for various other " sophistic " products, some of them of considerable importance for the study of Horace, we must wait until the corresponding phase of the Third Cycle.

THE THIRD CYCLE IN GREEK LITERATURE

The second cycle eventually consolidated itself into an almost entirely Attic one ; the third is originally, and in some degree always remained, Sicilian. In this it is geographically midway between Greece and Rome ; it was also that chronologically ; and in the one and only original literary form which it invented it provides, as we shall see, the single *institutional* (as opposed to purely stylistic) bridge between the two great national literatures.

---

[1] If it had been with *pity*, I could agree with those who find in Euripides a certain moral and humane advance on Aeschylus and Sophocles ; but of pity I cannot myself see the smallest genuine sign.

In its first phase, the Song, this cycle is not now represented
for us, but obvious relics of it are either echoed, or here and
there [1] actually embedded, in the Idylls of Theocritus. Sicily
had been from time immemorial a land of rustic revelry and
festal singing-matches ; its pastoral folklore had provided
material for the lyric poet Stesichorus ; and it is small wonder
that the vintage or harvest " revel-singing " passed into actual
" comedy " considerably earlier here than in Athens. The
first who literarised this comedy, Epicharmus, is dated 540-450
B.C. But the form he thus originated was not Comedy in the
Attic sense ; it was a special kind, the Mime.[2] It had no
chorus ; its prototype was presumably that antiphony of repar-
tee which we know to have been a regular feature of primitive
Sicilian and Italian festivals, and which is mirrored for us in
Theocritus ; this was developed, by Epicharmus' time, into
a wordy dispute, often of a curiously technical philosophic
character. That is not however by any means the only feature,
though it is the most primitive and, as we shall see not only
in Plato but in Horace, the most permanent, of this curious
literary form. Even as practised by Epicharmus, the mime
was very much of a medley, and included dialogue of a quite
general kind ; but its distinctive characteristics are, realism
in style and setting whether the characters are heroic or not,[3]
and a popular exposition of moral philosophy. The importance
of Epicharmus among Horace's literary antecedents will thus
be evident at once to anyone who remembers the general form
and content of Horace's Satires ; and there are other links
between them, one consisting in the food-catalogues which
figure among his fragments. What are they doing there,
what relevance have they to the essential idea (in so far as it

---

[1] E.g., the song " of the divine Lityerses," Id., X. 42-55, a series of
primitive verse-proverbs, arranged in couplets into a sort of didactic
poem.

[2] It is perhaps advisable to remind the reader that what the Romans
called mime was a very different institution.

[3] I do not believe that the works of Epicharmus are to be thought
of as in two categories. The mime and the satura could, like their
affinity the Satyric Drama, have heroic characters, and the tone be still
equally realistic, the matter equally disputatious ; cf. e.g., Hor., Sat., II.
v., based perhaps on a piece by Menippus of Gadara.

had any) of the Mime ? The answer is that they are part of its general didacticism, often (but I believe not always) ironical ; they were presumably put into the mouths of gastronomical experts [1] like Horace's Catius, a profession peculiarly and notoriously Sicilian. The mime tended to be a dissertation, and the dissertation was often upon such a subject as roast pig.

For our present purpose, the main point about Epicharmus is the fact that his works set the tone of the whole ensuing period in being, not moral—not, that is to say, by " direct action "—but moralising. Realism, often ironical, plus moralism, that is the formula for the mime ; and the mime is the characteristic and the only original literary form of this third cycle.

The mime is dramatic in form, or, to speak more strictly, in appearance. If it had been functional, we should have regarded it as " second phase." But the mime is not functional ; its contests in primitive obscenity or sophistic logic were quite frivolous ; its pictures of low life were mere realism, pointless and " photographic." It is a form of Abortive Drama, and belongs to the Third Phase.

By far its most important development, at all events for our present purposes, is the Philosophic Dialogue. That had two forms, a refined and a coarse. The former consists simply of the Σωκρατικοὶ λόγοι, the *Socratici sermones* referred to by Horace (*Odes*, III. xxi. 9) ; of these, the works of Plato are almost our only extant representative, as they were, of course, from the outset incomparably the greatest. This type is " serious " ; that is to say, it is serious as compared with the other type ; it can be elevated, even noble, witness Plato at his highest ; but it is never so serious as Tragedy, it always remains too merely intellectual—too dissertative—to be sublime ; and it is never absolutely secure from a lapse into triviality or flippancy. On the other hand it should be noted that the coarse type, the Diatribe (Horace's *Bionei sermones*, *Epist.*, II. ii. 60), although it was, on the contrary, hardly literature at all, could be and often was extremely " serious " in its way. It was popular-scholastic, jocose, and fundamentally vulgar ; but earnestly evangelical, and doubtless productive of much " uplift " among the innumerable simple-minded.

---

[1] Cf. Cornford, *Origin of Attic Comedy*, 165.

Plato " slept with Sophron under his pillow " ; [1] in other words, ancient tradition tells us that in the matter of literary form Plato's chief master was Sophron. As a matter of fact, the Platonic dialogue looks like a cross between Sophron and Epicharmus. It owes to Sophron its realism, of setting and of conversation ; to Epicharmus, its philosophic content.[2] The literary ancestor of the Platonic Socrates was a stock comic figure, the Learned Doctor.[3]

The Diatribe, in turn, derives from the Dialogue ; it was indeed frequently in monologue form ; but so, theoretically, are some of Plato's works ; and even then it included short imaginary dialogues.

Of all these sophistic writings Plato's alone are something more than sophistic. He had been educated in Homer and the tragedians, and in several of his works, when all the mere dialectic has been discounted, there remains, as in the last scene of his *Phaedo*, an element not merely moralistic but moral. But after him moral literature suffers a complete eclipse ; morals and literature, to the misfortune of both, become divorced. Morality is henceforth taken charge of by philosophers ; literature becomes non-moral, it is *ad delectandum* merely. The only good literature is academic, Alexandrine ; but then that does not strictly belong to this cycle ; it synchronises with it, but in point of *forms*, it is simply a continuation of the products of the preceding cycles. Theocritus, indeed, has one root in the native life of Sicily, and his work remains to show to what a height of poetry even the mime can attain, in the hands of a master.

LATIN LITERATURE AND ITS OWN SINGLE (ABORTIVE) CYCLE

The third cycle of Greek Literature is continued in Latin Literature through imitations ; and as the Latin writers

---

[1] Diog. Laert., iii. 18, Suidas *s.v.* Σώφρων, Duris Fr. 45 in Müller, *F.H.G.*, ii. 480.

[2] Not, of course, its philosophic matter, but *the tradition of presenting* philosophic matter in dialogue form under a guise of imaginative literature. Cf. esp. Diog. Laert., iii. 12-14 ; the passages of Epicharmus which he cites are really remarkable.

[3] Cf. esp. Cornford, *Origin of Attic Comedy*, pp. 136-8, 161.

explored Greek Literature backwards, the other cycles too presently found their Latin exploiters. It is, indeed, possible to argue that Latin Literature had *no* cycle of its own ; that, being from first to last not social but scholastic, it had no " cycle " at all. But there is just one exception, the " satura." Even this, indeed, was early invaded by Greek influences ; but in view of its precedent history and origin, and also of the fact that it retained even to the last, in some degree, its inherent social function, we must regard it as representing for us the only native Latin literary cycle, very imperfect as that is.

That cycle had a " first phase," of crude lyric, already referred to.[1] Of the two types of primitive ritual, the grave and the gay, only the latter, the " Fescennine verses," became regularised on its *dramatic* side. A combination apparently took place in Rome itself between the professional stage-show of Etruscan origin, in which there had hitherto been only dancing and music, and these Fescennines, which now supplied the third constituent of drama, words. This composite institution, which was the only form of drama to which the original stock of Latin " literature " ever extended itself, held the Roman stage for over a century, when it was displaced by the *fabula*, or play with a plot, that is to say simply by translations (how crude does not concern us) of Greek dramas. In the confused passage of Livy [2] which is our authority for these developments, the combination is called *satura ;* and if he is right, and if the derivation of *satura* which connects it with *lanx satura* (= mixed dish, hotch-potch, medley)[3] is to be

---

[1] P. 32.

[2] VII. 2. But it is only fair to add that several modern scholars (not all, however) follow Hendrickson and Leo in denying the existence of the *dramatic* satura altogether. Cf. D'Alton, *Horace and His Age*, pp. 256 foll. ; with whose criticism of Hendrickson on p. 263 I agree.

[3] Undoubtedly this was the generally accepted explanation of the word *Satura* in the time of Juvenal (I. 86), and probably earlier, since Varro (116-28 B.C.) is referred to in this connection by Diomedes (3, p. 486, Keil) as having explained that a sort of stuffing, made of raisins, pearl-barley, pine-kernels, and honey-mead, was called by this name. But a metaphorical transference of such a term to a class of writing is a thing that could only take place in a comparatively late stage of literary civilisation, and we have good reason to suppose (*e.g.*, Livy, VII. 2), nor has it usually been even questioned, that the *Satura* was a very old

credited, then the name may quite conceivably have been given in virtue either of the amalgamation of the two elder institutions, or of the entirely plotless and shapeless and therefore miscellaneous character of this entertainment. But Mommsen's suggested derivation, though it has not won acceptance, seems to me very much more probable. He held that *Satura* means the masquerade of the " full " (*i.e.*, replete) people or *saturi* (σάτυροι) after their harvest festival, thus connecting the word with what was undoubtedly a kindred institution, the Greek satyr-dance ; that this " comic dance or *Satura* beyond doubt reached back to a period anterior to the separation of the stocks " ; and that the Saturnian metre was so named as being simply the metre used for this masquerade, the lengthening of the first syllable being caused later by popular association with the god of sowing (Sāturnus for Saiturnus). From this it follows [1] that, as the amalgamation described by Livy did not take place until 364 B.C., the name must have denoted one of the original ingredients, obviously in fact the Fescennine, an identification to which the Greek analogy once more points.[2] Nor indeed does the language of Livy in the passage above cited definitely imply anything to the contrary. Of the two constituents, the Fescennine was clearly the one which gave to the theatrical *Satura* what character or significance it had ; and although the *Satura* in general underwent in the course of its history a good many vicissitudes and only secured its survival by adopting various shapes, we shall find that this feature of dialogue, not infrequently of a coarse and bantering kind, remained embedded in it throughout.

This theatrical type of satura held the Roman stage for over a century, until it was displaced by the *fabula* or play with a plot, that is to say by translations of Greek plays. Satura

---

institution. Mommsen's derivation has the great advantage of being in complete accord with the undeniable connection of *Satura* with the Fescennines ; and I hope that my analogy between the evolution of the Italian satire and that of the Sicilian comedy or mime may throw a very little further light on the matter. Nettleship (*Essays*, II. 24-5) is very guarded in his reference to the traditional etymology.

[1] Mommsen himself does not draw this inference, but his language at III. 179 seems hardly consistent with I. 35 and 288-90.

[2] Fescennine from *fascinum* = φαλλός.

however continued, though in a new form; instead of being acted, saturae were now published. Ennius, the founder of this new type, took his matter from Epicharmus; he wedded, in fact, Roman satura to Sicilian mime, a marriage of first cousins. His saturae were not functional; they were literary exercises, both in matter and form thoroughly *sophistical;* they represent " third phase."

The *historic* satura, the " sermo," the form invented by Lucilius and continued by Horace and his successors, follows in the footsteps of Ennius to the extent to which (and that is a great deal) it derives its matter from Greek popular philosophy. To that extent it is, indeed, merely moralistic. But it is also more than that; it is moral. It has a genuine moral tone, a moral appeal, and is therefore, so far, moral in action; and it is conscious of exercising a moral function in society. To that extent it is not merely third phase, but, being functional, it resembles the " Iambic " of Archilochus; it is the *ribald* counterpart of Lyric, in the first phase; its aim is the exorcism, the exposing and disarming, of social pests. This moral and social purpose it did *not* find in its Greek antecedents, the Hellenistic scholasticism which it used as raw material; no, this, *the* function of satura, descended to it from its prehistoric ritual source, the Fescennines which exorcised by means of abuse, obscene or otherwise. In satire, therefore, Latin litera-ture must be admitted to have supplied a new and original literary form, although a minor one. Whatever Quintilian exactly meant [1] by his famous " satura tota nostra est," there remains a sense in which he is right.

What is the upshot of all this? It is, that through Latin satire the old politico-moral function of Poetry is *to some extent* restored to Classical Literature, after having lapsed in the Greek Decadence. The barbarian Roman ultimately achieves results far nearer to the work of the old Greek masters than did ever their cultured but degenerate successors, because he writes, as they had done, animated by a national spirit. And this power he first finds in his native satire. It was after

---

[1] Excluding, that is, the latest interpretation, which appeared after this chapter was written; Mr. Rennie (*Classical Review*, xxxvii., p. 21) takes the meaning to be " in Satire it is we Romans who bear off the palm " (translation mine); and makes out a strong case.

Lucilius had " flogged the town " that Romans realised that literature is not a plaything but a weapon. It was not merely Satura, as has been often said, that he stamped for ever with the mood of indignant invective ; he prepared the way for that in Roman poetry in general ; he was in his rough fashion a pioneer for Lucretius and Catullus.

Similarly Horace, as we shall see, rising so to speak upon the shoulders of Satura, attains to pure form and to direct poetic moral action in his Odes, where he is following in the footsteps of the original Greek Lyric ; but fails to extend his triumph into the creation of a Roman analogue to Attic Tragedy, falling back instead, in his *Ars Poetica*, upon the old Sophistic Fallacy.

I have shewn, in so far as I have found possible by crudely summarising the results of an unmatured study of so wide a field of literature, that in regarding the poet primarily as a teacher ancient popular opinion was, so to speak, " archæologically " right. But I am also convinced that it was *a priori* right ; in other words, that this, or rather something like it, is the true theory of poetry. Something like it ; for although I have just said of the modern world, that it has in this respect never appreciated the difference between preaching and training, I cannot deny that the ancients themselves tended to confuse the two ; the real difference is that they admitted either into the sphere of poetry while the moderns reject both. It is the old trouble, the intellectualist fallacy ; the ancient theory of poetry, whether as we find it in Plato and the sophists generally or as we may gather its popular and pre-sophistic form from Aristophanes, does not in either case take sufficient account of the undeniable fact that the poet's function, however he may have some common cause with them, is not identical either with that of the philosopher, whose method is to convince, or of the moralist, whose aim is to persuade.

The poet, by contrast, desires to influence. The moral philosopher may prove to men that this is right and that is wrong ; the moralist may cause men to act rightly in this or that regard ; but the moral poet's object is to make men moral. Thus it is not, strictly, his business to argue or to preach at all, although of course there is no objection to his throwing in here and there (as in fact the great poets have generally done) either argumentation or exhortation, provided it promotes the poetry, as it well may. His business is to make men love the good, and to that end his first necessity is to present it as beautiful ; as desirable for its own sake, without any reasons. His primary appeal, then, is the æsthetic one ; though indeed, it is only in analysis, and not in actual fact, that this appeal can be at all separated from the moral. He appeals to the senses, and to the moral sense as one of them—for his purposes the most important. For it is a sense, just as for example sight is. That some people are born blind does not prove that none can see. That the normal man can see does not prove that matter has an independent existence ; nor, on the other hand, does it imply that phenomena are altogether illusory. So with morals. As the sense of sight is an instrument by means of which we " manage " in the world of matter, whatever matter may be, so is the moral sense in the spiritual world ; whatever spirit may be. The moral poet simply assumes this sense, and plays upon it as a composer plays upon the sense of hearing. Although it has usually been found convenient to speak of such poets as " teaching," in strictness they do not do that even ; they *train*. Their object is to produce an artistic pleasure *via* the moral sense ; which pleasure is in itself moral. In the result, therefore, they *exercise* the moral faculty ; natural exercise being, here as in physical matters, pleasurable. Some of these statements may seem platitudes, but it is neglect of such obvious truths that has landed literary theory, and with it criticism, in those opposite extravagances, one or other of which has generally prevailed ; that the poet's most important duty is to preach, or, on the other hand, that poetry by its nature has absolutely nothing to do with morals.

The true State is a moral organism, and poetry proper is, potentially, one of its greatest civilising instruments. Such was the spirit in which Horace wrote. His moral instinct may be defective ; but no one, I take it, has made better poetry of the same moral material. In the world of literature he has no betters who are not also his spiritual superiors ; and he has very few even among those.

CHAPTER III

HORACE'S OWN THEORY AND PRACTICE OF POETRY

Odi profanum volgus et arceo.
favete linguis ! carmina non prius
audita Musarum sacerdos
virginibus puerisque canto.

THE general view, given in the preceding chapter, of the origin of art and in particular of poetry, is in accordance with the prevailing ideas of modern archæology and anthropology. But the *theory* of poetry there stated, of its essentially religious and moral character and of its importance for the healthy life of the community, is widely at variance with the spirit of modern literary criticism and the practice of modern poets ; more than that, it is alien to the spirit of the age, which is in general materialistic, and which in its inevitable and continual reaction therefrom supplies with indulgence or frivolity or sensationalism the place that would naturally be taken by art. Even apart from that, the theory itself is hardly likely to find favour, not so much because the example of the eighteenth century has caused a deadly fear of theories as applied to literature at all, but because any attempt to combine abstract with archæological theory is felt to lead inevitably to the vitiation of either or both. For my own part, however, I cannot see much use or even interest in accumulating facts and deductions about the origins of art, unless these are to be interpreted and made significant for future artists by some consistent doctrine as to the nature of art itself and its function in the community ; nor, on the other hand, should such a doctrine much commend itself while unsupported by what small amount of archæological data may be procurable. This, at all events, was evidently the feeling of Horace himself about the matter ; his theory of the nature of poetry, his aims and hopes for its contemporary and future development, and his notions about its origin as a human and therefore social institution, are regularly made to throw light on one another or to back one another up.

And the theory of poetry outlined in the preceding chapter, whether objectionable to these days or no, is fundamentally the same as Horace's. Hardly less is the account of origins there indicated at one with his accounts. But I propose to review his theory first, because it is in several respects the more important. His excursions into the field of literary history are from the nature of the case both intensely interesting and extremely valuable, but it would be idle to deny that they have also, to a disconcerting degree, the interest of problems. In brief, they *can* be squared with facts ; but only with an enormous effort—a most careful adjustment of claims on either side. At the worst, it may well be, Horace confused the origins of Tragedy and Comedy! If he did that, then, no matter if it were his only blunder, the fact remains that we cannot rely upon the accuracy of any of his suspected statements. But even at the best, there are two things that should always be remembered. He was a poet ; however industrious and wide a reader, he read always as a poet ; it is idle even to expect from him, I do not say the accuracy only, but so much as the *attitude to* facts, which marks the scholar. But, more important still, in literary criticism he was a theorist ; and theorists do not make good antiquarians,[1] no more than the converse. His mind, on such matters, works *a priori ;* and when dealing with facts he must almost certainly have tended to blur them into conformity with his views.

Those who write on the Aesthetic of ancient authors are liable to be met with the objection that they are reading into them what is not there. " You must not expect from me," said Bywater [2] on the eve of the publication of his *Aristotle on the Art of Poetry*, with obvious reference to Butcher, " anything about fine art, for I don't think Aristotle said anything about it.

---

[1] The same is true of Aristotle, and should always be remembered in reading the *Poetics*.

[2] See W. W. Jackson, *Ingram Bywater*, p. 136.

I have looked it up in the dictionaries and I see that the term is much later." He need not even have gone to dictionaries to discover that the word " poetry " is also later, Aristotle not having known English.[1] I will not pretend that I am here presenting Horace's theory of poetry as he presents it, since that would be superfluous. He does not, indeed, properly speaking, propound a theory at all, his sphere is literature, not science, but he makes many pregnant utterances about poetry, which show that at the back of his mind there was throughout a steady and consistent idea of its place in life.

Horace's Theory of Poetry

However much he may at times ironically depreciate his own achievements (and elsewhere he speaks of them in very different tones), the vocation of poet is always represented by Horace as a high one. Towards the end of the *Ars Poetica* he has a passage [2] of seventeen lines the object of which is to impress a due sense thereof,[3] on the budding poet whom he addresses. In the epistle to Augustus Horace does, indeed, assume in one passage [4] a mildly deprecatory or rather perhaps apologetic attitude to his own profession ; but that is partly because he is addressing an emperor, partly because the Romans had hitherto, as he here indicates, been an unpoetical race and he wishes to convert them, and to convert them in the Horatian manner gently and craftily, finding it more effective almost to over-depreciate the wares he is desirous to commend. That is how he introduces his main statement of his theory of poetry, which amounts to this, that (again " if you grant that great things may be helped by little ") poetry has a function in the community ; bad soldier though he be, the poet is *utilis urbi ;* and the reason why his function is political is that

---

[1] To do him justice, it was Bywater who discovered the earliest surviving instance of the word *poetria*—in a seventh-century scholium to Horace's *Epistles*, see Jackson, *op. cit.*, p. 142.

[2] *A.P.*, 391-407.

[3] Cf. also *A.P.*, 275-308, and my remarks on that.

[4] *Epist.*, II. i. 93 (*nugari* includes poetry, cf. *tragoedis*, 98)—118 (error . . . levis haec insania).

it is religious and moral. The poet is, for Horace as for Aristophanes, the educator of the rising generation.

> os tenerum pueri balbumque poeta figurat,[1]
> torquet ab obscenis iam nunc sermonibus aurem,
> mox etiam pectus praeceptis format amicis,
> asperitatis et invidiae corrector et irae ;

and he teaches not only by precept but by examples, he does not merely moralise but trains :—

> recte facta refert, orientia tempora notis
> instruit exemplis.

More than that, he is even in the position of a kind of priest—

> castis cum pueris ignara puella mariti
> disceret unde preces, vatem ni Musa dedisset ?
> poscit opem chorus et praesentia numina sentit,
> caelestis implorat aquas docta prece blandus,
> avertit morbos, metuenda pericula pellit,
> impetrat et pacem et locupletem frugibus annum.
> carmine di superi placantur, carmine Manes.[2]

The last line shows us the poet as an informal ambassador between man and the powers of light on the one hand, the powers of darkness on the other ; just as Mercury, the inventor of the lyre and the patron of poets, is *superis deorum gratus et imis* (*Odes*, I. x. 19-20), and the priest Orpheus, the legendary first poet, charmed Hades with his song. Horace's theory of poetry and his view of its origin are so intimately connected that the passage of the *Ars Poetica* previously referred to may count as either, according to the degree in which " Orpheus " meant for him a symbol or an actual person. The purport is that the poet is nothing less than the *civiliser* of his fellow-men.

> silvestris homines sacer interpresque deorum
> caedibus et victu foedo deterruit Orpheus,
> dictus ob hoc lenire tigris rabidosque leones ;
> dictus et Amphion, Thebanae conditor urbis,
> saxa movere sono testudinis et prece blanda
> ducere quo vellet.
>
> (*A.P.*, 391-96.)

---

[1] *I.e.*, of course through the boy's learning the poet's verse *by heart*.
[2] *Epist.*, II. i. 126-38.

Accordingly poetry was originally of a didactic and gnomic character.

> fuit haec sapientia quondam,[1]
> publica privatis secernere, sacra profanis,
> concubitu prohibere vago, dare iura maritis,
> oppida moliri, leges incidere ligno.

(A.P., 396-99.)

It was in virtue of such services as these that the earliest bards came to be regarded as to some extent divine. So far all is well, but at this point Horace finds himself in a difficulty, and perhaps no one can more cordially sympathise with him than the writer of the preceding chapter. Pre-historic poetry has " suited his book " admirably, and so in a moment will the various main departments of the post-Homeric ; but Homer is, of course, uncomfortably secular, disconcertingly undidactic. The necessity of treating him as functional, however, must be faced up to somehow or other ; so Horace hastily disposes of him as excellent for recruiting purposes, throwing in at the same time Tyrtaeus, partly perhaps because he wishes just to hitch on the elegiac along with the other kinds, but chiefly because it provides a " zeugma " by the help of which this curiously inadequate characterisation of the *Iliad* and *Odyssey* may at least sound somewhat less harsh. And yet not so very inadequate after all, perhaps ; Aristophanes,[2] at any rate, had accounted for Homer on a similar principle in very much the same sort of way, or rather his explanation is if anything the more far-fetched ; and indeed the simple fact is that the implicit moral code upon which all the great main effects of the *Iliad* depend, is the primitive heroic warrior's. A good deal of the slight inconsistency visible here and there in the moral conduct of the narrative, a good deal that would fairly be called defective if the *Iliad* were (what we ought now perhaps to be reminded that it is not) a drama, is explicable by this fact. Moreover, if *mares animos in Martia bella versibus exacuit* seems at first a statement rather in need of instances to make it acceptable—there is the conqueror of the world. The best test of poetry, if only it were a more available one, is the material effect it has had upon men's actions ; and a poem

---

[1] If indeed such is the right reading; but there is a good deal to be said for Gow's *huic . . . quando.*

[2] *Frogs*, 1034-6.

which was the first and remained the strongest incitement to a Schliemann to explore and an Alexander to conquer, may surely be called efficacious. But for all that, the *raison d'être* here given by Horace for the Homeric poems *is* inadequate, and it is clear that he himself recognised it. Their moral content is much more copious and more varied ; and later, when he " re-read them at Praeneste," he realised some of their great main features of ethical and human significance, and gave his full and mature view of them in the epistle to Lollius.[1] For the present, however, Homer thus perfunctorily disposed of, Horace has no difficulty in designating all the main types of Greek poetry of the " second cycle " in terms which indicate some degree of religious or political value ; he alludes *summatim* to oracles, to the didactic and gnomic schools, to the international or Pan-hellenic character of the lyric poets, and to the essentially festal function of the drama.

But no one can properly be regarded as a priest, even in the figurative sense, unless we can point to some sort of religious system to which he stands in some relation, whether as minis-trant, promoter, or interpreter. In the service of what deity is the poet, according to Horace's view, a priest ? Primarily, of the Muses ; in his formal opening address for instance (*Odes*, III. i. 1-4) that is what Horace calls himself. The office, as will presently be seen, means very much more than so vague a title might appear to imply ; it practically amounts to being dedicated to the *literary* service of any Olympian deity. In the meantime, however, to complete our account of Horace's theory, it must be observed that the Muse, as a deity, has her special province, exercises her peculiar function for mortals and even, it appears, within limits, for gods. It is the privilege of the Muse to confer immortality. We have seen that the poet's func-tion makes him to a great extent a civilising agent. We further find that the Muse bestows immortality—the immor-tality of fame—in recognition, it is true, of prowess generally, but especially of prowess of a civilising character. It was a familiar idea among the ancients that individuals who had

---

[1] *Epist.*, I. ii. Here is another argument, not I think hitherto noticed, for the earlier of the two alternative dates of the *Ars Poetica*. Is it really conceivable that Horace could have written *A.P.*, 401-3, *after Epist.*, I. ii ?

rendered supreme services to the community became gods after their death. This idea we are apt to associate especially with Euhemerus, a Sicilian who flourished about 300 B.C. ; but Euhemerus was merely the first to account for the institution of gods in general by referring them all to such an origin ; he was the Ridgeway of his day. Long before Euhemerus, an Œdipus or an Ajax, a Prometheus or a Heracles had been deified for the intellectual or military qualities by which they were believed to have made themselves public benefactors ; the latter two in particular were honoured especially as agents of civilisation. Horace knows of Heracles in this connection ; of Castor and Pollux ; of Romulus ; it is as a mighty civiliser that in more than one passage (*Odes*, III. iii. 9-15, *Epist.*, II. i. 5-17) he couples with their names that of Augustus ; Bacchus himself is explicitly placed by Horace in this category.[1]

> Romulus et Liber pater et cum Castore Pollux,
> post ingentia facta deorum in templa recepti,
> dum terras hominumque colunt genus, aspera bella
> componunt, agros assignant, oppida condunt,
> ploravere suis non respondere favorem
> speratum meritis. diram qui contudit hydram,
> notaque fatali portenta labore subegit,
> comperit invidiam supremo fine domari.

Once gods and demi-gods, as institutions, had been thus historically and rationally accounted for, it was but the next step to explain their immortality. That was neither more nor less than an immortality of fame. Such is the view expressly formulated in the eighth ode of the fourth book, which, apart from a minor puzzle or two, is (as I see it) thoroughly and peculiarly Horatian, and has special interest and importance besides. The series Romulus, Hercules, the Tyndaridae, Liber, repeating that

---

[1] The civilising activities of such figures are closely connected with their overcoming or taming monsters ; an obvious modern instance is St. Patrick. That is the significance of the tigers yoked by Bacchus, *Odes*, III. iii. 13-15; cf. *A.P.*, 393, quoted above, p. 59 *fin*. Horace further regards Bacchus as a civiliser because he is one of those gods who are especially the patrons of poets ; cf. *e.g.*, *Odes*, III. viii. 6-8. Bacchus helps the Olympians against the Giants, *i.e.*, civilisation against barbarity, *Odes*, II. xix. 21-28 ; and like Orpheus, symbolic poet, and Mercury the poets' protector, he is a *persona grata* even in the nether world, *ibid.*, 29-32.

of the passage just quoted and of the other above referred to, is a fact that (however unaccountably ignored by editors in general and apparently not even noticed by all but one or two) must of itself tell strongly [1] in favour of the authenticity of the poem, even if it did not, as it here does, appear in connection with the same two ideas that are eventually associated with it in the epistle to Augustus—that to be celebrated in poetry is the appropriate reward and perpetuation of great political and philanthropic achievements, and that it is at least possible to regard it as preferable [2] to being memorised by the other, that is to say plastic, arts. " It is the Muse," cries Horace, and the emphasis has usually been strangely missed,[3] " it is the Muse who forbids great men to die ; it is the Muse who gives immortality." This is the sense, he continues—for only a paraphrase will represent the force of *sic*—this is the sense in which it is quite *true* that Hercules after his labours has attained to his Valhalla, that Castor and Pollux are identifiable with a tutelary constellation, that wine is a god with attributes and the power of aiding his votaries ; to the extent that poetic tradition has made them these things, that is what they are. Such a rationalisation is entirely characteristic of Horace's thought ; [4] that was the sort of thing, as we see from plenty of other examples, that he, like Lucretius and many a Roman of more intellect than imagination, accepted from Greek sophistic tradition as conveyed to them by the philosophic schools. It is not, we must remember, the same view as Ovid's clever

> di quoque carminibus, si fas est dicere, fiunt

or as Swinburne's

> And God, the shadow of the soul of man.

That idea also had been an old one, as old as Xenophanes. But the Horatian view regards poetry not as maker but as maintainer

---

[1] No imitator would have thrown in Aeacus, cf. 25-7.

[2] *Nec magis, Epist.*, II. i. 248, is a " litotes," as is *non . . . clarius* here, 19 ; cf. *Odes*, III. xxx. 1-5.

[3] *E.g.*, Wickham's note, and Landor's comment " poor." What Horace meant is what Landor means when he writes : *'tis verse that gives Immortal youth to mortal maids.*

[4] For same idea of immortality see *Odes*, III. ii. 21-2, and cf. Wickham's note. Remark *negata ; i.e.*, it is *in this sense* that greatness achieves what is *literally* impossible.

of gods. But for the poet there would be practically no difference between the hero and the sluggard, once both are dead. *Paulum sepultae distat inertiae celata virtus ;* and the preceding lines are too well known to have to be quoted in this connection.[1] So in our present ode, *neque si chartae sileant quod bene feceris mercedem tuleris.* In view of all which, it is of the utmost importance (Horace reminds his emperor towards the end of the epistle addressed to him) to take pains in the hope of ultimately securing the best poets available ; for " proved heroism, military or political " has a cult, and it is the poets who are its *aeditui* or temple-ministrants.[2]

Not to titillate, nor to admonish merely, but to persuade or prevail upon, is in Horace's view the supreme duty of the poet. He recognises of course that there are writers who are only alive to one or other of the two ends, to combine which is the whole art and difficulty.

> aut prodesse volunt aut delectare poetae,
> aut simul et iucunda et idonea dicere vitae.

For indeed there always have been in all the arts persons who have admired themselves and been admired for conjuring with one ball instead of twenty ; to do an obvious thing pretentiously is the way to make a reputation in poetry as elsewhere. But Horace makes it quite clear that in his opinion at any rate such writers do not count ; and he believes that in the long run they do not count with the world either. Even in their own day they cannot do more than attract a section of the community.

> centuriae seniorum agitant expertia frugis,
> celsi praetereunt austera poemata Ramnes.

While if it comes to a question of posterity, he wisely sees that it is only the *fusion* that makes durable material, that all else is the merest jerry-building :—

> Omne tulit punctum qui miscuit utile dulci,
> lectorem delectando pariterque monendo ;
> hic meret aera liber Sosiis ; hic et mare transit,
> et longum noto scriptori prorogat aevum.[3]

---

[1] *Odes*, IV. ix. 25-30.   [2] *Epist.*, II. i. 229-31.
[3] *A.P.*, 333-4, 341-6.

HORACE ON POETIC ORIGINS

Horace's principal statement of his theory of poetry, which as we saw occurs at *Epist.*, II. i. 118-38, is immediately followed and supported by a brief résumé of its Latin origins. He very properly begins, not with Livius Andronicus, who is the fountain or rather conduit of the mighty tributary, but with the tiny trickle in which he or his authority rightly recognised the true original stream. It is a mistake to think that line 139 begins one of those abrupt transitions which are common in Horace. Still less, I think, does it mark a *resumption* [1] of the main subject. We have just been told that song is acceptable not only to the heavenly but to the chthonic powers. Thus, continues Horace, the farmers of old time, in celebrating their festivals of harvest-home, performed rites to the Earth, and also to Silvanus (a vegetation-god), as well as to " the Genius." (The Genius as such is always a *good god*, so that he would at least not count as chthonic ; while we know from Varro R.R. 1.1.4. that Jupiter himself ranked along with Tellus as the chief god worshipped by farmers.) " It was in this way," he continues—*i.e.*, to please these gods, and perhaps especially to keep the Genius merry [2]—that the Fescennine verses with their licentious reciprocal banter were instituted. But he does not then proceed to trace the development of Fescennine into *satura*, and so to establish that the Romans possessed one original literary form. The simple reason is, that Horace did not *know* that satire was the product of the Fescennine ; he regarded it as having been founded by Lucilius ; [3] but as, in his idea, Latin did not possess any original literary form at all, to found one is to derive it from the Greek ; so he was driven to conclude, innocently enough, that the invention of satire had suggested itself to Lucilius from the Greek " Old Comedy." [4] Of course, so to account for Latin satire is not to account for it at all ; since even if a hippopotamus *could* be the father of an ape, this fact would not explain how the offspring turned out to be an ape and not a hippopotamus. The reason why Horace came to suggest anything so crude and childish is manifestly his predisposition to regard

---

[1] So Wickham, for example.   [2] Cf. Wilkins' note.
[3] *Sat.*, I. x. 48, inventore.   [4] *Ibid.*, iv. 6-7.

literature with an eye to its functionality; he saw that the Greek Old Comedy [1] and the Latin Satire had each the function of expelling or at least exposing social pests; and he made the mistake of seeing filiation where he would have been justified in seeing affinity.

But in the present passage, Horace is not concerned with the diverse literary forms at all. From line 118 on, as indeed throughout the epistle, he is thinking of poetry in general, but especially of dramatic poetry; partly because that was the direction in which the ambitions of Latin literature had from its commencement steadily gravitated, partly I suspect because, having shrunk himself from the attempt to do for serious drama in Latin what the Augustan age had done for the other great main forms, Horace in this address to his imperial patron has drama " on his conscience." Ostensibly, however, concerned with poetry in general, his present object is to show that what little is known of the native stock of Latin poetry upon which the Greek was grafted (very near to the root of course, but fortunately for the literary products) tends to support the theory of poetry he has just enunciated, namely, that it has a function, primarily delectable indeed, but nevertheless of the utmost value and importance, in the life of the community. He rejoices, of course, at the supersession of Italian by Greek influences, because that meant variety and smoothness of metre in place of the barren and rough Saturnian, refinement (comparatively speaking) of tone instead of coarseness and virulence. But it is the virulence that he principally stresses, in his brief account of the pre-Hellenic literature; in other words, he makes it quite clear that, in his opinion, the single sufficient reason why the Fescennine must be considered to have failed to justify its preservation, and to have made the introduction of Greek forms the only hope, is the fact that it had *abused its function.*

> libertasque recurrentis accepta per annos
> lusit amabiliter, donec iam saevus apertam
> in rabiem coepit verti iocus et per honestas
> ire domos impune minax. doluere cruento
> dente lacessiti; fuit intactis quoque cura
> condicione super communi.

[1] *Sat.*, I. iv. 1-5.

Enactments against libel were of some avail, but it was not until Roman literature became Hellenised that the *grave virus* (158) was really banished.

Other passages in which Horace deals with poetic origins (*A.P.*, 202-19, 220-24, 275-84) are too scrappy or too summary to add anything of much importance for our present purposes ; but it may be noted that he remarks their festal character in *A.P.*, 210 [1] and 224, that he points out the moralising tendency and oracular utterance of the choruses of Greek tragedy—

> et tulit eloquium insolitum facundia praeceps,
> utiliumque sagax rerum et divina futuri
> sortilegis non discrepuit sententia Delphis

—and that he notes that the " Old Comedy " abused its function in a manner similar to the Fescennines.

HORACE IN HIS POETIC PRACTICE

If it has seemed difficult to treat Horace's philosophy of poetry in complete separation from his theory of its origins, it is just as difficult to touch on his principles without yielding to the temptation of referring to his practice. The passage of the Epistle to Augustus previously considered reminds the reader constantly of features in Horace's own works. *Asperitatis et invidiae corrector et irae* reminds us of the admonitory tone of so many of the odes and epistles ; when he tells us that the poet specially addresses himself to " the rising generation," *orientia tempora*, we at once remember his own *virginibus puerisque canto ;* and lines 132-7, although, of course, applicable to the Greek choral lyric in general, are in part an obvious allusion to his own *Carmen Saeculare.* Again, when he lays it down in the *Ars Poetica* that *scribendi recte sapere est et principium et fons*, he is for the time being thinking of drama primarily, but it is evident how thoroughly his Satires, Odes, and Epistles are illustrations of this very principle. And at one famous couplet already quoted from the same works,

---

[1] Note Genius and cf. *Epist.*, II. i. 144 ; showing that he regards Greek Drama and Italian Fescennine as kindred institutions.

probably almost every reader at once feels the applicability
to Horace's most characteristic and most successful vein :—

> omne tulit punctum qui miscuit utile dulci,
> lectorem delectando pariterque monendo.

The fact is, Horace's views on literature are derived primarily
from himself. This statement may sound rather bald, but I
believe it to be true to a much greater extent than has been
yet realised, and if true, it has, as will be seen in a later chapter,
an important bearing on the problem of the sources, structure,
and significance of the *Ars Poetica*. It makes no difference
if he occasionally expressed those views in terms borrowed
(to a greater or less degree) from Neoptolemus of Parium or
others ; that is his regular habit in all his work, to transmute
his own experience into traditional forms ; that is at least half
the fun. His allusion to the better part of valour in Archilochus, an example already followed by Alcæus and Anacreon,
is hardly to be regarded as a proof that he never saw Philippi !

The position he takes up as a poet is fundamentally the same
in Epodes, Satires, Odes, and Epistles ; but in the two former
divisions there is a much larger proportion of exceptions of
various kinds—experiments, exercises, immature or formless
work. It will be most convenient as well as fairest to examine
Horace's practice first and most fully where we find him in
full swing. Throughout the *Odes* and *Epistles* that practice
(with a negligible exception or two) never changes ; once he had
hit upon or evolved his most congenial type of poem he never
really deserted it ; he had found the unity upon which he could
work out his infinite variety, the observance which secured him
freedom. His apprenticeship ends with the second book of
Satires ; after that all his work is mature.

The celebrated but not always attentively read passage
chosen as motto for the present chapter was intended by the
poet as a prelude to the series of " Roman Odes," the first
six of the third book. But every phrase of it is applicable
to much more of Horace's work than that ; and *Musarum
sacerdos* in particular practically defines his office as he finally
discharged it.

That is, of course, not the only place where he speaks of
himself as specially dedicated to the service of the Muses.

Vester, Camenae, vester, Odes, III. iv. 21 ; *vestris amicum fontibus et choris,* ibid., 25, and in the same poem he tells of his having been lost as a child and found afterwards mysteriously covered with leaves of " sacred laurel and myrtle," thus miraculously preserved. It is as her priest that he prays to the Muse Calliope :—

> descende caelo et dic age tibia
> regina longum Calliope melos—

and proceeds to sing the praises of her and her sisters. " The service of the Muse is my vocation—as truly a vocation as any other and more ordinary one " is the purport of the first ode of all, the introduction to the first three books (cf. esp. 29-34) ; and apart from the fact that in the later poem he speaks of his own reputation as now assured, the third of the fourth book is closely parallel ; [1] in form it is a sort of hymn of thanksgiving addressed to the Muse Melpomene.

But the priesthood of the Muses involves much more than might at first appear. Ever since the prehistoric period when these goddesses had become the daughters of Zeus,[2] their cult had been subordinated to his, and so in due course to the Olympian religion in general. Thus Horace is the missionary of the moral government of Jupiter, *Odes,* III. i. 5-8. But as the other Olympians are all subordinate to Jupiter, and one or another of them may be chosen at any time to act as his deputy or emissary (*Odes,* I. ii. 29-end), Horace and his Muse regard it as a part of their function to celebrate any Olympian (*Odes,* I. xii. 1-4), " after Jupiter " always understood or expressed *ibid.,* 13-18), according as the occasion shall direct. Thus in *Odes,* I. x. we have a hymn to Mercury, in I. xxi., IV. vi., and the Carmen Saeculare, to Apollo with his sister Diana, in II. xix. and III. xxv. to Bacchus, while I. xxx. is a prayer to Venus.

These deities are Latin in little else but name ; as anthropomorphic conceptions, they are Greek. In remote antiquity,

---

[1] Cf. also *Musis amicus, Odes* I. xxvi. 1, and that ode generally ; it may be regarded from one point of view as a short hymn to the Muses. In *Odes* I. xii. he begins by apostrophising Clio. In III. xxx. the formal epilogue to the first three books, he concludes with a brief petition to Melpomene.

[2] Hesiod, *Theog.* 25.

they had once been popular gods ; later they had become
national, bound up with this or that Greek State-religion ;
later still they passed gradually to a third stage, and became
either rationalised or poeticised. Zeus for Cleanthes was a
symbol of the principle of the universe ; for Callimachus he
was (as were also Demeter and Apollo) a literary lay figure, an
object of purely academic invocation. And for Horace, too,
this Olympian religion is primarily one of literary convention.[1]
That does not in the least mean that for him it was not to
be taken seriously ; far from it. His poetic religion shares,
like his poetry, in both his moods, the grave and the light ;
and in point of fact so far as the deities yet mentioned are concerned, the treatment he accords them is in almost every case
entirely serious. Moreover, Olympianism in Rome had long
ago begun a new lease of life by slowly becoming once more,
though in a very different way, a state religion ; it was gradually *adopted ;* Jupiter had been the great national deity in
Republican times, and the Apolline cult was now being made
a state one by Augustus ; so that when Horace deals with
these deities he is in his national vein. But *primarily*, for all
that, it is a *literary* religion ; he is a priest only in imagination,
and accordingly, as he is in the literal sense no priest at all, he
is the " Muses' priest " of a good deal that does not belong to
Olympianism and has only a partial connection with the organised religion of contemporary Italy, but does belong, as we shall
see, to this curiously accumulated religion of literary tradition.

Some divinities he celebrates which are not Olympian.
I. xxxv. is a hymn to Fortune, an abstract deity [2] of which the
Hellenistic age had been rather fond, but whose admission to
the literary pantheon dates at least as far back as Pindar
(*Ol.* xii.). III. xiii. is a hymn to a fountain ; and there was,
as a matter of fact, an Italian festival called the Fontanalia [3]
when rites such as those described here by the poet were performed to the presiding deities of fountains ; indeed the imaginary occasion of the piece is probably to be identified with the

[1] IV. vi. is, perhaps, as good an instance as any ; especially 25-8.
See Wickham on 28.
[2] See Warde Fowler, *Roman Ideas of Deity*, pp. 61-78, and esp. 150-
51 ; Murray, *Four Stages of Greek Religion*, pp. 113-15.
[3] Varro *L.L.* 5.

eve of that festival. But the real reason why Horace chooses to write on this subject is that certain famous legendary fountains—Hippocrene, Castalia—were traditionally regarded as sacred to the Muses, and the principal purpose of the hymn is simply to canonise Bandusia—"fies nobilium tu quoque fontium." III. xviii., again, is a prayer to another Nature-deity, the Faun, whom he identifies with the Greek Pan. All these deities had some form of cult or ritual in Italy itself; Faunus belongs to the oldest stratum of native agricultural gods, and had his festival, the *Faunalia* of 5th December, which Horace here describes ; Fortuna had not only her cult at Antium (*Odes*, I. xxxv. 1) but a still more important one at Praeneste, and one element in her composition certainly belongs to the old Italian " religion " of functional abstractions. But of the major features of her divinity Warde Fowler says that " all this is far too anthropomorphic to be pure Italian," [1] and however naturally Horace may have desired here and there to give his theological material a certain degree of local colouring—and did, according to the general policy of Augustan poets—it is primarily to literary tradition that he turns for his choice of " what god to celebrate." As poet, indeed, he must be national, but as priest of the Muses he must be prophetic, as missionary of Olympus he must be moral ; and where theology is concerned the latter purposes were for the most part practically incompatible with the former ; the native Roman religion was totally non-spiritual, " its object was not to make men spiritually good, but to protect them from material evil." [2] In Olympianism and its accretions, on the other hand, he had a theological system out of which every inherent moral potentiality had been continuously developed over a long period, first by poets, and then by philosophers.

The next extension of this literary religion is one which it is necessary first to glance at generally in its older development, before considering its Horatian examples.

There is a passage in Prof. Murray's *Ancient Greek Literature* with which I have never been quite able to agree. He says : " In studying the social and the literary history of Greece, we are met by one striking contrast. The social history shows us

---

[1] In *Companion to Latin Studies*, § 214.   [2] *Ibid.*, § 201.

the Greeks, as the Athenians thought themselves, 'especially god-fearing,' or, as St. Paul put it, ' too superstitious.' The literature as preserved is entirely secular." If it ever seems so to us, that must be because we have become accustomed to regard religion as something unimaginative and illiterate—something dogmatic, rigid, literal, obscurantist. The doctrinal element in ancient religion is much more elastic, the attitude of man to God much more open, frank, and I might almost say democratic, than anything within our own direct experience. There may be less reverence of the formal kind, but of the spirit of reverence there is surely a great deal more. It is true, indeed—and nqt only true but important—that the historical evolution of the Greek literary forms shows itself over and over again as a process of continual secularisation in regard to subject ; that was what happened to the Lyric, and within the Lyric that was what happened to the dithyramb. But what is more remarkable is the extent to which, throughout all such changes, the spirit remains religious and the tone and the style essentially sacerdotal.

In this secularisation one of the steps which is several times exemplified is the gradual transference of some institution from the honouring of a god to the honouring of a great man. We have seen, for instance, how in pre-Homeric times the hymn became slowly transformed into the heroic lay. What now concerns us more is the similar phenomenon in the development of the Greek Lyric, the general model of the Horatian Ode. There, as Jebb [1] succinctly puts it, " Stesichorus extended the scope of the choral hymn from gods to heroes ; Simonides was perhaps the first who successfully extended it from the heroes to contemporary men." But nothing is jettisoned ; indeed, it is rather a case of the secular being made sacred than the other way round. Greek Lyric is consummated in Pindar, and Pindar is represented for us almost entirely by his triumphal odes ; the triumphal ode or epinikion is, virtually though not in origin, a special form of " encomion " or song in honour of a living great man ; and what do we find in Pindar ? Praise of the victorious athlete or owner, but subordinated to the praise of heroes, and over them of gods ; [2] the whole fused

---

[1] *Growth and Influence of Classical Greek Poetry*, p. 136.
[2] Cf. of course especially *Ol.* 3, *init.*

together by a lofty moral and religious pervading spirit ; and the style both priestly and oracular. Lest I be supposed to be unduly prejudiced by my general preconception, let me characterise Pindar's quality not in my own words but in those of an authority of deservedly long standing. " He has also a priestly tone ; he is an expounder of religious and ethical precepts, who can speak in the lofty and commanding accents of Delphi ; " and again " as the Iamidae " the family who had an hereditary title to the priesthood of Zeus at Olympia " might have spoken from their altar in the Altis, so Pindar speaks from the *spiritual* vantage-ground of his relation with Delphi. That is, he speaks loftily, with authority ; and not seldom his phrases have an oracular stamp, being terse, strangely worded, or even enigmatic."[1] I should like to go further, and to say that, even as there is what Matthew Arnold called " the grand style," so there is also another kind of style which we may appropriately term " oracular." It is at least a *factor* in a good deal of Greek and Latin poetry ; but as the grand style belongs in a particular degree to Homer, so does the oracular style belong especially to Pindar among the Greek poets, and among the Latins to Horace.

For Horace as for Pindar the gulf between gods and men is not an absolutely bridgeless one. His religious ideas are really quite consistent. Although he portrays Jupiter with all the old anthropomorphic particularities, the Jupiter in which he himself believed was much more like the Stoic conception ; but he knows that as a poet he must be picturesque and concrete, that as priest of the Muses he must observe their time-honoured ceremonial. In a similar way, he really believes in demi-gods, to the extent that we have already seen.[2] It is not—as the modern world, with the strangely literal attitude to religion which it so long preserved from the middle ages, has been too apt to think—it is not either mere courtly flattery[3] or mere poetic ornament when Horace speaks of Augustus as the deputy or representative of Jupiter on earth, or as already

---

[1] Jebb, *op. cit.*, pp. 144, 154 ; italics mine.
[2] Pp. 62-4.
[3] This was written long before I had seen Prof. Conway's essay on Horace in *Uvae Falernae* (C.U.P. 1917), where I am glad to find the same view so ably stated.

partly deified.[1] His language is metaphorical, imaginative, half-traditional, as beseems a poetic priest ; when language deals with such themes at all, it has only two alternatives, the concrete and the abstract, and it is at least arguable that the modern worship of the abstract is the grosser superstition. So that we ought not properly to be either shocked or surprised when we find that Horace's sacerdotalism in form and tone and style is extended to poems in which he addresses a mortal and a contemporary. These are the fifth ode of the fourth book, a prayer to Augustus, who is here again placed on a level with the Greek demi-gods Castor and Hercules (35-6) ; and the fourteenth and fifteenth, which are hymns in his honour, and approach him practically as a god.

So far, we have seen our poet-priest in his serious mood. But once the rite has begun to be treated as no rite but an art, once you have begun to play with it no matter how gravely, there is no reason why the extension should not be carried still further. A hymn is written to a supreme statesman, because genius is after all, in a sense, divine. Other things also may be regarded as divine after a fashion ; a hymn to a wine-jar is indeed not so very big a step from a hymn to Bacchus, and if such a hymn be written playfully, with a half-suggestion almost of parody, it is perhaps all the more calculated to delight that god. Such a hymn to a wine-jar is *Odes*, III. xxi, and I hope to show that a little more point may be seen in it if it be regarded in that light. So far as poetic form is concerned the parody counts with its model ; and there are a number of other odes of Horace, generally reflecting his lighter vein, whose structure shows traces—probably unconscious for the most part —of the formal influence of certain peculiar types of hymn familiar to antiquity. But for the present I am concerned with Horace as fulfilling a religious office for the community, and here the serious poems must take precedence.

We have seen hymns and prayers ; there remain exhortations. This class constitutes the great bulk of Horace's work ; almost all the odes not classifiable as hymns or prayers belong

---

[1] *E.g.*, *Odes*, I. ii. 41-52 ; xii. 51-2 ; III. iii. 9-12 (where I take *bibet* to be the true reading) ; v. 1-4, and the odes presently to be mentioned.

to it ; and, of course, all the Epistles.   Here, again, his practice is consistent with his theory ; for a reference to the passages already quoted in illustration of the latter will show that he devotes much the greater space to this monitorial aspect of the poetic office.

"Sermons" we might call such poems, if we were thinking of the modern "priest," and the term "homily" has in fact been applied to some of them.   But in the ancient religious service there was no sermon.   Their prototype is the Oracle ; oracle pure and simple is *Odes*, I. xiv, oracle with brief narrative introduction (but doubtless contemporary application) is that which follows it.   They are not indeed all equally like an oracle in respect to the attendant circumstances which they pre-suppose ; but they are all essentially oracular in *style ;* that is to say not only that their language, but their whole manner and procedure, is in certain respects deliberately enigmatical. At the same time, "sermon" is undoubtedly the better label, since it can include poems addressed to a company.   The sacrifice tends very early to become the banquet, whereupon the sacrificial chant takes on a convival character ; the singer addresses the other banqueters.   From the earliest times much of Greek lyric had been more or less of this "sympotic" sort, yet this much of the original sanctity of the occasion remained, that such poetry was always of a moralising tendency.   A number of Horace's admonitory poems are thus addressed, not to a single individual, but to an assembly of some kind. Sometimes, as in *Odes*, III. i., it is evidently met for a religious purpose ; at other times the occasion is a feast ; not infrequently the poet imagines himself as addressing the body politic gener-ally.   An oracle itself, of course, might be given to, or at least would often aim at applying to, a whole people ; thus political advice can be strikingly conveyed in the oracular mould.

> Delicta maiorum immeritus lues,
> *Romane*, donec templa refeceris.[1]

Compare an oracle reported by Livy,[2] and thus restored by Baehrens to its original metre : " Romane, aquam Albanam

---

[1] *Odes*, III. vi. 1-2.   [2] V. xvi.

cave lacu teneri," etc. The twenty-fourth of the same book recalls to the modern reader the scene in Florentine history when the priest Savonarola incited his fellow-citizens to the " burning of the vanities." Of the more secular sort of setting for an admonitory poem a good example is furnished by I. xxvii. ; not a sermon in any official sense, it nevertheless represents the poet cleverly and tactfully calming down a convivial uproar by an attractive diversion, much as a sensible and easy-going padre might do at a mess dinner.

Schoolboys are sometimes told, or used to be, that after all Pindar did not write his epinicions in order to provide hard work for them. I am not quite so sure. At all events, I never will believe that Pindar intended his language to be understood at once—even by the " συνετοί." As for the redoubtable athletes in whose honour the poems were composed—what a champion wrestler made of the Seventh Nemean, or even just how much the Sixth Olympian conveyed to the doubtless highly gratified pugilist Diagoras of Rhodes—of such things there is unfortunately no record left ; but we may reasonably suppose that those worthies would have preferred " to take Quebec." Nowhere has this aspect of Pindar been better indicated than in Jebb's fine essay. But Landor's marginal comment on the great opening address of the third book of odes is " omnium gatherum." Contemptuous ; yet one can half-sympathise with him ; I remember the time when I was greatly puzzled by the apparent lack of connection in the stanzas following the first. It is important to realise two things ; in the first place, there really is a latent connection throughout ; there is a sequence of thought, a logical sequence, " between the lines " ; and I do not know that it is anywhere better expounded than in Wickham's summary.[1] But the second thing to realise is that Horace himself *did not intend* the connection to be too apparent. He wanted these stanzas to sound like a series of imposing priestly exhortations, each one to strike the mind afresh.

This sort of deliberate discontinuity is a regular and traditional feature of the oracular style, and it originates in the poet's wish to make his utterance *arresting*. As Jebb said :

[1] For my own account see pp. 103-4.

" Continuous epic narrative no longer sufficed for Pindar's contemporaries " ; and he also called attention to Pindar's " frequent and rapid transition from image to image," and again to " those rapid transitions from one tone of feeling to another, from storm to calm, from splendid energy to tranquillity, from triumphant joy to reflection or even to sadness, which in Pindar are so frequent and so rapid that they are reconciled with art only by the massive *harmonies* of rhythm and language which hold them together." He goes on to point out that in this respect " the movement of every modern language is slower than that of Greek," and that the real modern parallel is to be found not in poetry but in music, which " allows of transitions from mood to mood as varied and almost as rapid as Pindar's ; and here again," he says, " it is the framework of harmony which makes them possible."

That last sentence I feel to be, if anything, even more applicable to Horace. The movement of any modern poem known to me is very, very much " slower " than that of the language of Horace's odes ; and his art is essentially a musical one, not merely in the sense in which it is repeatedly and rightly so called, that is in respect of verbal sonority, but in the fundamentals of its structure ; and it would be extraordinary if it were not, because in poetic structure he is the disciple of Pindar, and Pindar's odes were choral compositions of which he wrote the words and the music alike. It is far indeed from an idle metaphor when Horace speaks of his lyre.[1] " Modulations " are a very great part of the secret of the *Odes*.[2] *Series iuncturaque pollet* he wrote, indeed, in a somewhat different connection,[3] but it is a great principle anyway, and he was undoubtedly thoroughly conscious of it in the structure, as well as in the surface, of all his mature work.

But, although it is primarily to Pindar that he is indebted

---

[1] It is quite otherwise with Gray's " Awake, Aeolian lyre, awake " ; which is addressed, at the best, to an instrument with but one string.

[2] That is the sort of statement that a certain type of scholar resents ; well, all that can be said is, there is an end ; there is no getting over the fact that, as Pindar pointed out, Typhon does not like music ; and people who do not care for music are generally, I think, not fond of Horace's *Odes*.

[3] Apropos of Satyric Drama, as he would like to see it written, *A.P.*, 242. I consider that he is referring to style; cf. p. 5 n.

for the artifice of the sudden transition, his actual use of transitions is not indeed to any great degree like Pindar's ; it seems to me, at any rate, stronger, simpler, altogether more telling. The analogy of modern music may actually help us in certain places to understand his artistic purpose. For example, *Odes*, I. iv. 13, where Landor complains that " *pallida mors* has nothing to do with the above." On the contrary, this abrupt change is the focus of the whole poem ; *iunctura pollet*. If a poet says, in effect : " Spring is here again, we all know that it cannot last for ever, nothing does, we ourselves must die, therefore enjoy yourself, live intensely while you can "— if he sings so, he will defeat his own purpose, for he will make his audience go to sleep. Horace gives no sign of moralising ; he begins with a picture of the spring—the melting of the snows, the West Wind, the beached ships being launched again, the cattle going to grass, the ploughman ; Cytherea with the Nymphs and Graces in the moonlight dance, Vulcan and his Cyclopes resuming the labours of the forge, garlands of myrtle and the early flowers, the Faun—and then abruptly, as abruptly as it comes in real experience, he strikes the note of death. But even then he will not weaken his effect by dwelling on it ; and he ends up with the remark that before very long all the girls will be in love with Lycidas.

Three odes later (I. vii.) comes a still bolder and more sudden modulation—one which not only perplexed Landor, but even led some of the ancient commentators to think that it must be the beginning of a new ode. The poem is a good example of Horace's structural technique, and especially of the artful way in which he will suppress his real purpose until he has established a firm hold on our attention, whereupon he springs it on us while we are off our guard. To the ancients the προπεμπτικόν or ἀποπεμπτικόν (at any rate as addresse to deities) was a regular type of ode, and it is clear that such effusions would tend to show a tedious similarity of form and treatment. To be interesting they must avoid the obvious. Horace supplies several examples, and in each case evidently took thought to prevent the poem from giving itself away at once. Here he begins by mentioning a number of famous cities that have been the favourite spot on earth for some person or other. He then cleverly captures the sympathy of

Plancus (to whom the send-off is addressed) by admitting that none of these ever held *his* affection so much as Tibur, the home of Plancus, which he (Plancus) must now leave for the wars. Having thus got *en rapport* with his disciple, he slips in the friendly counsel which it is the object of the ode to give, under cover of an apparently harmless simile. Even the cloudy sky clears *some* day ; so you, no matter whether you may be in camp or (since no place is a safeguard against calamity) at your own beloved Tibur, be manly and shake off gloom. One of the great heroes of old had to go into bitter exile, but on his last night at home he drank like a gentleman and encouraged his companions.

Like these last two pieces, the larger number of the sermons of this less official sort are addressed to single individuals. This, in fact, was Horace's favourite form of poem ; hence, partly, his great success in the Epistles. Each of these poems is given like an oracle to a definite person in connection with a particular occasion ; like an oracle it is calculated to be taken away and meditated on ; the drift, though unmistakable, is not too obvious, and is often introduced, at least, in some more or less figurative form, such as a simile. At the same time, needless to say, Horace has all the while one eye on posterity ; we have already seen that he regards it as his most important mission to educate the young, and so far as his future public is concerned he fulfils it by the very method which his father, the worthy rate-collector, used with him ; it is by no means only in the Satires that he shows an hereditary aptitude for making moral object-lessons of the virtues or defects of his acquaintances. A typical example in many respects is the 9th ode of Book II. "Nature, my friend Valgius, is full of change : it does not rain for ever : the worst weather will yet mend. You rain tears for your lost Mystes as if you would never stop. Remember the example of aged Nestor. Too much lamentation is unmanly ; there are even, let me remind you, some present reasons for rejoicing ; think about our recent victories." To Quinctius Hirpinus, on the other hand, two odes later, he says : "*You* think *too much* about the wars. Spring does not last for ever. Come and picnic with me, and let us invite Lyde, who will sing to us." The same sequence of ideas also forms the basis of the following ode.

In fact, it now becomes obvious that it is often Horace's *main purpose* to end on a different note from that with which he began. " Wreathe my hair," he prays to Melpomene, " with the Delphic laurel," and true to the traditions of Delphi he not only inculcates on Licinius and many other friends the doctrine " not too much of anything," but he observes it in his own poetic practice. Sellar notes, apropos of the careful order in which the odes are arranged within their books,[1] Horace's " strong determination to avoid harping too long on the same string," [2] and this principle is often just as evident within the scope of a single ode. To quote again from Sellar, " he acts on the principle he so well expresses in the words *neque semper arcum tendit Apollo.*" Not only are there many other examples [3] of this particular subdivision of the admonitory address—the kind that leads from one mood to a different one, or at least presents an antithesis of moods—but Horace has (as Pindar might say) a whole quiverful of different effects, some of them serious, some sportive, some delicate, and some arresting,[4] to attain which in various ways he uses this device of the change of mood. But consideration of these must be deferred to a later chapter.

This general examination of Horace's poetic practice has now shown us : (i) that he feels his function as Poet to be of a sacerdotal kind, to be, though not identical with, yet *strictly analogous to,* that of the Priest ; (ii) that he feels himself to be " priest of the Muses," that is, of a religion of a purely literary order, a religion which admits not only all deities already sanctioned by literary usage, but all which a skilful poet can represent as having decent credentials for admission ; such deities being frankly regarded as existing not in the sense in which metaphysicians, ecclesiastics, or other superstitious persons speak of existence, but simply in imagination ; (a religion, in fact, which neither has led nor need ever lead to

---

[1] Another case of an obviously deliberate observance of the principle *series iuncturaque pollet.*

[2] *Horace and the Elegiac Poets,* 142.

[3] *E.g.,* I. xiii. xviii. xxvii. ; III. xix.

[4] *E.g.,* III. xxvi. *fin.*

any excommunications, wars or torturings, and of which the only martyrs are the priest themselves, who thus prove their sincerity) ; (iii) that an ode of Horace is ostensibly either a hymn or a prayer or an exhortation ; (iv) that it is couched in an oracular style, is highly rhetorical, and being directed to the feelings rather than the reason, is apt to be characterised by striking transitions of mood, often abrupt. Further detailed application of these last two principles to the poems themselves is deferred to the separate chapter on the *Odes*.

CHAPTER IV

LIFE AND WORK

L ITERARY biography is not properly a part of literary criticism. The confusion has become too common nowadays; for people who are not really interested in literature can be introduced to it through personalities. Even in the case of Horace, the obviously intimate connection between his writings and his life does not in itself extenuate any such concession to popular taste; his experiences form part of the material of his art, no more; the man is interesting, but he is not the artist. Yet the forms in which he worked are all along so alien to us, and his tone at times so obsolete, that for any really careful study of his writings we must be glad of light from every source available; and poetry having been in ancient days a comparatively recognised profession, some consideration of his life and times will go far towards helping us to understand what aims his art proposed to itself, and what was, both from his own and his employers' standpoints, its political or social function.

Of the life-histories of the majority of the greatest poets we know really very little. But literary precedents and personal inclination alike invited Horace to be communicative. As the source of what we actually know about him, his own writings are almost all-sufficient. Unlike many authors, he clearly visualised posterity, and he tells us everything that he thinks fit; rather more, in point of fact, than we do. We cannot, indeed, be expected to accept authoritatively his most explicit statement [1] upon oath, made on its own showing at least some sixteen years beforehand, as to the date of his own death; it is to another source we have to turn to find that, so far as

---

[1] *Odes*, II. xvii. 8-12.

the year is concerned, this estimate is quite correct, and otherwise only a few months on the safer side. Nor could he, naturally, reveal to us more than a very little, and that indirectly, of his relations with the Emperor. For these and other details we are indebted to a short biography which has been preserved in certain [1] of the manuscripts of the poet's text, and which, on the strength of a passage or two, has been by general consent identified with the memoir by Suetonius (about 75-160 A.D.) to which the Horatian scholiasts [2] refer.

His *praenomen* is vouched for by *Sat.*, II. vi. 37 *orabant hodie meminisses, Quinte, reverti ;* his *nomen* by *Odes*, IV. vi. 44, *vatis Horati*, and *Epist.*, I. xiv. 5, *melior sit Horatius an res ;* his *cognomen* by *Epod.*, xv. 12, *si quid in Flacco viri est*, and *Sat.*, II. i. 18, *Flacci verba*. He was born 8th December, B.C. 65. This, too, he tells us (but for the day, which is given by Suetonius)[3] and tells us more than once ; he twice [4] refers (once with peculiar affection) to wine bottled in the year of his own birth, and so by naming the consul (L. Manlius Torquatus) enables us to identify the year ; and in the epilogue to his first book of Epistles he further indicates the month.[5] The place was Venusia, on the borders of Apulia and Lucania ; [6] Horace himself, however, seems to regard it as, if anything, rather in the former area ; [7] it has been noticed that he is fond of attributing to the Apulians all the Roman virtues. Venusia was picturesquely situated on the slopes of Mount Voltur,[8] and near the river Aufidus, to which, as to Apulia's legendary King Daunus, he several times refers.[9] Strabo, who was a contemporary of Horace, tells us that it was a town of importance.[10] It had, indeed, had something of a history. Founded as a " Latin " colony in B.C. 291,[11]

---

[1] φ, ψ, λ, ρ. It was also in the *vet. Bland.* Others have the beginning and end only.

[2] Porphyrion on *Epist.*, II. i. 1 ; Acron on *Odes*, IV. i. 1.

[3] *Vit Horat.* " natus est VI Id. Decembr. L. Cotta et L. Torquato Coss."

[4] *Epod.*, xiii. 6, *Od.*, III. xxi. 1. [5] *Epist.*, I. xx. 26-8.

[6] *Sat.*, II. i. 34-5 (of himself) :—Lucanus an Apulus anceps, Nam Venusinus arat finem sub utrumque colonus.

[7] See *e.g. Odes*, III. xxx. 10-12 ; *Sat.*, I. v. 77.

[8] Cf. *Odes*, III. iv. 9.

[9] *Odes*, IV. ix. 2, xiv. 25-6 ; III. xxx. 10-12 ; I. xxii. 14.

[10] Strabo, VI. i. 3. [11] Velleius, i. 14.

towards the conclusion of the third and last phase of Rome's long struggle against the Samnites,[1] with the record number of 20,000 colonists,[2] it had not long to wait for an opportunity of proving its fidelity and mettle. As a result of Pyrrhus's first victory at Heraclea (280 B.C.), it was soon completely isolated among the enemy and his converts, but stood firm. While loyal, it was none the less proud. " These so-called Latins, issuing from the Roman burgess-body "—thus Mommsen,[3] speaking of the Latin colonies in general about this time —" and feeling themselves in every respect on a level with it, already began to view with displeasure their subordinate federal rights and to strive after full equalisation." It had *tribuni plebis* like the parent city. At the beginning of the second Punic War, it was captured by Hannibal on his rapid victorious progress through Italy ; Polybius in stating this tells us it was well fortified and full of all manner of stores.[4] Hither fled the surviving consul from the disaster of Cannæ, and here he and some remnants [5] of the Roman army which streamed in after him were supplied and re-equipped, corporation and individuals alike rising nobly to the emergency. Through the ordeals of the next decade Venusia, like the colonies in general, remained loyal ; that it suffered severely is shewn by the fact that soon after the conclusion of the war it was reinforced by a fresh body of *coloni* (200 B.C.). But its situation on the great southern highway, the extended *Via Appia*, was an infallible safeguard, and in the period which followed it recovered its old prosperity, while resenting doubtless like the Italians in general its exclusion from Roman privileges and its exposure to outbursts of Roman insolence.[6] Though not among the very first, it soon joined the insurgents in the Social War of 90-88, and became one of their main strongholds ; they gained their point and the full franchise, one result of which was that when the *animosus infans* was born there some quarter-

---

[1] Cf. Hor., *Sat.*, II. i. 36, which shows that Venusia knew its own history and was proud of it.

[2] On the strategic value of the position, see Mommsen (Engl. trans.), i. 493.

[3] *Op. cit.*, ii. 51.   [4] Polyb., III. 90.

[5] The others had stopped at Canusium. Livy, xxii. 49, 50, 54.

[6] See *e.g.*, Mommsen, *op. cit.*, iii. 492 *fin.*

century afterwards, it was born a *civis Romanus ;* with the right, among others, of holding landed property, one which it was destined to exercise, as well as that of contracting legal marriage, which it was not.

Horace was thus only five years younger than Virgil, and " North and South Italy were again represented in the two great poets of a period, as they had been in Plautus and Ennius." [1] Sellar notices the fact that his birth falls in the same decennium as that of the other leaders in action and literature who played their part in the Augustan age, and adds two rather amusing and instructive comments with which one need not necessarily agree : " Had he been born a few years earlier he might have been too far committed to the Republican cause ever to become reconciled to the new government. Had the date of his birth been somewhat later, he would probably have been as little interested in the national fortunes, as little braced to manliness in thought and feeling, as Tibullus and Propertius." [2]

The enjoyment of the rights above-mentioned had not been long in the family. Horatius senior had originally been a slave, so that strange to say we cannot even be quite positive about the race of the writer of the great Roman odes. But the probability is that he was of Sabellian, [3] that is to say pure Italian blood, the servile status having been a legacy of the old Samnite wars. The father was by occupation a collector of taxes or other dues, [4] a function which he would naturally exercise as a public servant of the municipality ; and in that case the name is explained ; for on acquiring his freedom, which in time he did, he would be under the necessity of taking a Roman name ; slaves manumitted by a citizen took the gentile name of their late master, and since Venusia as a colony was enrolled at Rome in the rural tribe called *Horatia*, that would provide an obvious source. [5] On the analogy of L. Cornelius Chrysogonus and the like, we may take it that Flaccus (" Flap-ear ") had been his slave-name. Gossip in Suetonius's time said that

---

[1] J. Wight Duff, *Literary History of Rome*, p. 497.
[2] *Horace and the Elegiac Poets*, p. 8.
[3] Sellar, *op. cit.*, 9 ; Sonnenschein, *Class Rev.*, xi. 339 ; xii. 305.
[4] *Sat.*, I. vi. 86.
[5] This was first suggested by G. F. Grotefend.

his real occupation had been the still humbler one of dealing in salt fish. The ancients seem to have had an idea [1] that a running nose is a fruitful source of human error, and Latin in its terse and homely fashion expressed this in the phrase *emunctae naris*,[2] " with one's nose well wiped," as a picturesque equivalent for being what we should call " all there," for having all your wits about you. It is evident from the son's picture of him that the elder Horace was a man of shrewd observation and (for his age and environment) no small insight into men and manners. We are told by Suetonius that the poet was once taunted with the fact that his father had been often seen, in the exercise of the last-named profession, to wipe his nose on his shirt sleeve. Perhaps we may plead that so long as the desired result was attained, we ought not to be too inquisitive about the method.

He never so much as mentions his having had a mother, and one might conjecture from his matured character, which shews no feminine influence, that she had not survived his infancy.[3] He seems, moreover, to have been an only child. Apart from the difference between *de iure* and *de facto* servitude, many a slave in the ancient world had no lower a status and perhaps no worse a life than what is now called an employee, and Horace's father apparently saved quite a decent sum from his earnings ; at any rate he had succeeded in buying a small farm ; [4] and in due course, when the boy became of an age

---

[1] Cf. *e.g.*, Plato, *Rep.*, 343 A (Davies and Vaughan's translation) :— When we had arrived at this stage of the discussion . . . Thrasymachus, instead of making any answer, said, " Tell me, Socrates, have you a nurse ? " " Why ? " I rejoined : " had you not better answer my questions than make enquiries of that sort ? " " Why, because she leaves you to drivel, and omits to wipe your nose when you require it, so that in consequence of her neglect you cannot even distinguish between sheep and shepherd." Cf. Sophocles, *Ichn.*, 363 ; Lucian, *Navig.*, 45 ; Pliny, *N.H.*, xx. 7, 26.

[2] Hor., *Sat.*, I. iv. 8 ; Phædrus, 3.3.14 ; similarly Hor., *Sat.*, I. iii. 30. The metaphor in " terse " itself is not very far distant ; cf. *emunctus* of a clean style, Quint., xii. 10, 17.

[3] Other considerations pointing to this are given by Sellar, p. 11. Cf. also *Odes*, III. iv. 10, which indicates that as a small child he was in charge of a nurse (*Apuliae* being an impossible reading ; I consider Bentley's *sedulae* the best conjecture).

[4] *Sat.*, I. vi. 71, *macro pauper agello.*

to go to school, he was able (since he did not consider the local one socially good enough) to take his son to Rome and for the time being fix his abode there. The school of Orbilius [1] was a fashionable one, and thither the freedman's son, now duly accompanied by a small retinue of slaves, proceeded daily, to acquire the same education as the sons of Roman knights and senators.[2] The father himself accompanied him to and from his classes, a service usually assigned in Roman families to the tutor or παιδάγωγος, who was, of course, a slave. Under Orbilius Horace was instructed in the " poems " of the earliest patriarch of Latin literature, Livius Andronicus, and in mature life was charitable enough not to wish for their destruction. In due course, he must have learned much more ; it was doubtless in his school-days that he laid the foundations of that general acquaintance with Latin literature which his writings indicate ; and he himself speaks [3] of having read, or read in, the *Iliad*, before he left Rome for University life in Athens, which he did not later, doubtless, than 45 B.C.[4]

At Athens he attended the lectures of the school of philosophy called the Academy, founded by Plato. He speaks of having studied geometry, and also philosophy generally. It may be presumed that he here extended his readings in Greek poetry. That he did not afterwards appear a professed Academic is probably due to the simple fact that the doctrine of that school was so " academic." The really living philosophies of the age were Epicureanism and Stoicism, ard it is in these that his *Satires* and *Epistles* show him interested. But it was now, and in the Academy, that he first became acquainted with those questions of morals which were to prove the chief and growing concern of his later years. He looked back on his University life with a sort of affection, or wistfulness ; at least he applies to Athens the same epithet as he did—retrospectively—to Cinara, *bonae*.

Hither came, some three and a half months after Horace's twentieth birthday, the sensational news that Julius Cæsar had been assassinated ; and as a result the young poet's University career was soon to be cut short, like many a recent

[1] *Epist.*, II. i. 71.   [2] *Sat.*, I. vi. 76-8.   [3] *Epist.*, II. ii. 41-2.
[4] Cicero's son went then, and he was born in the same year as Horace ; *ad Att.*, XII. 2.

University career, by a world-war. It was in the Autumn of 44 B.C. that Brutus, on his way to the province of Macedonia assigned to him by the late dictator, came to Athens, where he was received with enthusiasm by the Greeks themselves,[1] and soon found no difficulty in winning to his side the numerous young Roman students.[2] Having murdered his friend on principle, he proceeded to attend lectures on philosophy, among others those of Theomnestus, the head of the school at which Horace was studying; it was doubtless in this connection that they met, and the Republican general in due course jobbed the proficient in moral science into a military tribuneship.[3] Thus did the future laureate of Augustus begin his political career in the opposing camp. From the episode recounted in *Sat.*, I. vii., as also from the familiarity with Aegean islands and cities of Asia Minor shewn in *Epist.*, I. xi., it is clear that he accompanied Brutus eastwards in the following year. It is probably hardly necessary to remind any reader of this book of the passage in which he alludes to his share in the final rout at Philippi. That tragic farce concluded, he obtained, like many another in his position, the pardon of the victors,[4] and returned to Rome " with his wings clipped " (*Epist.*, II. ii. 50). His father was by this time dead, and he would have inherited the property at Venusia, but he was now to pay for his Republicanism [5] by the forfeit of his estate. It was doubtless his first step to secure—by purchase—a situation as a clerk (*scriba*) in the Treasury.[6] This and other such clerkships were often held by freedmen.[7] His meagreness of means now drove him, he tells us, to write verse. This is the very last thing a man would

---

[1] Tac., *Ann.*, ii. 53. [2] Plut., *Brut.*, 24.

[3] About = Lieut.-Colonel.

[4] " τελευτήσαντος δὲ αὐτοῦ [Brutus] τὸ μὲν πλῆθος τῶν στρατιωτῶν αὐτίκα ἀδείας σφίσι κηρυχθείσης μετέστη. Dio 57, 3. But it seems probable that some special act of grace relieved Horace " [*i.e.*, the pardoned officers generally] " from further consequences. The soldiers would be simply amalgamated with the victorious army. Suetonius says *venia impetrata*."—Shuckburgh, Introd. to his ed. of *Epistles*, I., p. xii., n. 20.

[5] The confiscation *may*, however, have had no relation to his past politics ; Appian, *Bell. Civ.*, iv. 3, mentions Venusia as one of the towns where lands were assigned to their veterans by the triumvirs after Philippi.

[6] Cf. *Sat.*, II. vi. 36-7. [7] Cf. *Sat.*, I. v. 66-7.

do nowadays from such a motive ; but in that age he could naturally hope that he might thus secure a certain amount of patronage ; as, in fact, Horace ultimately did. The " verses " in question are doubtless partly represented for us in the very earliest of the *Satires* (I. vii,[1] I. ii. possibly also iv.) and *Epodes* (xvi.[2] and perhaps a few others) ; but they were as yet unpublished. As I understand Epode xvi., his sentiments during the Perusine War were still distinctly Republican ; [3] and not unnaturally.

In the meantime, Virgil too (who was now writing his *Eclogues*) had known what it was to be ejected from his farm to make room for a soldier, though he, more fortunate, had been reinstated on appealing to Octavian. This would naturally dispose him to extend his sympathy to Horace, once they had met ; and they doubtless met in some literary circle, though exactly how, or when, it is not possible to say.[4] The obvious resemblance between the sixteenth Epode and the " Messianic " Eclogue seems to point to intercourse between them in the year 40 ; in which case I believe, myself, that the more famous poem—and incomparably more beautiful— was the derivative one. Horace also became acquainted with Virgil's friend and fellow-poet Varius. They were both his elders in political development as well as in years, and through their patron Maecenas,[5] the diplomatic right-hand of Augustus, were on a good footing with the dominant party. First Virgil, then Varius, recommended him to the great man ; in due course he was summoned to an interview ; but Maecenas had the second as well as the first qualification for a true patron of poets, he was cautious as well as liberal, and it was another

---

[1] *Not* written in 43 ; cf. p. 128.

[2] End of 41 or early in 40. Cf. p. 131.

[3] Cf. p. 132 ; also Gow, Introd. to *Odes*, p. xii.

[4] The question was made the subject of a paper by Prof. Ramsay [*Expositor*, May and August, 1907]. I incline to a general agreement with his view that *Ecl.*, iv. is a sort of *answer* to *Epod.*, xvi.

[5] The best and most convincing study known to me of the character of this extraordinary man is the admirably written essay which Mr. Francis Holland has appended to his *Seneca* (Longmans, 1920), where emphasis is rightly laid on the *breach with tradition* which his influence represents.

nine months before the youthful satirist, now in his twenty-seventh year, was again summoned, this time to be told that he might consider himself Maecenas' friend ; in other words, that he need not in future consume his genius in the effort to earn his own living. A friend, however, in the most intimate sense, he very soon became. Even to begin with, the arrangement was no unequal one ; the minister's interest in literature was no mere dilettantism, but connected in the most vital manner with his whole policy, which was, to establish the new régime in the strongest possible way, by commending it indirectly to the imagination of the public. As for Horace's Republicanism, it may be questioned whether it had ever been a matter of principle. When Brutus was at Athens he practically had no choice. After Philippi it was the only active outlet for his grievances. But we know he had a strong sense of the concrete and the practical to save him from the intransigence of the *doctrinaire ;* and his gradual conversion to the Cæsarian party on its better side was perfectly consistent with political integrity on his part, once he had discovered that they had, what no party had had in the whole awful period since the Gracchi—and no leader but Octavian's great-uncle—namely, ideals.

And the next best thing—ideas—they had likewise ; in particular, two ; two which have never yet been refuted, and in the whole of history have only twice or thrice been tried ; and never except on this occasion actually experimented with in combination. One is, that the welter of human barbarism will never cease, until the whole world is organised, and therefore in some way or other [1] centralised ; the second is, not merely that nothing more than the most trivial and transitory benefits can be conferred on the community by the (so-called) statesman whose policy and influence are not primarily moral —for that idea is found in Plato [2]—but that the one and only way to make a people moral, assuming that to be possible at all, is to appeal to their moral sense *through the imagination,*

---

[1] The League of Nations is an endeavour to centralise it *in a new way ;* that is its chief historical importance. The Persian Empire represents the first attempt ; Alexander the Great the second ; the Roman Empire the third and most successful ; since when we have used no other.

[2] *E.g., Gorgias.*

that is to say, through the arts and especially through poetry. Art—poetry—to the ancients these things implied, what (to put it mildly) they do not imply to us, religion. Hence the famous Augustan Religious Revival. It was not a " religious " revival in the sense in which the phrase is apt to be used nowadays ; it was no sudden epidemic of evangelical fervour. It was not, specifically, mystical ; it was indicated by policy rooted in an enlightened humanism ; but to think that it was merely dynastic is as erroneous as to call it unimaginative. It may be objected that this amounts to attributing to the reformers nothing less than a conscious endeavour to introduce the millennium. It does. The evidence is the fourth Eclogue.[1] World-wars, or far-reaching political cataclysms, have regularly been followed to a greater or less extent by hopes of a golden age ;[2] on this occasion these went the length of a concrete experiment. How much that experiment did for humanity we are perhaps even yet not quite in a position to estimate in full ; exactly why it proved ultimately a failure is one of the most important questions in history. Nor is it a question irrelevant to the life-work of Horace, since that was a main agent in the reconstructive enterprise ; and in so far as his share is concerned, a slight attempt to indicate where the failure lies will be made in my final chapter.

Whose, originally, was this idea of reconstruction via religion and public morals ? Dion Cassius attributes it to Maecenas himself, in a speech which he represents him as delivering to Augustus, subsequent to the victor's return from the East after the final decision of Actium.[3] There is every reason to suppose that he is right. But the general policy had, as we have seen, been conceived long before that ; at least twelve years before 28 B.C. By 29 B.C. Virgil had finished his *Georgics;* he had begun them in 37. It is natural to

[1] I have no doubt, myself, that the " boy " was the unborn Julia. This idea has been ridiculed, *e.g.*, by Sidgwick, but see the very interesting *Virgil's Messianic Eclogue*, by Mayor-Fowler-Conway, 1907. It is remarkable that the junior triumvir should have been entertaining dynastic ideas so soon after Philippi ; doubtless Perusium is his justification.

[2] This was pointed out recently in a leading article in *The Times Literary Supplement* (reference unfortunately mislaid).

[3] Dion Cassius, lii. 14-40.

inquire what Maecenas can have seen in *Epodes*, xvi. and any or all of ii., iv., v., vi., viii., x., xi., xii., xv., xvii., and in *Sat.*, I. vii., ii., and probably iv., to make him think the writer a promising employee. Some sort of a standard of conduct, at most ; that is the answer ; and the least in that line is a thousand times more hopeful than nothing at all. There is in a number of these pieces a good deal that is objectionable, in various directions and degrees ; but there is also in most of them a sense of the claims of public decency, and further even, a genuine moral *reasonableness*, which to an Ovid or a Propertius it somehow or other simply did not occur to have.

> Me sine, quem semper voluit Fortuna iacere,
> Hanc animam extremae reddere nequitiae

is interesting, moving even, as contrasted with some of the just-above-mentioned and readable compared to others ; yet not at any period of his life, the fact remains, could Horace possibly have descended to it. Of course it was not this consideration in itself that can have decided the patron ; it must have been the fact that there was an obviously very exceptional command of terse and precise and rhythmical language which made this as yet very faintly perceptible ethical value worth considering and building hopes upon. But probably the point was decided less by the literary factor at all than by the personal one ; here was at least a young man with " character." As often enough noticed by modern readers, the tone of Horace's writings takes a huge stride forward after his becoming really intimate with the great statesman.[1]

Maecenas was popularly supposed, or perhaps himself affected, for good reasons which it is not difficult to imagine, to be a luxurious and effeminate liver ; but his official life, at least, seems to have been strenuous enough. Between 40 B.C. and the Spring of 37 inclusive, he made no less than four separate journeys to Brundisium [2] to patch up the increasing chasms in the uncordial *entente* between the two acting triumvirs ; and on one of these, partly for social dis-

---

[1] In *Sat.*, I. v. it was still patronage, not intimacy.

[2] In the Spring of 38 he probably stopped short of Brundisium, since Antony had not waited, but in the Autumn of the same year he went to Brundisium and thence to Athens.

traction and partly doubtless to observe him further, he took
his newly-adopted client with him, besides, of course, a considerable and distinguished suite, including Virgil and Varius.
It is now generally agreed that the journey described in *Satires*,
I. v.—which is certainly far less interesting than one who
was less of an " introvert " could doubtless have made it,
but is interesting, nevertheless, as it was bound to be—was
the last of those four, *i.e.*, it took place in the Spring of 37.
The first two are out of count, and the third was in Autumn ;
in line 14 Horace refers to the frogs of the Pomptine marshes
whose croaking kept the company awake at night ; and as
the cackling geese saved the Capitol, so do these humbler
creatures seem to have preserved the identity of this diplomatic mission, as it is stated on the authority of distinguished
naturalists familiar with the frog species of Southern Italy,
that although one may give an occasional croak as late as
August, they " do not croak in concert except from about
February to April, *i.e.*, in the breeding season and for some
weeks afterwards." [1] However that may be, there are things
in the piece—such as the account (51-70) of the efforts made
(successfully, it appears) by the two professional entertainers
to amuse the party—at which, it may be supposed, even a
frog would croak.

During these first three years or so of his dependence on
Maecenas, Horace was engaged in the composition of those
satires (I. v., viii., i., iii., ix., vi., x.) which he presently added to
the three above referred to as already written, publishing all
ten together as the first book in 35.   Though it is not possible
to say that he had begun to write epodes first, it seems a fact
that before his introduction to Maecenas he had been mainly
engaged [2] on that form of composition.   Set beside the positive
beauty and constructive tendencies of Virgil's *Eclogues* and
Georgics, the ostensible purpose of all the early work of Horace
is negative by comparison.   But it is important to realise
that it has such a purpose—the " neutralisation," by exposure,

---

[1] Gow, Introd. to *Sat.*, I. v., and *Class. Rev.*, 1901, p. 117.

[2] So far at least as his extant work is concerned ; but the amount
of self-defence in *Sat.*, I. iv. (pre-Maecenas) might seem to point to his
having previously circulated something more in the way of satire than
I. vii. and ii. merely.

of enemies of society. The Epodes themselves attack the
vulgar profiteer, the vicious matron, the adulterer, the base
poet ; and even that early second satire of the first book
has its justificatory basis of protest. That in Roman society
verse of this sort could be a damaging weapon is clear from the
outcry which Horace presently (*Sat.*, II. i.) tells us has been
raised against him because of his first book of satires. And
in the second place, even in the work of his first period, the
Epodes and both books of Satires, there is clearly traceable a
progress in moral value. The first step in that is now before
us. Crude in tone as the satires of the first book often are,
they are on the whole less crude than the epodes ; and besides,
the very choice itself of the *satura* in preference to the ἐπῳδός
marks an advance in the poet's work. In the epodes he is
following a Greek model, Archilochus, and a very ancient one
at that ; some of them count for little more than academic
exercises. In the satires he is not only working in what was,
as we have seen, the only literary form original to Latin, but
he is taking up a special development of it invented by a Campanian writer whose floruit had been just a century earlier and
whose work in that line had enjoyed an unprecedented popu-
larity. Lucilius, 180-103 B.C., was no artist, and he did not,
indeed, give to the " miscellany " any more unity of the formal
kind than he had found in it as it slid from the hands of Ennius ;
but he did impart to it a unity of tone or tendency ; he it was
who first impressed upon Latin Satire that censorious character,
which we, owing to the fact that its two most famous exponents
Horace and Juvenal were his disciples, now regard as its essential feature.[1] It was still a hotch-potch ; but he succeeded in
pervading all his puddings with something of the same acidity.
He " lashed Rome " (Persius) ; he inveighed incessantly
against corruption of every kind. Thus, whereas the characteristic pieces in the book of epodes (or the majority out of
so heterogeneous a collection) are " satirical " chiefly in our
sense—light, rather ironical, not so serious as they look—the
" satires," on the contrary, are not so much satirical as po-

---

[1] In so doing he was, of course, whether consciously or not, reverting
to the ancient function of the " fescennine verses " to which the *satura*
is ultimately traceable.

lemical. The increase of seriousness is marked by a comparative absence both of raillery on the one hand and of violence on
the other. And, though Canidia is still pursued (viii.), for the
most part the objects of attack are now of a less obvious character than were those in the Epodes ; by way of social nuis-
ances, it is the pushing young author (ix.) or the pedantic
critic (x.) that are held up to our derision. For the rest, the
theme of the satirist is rather those failings which are common
to mankind in general ; the restless discontent of each with
his own occupation or lot (i.), the idolatry of money (i.), uncharitableness (iii.) ; or he attacks, not an individual, but a
sect, the Stoics (iii.). But perhaps more significant still is the
fact that behind all this destructive criticism there begins to
appear a constructive element ; some sort of a positive lesson
is drawn ; the first step towards a cure is a sound diagnosis,
and in the opening piece of this collection we see the satirist
recognising that the general unhappiness of mankind is symp-
tomatic and desiring to trace it to its real source ; this he
finds in their insatiable greed for money ; it is because they
are always longing for what they have not, that they are
always unable to enjoy what they have. Of this truth, so far
as it goes—and it still goes a long way, for that sort of spiritual
disease is one of those which are most apt to thrive subcon-
sciously—of this truth Horace never lost sight. We have
here the earliest of those many declamations, rhetorical or
lyrical, which he made against materialism and capitalism ;
a theme which inspired many of his most trenchant utterances,
things of so pure a crystal that their brilliance ceases to be
metallic and becomes live and luminous as of a star. Such
things indeed are not yet ; but we may note that his work is
becoming more considerable, and that his character is developing. He is at that phase of adolescence which regularly expresses itself in the thinking-out of current problems of moral
science. In the physical sense, indeed, his adolescence was
now long past, it had clearly been what we should consider
very early ; but in psychical development, the third satire of
this book shows him, not far from his thirtieth year, more
or less at the stage of the modern clever undergraduate ; [1]

---

[1] Or don.

concerned to maintain that there is no sanction in " Nature " for morals, that they rest only on conventions established by society for its own protection. Still, whereas in the early group of epodes he has shewn no concern for such matters at all, it now appears that he is, despite even the youthfully dogmatic tone of *Sat.*, I. iii., feeling vaguely out for some sort of guiding principles of conduct ; in the first piece, which is probably the last written except (x.) the epilogue, he is even found asserting some sort of a connection between the constitution of the universe and morality (106-7, and *intra naturae fines viventi*, 50). But he is still " unconverted."

Few things are more potent to reconcile a man to " Nature " (or as it is now more usually called, the universe) than— nature. Horace had already shewn himself susceptible—for a Roman, remarkably so—to the charm of natural scenery ; for the notion that the second epode is a satire is not worth serious consideration. It was shortly after the publication of the first book of satires that Maecenas presented the poet with a small estate in the Sabine hills. The site was identified in the eighteenth century by the Abbé Capmartin de Chaupy, whose work on the subject runs to three volumes.[1] Quite recently, a very clear account of the physical features of the neighbourhood and the actual position of the squire-poet's own villa was given by Sir Archibald Geikie in an interesting article [2] dealing generally with Horace's life at this Sabine farm. It was situated near the top of a narrow glen opening from the north into the valley of the Anio at a point about eight (English) miles above Tibur, the modern Tivoli ; thirty-two Roman miles separated the bard from Rome. There are still there, and in process of exploration, the remains of a house popularly known as the " Villa d' Orazio," which, though mainly post-Augustan,[3] almost certainly represent for us the position

---

[1] Published in Rome, 1767-9. The best-known modern account is that of Boissier, *Nouvelles Promenades Archæologiques—Horace et Virgile* (6th ed., 1907). [The latest is Mr. G. H. Hallam's scholarly and delightful *Horace at Tibur and the Sabine Farm*, which appeared while my book was in the press.]

[2] *Nineteenth Century.*

[3] I doubt if much can be built on the argument that they are too luxurious (with their mosaic floors, baths, and elaborate heating arrange-

of the poet's dwelling, where, it is very plausibly suggested,[1] some later owner proudly erected his mansion. Horace's estate was large enough to have five tenants; his own farm had eight hands or "slaves" with a bailiff or foreman to look after them. The place-names he mentions are still quite recognisably preserved; the river that runs down the valley, his Digentia, has, with the time-honoured Italian facility for turning d's into l's, become Licenza; his little town of Varia not far away is now Vicovaro. "Men may come and men may go, But I go on for ever "—from a cleft in the rocky slope above there still gushes forth the spring which (there is good reason for thinking) he himself in due course named "Bandusia" after another in his old native haunts of the south, and upon which, in the poem taken as a *point de départ* for the present book, he was to confer the gift of a parallel immortality.

He seems at once to have begun to build himself a house on this property,[2] and was established therein at any rate before [3] December, 33 B.C. It would be difficult to exaggerate the beneficent influence of this event on his character and his work alike. If the acquaintance with Maecenas had begun his redemption, this gift of material freedom confirmed it. All his subsequent writing, though in it too there are different grades, is artistically far firmer than what preceded, and at the same time indicates a much mellower mentality in the writer.

In the meantime, the political kaleidoscope was changing, and the breach between the world's two rulers becoming steadily more irreparable. In 32 war was declared ostensibly against Cleopatra, virtually against Antony, and Octavian commissioned with the conduct of it. Early in the year the two consuls, foreseeing the inevitable, had left Rome to join Antony, and they were followed by many senators; to that juncture, I suspect, belongs the seventh epode, and it is to

ments) to tally with Horace's account; quite apart from his habitual εἰρωνεία, I often suspect that we underestimate the extent to which the conventional material standards of ancient literature are plutocratic.

[1] Sellar, 32 n.; Geikie, *op. cit.*, p. 485 *fin.*

[2] *Sat.*, II. iii. 308, where *aedificas* is retrospective (cf. 312) and refers to the house now completed, which is the scene of the conversation.

[3] *Ibid.*, 5 and 185.

those departing Antonians for whom the astute Octavian openly proclaimed entire freedom of action, that its opening protest is addressed, *Quo quo scelesti ruitis ?* [1] The gloomy picture which it draws is not prompted by any actual despair of the writer, but is calculated to shame the men who are preparing to draw once more swords that had seemed to have been finally sheathed. It used to be thought that Maecenas was not present at the battle of Actium, since Dion (51.3) says that during the campaign as a whole he was left in charge of Rome and Italy ; but it would be very natural that he should be with Augustus until victory was assured, and then be sent back to Rome, whither Augustus did not return until late in 29 ; and his presence at the battle is alleged by an extant elegy on him, belonging probably to the first century A.D. Accordingly it is now agreed that the first epode is to be taken at its face value. Maecenas is going to the wars ; Horace has been bidden by his patron to stay behind, but respectfully urges that he cannot ; he must be allowed to face all the risks faced by his benefactor. That this was no empty profession appears from the ninth epode, composed, it is now quite clear, not in Rome just after the first vague news of the victory, but at Actium itself, on shipboard ; the poet is suffering from sea-sickness (35). " Whenever shall I be drinking champagne " —Caecuban, dry and tonic—" in honour of peace ? " he begins by asking wistfully. The answer appears in the beginning of *Odes*, I. xxxvii., " *Nunc* est bibendum." And likewise, " nunc pede libero pulsanda tellus." The century of civil wars was over ; the revolution had ended in a dynasty. Horace began to write his odes.

But first he had to get rid of his existing works. In the year after Actium he published his second book of *Satires*, and about the same time the other egg, already rather long in danger of becoming addled, the collection of Epodes ; of which latter it may truthfully be said, that parts of it are excellent ; for the purposes of the present chapter, enough on this, the slightest of the works of Horace, has been said already, except that we should note the remarkable foretaste of the manner of the *Odes* in number xiii. The eight satires of the second

[1] See p. 144.

book, in addition to a marked improvement both in technique and in art, show an advance in the writer's own character, the sort of advance that directly affects their literary value; there is at once more seriousness and more humour, more archness and more charm. In contrast to the anti-Stoicism (accompanied by marked Epicurean features) of the first book, this shows an obvious softening towards the austerer system in iii. and vii., and consistently therewith a general preaching throughout the whole book of an ethical idealism of strongly Stoical colour. This is to be noted for its bearing on the development of Horace's character; but its significance is not confined to that. A much larger watershed than is usually realised has thus its apex between Horace's first and second books of *Satires*. Roman Satire before that point, and the remark may be extended to include the antecedent Greek diatribe, has been anti-Stoical; from now on, satire or diatribe Greek or Roman, it devotes itself to the exposition and furtherance of Stoic doctrine with all the zeal and industry of the sudden convert. Horace's own *Epistles* are still more Stoical than *Satires*, II.; Persius is nothing if not Stoical; Juvenal is deeply tinged with Stoicism.

Quite apart from the political aspect of this indirect attempt to elevate the tone of Roman social life, there are even in the *Satires* streaks of reconstructionist propaganda of a more concrete order. It was not until 28 B.C. that Augustus was able to restore the temples which a generation or more of intermittent anarchy had let fall into various degrees of ruin. But as early as in *Sat.*, I. vi. 34-7, that is to say about 36-5 B.C., we find Horace saying :—

> sic qui promittit, cives, urbem sibi curae,
> imperium fore et Italiam, delubra deorum,
> quo patre sit natus, num ignota matre inhonestus,
> omnis mortalis curare et quaerere cogit.

The first two of these lines fit Octavian excellently; and they fit no one else at the time.[1] What are we to think? Has the triumvir already matured his plans, and circulated a hint or two on preparing public opinion? Or, as Professor Conway

[1] As to the second two, see Suet. Oct. 2, 4. Cf. on this passage generally, D'Alton, *Horace and His Age*, p. 94 *fin.*

has quite recently suggested,[1] was the Augustan reconstruction to some extent " dictated and inspired " by the poets ? On such questions as marriage reform and imperial apotheosis Horace in his *Odes* is certainly ahead of history. But it is generally agreed that at the time of the *Satires* the poet had no actual acquaintance with the future emperor. On the other hand, it is at least surprising, as D'Alton points out, that Horace while still under Epicurean influence should display so much solicitude for the temples of the gods. In point of fact, there is at all events nothing inconsistent with such evidence as we possess, in supposing that Dion Cassius' account already referred to is substantially correct ; and that the policy in general was derived, by emperor and poets alike, from the blue-blooded Etruscan and astutely professing sybarite who was the original means of their being brought into co-operation. The same hint is repeated later, in a patriotic context, II. ii. 104, the lesson being the right use of riches :—

> quare
> templa ruunt antiqua deum ? cur, improbe, carae
> non aliquid patriae tanto emetiris acervo ?

Interesting pictures of his private life at Rome or in the country, both before and after the gift of the Sabine farm, are given by Horace in *Sat.*, I. vi. 104-31, and II. vi. generally. By his own account he managed on two meals a day, lunch and dinner ; but we may presume that he did not think it worth mentioning that he breakfasted in bed.[2] Waking about seven, he wrote or read in bed till ten ; then got up and took exercise, a walk or game, until mid-day, when he resorted to the public baths. After lunch he " took his ease at home." So far it seems a " simple life " in externals at least ; but then, at his dinner he was waited on by three slaves. And, of course, in any case it needs (failing private means) a Maecenas ; when he talks (I. vi. 129) as if everybody might be enjoying that sort of life if they would only have the sense to give up being on the make, he is, in the naive pagan way, thinking only of the leisured class.

In the year after the publication of these works, Augustus

---

[1] *New Studies of a Great Inheritance*: " Horace as Poet Laureate ": p. 54, cf. 62.

[2] I. vi. 127-8 is not really inconsistent with this.

having at length wound up affairs in the East returned to Rome. He was now in actual fact master of the civilised world, and celebrated an appropriate triumph.   The closing of the temple of Janus on 11th January 29 B.C. can hardly have been less welcome in Rome and Italy than was the news of the armistice of 11th November, 1918, throughout Britain ; for though the agonies that preceded it had been less violent, they had lasted for twenty years instead of four-and-a-quarter, if indeed they are not to be reckoned from still further back.   And peace then likewise brought with it the necessity of immediate and far-reaching reconstruction.   As we have seen,[1] the adoptive son of Julius Cæsar had already, less than two years after Philippi, anticipated succeeding to his position of virtual monarch, and formed plans for the regeneration of society ; and now that power came to him, it did not find him unprepared. To review the methods by which he tackled the problem, and to compare them with the spirit in which it is being approached to-day, is too large a subject for consideration here, though not, as a matter of fact, irrelevant ; the inquiry should be instructive, salutary perhaps, but hardly encouraging.   He did not neglect the humblest aspects of what is essentially a single even if a highly complicated task, but he was as far perhaps as any great statesman has ever been from interpreting reconstruction in the terms of twentieth-century materialism. He repaired the drains ; but he also rebuilt the temples.   He instituted metropolitan police and fire-brigades ; but he also made moral and social reforms.   He gave Rome a regular water-supply ; but he also purified the civic sense and stimulated the highest kind of patriotism.   He saw, in fact, that without a serious appeal, on a large scale, to the national imagination, national reconstruction is simply impossible. With this end in view he made his chief sphere of reconstruction that of religion and morals, and his chief agency poetry.   In the case of one reform after another, we can see him preparing public feeling for it through the poets ; all along we can see him using them to awaken and inspire the sense of nationality and (still more important) of a great racial *mission*.   In our own enlightened age we can, perhaps, afford to smile at such

---

[1] P. 91, n. 1.

simplicity; we have learned many things he did not know; Evolution, for one thing, so that we can carry on in our old ways and wait for history to evolute, secure in the certainty that it is a principle which works mechanically; Art for Art's sake, also, so that we have apprehended the great truth that Art has no use, and can enjoy without misgivings the unalloyed beauty which has so markedly characterised the arts since that other revelation of mid-nineteenth-century.

Inventas aut qui vitam excoluere per artes—to the ancients, on the other hand, unblessed with our distinction between fine and applied art, the arts one and all, the highest as the humblest, existed for the practical refinement of human life. Their craftsmen were artists, where ours are mechanics; their artists were craftsmen, where ours are dilettanti. For them the poet was primarily a civiliser. It was in that capacity that Augustus used the poets of his age. Before Actium, Maecenas, with the prescience that perhaps more than anything else constitutes him a genius in statesmanship, had already employed them in the preliminaries of this work. But it was not till now that there had been an absolutely free field; and now the business of national regeneration through poetry began at once in real earnest. Between 29 B.C. and his death in 19 Virgil was engaged on the *Aeneid;* between 30 and 23 Horace was writing his first three books of *Odes.*

During just that period the emperor himself was less occupied with national reconstruction than with imperial organisation;[1] and as has been remarked,[2] the details of provincial administration are not for poetry. It was not until the end of the year 19 that Augustus turned his principal attention to the problems of domestic reform. But, as already indicated, his use of poets was to no small degree of a pioneering character. And the odes of these three books, while, of course, they do contain a good deal that is of immediate reference, and in a number of indirect ways inculcate the lesson of Virgil's *Tu regere imperio populos Romane memento*, supporting Augustus' policy of making the Italians feel themselves to be a people with an imperial mission—these odes are nevertheless in other

---

[1] Pelham, *Outline*, 377-8.
[2] Wight Duff, *Lit. Hist. of Rome*, p. 524.

ways largely prospective, and herald the religious and moral reformation associated with the series of " Julian " laws.

A modern writer advocating general lines of reconstruction would instinctively proceed by a method totally different from Horace's, in at least two respects. He would employ prose, not verse ; and he would write scientifically, not imaginatively. He would use the technical terminology and the abstract conceptions of political science. By far the most widely read book on the European question since the conclusion of the war has been concerned entirely with Economics.[1] That could not have happened in any other period of history, however brilliant the book. The ruling interests of this age are Science and Finance. Horace's terminology is entirely one of imaginative associations ; no matter whether he is dealing with religion, or morals, or politics. The gods of various strata, Greek or Roman, barbaric or civilised, Olympian or popular, which appear in his odes, define the drift of the poem according to what they stand for, what they suggest. Jove is the Zeus of the Greek age of the city-state ; the King of the Olympians, he represents civic order, and civic order centralised in a ruler who is, if benign, yet absolute. He is also the Zeus of the Stoics, the personification of the moral law. But he is also in Horace, what he had been in history more or less by accident, the great god of the Roman *Republic ;* and just as Augustus was careful to emphasise the continuity between the Republican and the Imperial constitutions and to make out that the latter was no violation of the former but a development of it, so is Horace careful to show that the various gods —such as Apollo, for example—whom he represents, in accordance with the Emperor's religious predilections, as patrons or guarantors of the new régime, are after all but the time-honoured executants of the will of Jupiter.[2] I was long puzzled by the fact that what the poet puts in the forefront (since the opening stanza is but a formal "¡Oyez ! ") of the ode which in its turn he puts in the forefront of the great series that begins the third book (those six poems which have been universally recognised as the centre of emphasis of the whole collection),

---

[1] J. M. Keynes, *The Economic Consequences of the Peace.*
[2] Cf. esp. *Odes,* I. xii. and esp. 49-60. See pp. 105, 107.

seems at first little more than a turgid commonplace asserting the supremacy of the god whom all the classical tradition had in fact recognised as supreme. But what he means is: " The new government stands for the restoration of civil order, of morality on a religious basis, and of the old Roman traditions " —all three of which ideals had lapsed grievously in the preceding century ; " it also stands for " one *new* principle, *viz.*, " centralisation in a personal ruler." Yet even that is not quite all he means. The victory of West over East at Salamis had been idealised in 5th century Greek art as one of civilisation over barbarity, and symbolised in sculptures depicting men victorious over monsters.[1] Augustus too, as is well known, did all he could to represent Actium as another triumph of Western against Eastern ideals ; and the old Greek imagery is requisitioned by Horace for this purpose. That is, for example, why he repeatedly calls the great enemy yet remaining " Persians " instead of Parthians ; and in the third line of our present stanza is a significant echo of Periclean symbolism recalling the preceding great age of reconstruction after a world war.

> Regum timendorum in proprios greges
> reges in ipsos imperium est Jovis
> clari Giganteo triumpho,
> cuncta supercilio moventis.

If *regum—reges* is not quite an allusion to Augustus, it has his position definitely in view. There comes a time when men get sick of the dismal results of collaboration with its mechanical methods, and turn again, in politics or art or both, to the idea that the greatest efficiency is secured rather by that vital unity in the product, which can only be conveyed to it by an individual character. *Rex* is one of those words like *vates* which become restored to honour in the Augustan period ; by Horace it is usually employed in a good sense,[2] never with Republican odium. The Elizabethan age, too, combined a sense of the

---

[1] Cf. E. Gardner, *Handbook of Greek Sculpture*, p. 215.

[2] This is partly of course due to Stoic influence. But *Odes*, I. i. 1 and III. xxix. 1, are not the sort of compliments that Roman poets would have paid to their patrons outside the Augustan period.

mortality and human impotence of kings [1] with a belief in the monarchic constitution, and this first ode of the third book is in effect [2] an acceptance and inculcation of the principle of " Degree " in human society—to give it the term applied to it by Ulysses in his famous speech in Shakespeare's *Troilus and Cressida.*

We may now glance at some of the chief instances of these two main kinds of symbolism, the theological and the historical.

The odes in which the former kind figures most are : I. ii., xii., III. iv. ; and (since it will be convenient here to anticipate later works) IV. vi. and the *Carmen Saeculare.* In both the first-mentioned, as in the tonic stanza above quoted from the beginning of III. i., we find Jupiter at the head of the hierarchy (I. ii. 29-30, xii. 13-18, 49-end). Under the " principate," as it might be termed, of the Roman national god, now augmented with his Hellenic attributes as Roman life was by this time intensified by Greek culture, comes a hierarchy of Olympians and heroes, all deliberately selected for their value as political ideals. Of these Apollo is evidently first in importance. [3] This position in the Horatian pantheon he owes to the fact that Augustus had, for a variety of reasons, [4] made a very special feature of the Apolline cult in his religious reconstruction ; but what Horace has to do is to make that cult *mean* something. The sun-god means " light " in Matthew Arnold's sense ; " clearness of soul," to use the phrase of another poet ; poetry, harmony, " sophrosyne," simplicity of life—that is the message which the Delphic god is to bring in Greek culture to the future Roman world. [5] With Apollo goes necessarily his sister ; chastity, not for all women (there will be a place for Venus presently), but for the free-born, is to be an ideal of the new era. Apollo is the patron of Augustus ; with a select company of other deities the Emperor associates on

[1] *Odes,* I. iv. 13-14 ; *Lear,* generally ; 2 *K. Hen. IV.,* II. ii. *init.*

[2] See p. 69.

[3] Despite I. xii. 17-20, which cannot mean much, considering that 18 is contradicted by 51.

[4] On the significance of Augustus' Apollo-worship see J. B. Carter, *Religion of Numa,* p. 166 foll.

[5] See esp. I. xxxi.

equal terms ; these are often mentioned ;[1] Quirinus, that is
Romulus, the earliest of Roman sanctified rulers ; Hercules,
the destroyer of monsters (compare Periclean art again) the
civiliser of the world ; Castor and Pollux, benefactors of the
race, genial[2] influences ; and Bacchus—but what is the wine-
god doing in that *galère* ? He also is a *refining* influence ; a
tamer of unruly monsters ;[3] he is, like Apollo, a friend of the
Muses,[4] a source of inspiration,[5] and a patron of poets ;[6]
" Who in his cups would talk of campaigning ? " (I. xviii. 5)—
Bacchus stands for the Grace that is to come into the new life
and wipe out the memories of the civil wars. Venus, like
Apollo, owes her position primarily to mythology, being the
mother of Aeneas and so ancestress of the Julian house ; but
she too, on the symbolic side, represents one aspect of the
motif of grace, charm, relaxation ; so I. xxx., where she appears
in the company of the Graces and of Mercury. Mercury, however, it is who is most clearly and vividly portrayed as the
divine emblem of this new ideal ;[7] a very pleasing sketch of
him is given in I. x ; and how closely all that is to be connected in our minds with the Augustan régime is shewn by
I. ii. 41-4, where the poet even goes the length of suggesting
an identification of the Emperor with an avatar of this god.
And, of course, there are the Muses, whose political significance
is similar, but whose province is more particularly literature ;
literature, however, in which the element of *counsel* is an
essential. The poem which most definitely establishes this
political and reconstructive value of Horace's Olympians is
perhaps III. iv ; there we have the legend of the battle between
the gods and the giants with all its profound import as figured
forth in Periclean sculptures, and here explicitly asserted :—

[1] I. xii. 21-33, III. iii. 9-16, IV. viii. 22-34; *Epist.*, II. i. 5-12 all
give the series complete.

[2] I. xii. 27-32.

[3] III. iii. 13-15 ; II. xix. 29-32 ; and cf. III. iv. 42-80, in the light of
Periclean symbolism, with II. xix. 21-24, shewing that Bacchus is on
the side of the Angels, of Apollo, etc.

[4] *E.g.*, I. xxxii. 9.

[5] *E.g.*, I. xvi. 5-6 ; II. xix. 6-7.

[6] *Epist.*, II. ii. 77-8.

[7] On the significance of Mercury for Horace, see Ch. VII., p. 220.

> vis consili expers mole ruit sua ;
> vim temperatam di quoque provehunt
> in maius ; idem odere vires
> omne nefas animo moventes.

With Apollo and Diana [1] on the side of civilisation and Jupiter, is " matrona Juno " the patroness of the sanctity of marriage ; the conclusion is partly conditioned by the fact that " Pirithous " is a gloriously-sounding name to end with ; [2] but not only ; *amatorem* is, unless I am super-subtle, a glance at Antony ; [3] the new government is to be especially discouraging to the expense of spirit in this direction. And of that ode it is the Muses who provide the pivot ; by virtue of them the first and second halves make one poem and not two—

> vos lene consilium [4] et datis et dato
> gaudetis almae.

And it is they who connect the whole with Cæsar, whose literary patronage is no mere cold instrument of dynasty but genuine and whole-hearted—

> vos Cæsarem altum, militia simul
> fessas cohortes reddidit oppidis,
> finire quærentem labores
> Pierio recreatis antro.

Only the spirit of Dr. Johnson on *Lycidas* would protest that Augustus never took his recreation in a cave. To a Roman, Pallas could not mean so much as the deities just mentioned ; but all this symbolism, in this signification, was invented by her city, and therefore she is naturally here ; she is also in I. xii. 20, momentarily in a position of high honour which she has already lost in the 51st line of the same poem.

As for the *Carmen Saeculare*, that is mainly in honour of the specially imperial Apolline cult ; but it is now known [5] to have been performed not only on the Palatine hill before Apollo's temple but again on the Capitol sacred to Jupiter and Juno, who are referred to at 45-52 ; and in the last four lines

---

[1] 71. Haupt bracketed 69-72.   [2] Cf. IV. vii. 28.
[3] Cf. I. xv. 19 *adulteros crines ;* see p. 110, n. 3.
[4] The connection is established by *consili*, 65.
[5] See p. 215, n. 3.

the approval of the older national deity is duly asserted for these praises of Phœbus and Diana. Of these lines Warde Fowler has recently written : [1] " This is an extremely clever stanza ; Horace contrives to bring in Jupiter as after all the presiding genius of Rome, upon whose good will the future of the state depends. . . . But at the same time Horace has most dexterously managed to make the final touch an Apolline one." The same writer remarks that this Apolline part of his task must have been a congenial one to the poet who believed that—

> spiritum Phœbus mihi, Phœbus artem
> carminis nomenque dedit poetae.

The ode in which he says so (IV. vi.) is a sort of prelude to the Secular Hymn ; and in it he brings out still another aspect of Apollo which must have helped to make his cult an appropriate one for the political purposes of Augustus. It is now recognised that the idea of transferring the capital of the Roman empire to the East, in point of fact to the Troad—" a project almost literally carried out by Constantine some 350 years later " [2]—was seriously entertained as part and parcel of the Cæsarian policy inherited from Julius. To Julius it is explicitly attributed by Suetonius ; Augustus eventually decided definitely against it, and both Virgil and Horace urge or acclaim that decision.[3] Apollo himself, we are reminded in this ode, Apollo the patron of Troy, had had to submit to the destruction of the offending city, and to realise that the new settlement to be founded by that Aeneas for whose survival he interceded was destined to be founded with better omens. In III. iv. we had been made to feel that powerful divine influence was against the centralisation of world-empire in the East ; powerful, because Juno, the speaker there, was a great Roman deity. But then Juno had always been the implacable enemy of Troy. Here we are assured that a god of still more authority who had been from the first as con-

---

[1] *Roman Essays and Interpretations*, pp. 124-5.

[2] R. Conway, *New Studies of a Great Inheritance*, p. 61 ; cf. Walter Leaf, *J. Phil.*, xxxiv. 68, p. 286. See both contexts for the question in general.

[3] *Odes*, I. xiv. (see Dr. Leaf, *loc. cit.*), III. iii. *Aen.*, xii. 823-8 (see Conway, *loc. cit.*).

sistently philo-Trojan [1] as a moral god could be, had long ago
yielded to the necessity of the Western policy ; whence we
may rest in the assurance that Rome's position is indeed
secure, and that the old unhappy feud of East and West which
had shaken the world at intervals from the days of Helen to
those of Cleopatra, is now past for ever.

This brings us to the consideration of the other main type
of Horatian symbolism.

Here again Horace utilised a whole complex of associations,
or system of poetic imagery, that had already been made
familiar by Greek literature. The idea of a series of struggles
between East and West meets us in Herodotus and Thucydides ; the latter makes it begin with the Trojan War. One
such contest, a mythical one, is represented as a struggle of
lawless violence against Hellenic " sophrosyne " as early as the
Supplices of Aeschylus. In his *Persae* we see an *historic*
instance of the same feud made to symbolise the defeat of
Oriental delicacy, pride, effeminacy, luxury, and godlessness
by the opposite ideals. In his *Agamemnon* the victory of
Greek over Trojan is clearly and repeatedly invested with a
similar significance :—

KΛ. τί δ' ἂν δοκεῖ σοι Πρίαμος, εἰ τάδ' ἤνυσεν ;
ΑΓ. ἐν ποικίλοις ἂν κάρτα μοι βῆναι δοκεῖ.

Then there are the fifth-century sculptures. " The struggle
between light and darkness, between freedom and tyranny,
between Europe and Asia," writes Prof. E. Gardner [2]—and he
might have extended the spiritual antithesis—" is the true
theme of all the battles between gods and giants, or Greeks
and Amazons, or Lapiths and Centaurs, and all are regarded
as antitypes of the great struggle from which the Greeks themselves had just emerged victorious." To which particular
source, if any single one, Horace was indebted is perhaps
not evident, but it is obvious that the symbols of Periclean
reconstruction and civilisation are transferred by him to help
in voicing the spirit of Pericles' immediate successor in the
lamentably slow history of the political redemption of a world

---

[1] III. iv. 66, *auctore Phoebo* throws up the significance of IV. vi.
[2] *Handbook of Greek Sculpture*, p. 215.

that is only too manifestly barbaric still. In particular, the Roman poet employs for this purpose the names of Troy and Persia. It would scarcely be possible to make too much of, nor, I would add, to overpraise for poetic felicity, economy and force, the juxtaposition of the two concluding poems of Book I. Impotence, effeminacy, intoxicate infatuation, monstrosity, and an almost sublime perversity of daring, are the qualities he sees in the cause of Cleopatra whose defeat he celebrates in the 37th ; in the 38th he denounces " Persian " (that is, Oriental) magnificence, and inaugurates the era of the simple life. This I believe is more than half the reason for the prominence (it has naturally been thought surprising) [1] assigned in many a passage of the *Odes* to anti-Parthian campaigns or projects ; for Horace they are what he almost always calls them, " Medes " or " Persians," and all that the name involves must be subdued.

And not even Rome's own Trojan derivation can efface the significance in Greek poetry of the sinful city. It was, indeed, convenient, as we have just seen,[2] for Augustus' political purposes, that the curse which rested upon Trojan soil should still be fearfully remembered. But the significance of " Troy " in the *Odes* of Horace is not limited to a warning against the establishment of an Eastern capital as a rival or successor of Rome. It is meant to be a general warning against Oriental ways of life ; against what Antony had stood for (or at least was by Cæsarian propaganda made to stand for) in the Roman imagination, and what Augustus now stood increasingly against. In I. xv., a poem which has been dismissed as a mere mythological verse-exercise because readers have not felt throughout how it must have sounded within a year or two after Actium,[3] the Trojan cause is associated with effem-

---

[1] See *e.g.*, D'Alton, *Horace and His Age*, p. 13.

[2] Above, p. 108.

[3] Of course all this is really about the Civil War from which the Roman world had just been delivered. In *Eheu, quantus equis, quantus adest viris Sudor ! quanta moves funera Dardanae genti !* he is in the vein of II. i. 20, 21-2. In *serus adulteros Crines pulvere collines* he is glancing at Antony. In his catalogue of Achæan heroes, 21-8, he is thinking generally of the good men who had ranged themselves against that perfidious one. His Nereus is oracular. If this is not true, then the poem is meaningless and trivial ; *reductio ad absurdum*.

inacy (for contrast see III. ii.) and adultery (then read III. vi.). In III. iii. it is contrasted with the strong and just policy explicitly attributed to Augustus, and is associated with moral and political dishonesty and matrimonial laxity. Henceforth Rome is to be the ruling power, a Rome true to Roman ideals ; she is to triumph over—" the Medes " (44). Since both mean " Oriental," Medes here amounts to the same as Trojans elsewhere in the poem. Why did he write " Medes ? " Not *only* because he was speaking of the future and therefore thinking of the Parthian danger. If we do not of ourselves think at this point what " Mede " meant for Aeschylus, the stanza 49-52 will remind us. " Gold " and " sacrilege " ; the *Persae* is full of both. The new era is to discourage capitalistic materialism and to encourage true religion. And as the *justus et propositi tenax* principle of government is explicitly attributed to Augustus, so, no less unmistakably as it seems to me, is the whole " Trojan " or Oriental side of the antithesis identified with the cause of the recently defeated Antonians. In 61-4 Juno is made to glance at their venture as a rehabilitation or renewal of " the fortune of Troy "—its " cause," we should call it—and to prophesy their downfall.[1] Then in the following stanza is

[1] The editors (all of them, if I am not mistaken) have strangely missed the point of 61-4, and by consequence (though to a less degree) of 65-8. According to the regular view, the latter of these two stanzas merely repeats the purport of the preceding, a phenomenon surely without parallel in the *Odes ;* and is it good Latin to have both a participle and a future indicative investing one another with a conditional sense which neither can of itself originate ? Why should not 61-4 mean what it says ? I understand Juno to declare (i) that it is a condition of Rome's success that Romans refrain from rebuilding Troy ; (ii) that in proof thereof " the fortune of Troy " will some day yet be resuscitated, only to end in a second disaster ; and (iii) that if a *third* revival should be attempted, though the walls were strong as brass and Phœbus himself (? *via* Augustus) approved of it, its doom would be the same. There is no reason why Juno should not have taken the credit of Actium to herself ; she was presumably among the *magni di* of *Aen.*, VIII. 679, which included Neptune and Venus and Minerva (*ibid.*, 699). *Ter* is not " numerus poeticus " (Orelli), which would be pointless in a hypothetical context (*Georgics*, I. 281-3 is another matter) ; it is literal, as is shown by the clear antithesis with *iterabitur*. That the difference between the 2nd and 3rd revivals is one of fact *v.* supposition, is enforced by the constructions used. Finally, the main warning of

embodied the main *tendenz* of the poem ; do not let us transfer the seat of government to the East ; which, it has been implied, would only result in imbuing our world-empire with the Eastern vices already indicated. To the considerations advanced by recent writers in explanation of the somewhat unexpected emphasis given by Horace to what the tradition has never bade us regard as a really burning question of the day, one more may be added. The miseries of the last civil wars had caused vague schemes of migration to be mooted since a decade or more ; and Horace himself may well speak feelingly here, in so far as this poem is his " palinode " to *Epode*, xvi. It is in Rome itself that the new Golden Age is now to be inaugurated.

Such are the chief symbols, the concretes for abstracts, which the poet requisitions to make his gospel clear and telling. The positive content of that gospel, the antidote to " Persian extravagances," is stated literally and succinctly and illustrated with object-lessons, over and over again. The simple life ; [1] the subordination of money [2] and of material interests generally to the spiritual health and happiness of the individual ; that is the means by which he hopes to regenerate Rome and avert another world-war. The simple life means, on the one hand, a certain austerity ; the young Roman must be physically fit, and hardened in military exercises or frontier service (III. ii.) ; a severely " manly " ideal is voiced in stern language in such poems as III. v., vi., xxiv. But it has noticeably its other side. " We must have some new element of *grace* in our life " is the contribution to a practical policy of reconstruction made by a very considerable proportion of the *Odes*, and I doubt if this has been sufficiently realised. As contrasted with the tone and language of the four last-mentioned pieces, all of which would have been whole-heartedly endorsed by any Roman of the old school from Cato to Cincinnatus or further back, this doctrine was a comparatively recent heresy whose

the poem thus receives much more force ; the most concrete argument against the Eastern scheme is after all, says Horace, the fact of Actium. It may be added that 65-8 also came true in course of time, when Rome herself became largely Orientalised, and fell.

[1] Characteristic " simple life " odes : I. xxxi. ; II. xv., xviii. ; III. xv.
[2] Typical anti-capitalism odes, II. ii. ; III. xvi.

introduction scarcely precedes the younger Scipio. The fusion which meets us in Horace of these two diverse but not irreconcilable ideals had been conspicuously rare in Roman history, and the nation had suffered thereby The gospel of grace according to Horatius may include a good deal of which our modern age would approve, or to which it would at least give lip-allegiance ; it may also include some things totally at variance with modern ideas of " grace." But however repugnant to us, and however rightly repugnant, may be certain social and moral evils which a number of the *Odes* must recall to almost any modern reader, it should not betray us—as, I believe, it has partly betrayed Ferrero—into imagining that Horace in writing those *Odes* was in the least degree affected by, or even aware of, any such standpoint as that of an advanced modern with regard to prostitution and fornication. There is every evidence that he was not, nor indeed had such views come into existence then ; and in consequence Ferrero as it seems to me quite misconceives the *relation* of the " erotic " poems to the rest of the collection, as well as to the political tendency of the work as a whole. On that question I must refer the reader to my epilogue, pages 293-4. In the meantime, so far from viewing the erotic odes as " external to the poet himself," impersonal reflections of his age, ironical, inconsistent with the serious side of his political and social morality, I think that his recommendations to light love are just as genuine as his recommendations to moderate drinking, and that both are as genuine as those dissuasions from worry, money-making, and political ambition, of which they are, in fact, the simple obverse. The erotic odes are, doubtless, to some extent, jam round the political pill ; but they are fully intended to be swallowed with it, as contributory to the same effect. It is no small part of his monarchist propaganda to persuade the Roman noble that life is not to be taken too seriously. We must reserve a decent degree of leisure, which we must devote to literature, Greek culture, and—as they were then regarded—the innocent delights (in moderation) of drinking and light-love-making.[1] Hence such odes as I. x.

[1] That this is the relation of the convivial odes to Horace's general reconstructive scheme is clearly shown by such passages as profess to describe the realisation of that scheme, *e.g.*, IV. v. 29-40, xv. 25-32 ;

8

with its picture of Mercury ; I. xxxi. (*Quid dedicatum*), especially its last stanza ; hence " literary " hymns to Greek deities,
like I. xxi. (*Dianam tenerae*), II. xix. (*Bacchum in remotis*) ;
hence " the Graces," [1] in such places as III. xxi. 22 ; hence
(one of our old puzzles) [2] III. xvii., advising the blue-blooded
scion of an old Roman family to make preparations for giving
himself a good time ; and all the other pieces of a generally
Epicurean tendency ; and the erotic odes *en masse*. Hence
III. xiv., which nicely indicates (to the modern critic, not of
course betraying itself to the ancient contemporary reader)
the very close connection of this whole vein in Horace with his
monarchist propaganda. And finally, the gospel of grace is
duly accorded a position in the frontal façade of Horace's
poetic edifice, the six odes opening Book III. ; of which the
fourth is in praise of the Muses and recognition of their function
in life.

Finally, mention should be made here of those odes which
are concerned in whole or part to denounce civil war as a crime,
as *nefas ;* II. i., I. xxxv., for example.

That Horace is by nature both a subtle and an economic
poet, who seeks to convey his meaning not only by what he
says but by *where* he says it, is further borne out by the obvious
deliberation and suggestiveness in the arrangement of the odes
in this collection—and also, as a matter of fact, in the subsequent Book IV. All of which has before now been sufficiently
well expounded. [3]

These first three books of *Odes* were published together in
the earlier part of 23 B.C. [4] The next clear date for any publication of Horace's is that of the first book of *Epistles* in 20.
But I am of those who are persuaded by the arguments of
various scholars [5] that the poem entitled *Ars Poetica* belongs to

and of the erotic, by *e.g.*, IV. i. 7-28, where it is hinted that the young
man's efficiency is greatly increased by his taking relaxation of this sort
in what the writer regards as a proper spirit.

[1] The *function* of the Graces is seen from III. xix. 15-17, tris prohibet
supra | rixarum metuens tangere Gratia | nudis iuncta sororibus.

[2] See Ch. I., pp. 4-5.

[3] See *e.g.*, § II. of Wickham's Introd. to *Odes*, I.-III.

[4] See *e.g.*, Wickham, § I. of Introd.

[5] See Ch. VIII., p. 233 ; and for an admirable statement of the case,
Wilkins' *Introduction* to the poem.

about the same period. I take it to have been written either at some time between 23 and 20, or at intervals during that period.[1] Moreover, I think (see Ch. VIII. *init.*) that of these two publications it is the *Ars Poetica* that represents the earlier stage of the writer's poetic evolution. The relation of this work to the circumstances of the time and to the general part played by Horace as a national poet is such as may perhaps excuse a rather detailed consideration.

THE " ARS POETICA " AND THE FIRST BOOK OF " EPISTLES."

Epic, Lyric, and Dramatic—these are the three types of poetry, and Epic is just narrative, mere description ; for the direct expression of emotion there are left only two. Youth sings, instinctively ; but when a man has reached the stage at which he feels, whatever others and the world may think, however small his output, that he can write the sort of poems it had been his hope to write, and that though energy or opportunity may desert him, the power at least is his—from that time on, visits of the lyric afflatus may bring their exhilaration certainly, but he cannot experience the full thrill, the sense of doing what he had half feared he could not, unless he attempts the conquest of some new poetic sphere. For the bold poet, for the complete poet, the natural sequel is the Drama. As inevitably as harmony comes after melody, does distributed poem suggest itself from poem. Rather, perhaps, true poem is in itself dramatic. Dramatic, in a perfectly legitimate and approved sense of the term, are the performances of the blackbird and the nightingale, with the playful surprises of the one and the swift emotional transitions of the other, almost suggesting—in their livelier or lighter moments—an impersonator. And not only do the inexhaustible possibilities of vivifying single expressions of feeling by an illuminating context, or still more, of using language as an artist uses line, to make the

---

[1] I would add here three considerations :—(i) that Horace was then giving encouragement and criticism to young poets generally, we see from *Epist.*, I. iii ; (ii) in *Epist.*, II. i., written 13 B.C., Horace evidently despairs of a revival of the literary stage-drama ; this shows that *A.P.* was written at least some years earlier ; and the only alternatives open to us anyhow were, as Wickham has shown, 23-20 or 10-8 ; (iii) see Ch. III., p. 61, n. 1.

reader feel what is not there but is led up to or implied, attract and challenge the aspirant, but his growing moral sense and interest in humanity as such, his discovery that the only real validity and fulfilment or rather immortalisation of emotion is in action, inevitably point him along the path to Drama.

Horace had now reached this stage ; he had written lyrics of a quality which at least satisfied his own ambitions, and he had written as many of them as he cared. He regards himself as finished with lyric.[1] And there seem at first good reasons why he should have proceeded straight to Drama. The literary drama, after its eclipse in the Ciceronian age, had become once more a living pursuit ; first Asinius Pollio,[2] and later Varius[3] had distinguished themselves in tragedy, and that not mere closet drama, but getting the length of stage production ;[4] Ovid was soon to write, if not now writing, his *Medea*. Augustus had perhaps, in the way of *direct* service, done more for this branch of literature by the destruction of his unfinished *Ajax* [5] than by the writing of it ; but with his statesmanlike recognition of the power of imaginative literature as a reconstructive agency, he could not conceivably have ignored as patron the most immediately and widely influential branch of all ; if he did, he is not worthy to be ranked with Pericles and Elizabeth ; but in point of fact, such meagre evidence as we possess could not more clearly indicate, not only that he encouraged it most handsomely,[6] but that he did what he could to make it national. His return from the East in 29 B.C. was the occasion of his first appearance in Rome after the victory of Actium, and this was signalised by a colossal ovation, into the details of which it is not necessary to enter here ; at the games associated with it was acted a tragedy, *Thyestes*. The acknowledged master [7] of Roman tragedy was doubtless still Asinius Pollio ; but Pollio

[1] *Odes*, III. xxx.   [2] *Sat.*, I. x. 42-3 ; *Odes*, II. i. 9-12.

[3] Quint., X. i. 98 ; Tac., *Dial.*, 12.

[4] *Odes*, II. i. 10 ; Cod. Paris. Lat. 7530.

[5] Suet., *Aug.*, 85.

[6] For his general encouragement of Varius see *Epist.*, II. i. 245-7. *Ibid.*, 214, *verum age et his*, at first sight very surprising, ceases to be so when it is seen to imply that Augustus had done a great deal to stimulate the drama.

[7] Verg., *Ecl.*, viii. 10 ; Hor., *Sat.*, I. x. 42-3.

had been at first a supporter of Antony and then a neutral. The commissioning of a tragedian for the occasion had been doubtless in the hands of Maecenas, who was driven to have recourse to one who was properly an epic poet—the senior member of his own literary circle, Varius. In epic had Varius some time since won pre-eminence,[1] and to epic he was to return;[2] but for the nonce he stepped into the breach, and "after exceedingly hard work" produced this tragedy. Augustus is said to have given him the equivalent of £10,000.

Augustus' object (or Maecenas') was evidently to *replace* the old national classics by new ones which should be just as Roman without being so Republican—neither more nor perhaps less Republican than his own constitution was—and which should eclipse their predecessors by dint of sheer literary and artistic superiority. In this way had Horace tried to take the wind from Catullus' sails, in this way was Virgil labouring to better Ennius. It would have been in any case unlikely that the state department which unofficially inspired these efforts should have neglected to make all possible provision that what was being done for Lyric and Epic should be effected for the Drama also; considering the eminence (among their compatriots) of the Republican dramatists and the veneration in which they were still held, it is incredible. Notwithstanding, the thing was not done; even the *Thyestes*, though it survived till the eighth century, has left little trace of itself in literature beyond an allusion in Horace[3] and the tribute of Quintilian, who evidently thought it as admirable as Euripides, but whose judgments on the Greek tragedians are so bad, that even if he had thought it as crude as Aeschylus it would have mattered little. The fact remains that, like our own Victorian age which it in several ways resembles, the Augustan was one of those literary generations that have made repeated attempts at drama and yet failed to produce anything of permanent value—except in criticism.

In both cases, the most essential factor was not there— dramatic genius. Martial (VIII. xviii. 8-9) makes the interesting observation that Virgil could have done better at tragedy

---

[1] *Sat.*, I. x. 43-4.   [2] *Epist.*, I. xvi. 25-9, and schol. on 25.
[3] *Odes*, I. vi. 8, and cf. 2 ; after the *Thyestes* Varro's true sphere is still said to be Epic.

than Varius, but obligingly refrained from competing with him.
He is, however, hardly serious, and it may be said that Virgil,
though he had the rhetorical ability, had not nearly the range
of characterisation, nor the constructive firmness, nor the
ethical pre-occupation, required for tragedy. But Horace is
another question ; he had already given evidence of a number
of special qualifications of various importance for dramatic
writing, some of them rather rare. He had shewn an aptitude
for sudden effects—the beginning *in mediis rebus*, the abrupt
introduction of a professedly new topic, the unexpected change
of mood, the paradoxical wind-up. He had shewn, in an
unusual degree, the sense of one of the most tragic elements
in human nature—the combination of defects with qualities.
He had shewn that he could write lifelike dialogue, a rock on
which many dramatists have split. He had shewn humour,
irony ; could put an effect " between the lines " instead of
talking about it ; could tell a tale or suggest a scene which
had at least Aristotle's immortal desiderata of a beginning,
middle, end.

It is true that, at least as artist, he was not quite adequately
equipped in feeling. But lyric as well as drama requires feeling, and he had shewn that he had at all events enough of it
to produce, when combined with subtle judgment and patient
industry, great lyric. Perhaps the difference consists in this,
that drama seems to demand as well a generous and fertile
temperament. It may be that the only reason why Horace
did not make Roman Tragedy was that he was, not too unemo-
tional, but too lazy (especially after the call that had been
made on him by the first three books of *Odes*) to make the
necessary emotional effort. But it is also quite possible that
there is a deeper reason still. It may be that even if he could
have made the effort, he was just not good enough.

What is the best single piece of advice to give to a young
man who is about to attempt serious drama ? Perhaps it is,
that he must first understand a certain fundamental spiritual
truth. This truth itself is quite a simple one ; it is the statement of it in simple terms that is so difficult. " Poetic justice "
is a good phrase, but rather spoiled by the too mechanical interpretation usually put upon it. Whoever would write true
tragedy must understand the spiritual paradox ; that in spite

of all the obvious appearances to the contrary, the virtuous
do prosper, and all the more because their final prosperity is
not of a material kind. " Virtue is its own reward." To
deny the moral law is simply to reveal that you have not gone
deep enough, that you are still judging (though you may not
think it) to a greater or less extent by material, that is to say
external, standards. You would shew your audience truth ;
you must first understand the most important or rather only
ultimate truth, spiritual truth. But this in effect is just what
Horace says. *Scribendi recte* (he is speaking of tragedy) *sapere
est et principium et fons.* *Sapere* here means *sapientia,* and
sapientia means Stoicism, and Stoicism meant simply the
spiritual paradox. Horace felt deeply the truth of this paradox,
it is if anything his favourite topic, he harps on it in *Satires,
Odes, Epistles* to the nausea of all those who are ignorant that
they have never understood it. Men have made great reputa-
tions in serious drama who never even glimpsed this basic
principle ; Euripides and Ibsen for example. How comes it
then that Horace who understood it wrote no plays ?

Where fools rush in, of course, it will often happen that
the *sapiens* may fear to tread. But the right explanation is
more deep than that ; it is indicated by the line which follows.
" And for the spiritual paradox, see—the Socrates of the
Platonic and other dialogues." Up to a point, yes ; see passages of the *Gorgias,* for example, or of the *Phaedo* or *Republic,*
for a *statement* of it, eloquent, earnest, even beautiful, but abstract ; based upon utilitarianism ; a spiritual utilitarianism,
certainly, yet of a sort essentially egotistic. But for all practical purposes, no ; see rather Aeschylus ; see rather Sophocles ; [1] see rather even Thirlwall on Sophocles ; for there
you do not merely hear *about* the spiritual paradox, you see it ;
see its *working,* not in abstract argument, but in concrete life,
so that you simply cannot doubt it, unless you either deny the
evidence of your senses, or go to those authors with your senses

---

[1] *A.P.,* 268-9 (vos exemplaria Graeca, etc.) is merely apropos of
metric. The *A.P.* as Wight Duff remarks (*Lit. Hist. of Rome,* p. 532)
shews " no inkling of the moral grandeur . . . of Greek tragedy. It
strikes one as an extraordinary limitation that . . . Horace should
have failed to grasp the universal import of the plays of Aeschylus and
Sophocles."

shut. There you are shewn the greatness, the more than Stoical invincibility and invulnerability, of Antigone, who does what she feels is right even when " the argument " is against her, even when she believes her act is *not* supported by the powers that rule the universe, simply because she acts from love ; there you are shewn this world in all its harshness, a world in which it is not possible to be good by reason only, since unfortunately reason unaided does not point that way— hereby distinguishing it from the world of moral philosophers. But the " Age of Illumination " could not see this simple truth ; the sophistry substituted for it by Plato has exercised its paralysing influence to this day. The natural emotions are still, in much modern thought and habit, scarcely less suspect than they were in Horace's time, than they were even to a post-Christian Stoic like Epictetus ; men blame them instead of the morbid manifestations of them which prevailing suspicion and superstition engender. After Sophocles, moral drama lapsed till Shakespeare ; the emotional basis of morality was reasserted, and in an infinitely deeper and more vital form, some quarter of a century after the death of Horace by him who was crucified under Augustus' own successor ; the distinctive quality of Shakespearean tragedy is that it is Christian. But the world in general is still far from understanding Shakespeare, as it is from understanding Christ.

And *didicit* in 312 similarly betrays the flaw. To be a dramatist it is *not* enough to know what duty is. If it had been enough, then Bacon (who was, at least, a moralist) might have conceived the plays of Shakespeare ; this is *reductio ad absurdum*. Seneca knew what duty is, and yet he could do no better than Senecan tragedy. The gulf between knowing the right and making drama is just as great as that between knowing the right and doing it. That making drama is an act can hardly be too much insisted on, though it is action in a different phase. Bacon took bribes ; and Seneca was Nero's tutor. The fact is, to be a good tragedian, no less than to be a good man, one must not be moral only, one must be religious. It is, ultimately, a matter of emotion ; of emotional relation to something not actual ; of love of God, or love of your own puppets. And Stoicism, after all, was not properly speaking (though it is often convenient to call it so in comparison with the Thales-to-Aristotle philosophy) a religion at all ; it was no more a religion than its modern counterpart Christian Science, a popular metaphysic which seems to have brought comfort 'and stability to many. Nor is it easy to imagine Horace becoming whole-heartedly devoted to anything external to himself.

In plain language then, whereas with a completely-endowed poet who is on the threshold of his dramatic period a concentration takes place of all his genius, the genius of Horace at this crisis split. His output between 23 and 20 B.C. is magnificent, but it is in two directions. His first book of *Epistles* has the mature moral insight which is one out of the two great features distinguishing the drama from the song ; but it has not the other ; it has not the *action*. His understanding of character is at once subtle, deep, and wide ; but it is intellectual merely ; he regards human nature sympathetically as well as wisely, and yet always from the outside. He was not indeed altogether devoid of, but congenitally deficient in, that more passionate and potent sympathy which *becomes* the character it contemplates, so that the puppet, now living, needs must act. He may have known, or felt, or not known, that the too scant leaven of vitality which had still lurked in his imagination might, if it had been far stronger, have burst out into something more wonderful than an epistle. At all events, there was that in him which was not satisfied even with this first book of *Epistles* as he achieved it ; and which, small as it was, must have its expression somehow. And so he did what all who are just not good enough for some art fall back on ; he wrote about it ; tried to shew, generally, the *sort* of way in which it could be done ; outlined a theory of it, threw off a few principles, and added, within decent limits, rules. That is the chief (though not the only) reason why drama—certainly not its ostensible theme—remains in point of fact the main subject of the *Ars Poetica*.

For the rest, the chief biographical interest of *Epistles*, I. is the indication it gives, all but everywhere, of the direction in which the writer's " philosophy of life " had by now definitely matured. In the first book of *Satires* we have seen him rather harshly opposed to Stoicism, in the second, despite a smiling pretence of reluctance, executing a sudden change of front

and becoming fascinated by it. In *Odes*, I. xxxiv. he announces
in part allusively but in effect unmistakably, his conversion
from Epicureanism to Stoicism. The reason given remains,
after all that can be said, a strange one for the modern reader ;
but I do not doubt, myself, that Horace is here entirely serious.
So far from being able to accept the view that " as the Horatian
quietism and indifference gradually become disturbed by the
political necessities of Augustus, the poet develops a kind of
quasi-religious feeling in three ways," [1] I seem to see that it
was the growing seriousness of his character that turned him
to Stoicism, and that it was Stoicism that provided for him
the bridge to, such a theology as the *Odes* present us with. It
was the abstract or cosmic " Zeus " of Stoicism that weaned
him from the physical gods of Epicurean theory, and caused
him to celebrate in language of clearly genuine reverence not
only such a half-Roman half-Hellenistic *numen* as Fortuna
(the moral aspect of Accident, which so often tests out man
from man ; the whirligig of time that brings in its revenges ;
" God in History ") but also the *poetic* Zeus whom he identifies
with the philosophic one ; and so, through the Zeus of poetry,
opened out for his sympathetic treatment as poetic and religious symbols the whole Greek Pantheon. At all events,
the first book of *Epistles*, though it has its light moments,
is pervaded and dominated by Stoicism ; not merely by the
technicalities of Stoicism ; it is Stoical in *tone*.

LAST YEARS, 19-8 B.C.

Horace had now published his three masterpieces, *Odes*,
I.-III., a masterpiece of creative literature ; *Epistles*, I., of
ethical literature ; *Ars Poetica*, of the literature of poetic
theory. No Roman poet before or after showed anything like
so wide a range of poetic thought. His great period was now
over.

But he was still to write poems of some importance and
interest. Another *Epistle* was composed soon after, perhaps in
the next year after, the publication of the first book. It is

---

[1] Warde Fowler, *Roman Ideas of Deity*, p. 153. I trust that no one
will misconceive it as impertinence if I say that this sentence strikes me
as extremely funny.

addressed to his young friend Florus, the recipient of *Epist.*,
I. iii., who was on the staff of the future Emperor Tiberius.
The occasion is a friendly protest from the young man at his
continued refusal to follow up the great collection of *Odes* with
further exercises in the same kind. He pleads, among other
and perhaps more real reasons, that it was only to save himself
from destitution that he had in the first instance taken to
writing verse at all ; philosophy had been his original choice,
and to that, now that his material freedom is secure, he is
ever more and more returning. To enforce this point he has
to give a brief outline of his early life and so add another to
his autobiographical passages. He repeats (*Epist.*, II. ii. 55-7)
the protestation of, perhaps, four years back (*Epist.*, I. i. 10)
that advancing years are taking away from him the desire to
write. He is still only in the middle of his forties when he
writes

> eripuere iocos, Venerem, convivia, ludum ;

though Edmund Spenser—for example—at forty-one was recording in a sonnet [1] that it was but a year ago that the winged
God " began in him to move."

From about B.C. 20, if not earlier, it seems that a certain
coolness sprang up between the Emperor and Maecenas ; their
friendship began, says Tacitus,[2] to be more apparent than real.
Up to this time Horace had not, apparently, been specially
intimate with the Emperor himself ; *Epist.*, I. xiii. indicates no
more than that respectful homage from a national poet to his
sovereign, of which history shows many examples. But he
had been enough about the Court to address to the future
Emperor Tiberius a letter (*Epist.*, I. ix.) of recommendation in
behalf of a friend. Augustus, however, is known from Suetonius
to have had a very high opinion of the work of Horace and a
belief in its immortality ; and it is evident that when his
estrangement with Maecenas occurred, he took steps to prevent

---

[1] *Amoretti*, lx.

[2] *Annals*, iii. 30 *fin*. Suetonius, *Aug*. 66, says that Maecenas had
betrayed to his wife Terentia state secrets relating to the detection of
the conspiracy of (her brother) Murena. An *alternative* explanation
(Shuckburgh strangely confuses the two) is that of Dion Cassius, liv.
19, that Augustus had an intrigue with Maecenas' wife.

its extension to the poet by making advances to him direct. Another event contributed to this result ; in 19 Virgil died. This, of course, left Horace easily the supreme poet in Rome.

One of the first results of all this was that Horace was prevailed on to yield to imperial urgency what he had denied to his private patron and other friends ; he resumed lyrical composition. In the year 17 the first decade of the Empire came to an end, and partly for that and partly for general reasons, Augustus wished to hold a national festival on a properly magnificent scale. By a decent juggling with dates and straining of records, it was discovered that the *Ludi Tarentini*, a primitive festival in propitiation of the powers of the underworld, supposed to be celebrated once in every *saeculum* or " century " of 110 years, fell due to be performed in this year. Augustus decided not merely to repeat it but to transform it. In the result the *Ludi Saeculares*, as the festival was called on this occasion, took the united form of a national anniversary, a thanksgiving for the successful establishment of a new epoch of peace and prosperity, and a prayer for its continuance. The procedure was too complicated, and the deities honoured too many, to be recounted here ; but the place of honour among the latter was given to the specially Cæsarian god Apollo (this was easy since the games were supposed to be taking place according to the prescription of the Sibylline books, in Rome always closely associated with the Apolline cult), and the climax of the ceremonies was the performance of a specially composed hymn to that deity (his sister Diana of course included) by a choir of twenty-seven boys and the same number of girls. Horace was appointed to write this hymn. It must have been an exciting moment when, in September 1890, an inscription discovered near the Tiber bank on the remains of a memorial column, recording various matters relative to this celebration, including the order of proceedings, was duly found to refer to the *Ode* and to mention its author by name :—

Sacrificioque perfecto pueri [X]XVII. quibus denuntiatum erat patrimi et matrimi et puellae totidem carmen cecinerunt, eo[de]mque modo in Capitolio. Carmen composuit Q. Hor[at]ius Flaccus.

The poem itself, however, is not exciting. " The impression it always gives me," writes Warde Fowler, " is that Augustus wrote out in prose what he wanted put into it, and that his laureate did this with consummate skill and *concinnitas ;* but the result, for me at least, is that it is as flat as such compositions usually have been." That is not unfair. At the same time, anyone who is inclined to condemn it too hastily or too wholly might do well first to read through *God Save the King*. Immediately several conspicuous merits will stare out at him from the less barbaric expression of national sentiment.

It is, however, as Warde Fowler suggests, very probable that Horace had learned at some cost the difference between a disinterested and an imperial patron ; and he was to have further experience in the same kind. For during this last period of his poetic activity it is not Maecenas, but Augustus himself, who stands to him in this capacity. The poet's position was doubtless one of some delicacy, but we can hardly suppose that the good social sense of a Horace was not equal to it. There is certainly every reason to believe that he maintained perfect loyalty to his first benefactor. The Emperor at one time pressed him to become his private secretary ; Horace must have known that he risked a monarch's displeasure by his firm refusal ; though as a matter of fact Augustus not only bore him no resentment, but afterwards heaped further favours on him, including (probably) a house at Tibur.

After the *Carmen Saeculare*, other commissions or commands followed. In 15 B.C. the princes Drusus and Tiberius waged in the Eastern Alps a double campaign in which both were victorious, the former against the Vindelici, the latter against the Raeti. The two *pièces de résistance* of the fourth book of *Odes* are provided by the poems which celebrate these exploits ; [1] they appear as the fourth and fourteenth of the collection. The other principal official odes are placed after them ; the fifth and fifteenth both sing the praises of the Augustan régime, its peace, prosperity, and honour. The moral reforms so

---

[1] That these are the nucleus of the book is vouched for by Suetonius (*Vit. Hor.*), *eumque coegerit propter hoc tribus carminum libris ex longo intervallo quartum addere.*

forcefully urged in the third book are here exhibited as now in successful and harmonious operation. The sixth ode purports to be a prelude—in inception it was more probably an overflow—to the *Carmen Saeculare*. The official basis of the collection is deftly camouflaged by an overture in the erotic vein (i) followed by two pieces ultimately on the stock Horatian theme of the praise of poetry ; it is redeemed by an occasional fine poem or two (vii., xiii.), and eked out by an occasional bad one (x.). Published in 13, it reflects very clearly the change of patron. Maecenas had figured in all the most prominent places of the former collection ; in this there is only one mention of him, in xi., which purports to be on the occasion of his birthday. More would have been, not probably injudicious, but out of keeping with the general tenor of the book ; the terms of this single reference preclude any idea of diminished regard. But if the last stanza of the same poem is any clue to the writer's general state of mind at this time, it speaks unmistakably, both in the matter and the manner, of diminished happiness and lowered vitality :—

> (non enim posthac alia calebo
> femina) ; condisce modos, amanda
> voce quos reddas ; minuentur atrae
> carmine curae.

Horace's lyrical vein was now evidently worked out. The manner of the epistles, however, had for a long time been far more congenial to him, and his one remaining work was to be a last achievement in that style. The Suetonian life tells us that Augustus, after reading through several of the poet's " sermones " (which may mean either satires or epistles), complained with mock indignation that a majority of them ought to have been addressed primarily to himself. " I hope you don't think," he added ironically, " that it would tell against you with posterity, if you were to appear as having been on intimate terms with me ? " Horace took the hint, and composed an epistle of 270 lines addressed to his Emperor, which he prefixed to the older one to Florus, publishing both as the second book. Like its companion, but to a greater extent, it deals with literature, and combines a general " apologie for poetrie " with a particular defence of the Augustan school of poets ;

and indirectly with a special justification of his own renunciation—or refusal to do more than he had actually done. In the
last regard, he explains not only that he had not written more
national odes because he did not feel himself qualified for themes
so great, but that he had not attempted drama at all because
of the hopeless frivolity and vulgarity of the public taste in
spectacular performances. The praise of the Emperor himself
as a literary patron provides the element of personal compliment.

The style is still terse and vigorous ; but it was long since
he had written without external stimulus, and in further default
thereof he wrote no more. He had, as we have seen, aged
prematurely. Early in 8 B.C., Maecenas died, leaving (in his
will) the message for Augustus " Horati Flacci, ut mei, memor
esto." On 27th November of the same year the poet fulfilled
his own prophecy that he would not long survive his patron.

CHAPTER V

EXPERIMENT—THE EPODES

THAT the infant Horace was covered by doves with bay and myrtle leaves we need not necessarily believe, but his self-chosen apprenticeship to the Muses must have begun when he was very young. Even his earliest extant compositions—*Sat.*, I. vii., and *Epodes*, vii. and xvi. and perhaps ii.—though the first is poor in humour and some of the others are even (a strange thing in Horace) diffuse in execution —even they are pretty surely not the work of an absolute beginner. He had probably learned something from those early exercises in the writing of Greek verse, of which he tells us in *Sat.*, I. x. 31 ; but we may naturally infer from the imaginary incident which follows that he had soon desisted from what he felt to be an unprofitable and dilettante practice. Considering the state of Latin metrical technique at the time, the precision and finish even of the early poems just mentioned can hardly have been attained without some previous versifying in his native tongue.

The seventh satire of the first book provides the most natural *point de départ* in the consideration of Horace's works. Palmer, indeed, considers it the earliest extant, and dates it 43 or 42 B.C. ; Wickham, too, puts it before the death of Brutus. That it is the earliest I am prepared to believe, but not that it is so early. The episode recounted probably took place late in 43. But the piece is quite clearly written as from Rome, not from Clazomenae. Persius is introduced and described, while the character of Rupilius Rex is at first merely alluded to (1 and 6) ; " ad Regem redeo " as a phrase for passing to the story shows that it is the latter who is the centre of it. The sore-eyed and the barbers are, certainly, proverbial gossips in the Greek as well as in the Roman world ; [1] but in this case, as there is no local specification, we should naturally assume that it is those of " the city " that are referred to ; and besides, it obviously is, because the joke [2] of the foul-mouthed Roman ex-magistrate's having been crushed by a mere Greek banker would only be a joke where Rupilius was well known. [3] The story, then, is spoken of as having reached Rome ; and this it could not do until brought by those of Brutus' following who had been amnestied after Philippi. That there is " no allusion to the sad fate of Brutus " (Palmer) or that "the joke on Brutus's act is one most naturally made before his tragical end "—these arguments for its having been written previously to Philippi are negligible ; a Roman's ideas of delicacy were not an Englishman's. On the other hand, it is quite true that Horace is very unlikely to have made fun out of Julius Cæsar's assassination when once he had begun to get in touch with the outskirts of Octavian's party, that is to say when he became a friend of Virgil and Varius. I think the piece was written very soon after his return to Rome, for the story is spoken of (line 3) as a current one, and it is not, at the best, of a kind likely to be treasured long even by sufferers from ophthalmia. In view of its wide circulation, Horace comes forward with a version which professes to be authoritative, as coming from an eye-witness. But the main interest of this satire for our present purpose is that in relation to Horace's artistic evolution it is distinctly primitive. We see him here making his début with bare narrative ; there is no mise-en-scène, nothing dramatic, no addressee ; we can just (in view of *opinor*, line 2) say that he speaks in his own person ; but the first-personal element is here, as in the second of this same book, practically unessential to the piece ; which is therefore very nearly [4] lacking in all the structural

---

[1] Lysias, xxiv. 20, quoted by Gow.

[2] Despite the editors, the joke does *not* consist mainly in the pun which forms the climax.

[3] He was an *eques*, had been elected praetor in 43, and may be credited with a faculty for making himself unpopular, as he had been exiled by his Praenestine fellow-citizens.

[4] In view of the third line it may just be said to have an " occasion." That, incidentally, is never an essential factor of the earlier type of Horatian satire. *Sat.*, I. ii. (a very early one) has it quite distinctly,

constituents of the fully-developed Horatian composition, and is even lacking in some of the most characteristic features of the Horatian satire. Pure narrative, in fact, was not, as a poetic form, congenial to him, as apparently he soon discovered ; he had, indeed, the gift for the *short* story, no writer more so ; but the bent of his imagination was predominantly dramatic, and he only twice attempted the narrative form again, once without success in the " Journey to Brundisium " and once with it, and remarkably so, in the " Encounter with a Bore."

And other signs of immaturity are not far to seek. When you intend to make your readers amused by something, it is fatal to tell them that as a matter of fact the eye-witnesses *were* amused (like 22). But perhaps this should be discounted as to some extent characteristic of Roman humour in general, where a joke is often signalised ; [1] Horace himself explains at *Sat.*, I. i. 23 that he has been in fun, and in *Epist.*, I. i. 91 makes the even more fatal mistake of giving the cautionary command to smile (like a professional photographer) ; while Cicero in a letter [2] to Trebatius considerately introduces a playful passage with the hint " rideamus licet, sum enim a te invitatus," and concludes it with the declaration " sed iam satis iocati sumus," thus leaving the reader no reasonable doubt, not only where to laugh, but for how long. No, the real weakness of this piece is the anti-climax of the conclusion ; for it is only a partial mitigation to assure us, as Wickham does, that this sort of pun " gave especial pleasure to Romans " ; the fact is that the story as Horace tells it is not, and can hardly have been even to a Roman, funny. Yet with a big effort of the imagination it is possible to conceive that the incident itself was ; it was probably the suddenness and impudence of the remark, and the feeling of its being innocently addressed to the last person in the world who could view the act referred to (or indeed anything) in a humorous light—" Couldn't you suppress this ' King ' ? Wouldn't that be rather in your line, my lord ? " to Brutus !—it was probably something of that sort

but uses it only as a peg ; *Sat.*, I. x. is the only other of the first book that can be said to have it at all. The majority of those in the second, being dialogues, do not need this sort of topical " occasion," as they already have their dramatic one.

[1] Cf. also *Sat.*, I. v. 57, 70.   [2] Ad Fam., vii. 10.

that made all the young subalterns burst out into a roar, and perhaps even, in due course, and after he had recovered from his surprise, brought a faint sour smile into the features of the conscientious and philosophic betrayer and friend-murderer himself.   At all events, if it ever was funny, Horace has failed to fix and convey the subtle thing that made it so ; everyone knows how easily and apparently unaccountably the comic element in an episode will vanish in what seems to be the most faithful relation possible ; but it should be said in justice that he has got in all else.   The contrast between " the half-Greek trader, courtly, fluent, witty, and the country-bred Italian, thick-skinned and heavy-handed in his sarcasm " [1] —the irony of the indirect and mock-heroic suggestion that between these two costermongers there was, in the matter of gallantry, nothing to choose [2]—the neatness and aptness of the illustrations, down to the interesting little vignette of 29-31— these things are all far more skilled work than might at first sight appear.

Of the more or less datable pieces the next in order is an epode, the sixteenth ; but here again I cannot feel quite satisfied with the generally accepted view.   This epode is commonly bracketed with the seventh, and both are taken simply as expressions of a patriotic neutral's indignation [3] at this or that renewal of civil war.   But the tone of the sixteenth at any rate is not particularly patriotic, nor does it strike me as neutral ; the mood is less like indignation than like bitterness become sullen.   Orelli suggested that the poem was composed on the outbreak of the " Perusine " war in 41 B.C., when Mark Antony's wife Fulvia and his brother Lucius came to hostilities with Octavian ; and such has been the usual view.   Yet the language of the first line (unlike that of *Epode*, vii.) does not suggest an *outbreak*.   I believe it was written later, towards the end of this year or the beginning of the next ; at all events, soon after it first became apparent that the cause of Lucius was doomed.   Take lines 15-16 ;

---

[1] Wickham, preface to translation.

[2] Cf. *Sat.*, I. v. 51-6.   At 10-11 of the present piece I follow Krüger as reinforced by Gow.

[3] *E.g.*, *liberrima indignatio* (Orelli).

considerations of Latinity [1] demand the rendering " Perhaps you inquire what is to the common interest, or seek (at least the better part of you) to live without these cruel distresses." Now probably one reason why this inevitable rendering has been so much jibbed at is that it should naturally be the other way round ; it is all and sundry who should care only to get rid of trouble.   It is " the better part " who should take counsel for the commonwealth.   The solution is this ; *melior pars* is, of course, the writer's own party ; and their longing to migrate is due to the fact that they are only too obviously beaten ; beaten beyond any possibility of hope.[2]   The lengthy and fervent description of the Islands of the Blest is a throwing up of the sponge.   It was when the game was up that Sertorius (according to a story which may well have been in Horace's mind here) conceived such a yearning to sail thither.[3]

That Horace should have deplored the outbreak of the Perusine war is surely most improbable.   However accidental may have been the causes of his originally having been swept up into the Republican army, Philippi committed him ; he returned to find his property confiscated ; he was without a home.   Any throw of the dice is at least better than the lowest ; the destitute have never been notorious for their disapproval of new political movements ; their characteristic is rather a general ferocity—such at all events was the view of Horace himself.[4]   But in any case, we happen to know that Lucius and Fulvia's venture owed its opportunity entirely to the widespread resentment caused by Octavian's evictions.[5] It rapidly took the form of a " recrudescence of the Republican

[1] Succinctly put in Gow's note, from which I have taken the translation.

[2] " At Perusia a blow was struck at the old Republican party . . . from which it never recovered."—Shuckburgh, *Life of Augustus*, p. 97.

[3] *Ad insulas fortunatas Sallustius in Historia dicit victum voluisse ire Sertorium*—Acron on l. 42 of this epode, confirmed by Servius on Verg., *Aen.*, v. 735.   Cf. Plutarch, *Sert.*, 9.

[4] *Epist.*, I. xv. 26-29, II. ii. 26-29.   In applying the latter illustration to his own case. the only outcome of *audax paupertas* which he mentions is the writing of (scurrilous) verses (51-2) ; but any time after the Sabine presentation an allusion to past Fulvian sympathies would surely be inexcusable.

[5] Dio, xlviii. 5 foll.

opposition lately headed by Brutus and Cassius," [1] that party now welcoming any sort or kind of civil war that might end in the destruction of the triumvirate. Under all these circumstances it is surely incredible that Horace did not even wait to see what might happen before crying out, but very natural that on the surrender of Lucius his first feeling should have been one of complete despair.[2]

This poem, too, in certain ways betrays the novice. There is a slight redundancy,[3] so slight as to be hardly worth remarking in any other poet ; but it is interesting to see that even Horace's terseness had to be won, though it was won very early. The fulness of description is paralleled in Epode ii., which is therefore probably of the same period. *Pluraque felices mirabimur* is a poor device to hang fresh details on. He has obviously not yet fully learned what he was so soon to be a master in—poetical economy. The picture of the happy isles is mere embroidering.

But of much more importance than any such shortcomings is the fact that this exercise, when compared with that previously discussed, marks a considerable advance in the writer's poetic art by his new choice of form. I do not mean that this is necessarily his earliest epode ; on the contrary, I think it is pretty obviously not. Its metre stamps it as written under the influence of studies in Archilochus ; but viii. and xii., and I am disposed to think xv., and (though perhaps in a less degree) vi. and x., are much more Archilochian in style and spirit ; the first three at least I take for that reason to be earlier.[4] But as contrasted with the Rupilius-Rex satire, this piece has the formal *raison d'être* which characterises the typical Horatian poem ; it has a definite occasion ; an addressee, the Roman public ; and an avowed practical purpose. If it is not certainly

---

[1] Shuckburgh, *Augustus*, p. 94.

[2] Compare the case of Propertius, who in I. xxi. refers to the siege of Perusia in an anti-Cæsarian spirit, and was afterwards converted.

[3] Repetitions :—(i) objectionable, 18 and 36, 15 and 37. (ii) not without point, but un-Horatian, 63 and 66 *pius*, 64 and 65 *aere*. The laxity of this piece in general does not seem to me to warrant either the obelisation or the transference of 61-2. " Out of place " says Gow, but would he have said so if it had consisted of four lines instead of two ? That would be unjustifiable, as 53-6 and 57-60 have no closer connection.

[4] If not, one would naturally assume that there were such earlier imitations, but that they were not preserved.

the earliest work of Horace to present all these features, it is
perhaps the earliest mentionable or considerable ; it is in any
case the first in which we find a foretaste of that hortatory
and at times sacerdotal tone which was to become the most
essential characteristic of all his mature work, and in particular
of his political odes ; and this we do find most distinctly. He
takes it upon himself, even at the age of twenty-four, to con-
front his fury-blinded countrymen with the whole enormity of
what they are doing (1-14) ; having thus shamed into attention
those of them who are not already past saving, he urges on
them the only remedy which in his bitterness he can conceive ;
and he urges it as a priest and prophet—*vate me datur fuga.*
The counsel of despair, though its elaboration was obviously
congenial to his present mood, was not even then, it is probable,
put forward seriously. Its object is possibly to shock his
hearers into sense, as (I take it) in the ostensibly despairing
conclusion of *Epode*, vii. I am more inclined, however, to
think that it has a different bearing of a positive kind. It is
remarkable that this poem forecasts the typical " admonitory "
ode in still another point—its structure ; like such pieces as
Odes, II. ix. and xi., it attempts to lead its audience from one
frame of mind into the opposite, and to influence them by dwelling, in what might otherwise appear an inappropriate manner,
on the mood desired ; hence the last third of it is in a totally
different key from the rest. This would imply that that passage
is, after all, intended to have some practical application ; nor is
it difficult to see what that could be. " Quod petis, hic est "—if
you can behave yourself. The migration is figurative ; the
poet is not advising a change of *caelum* but of *animus ;* he is
yearning for a New Age, which, if it comes, will seem by comparison to be another Golden one. It was just this yearning
for a New Age that ultimately did (when it became general)
produce the cure, by making all parties only too thankful to
accept the rule of Augustus ; so that even *vate me* is not altogether a piece of empty poetical verbiage ; although the goats
did not immediately come unbidden to the milk-pail, and
although the necessity for ploughing continued for some time
to be felt, still the fact remains that agriculture did begin to
revive again, and Horace himself, once he attached himself to
the right party, got his goats with his Sabine farm—his *arva*

by which he was made *beatus ;*[1] even line 56 of this poem has its echo in *Epist.*, I. xvi. 8, *temperiem laudes.* Indeed, it was only some months after this epode had been written (assuming my date to be correct) that a real attempt was made at a clean start ; Asinius Pollio assisted in negotiating the treaty of Brundisium, and Virgil, obviously expressing the mood of fervent hopefulness then prevalent in some court circle, addressed to him the eclogue which heralds, in language and ideas that surely (all things considered) owe their origin to this very epode, the dawn of a new Golden Age.

But it was not to come so soon. Virgil's prophecy proved to be more visionary, or less verbally safe, than Horace's. Horace had said (25-34 of this epode) that the seekers after El Dorado would be prepared to settle down in Rome again only after the apparently inconceivable occurrence of certain prodigies. In the second ode of the first book he, as spiritual spokesman of the Roman people, hails the advent of the now manifestly Heaven-appointed saviour of society Augustus ; and it appears from the opening stanzas of that poem that just such prodigies had by then occurred ![2]

We may now consider that we have seen Horace definitely set up as a poetic artist, and since the attempt to trace his progress from poem to poem any further must be tedious as well as full of uncertainty, it will be convenient to consider his work in certain groups, into which it naturally falls while we examine it with a view to following out his general artistic evolution.

THE EPODES

The book of Epodes is rather a jumble. Never again did Horace publish so heterogeneous a collection. It *has* a unity, but in one respect only ; a unity of verse-form. It has no unity of poetic form. Several of the poems, for example the first or thirteenth, are not satirical at all. Still, the majority are ; and the book is most conveniently treated as a small collection of lampoons, tirades, or other invective pieces, with a few others of different categories thrown in.

---

[1] Satis beatus unicis Sabinis—*Odes*, II. xviii. 14.
[2] Cf. 25-34 of this epode with *Odes*, I. ii. 5-12.

The invective pieces are quite evidently regarded by Horace as having a function, and that a social one. This is most clearly stated in the sixth Epode, where he speaks of himself in the similitude of a sheep-dog. He is not, like the writer he is here warning, a bully, he does not attack inoffensive persons ; he is the enemy only of those who are themselves the enemies of civilised society, that is of " wolves " (line 2) and of " wild animals " (line 8) generally. In other words, his lampoons are not vexatious and malignant, their ultimate purpose is the protection of the community. This it is which primarily distinguishes Horace's Epodes from those of his formal model Archilochus. Archilochus in his animosities had been purely personal ; in its original association with the ritual of Demeter and Dionysus the iambic may well have had, to superstition at least, an " apotropaic " social function, but Archilochus neither shows any consciousness of this nor ever appears to use it so. With Horace, on the other hand, the legitimate use claimed for iambics is very much the same as that which he claims elsewhere for satire. In *Sat.*, I. iv. 65-8 he says that it is only robbers who need fear the satirist,[1] and in the beginning of the same piece he indicates that this literary type performs the same service for the Roman community as the Old Comedy did for Athens, the service of branding malefactors ; and again in *Sat.*, II. i. 34 and 60 foll. he clearly declares himself a follower of Lucilius in the matter of exposing hypocrites. All this is quite consistent with his regarding his frays at the same time in a personal light, as the dog doubtless does. Who hates my dog (if it is an unaggressive animal) presumably hates me. In that connection he makes two claims, and he makes them in regard both to his Epodes and his Satires ; his bite is purely defensive, and it is his natural weapon. *Nemo me impune lacessit* is the purport both of this epode and of *Sat.*, II. i. 44-60, and these two passages are further connected by the imagery ; his sharp pen is to him what the horns are to a bull ; his utterance is a warning bark (*ibid*, 85 *latraverit*).[2]

---

[1] True, he there dissociates himself from the satirists mentioned ; but the distinction no longer applied once he had begun to *publish* his satiric works.

[2] Cf. further Ch. VI., p. 162, n 1.

But although Horace thus differentiates his function, he does not himself recognise the distinction thereby involved between his own invective and that of his Greek exemplar. In *Epist.*, I. xix. 24-5 he expressly says that he had reproduced the *spirit* of Archilochus, and in this present epode he compares himself to the " rejected son-in-law of Lycambes." And in point of fact some few of the epodes are merely personal attacks. It has been reasonably suggested that the most Archilochian are the earliest ; and it is certainly convenient to get viii. and xii. out of the way as soon as possible. We know from fragments of Archilochus that he did not avoid indecency when occasion offered, and from tradition that he railed against a woman ; that he did both together seems to be a mere assumption. However that may be, the pair of pieces last mentioned are customarily regarded as imitations of him.[1] There are, however, different sorts as well as different degrees of obscenity ; nothing really resembling these in either appears in the extant fragments of Archilochus ; and the heavy slogging style of the abuse is perhaps less Greek than Roman.

The real nucleus of the collection consists in those epodes where the sheep-dog barks at his *bêtes noirs*. In vi. it was, naturally enough, another dog ; a cowardly dog, whose bark was worse than his bite, and whom anybody of bad intentions could bribe off with a bit of meat. In iv. it is a wolf ; for in the first line I take it that, though Horace is not to be identified as one of the " lambs," he is again at least half-thinking of himself as the dog who is on their side ; the lambs are rather the citizens of line 9, who look askance at the alien and intruder, and of whom Horace makes himself the spokesman in the latter half of the piece. The wolf is a certain freedman [2] who has managed to acquire enough wealth to rank as a " knight " and to get himself appointed a military tribune. He has

---

[1] *E.g.*, Orelli uses the phrase *Archilochio modo* of both. Plüss contests the view ; but I can only agree with the negative part of his article on this epode.

[2] Surely *not* Menodorus, as alleged by the scholiasts ; a mere conjecture, probably from line 19, but anyone except an ancient grammarian would probably feel that this suggestion at once robs that line of its whole point—irony.

entered into the sheepfold by an unrecognised avenue ; " the same is a thief and a robber." This is the implication of *latrones* in line 19 ; it is of *latrones* that the satirist as such is the avowed enemy—we gather this from *Sat.*, I. iv. 67, where Sulcius and Caprius are described as *magnus uterque timor latronibus*, and from *Sat.*, II. i. 42, where Horace himself asks why he should unsheathe the pen which is his sword, so long as he is *tutus ab infestis latronibus.* Here he cries out against the inconsistency of waging war against the slaves and pirates who manned the fleet of Sextus Pompeius, while at the same time admitting an ex-slave into the best society. But I cannot resist one more Scriptural reminiscence apropos of this epode ; what about the unjust steward ? One remembers a certain other appointment that had also caused great indignation, where the son of a freedman became a *tribunus militum.* He might have made his case against the despiser of Otho rather more telling if he had been able to bring up against him some more heinous crime than the wearing of an ample toga.

Similar to these in spirit is number x. Formally, this is a prayer, more specifically a curse, or, to employ an ancient technical term, it is a προπεμπτικόν, a send-off, though of an inverted kind, as may be seen by comparing it with *Odes*, I. iii. That invokes a fair voyage for Virgil, this imprecates a foul one culminating in shipwreck for one who was an enemy of Virgil's as well as Horace's, the bad, fat, stinking poetaster Maevius. It is in the mock-heroic vein with which Horace not infrequently amuses himself, and that is its main point ; it probably meant at least as much to Horace's circle as a good parody means to us ; they were doubtless greatly tickled by the appearance of regulation features of the ancient full-dress ode, such as the allusive glance at a relevant myth (11-14) and the conclusion with a vow of sacrifice.[1]

All the five pieces just considered are frontal attacks. The person inveighed against is directly addressed, the poem is in form a lampoon as well as in effect. We feel it is an

---

[1] Incidentally, I suggest that the point of l. 17 is got by realising that *illa* and *non* are both emphatic. *Eia, viri*, is the Latin for " Yoho my lads." Horace says, " Your sailors will fairly sweat, and *your* ' eia ' will not be at all of the ' virilis ' kind," *i.e.*, it will not be an *eia* but an *ei. Non virilis* cannot be a mere synonym for *muliebris.*

advance in art at least when the satirising is done indirectly. Certainly the fifth and seventeenth epodes are vastly more entertaining. They resemble a certain other well-known witch-satire in being essentially *spirited* productions ; there is pace, colour, vitality. This is partly because Horace is inspired by his theme ; witchery gives endless opportunities of imaginative effect and singularity of detail ; classic though he is, he is here exploiting the same field which has attracted so many of our own Romantics since the very beginnings of the movement. But it is also because Horace is stimulated by his poetic form, which in these two pieces is semi-dramatic. The latter is actually a dialogue, the earlier, though strictly speaking a narrative, and to that extent uncharacteristic, is rather to be considered (in virtue of its beginning and end) as a dialogue in which the speeches happen to be connected by narrative, which is here really just a sort of extended stage direction. Both have been aptly compared to a Greek mime.

The purpose of these pieces is, of course, to blackguard the witch Canidia, but neither in them nor in the companion *Satire* (I. viii.) is the tone at all serious ; Epode v. in particular by its grotesque combination of humour and horror, and (*exceptis excipiendis*) the scarecrow's story, are perhaps the only things in classical literature suggestive of the Ingoldsby Legends. This sort of thing is, in fact, not " classical " in the strict sense ; the amused interest in magic, and the *genre* quality of the occasional flash-pictures of low life,[1] are Alexandrian, and as such worth noting in Horace, who was the least open to Alexandrian influences of all the Latin classic poets. " Baby-killer " has been a stock reproach in all ages, our own has heard it of suffragettes and Germans, and, of course, it has figured among the items of indictment against witches. But if Horace had really hated Canidia, he could hardly have dwelt with such obvious relish on each successive gruesome and (characteristically) graphic detail of this child-murder. Highly successful too in its absurdity is the impression given of Canidia's passion, of the ferocity of her appetite and the aggrieved and vindictive spirit in which she woos with threats her ridiculous old gallant ; she too has her *odi et amo !* The mock-heroic

---

[1] Cf. 41-4 with *Sat.*, I. ii. 1-3.

is again exploited, for example in the witch's invocation and peroration, and the ludicrous Nemesis-motif with which the whole concludes. In its peculiar kind, it is a masterpiece.

The seventeenth is mock-heroic from beginning to end ; that is the joke—or rather was the joke, for the elaborate epic and other allusions can hardly now appeal to any but scholars, and to most of them rather by way of interest than of amusement. But the skill of the word-weaving is still appreciable, the colours are lively, the texture strong, all is well-packed and explicit, yet the effect is one of speed and not of effort. Speaking in his own person, Horace begins with a mock-abject supplication to Canidia to release him from her spells, beseeches her to name once and for all her final " war indemnity," and undertakes to go to any lengths in his prospective gratitude ; he will actually praise her chastity ; he will gallantly declare that she has illegitimate children—by which, of course, it is intended that she is too abandoned even for that. Canidia replies, inexorable, and is made to give herself away in almost every line. It is in the subtlety of the insinuations that the ingenuity consists. All of which does not sound promising, for modern tastes ; yet one of the few passages in the whole book that are, or would be out of their context, poetical, is supplied by this epode :—

> optat quietem Pelopis infidi pater
> egens benignae Tantalus semper dapis,
> optat Prometheus obligatus aliti,
> optat supremo collocare Sisyphus
> in monte saxum ; sed vetant leges Iovis.

The piece refers to, and is therefore later than, not only the companion Epode, but the companion Satire (*Sat.*, I. viii.).

So much for the lampoons. The next group may be said to be one degree less " iambic " in tone ; it consists of pieces perhaps more or less, and perhaps here or there, satirical, but characterised on the whole rather by a playful spirit, which amuses itself periodically with light excursions into the mock-heroic.

The second epode, for example, is in an idyllic vein. The last four lines pretend to invert it into a satire, but only humorously ; proportion cannot be so entirely discounted, any more than the light ending of *Odes*, ii. 1 could be said to cancel the seriousness which has there deepened into pathos. The notion that it is an indirect protest against the fashionable affectation of a delight in country life is too far-fetched to need refuting. The plain fact is that we have here the earliest example of one of our author's favourite structural devices, the *volte-face* ending. The praise of the simple as against the capitalistic life is one of Horace's favourite themes ; true, the tone here is light—*descendat in ventrem meum* serves to remind us that this is an epode and no ode—but the description of rustic pleasure is obviously " sympathetic." Alfius, of course (the usurer into whose mouth the idyllic dream is put) decides at the eleventh hour to stick to his profession ; but that is just what men will do, according to Horace—compare *Satires*, I. i. 1-19. Such anticipations are worth noting in a piece which is obviously one of the very earliest ; for it is deficient in the formal constituents of the Horatian poem, though these are found in the majority of the epodes ; it cannot properly be said to have an occasion, and it has no addressee ; it is, in fact, simply an exercise on a given theme ; it is Horace's *L'Allegro ;* and the profusion of descriptive detail as well as the yearning for a rustic Golden Age connect it with the sixteenth, and incline me to think that it was written soon after that poem (at twenty-five political despair gives place to *insouciance* much faster than style changes) and is therefore one of the earliest epodes. The Horatian explicitness is evident throughout. Language and theme are pleasing ; the descriptions are characteristically graphic ; [1] but the effect is not very lasting ; this is not one of the pieces one is accustomed to re-read. *Haec placuit semel.*

Vocabulary and matter alike connect the queer effusion that follows it with the Canidian epodes and particularly xvii. This is presumably Horace's earliest poem to Maecenas ; but it is not respectful. It is " occasional," though what the occasion was is hardly easy for modern readers to appreciate. The poet is suffering from indigestion ; if the patron has *really* had too much garlic surreptitiously introduced into some dish

---

[1] There would be one exception to this statement if *fontes* were the right reading at 27, but for my own part I believe in Markland's *frondes*, and would cf. Theocr., I. 1-2.

with which he had entertained him—if Maecenas has really, as we are asked to believe, done this " for fun "—then all that can be said is, that it is very difficult to imagine any standpoint from which that can possibly appear funny. However, in the epodes the fun is generally of a gruesome kind. But it is perhaps more likely that Horace pretends, " for fun," to attribute to a practical joke on Maecenas' part what had in reality been a mistake of his cook's, caused them both the same discomfort, as they both well knew ; that, in fact, on that very evening, when in due course the consequences became unmistakable, the host had apologised, and that this is Horace's way of reassuring him by showing how entirely humorously he regards the whole episode. Yet after all it does not matter what it is. Ostensibly (19-22) a curse, it is in effect playful and mock-heroic, and so let it pass.

Three may be called, in respect of subject at any rate, erotic. The eleventh is so far a satire in that it satirises himself ; he has lost all delight in verse-writing now because he is always in love with somebody or other ; he is cured of one passion only by becoming the victim of another. The object of derision in the fifteenth does not transpire until the last word ; it is his successor in the favour of Neaera, soon to be his successor in experiencing her fickleness. The first half-dozen lines of this piece are one of the very few passages of real poetry in the whole book ; in the third line the future participle is especially good ; though neither of them then knew that she was to be false, it was already destined. But the particular eternities she elects to swear by may perhaps not unaptly be felt to spell a lapse for the poem no less clearly than for herself, however unconscious the poet may appear to be of either ominous infelicity. *Si quid in Flacco virist* is hardly reassuring in the light of the idea of " manliness " (*virtus*, 11) indicated by its context.[1] The piece may be regarded as a sort of anticipation of one of the odes, the well-known favourite *Quis multa gracilis ?* (I. v.). In the preceding, Horace employs the old trick of the " Lines to a Blank Space " by making his inability to produce enough poems to fill a volume the occasion of one further poem. Maecenas, we hear, has been reproaching him,

---

[1] 13-16 ; incidentally at 15 I accept *offensi* (Gogau, Gow).

asking "how he has come so early by this lethargy";[1] a question which it appears the defaulter in this case cannot meet with the same assurance as did Sir Toby. The style, too, seems to mark it as one of the latest epodes; it is terse and forcible; the elliptical abruptness of the beginnings of lines 6 and 9 is good;[2] the brief plaint rises to a climax in the last sentence, and that to a climax in its last word.

The third group consists of the four remaining poems. The aspect of world-politics has suddenly once again grown serious; the final convulsion in the change from Republic to Empire is now threatening; men are everywhere having to choose on which side they will fight. From Horace as an ex-Republican by this time definitely committed to dependance on Cæsarian patronage, this crisis must have demanded the final severance of all his original party predilections; and however Roman sentiment was scandalised by the Orientalism of Antony, the process must have involved enough of a wrench to bring out to the full both his moral conviction and his personal devotion in favour of the party of his considered choice. The thirteenth, seventh, and first epodes seem to reflect this period in a seriousness of tone quite foreign to the remainder of the collection, though the fact has been obscured by the subsequent placing of *Ibis Liburnis* first. That the inclement weather which provides the ostensible occasion of the thirteenth is a symbol for political storm and anxiety is indicated later in the poem itself (7-8). The particular application, indeed, has been otherwise explained; but as on this count we are practically required to date the piece very early if we do not put it among the latest, I prefer the latter alternative on the ground that this is the only one of the epodes which in style and diction, as well as in its hortatory tone, resembles the more serious type of Ode;[3] so much so that it could be placed among the Odes without any incongruity. It is a fine poem, particularly the last seven lines, which are in the purest classic style.

[1] *Twelfth Night*, I. v.

[2] I suspect that it was *deus deus nam me vetat* that consciously or not suggested to Matthew Arnold his own much finer " A god, a god their severance ruled ! "

[3] The two previously considered, xv. and xiv., resemble in structure one of the lighter types of Ode.

By almost [1] all scholars the seventh has been dated considerably earlier, either 41 or 38 or 36, all of which years were marked by renewals of hostilities.   But *dexteris aptantur enses conditi*, as well as the whole language of the poem, points to a sudden outbreak after a peaceful interval,[2] of what is evidently civil war in the fullest sense.[3]   Moreover, the words

> Parumne campis atque Neptuno super
> Fusum est Latini sanguinis ?

are surely best explicable as glancing particularly at the operations against Sextus Pompey in 36, which had not culminated in his defeat without serious naval losses to the victors.   Accordingly I cannot help suspecting that the occasion is the final breach between Octavian and Antony in 32, and that the piece is addressed not to Romans in general but to the Antonians, many of them Senators, who were now hurrying away from Rome to join their leader.   As against this, it has been remarked [4] that there is not here any expression of partisanship, "which would certainly have appeared before the final conflict with Antony."   True, there is not ; and for the best of reasons. The poem has, or at least purports to have, a definite purpose, that of shaming the offenders into a better mind.   The last four lines are not at all to be understood as an utterance of political despair comparable to the commencement of Epode xvi.   What he says here about the fratricidal fatality that haunts Rome is the opposite of what he really believes, and he says it to frighten his hearers into sense.   In this epode, satire is replaced by political indignation culminating in bitter irony.

The metre originally used by Archilochus to express personal animosity is employed in Horace's first epode as the vehicle of a tribute to friendship.   It is the earliest poem devoted to his affection for Maecenas.   The occasion is the imminence of a

---

[1] Sellar states favourably a case for 32 B.C., but seems to prefer 41 or 39, for the reason to be dealt with presently.

[2] Is *enses conditi* appropriate to the malcontents of the Bellum Perusinum ?   In any case, I take the view that Horace had then been still in sympathy with the disaffected ; cf. above, p. 132.

[3] For that reason the wars against Sextus are surely to be ruled out as too departmental merely.

[4] Sellar, 123.

great naval battle—Actium as it turned out. " You are going to the scene of action, ready to risk your life for Cæsar. What am I to do ? What *can* I do but accompany you ? " The poem somewhat resembles that type of Ode which in its turn resembles an Epistle ; and ends with just a hint of the moralising which characterises both those types.

The latest written of the Epodes was evidently the ninth. This is an " occasional " poem in the fullest sense ; it is not merely ἀ*propos* of something, but it has a dramatic setting, and it was the failure to interpret it from this standpoint that so long prevented its being quite understood, while it was assumed to have been written in Rome on the first reception of the as yet vague account of the victory of Actium. So long as no other occasion was suggested, commentators had to follow the scholiast in supposing that when at line 35 the poet calls for a special wine of anti-emetic virtues, he is anticipating the effects of too copious a celebration of the good news. It was not until 1878 that the happy suggestion was made, by Bücheler, that the " nausea " here complained of is nothing less reputable [1] than common sea-sickness ! The poem, in fact, pretends to be writing itself (and almost certainly [2] was so written) on board Maecenas' galley rather early (I suggest it was read out to enliven the lunch-party, for it has the character of a " sympotic lyric ") on 2nd September, B.C. 31, the actual day, though this, of course, could not yet have been predicted confidently, of the naval battle which was to prove the final victory. The poet speaks in his own person. The tone is light, for victory, though not yet certain, is already highly probable. We must take it [3] that there was a standing joke against Horace in

[1] " Eum vomitum narrare Horatius credendus est, qui nulli turpis est nec vitabilis . . . Non indecora laboravit nausea belli pericula in mari temptans." Most editors since then have accepted this view ; but not all ; *e.g.*, L. Müller even in 1900 still clings to the old *Katzenjammer* explanation.

[2] It not only makes no reference to, but practically proves ignorance of, the salient facts of the battle itself. See Housman, *J. Phil.*, X. (1882), 194-6. Here again L. Müller attempts to reassert the old view, which still numbers adherents among those who are orthodox on *nausea ;* *e.g.*, Kiessling-Heinze, 6th ed., 1917.

[3] This is a pure conjecture on my part, but the fact that the poem begins and ends with a mention of Caecuban *must* (in Horace) have some

10

Maecenas' intimate circle about his weakness for Caecuban wine, and that he responded to frequent chaffing on this subject by assuming a naive resourcefulness in finding occasions for its consumption. " When will it be ? "—he cries excitedly at the officers' mess-table, with the implication that it *may* be very soon —" When shall I once more be drinking Caecuban with you, Maecenas, to celebrate the peace which will follow Cæsar's *final* victory ? Roman soldiers, it is true (though the time will come when it will be incredible) are still in arms against us under a barbarian queen ! Yet [1] 2000 Galatians have deserted to us from the enemy ; and his ships are afraid even to come out of harbour. Come then, Triumph-god, up ! delay no longer. Why should you hesitate, when (i) you gave your favour to Marius and Scipio and our leader is in himself [2] a greater man than either of these, and (ii) Antony (already suffering from losses on sea and land) [3] has evidently despaired and is doubtless even now in full flight." Then, as hopefulness [4] begets itself—" Come, waiter, more wine, Chian or Lesbian or—oh do let us have some Caecuban—if only to stop this feeling of sea-sickness ! " This latest of the Epodes naturally reminds us that Horace was soon to begin writing his Odes, of which I. xxxvii. (on the death of Cleopatra) is one of the earliest ; the answer to the *Quando ?* which opens the present poem is the *Nunc* which begins that ; for from the fifth line of the later poem it appears that in due course he got his Caecuban.

point, especially as the later reference flatly contradicts the spirit of the first. Very few editors have mentioned this, none explained it.

[1] Reading *at huc*.

[2] *Reportasti* in its context is no warrant whatever for the assumption always made that the poet is here speaking (whether historically or prophetically) of the *victory* of Cæsar.

[3] A conjecture of the poet's ; there was no land-battle.

[4] Despite Prof. Housman, *loc. cit.*, I cannot believe that *curam metumque* in 37 means very much. I think it means, as surely it naturally might, that he will drown in wine the *remnants* or *memories* of those feelings ; the feelings themselves are supposed to have been dispersed by the reassurance of 17-32. The tone of the whole is light and spirited.

CHAPTER VI

FEELING AFTER FORM—THE SATIRES

Invest me in my motley ; give me leave
To speak my mind, and I will through and through
Cleanse the foul body of the infected world,
If they will patiently receive my medicine.

THE Roman who addressed himself to his public through the medium of the *satura* was certainly putting on about as " motley " a poetic uniform as has ever existed. Lyric, epic, drama—the terms all suggest something ; these are obvious modes. The *satura,* as in content it was about everything, and therefore in itself about nothing at all, so in form might be practically anything, a monologue or semi-dramatic, a diary, a dissertation, a letter, a tirade ; in fact, one formal characteristic it had alone, and that was formlessness.[1] Horace we can now see to have been the one writer who was by nature primarily an artist in a litera- ture whose practitioners were for the most part not artists at all. How came he first to select this medium ? Several answers may be given. His own account is that all the others already had their acknowledged living masters. The simple fact perhaps is this, that there was now arising a general desire to make Roman poetry more national, and there was no al- ternative way of doing so between Romanising a Greek form, or writing *satura ;* and until he presently hit upon the idea of imitating Archilochus (not at first by any means an obvious idea), there probably did not seem much chance of a new departure in the former direction, Greek Lyric having been

---

[1] Cf. Mommsen, V. 484, " In fact the Roman *satura* in general was not properly a fixed species of art, but only indicated negatively the fact that the ' multifarious poem ' was not to be included under any of the recognised forms of art."

broached by Catullus without apparently any promise of a copious result. Besides, it is not at all improbable that he may have been positively drawn to the *satura's* last successful exponent, and so tempted to follow in his footsteps, by the strong Republican sympathies which there is good reason to think he entertained in the year or two after Philippi.[1] Pompey was the son of a niece of Lucilius, and consequently scholars of the Pompeian circle had taken a special interest in that writer, whose tone was in any case critical and, as Mommsen says, " oppositional," and therefore likely to be congenial to the disinherited clerk. And apart from all that, it is evident that Horace, although a born artist, took some time to discover it. To trace the progress of his artistic apprenticeship is one of the main interests of a study of the earliest of his three periods of work.

The *satura*, though it had no form, had, indeed, some sort of a tradition ; but that was (according to the view taken of the various grades or modes of literature in my second chapter) a debased one. In that chapter it has been shown that this class of writing was from its origin akin to the Greek " mime "—in the wide sense there given to that term. But it was not only akin to it ; at a point in its history it came into direct contact with the Greek tradition of the great " mime " period, and it was the access of rank and voluble vitality which it then received from that vast sophistic literature, it was the connection which it then established therewith, that ensured its continuity as a literary practice. That junction was effected by Ennius, and the association was preserved by Lucilius, and reinforced (to this extent we may include his *Epistles*) by Horace ; it was kept up, in their ways, by Persius and Juvenal. Roman satire became with Ennius, and remained to the end, the recognised vehicle for Greek popular philosophy.

The poet attempts to make men good by simply putting the noble and the beautiful before them, on the assumption that " we needs must love the highest when we see it " ; the moralist by other methods, by exposing the bad and denouncing it, by appealing to the reason, by preaching. Horace was to tend, indeed, towards the poetic method ; but he began at the

[1] Cf. above, p. 132.

wrong end. His progress in choice of models is similar to that of Roman literature in general. Roman literature began upon the later and inferior writers or kinds, and from them (as a rule) worked back. In its merely imitative stage, it began in tragedy with Euripides, in comedy with Menander; when its operation was more free, it still began upon Alexandrine methods; it is the Augustan age that sees the general reversion to the older poets and the purer forms. Characteristic, then, of their national literature, are Virgil's reaction from the exploitation of Theocritus to that of Hesiod and then of Homer, and Horace's sudden leap from a model which ultimately derives from the Sicilian mime and the " Socratic discourse " [1] that had arisen as a by-product thereof, to the wellspring of Greek Lyric, and to an interest, at least, in Greek Tragedy.

For it is important to realise that in his satires Ennius (239-169 B.C.) was simply grafting the Sicilian mime on the coarser but kindred stock of Roman *satura*. Born in South Italy, by race partly Greek and by education almost entirely so, he became deeply imbued at once in the kind of philosophy that formed the content of the mime of Epicharmus and his disciples, and in the style in which that class of literature presented it. Which of his writings that are not dramatic or epic are to be regarded as *saturae*, and which are not, is not perhaps quite apparent; but it does not greatly matter. His *Epicharmus*, in which he embodied a hash of the Pythagorean didactic passages of the old Sicilian, was written in trochaics, a favourite metre of Epicharmus himself and one of the metres of Lucilius; and its general connections with Greek mime on the one side and Roman satire on the other are obvious enough. His *Euhemerus* indeed seems to have been in prose, but satire (like mime) could be in prose when and where it liked. The important point is that these widely read works of the first writer of *saturae* begin in Roman literature certain traditions which it at once fell to the *satura* to continue; and chiefly two. His *Epicharmus* begins the popular preaching of philosophy, not according to the technicalities of the schools—for the schools tend to be derided in this tradition—but as a *way of life*, the old Pythagorean conception of philosophy which, no matter

---

[1] *Socratici Sermones, Odes*, III. xxi. 9.

what we may think on the now vexed question of the Pytha-
goreanism of Socrates, was certainly the view taken of the
function of philosophy by Socrates' most influential philosophic
progeny the Stoic school. His *Euhemerus* similarly begins that
rationalising of myths, especially of religious myths, which
was to be, for example, an interesting feature of Horace's
works in the *satura* kind. As for his *Hedyphagetica*, a gastronomical treatise after another Sicilian original, the poem of
Archestratus of Gela, that is the first appearance of what is
obviously a frequent topic in Roman satire, from Lucilius and
Horace to Juvenal. It is not properly, however, a separate
tradition from the two just mentioned ; it is a part of the
general inculcation of a " way of life " or δίαιτα (the word
from which we ourselves get " diet "), for ever since the Pytha-
goreans had dietetics ranked as one of the most important
aspects of right living. In the general treatment of this topic
in Roman satire, and doubtless in its Sicilian antecedents also,
it is sometimes the simple life that is seriously recommended
(as in Horace, *Sat.*, II. ii.), sometimes the luxurious that is
preached ironically ; but whether the tone is earnest or light,
the pulpitorial style is always present, appearing in the latter
case in the form of the mock-heroic. This is well seen, for
example, in the fourth satire of Horace's second book, with
its " ipsa memor praecepta canam," its authoritative solemnity
of diction, its final reference to the doctrines as " vitae praecepta
beatae." All this is ultimately derived from the original mime,
in which, as Mr. Cornford has shown,[1] the Learned Doctor who
was one of its prime constituents often figured as Professional
Cook. If we remember that in primitive times the priest
and medicine-man are one, we shall see that even in this comparatively humble feature Roman satire preserves a formal
trace of the original and theoretically essential function of
poetry as an instrument of the priest. Other information that
has come down to us about Ennius's *saturae* is, though meagre,
certainly significant. Dialogue, of course, had already existed
in the old perfotmed *satura* of the capital in the days before
Livius Andronicus ; but a dialogue between Life and Death,
such as Quintilian [2] tells us occurred in one of Ennius's pieces,

---

[1] *Origin of Attic Comedy.*   [2] Quint., IX. ii. 36.

further suggests Greek influence from the age of popular moralising ; Quintilian indeed mentions it in connection with the fable about Virtue and Vice by the sophist Prodicus. Another element in the Ennian satire was apparently fable,[1] used, as we can see from the tag preserved, to point a moral ; and this, too, remained a feature with Lucilius and Horace.

Diversity of topic and discursiveness of style, general moral tendency, absence of structure in the separate pieces, range of metres from hexameter to trochaic and iambic—these are the major features of the Ennian satire which were still preserved by the next successful practitioner, Lucilius (180-103 B.C.) His main innovation has already been noticed ; [2] he it was who gave to Roman satire what afterwards remained the distinctive feature of the genre, censoriousness of tone. At the same time he invented for his effusions a new descriptive label, which, while it did not oust the old one, was retained along with that by Horace, and which is certainly still useful as denoting another original characteristic of the Lucilian satire distinguishing it from that of Ennius. Instead of referring to his own poems as *saturae* he called them *sermones*,[3] " discourses," a term including *causeries*, conversations with an imaginary interlocutor, and letters. It would really be fair, and certainly convenient, to use these two terms regularly for the two main types into which Latin satire now divided itself. Such works as those of Varro and Petronius are true " miscellanies " somewhat after the manner of Ennius. Horace's own " satires " and " epistles " are both *sermones* (as he himself on occasion calls them),[4] and the works of Persius and Juvenal also have the *sermo's* distinctive traits. Ennius had not written as personally addressing himself to anybody ; Lucilius regularly did. Sometimes there is a definite individual addressee ; sometimes it seems to have been the public ; but even in other cases, even when, for example, he affects to report another's homily as Horace does in *Sat.*, II. ii., he almost always

---

[1] Aulus Gellius, ii. 29.   [2] Ch. IV., p. 94.
[3] Cf. *Marx, Lucil. Carm. Rel.*, I. xiii. *fin.*
[4] He calls his satires *saturae* within the Satires themselves, but in the Epistles he refers both to his satires (*Epist.*, I. iv. 1, II. ii. 60), and his Epistles (*Epist.*, II. i. 4, 250) as *sermones*.

writes in such a tone as to give the impression that the author is personally addressing the reader.

For the rest, Lucilius is continuing the work of Ennius, the " grafting " already alluded to ; he is, indeed, generally more *national* than Ennius, but that in itself is a following of Ennius' own lead and of the natural course of Latin literature. But while there is a fairly clear distinction between the *satura* and the *sermo*, it is essential for the scientific study of literary evolution to recognise that they are, and remain throughout, fundamentally one and the same kind.[1] Through the garrulity of a Varro no less than in the invective of a Juvenal runs a tone of protest against, or irony at the expense of, the various corruptions of contemporary Roman life ; the medley and the discourse are both full of Greek popular philosophy. It is unfortunate that we do not know more about the nature of Lucilius' models apart from Ennius. It is the more unfortunate because Horace's statement on this point has won general acceptance. Lucilius, he says (*Sat.*, I. iv. 1-7), is entirely derived from the Greek " Old Comedy "—he changed nothing but the metres ! The patent absurdity of such (to say the least) exaggeration should have warned us from accepting the statement at all. Horace's idea in making it I have already [2] shown. There is no direct influence whatever ; only a sort of *ex post facto* distant affinity (political advice given amusingly and as from the poet in person) which Horace has noticed and takes advantage of for his own ends. " Eupolis atque Cratinus Aristophanesque poetae " are never mentioned, or alluded to, in the extant fragments (some 1300 lines) of Lucilius. Nettleship said that this was " probably an accident." [3] But neither is there any sign that he imitated them, either in spirit or in style.[4] In plain language, Latin literature had not yet got so far ; indeed it never did. It was still concerned almost entirely with the Greek literature of the great Sophistic

---

[1] Cf. Nettleship, *The Original Form of the Roman Satura* (in Lectures and Essays,, II.), p. 40.

[2] See Ch. III., p. 66.   [3] Nettleship, II., p. 42.

[4] As to matter, he does seem to be some twice " indebted " to the Old Comedy ; 836 *quis tu homo es ? nemo sum homo*, where Marx cites Aristoph. Vesp., 184, τίς εἰ ποτ', ὦνθρωπ' ἐτεόν ; Οὔτις νὴ Δία, and 978 which is paralleled by a fragment of Pherecrates.

period, the tradition of which had begun in Sicily (alike with the earliest sophists and the earliest mimes) and was transmitted *via* Sicily to Rome. Lucilius, of course, as a highly educated man,[1] knows Homer well, and shows an acquaintance with Archilochus; but for the rest, his own references, such as they are, show his Greek reading to have been practically confined to the period of the decadence ; the writers whom he chiefly exploits are the philosophers, and of all schools, Academic, Peripatetic, Stoic, and Epicurean. He has a clear reminiscence of Plato's *Charmides* in 830-3 (Marx), and an unexpected echo even of the *Laws* (1234) ; he refers by name to the " Socratici charti " (709) ; [2] and to Aristippus as a Socratic (742). He seems to have ridiculed Stoic professors as Horace was to do after him,[3] and as Greek sophistic did the Cynics and others. He discussed Euripides (1169) and borrowed from Menander (974). He knows of the theory of the Sicilian Empedocles, mentions his own contemporary Carneades, and alludes to the conversion of Polemon (cf. Hor., *Sat.*, II. iii. 254). Such is the sort of literature on which his mind runs. But what of his general model ? A tradition, preserved by Joannes Lydus, says that it was Rhinthon of Tarentum, whom we know to have been a writer of the time of the first Ptolemies and the inventor of the burlesque tragedy. The same authority says that Persius imitated Sophron. We know independently that Ennius reproduced Sophron's predecessor Epicharmus and Rhinthon's contemporary Sotades. All this points undoubtedly to a general dependence of the Roman satire, for its materials, on the Greek mime. But " burlesque tragedy " does not explain the character of Lucilius's remains in the least, so his indebtedness to Rhinthon is not believed. It seems, however, to be in this cycle of Greek literature that his model should be looked for. And his *sermones*, from all that we can gather, bear a quite distinct resemblance to the class of " literature " invented by one who was for a considerable period a very notable and popular publicist of this cycle, and who was characteristic of it ; and they are the earliest Latin writings to do

---

[1] *Eruditio in eo mira*—Quint., X. i. 93.
[2] Cf. Hor., *A.P.*, 310.
[3] Cf. Sellar, *Roman Poets of the Republic*, p. 243 *fin.*

50. Bion of Borysthenes, who flourished at Athens about the beginning of the third century B.C., belonged at various times to almost all the philosophical schools then existing, but to judge from his general outlook was obviously most appropriately placed when he was an adherent to the Cynics. He invented the " diatribe " ($\delta\iota\alpha\tau\rho\iota\beta\acute{\eta}$). What Bion's master Diogenes was to Plato's master Socrates, that was the diatribe to the dialogue ; a vulgar, coarse, illiterate, but vigorous and popular form thereof. Both these literary types flourished much more than we should deduce from their remains ; the popular especially [1] (as time and degeneracy went on), though very little has survived of it at all. They are both, of course, forms of mime ; the Latin term comprising both is *sermo*— *Socratici sermones*, Hor., *Odes*, III. xxi. 9, *Bionei sermones*, *Epist.*, II. ii. 60.[2] Plato's dialogues are at least partly indebted for their form to the oral teaching of Socrates ; this lends further probability to Wendland's view that the conversation of Diogenes is the historic prototype of the diatribe.[3] Though our remains of Bion are fragmentary in the extreme, we can get some idea of the nature of his diatribes partly from a report or two, partly from extant later writings which more or less belong to that category, such as the six lectures of his imitator Teles (about 250 B.C.), the moral epistles of Seneca, and the harangues of Epictetus. To make a long story short, it seems fairly clear that a considerable number of the general features of Roman satire are ultimately traceable to the diatribe. The " form," to begin with ; an address, sometimes to an individual, whether imaginary, or a real person used as lay figure, in which case the address is liable to take the semblance of a letter ; at other times to a company, such addresses being frequently interspersed with brief abrupt dialogues with an imagined

[1] Wendland, *Hellenistisch-Römische Kultur*, 78, in a chapter to which I am indebted for several facts relating to the history of the diatribe. See also Powell and Barber, *New Chapters in Greek Literature*, p. 1 and foll.

[2] It is also Cicero's term for his philosophical dialogues.

[3] But I believe we should go further back, to Socrates himself, whom Plato represents (*Apol.*, 37, D) as describing his discourses by this very term $\delta\iota\alpha\tau\rho\iota\beta\acute{\eta}$. [Since I wrote this, Prof. Burnet, using, however, the term $\pi\rho\sigma\tau\rho\epsilon\pi\tau\iota\kappa\grave{o}s$ $\lambda\acute{o}\gamma os$, has expressed a similar view, see *Legacy of Greece*, p. 79.]

interlocutor. The content ; on its negative side, criticism, generally derisive, of philosophers and of moral poets ; on its positive side, propaganda in favour of the simple life. This last especially, a pervading feature of Lucilian and Horatian satire, undoubtedly derives primarily from the Cynic school, however it may take on in certain forms an Epicurean or even a Stoic colouring. These traits especially connect Lucilius and Horace with Bion ; and so does one other (in contrast, for example, with Persius or Seneca) and that is, anti-Stoicism, such as is seen in Horace's earlier satires ; [1] and another, anti-capitalism.[2] With all these features in common,[3] which of the two, Lucilius and Horace, is more likely to have chosen the model ? the earlier or the later ? The conclusion would seem almost inevitable already, that Lucilius, the inventor of the *sermo*, derived the form from Bion, and that Bion is therefore his true Greek antecedent ; and it is further borne out by two important considerations.

The reason why it is always said, not that Lucilius, but that Horace, first Romanised Bion, is that Horace, speaking in a comparatively late work of his various friends' different preferences in regard, not so much to his past writings, as to further productions which might be supposed to be desired from him, says, one likes odes (*carmen*), one epodes (*iambi*), another " Bion-esque discourses " with their " coarse wit." But he is not exactly *alluding* to his own two books of satires ; he is, of course, glancing at them, and obviously in a depreciatory manner, and presumably with special reference to the very earliest ; but the whole phrase is simply a perphrasis for " satire." There is nothing here inconsistent with the attribution of the imitation of Bion, not to himself, but to the inventor of the *genre ;* I take it that by this time Horace has learned the fact of which he had not, in his somewhat cavalierish manner of literary theorising, troubled to inform himself when he wrote *Sat.,* I. iv. But the really significant part is the phrase *nigrum*

---

[1] For anti-Stoicism in Lucilius, see above, Ch. IV., p. 99 ; for Bion's, Athenaeus IV. 162, D, Diogenes Laertius IV, 46-58.

[2] Stob., X. 38, Βίων ὁ σοφιστὴς τὴν φιλαργυρίαν μητρόπολιν ἔλεγε πάσης κακίας εἶναι.

[3] Cf. Tyrrell, *Latin Poetry*, p. 180, on the " basis or frame " common to many of Horace's and Lucilius' satires.

sal, which is, by all that we can see, far more applicable to
Lucilius than to Horace himself.[1] Palmer observes that
" Horace's satires have with one exception little or nothing
of the cynical profligacy which seems to have marked the
writings of Bion." Of that sort of cynical profligacy, on the
other hand, there is in Lucilius, despite his high-toned ful-
minations in certain other passages, a quite obvious vein.
And in the second place—and I cannot see why it should
have been so much ignored—there is the tradition preserved
in the explicit statement of Acron : " sunt autem disputationes
Bionis philosophi, quibus stultitiam volgi arguit, *cui paene
consentiunt carmina Luciliana.*"

Thus, then, by Ennius and Lucilius, are the two new types
of Republican *satura* inaugurated ; by the two gates they
opened is the whole herd of Greek mime-literature let in to
that rank no-man's land. For, motley though the herd is,
they *are* ultimately all of the same genus. " Attic salt " or
" black salt," the wit is always a different thing from the
imaginative humour of Aristophanes. We need not be surprised that the exploitation in Latin of Epicharmus and Bion
leads on in time to that of Plato himself ; we need not think
it incongruous that Horace squeezed that author close against
Menander when he packed up for his country house. It is not,
in Horace, so much a case of using Platonic material,[2] as of
asserting, through the satire, coarse medium though he found
it, a doctrine not very far removed (and in the Odes and Epistles
the distance was to be still less) from the great spiritual paradox,
the doctrine which Plato, in his dialogues of best literary and
moral value, puts into the mouth of Socrates, that materialism
is literally nothing less than a snare and a delusion, and that
it is only within himself, that is to say in health of soul, that
a man can hope to find anything other than misery.[3] The
reason why all this should not surprise us is that between the
Platonic dialogue and the Bionian diatribe there are significant

[1] Cf. his phrase about Lucilius, *sale multo urbem defricuit*, Sat., I. x.
3-4.
[2] Note, however, that on occasion he does so ; *e.g.*, *Epist.*, II. i. 114-17.
[3] " Horace " it may be objected " simply got that from the Stoics."
But their effusions were merely technical ; my point is that Horace
in literature is the successor of Plato.

general features in common ; propaganda, through more or less realistic conversation, of the principle that the *true* utilitarianism is *opposed* to materialism ; criticism of rival schools and especially of pedantic ones ; carps and sneers (betraying the intellectual or the plebeian) against the masterpieces of imaginative literature. In a well-known passage of the *Republic* (III. 388 A), the Homeric Achilles in the violent physical manifestation of extreme grief is deprecated as a demoralising spectacle. Bion we know [1] directed his caustic wit at Homer and other poets, and Cicero has preserved for us an example which indicates quite clearly how very like Plato's, allowing for the homelier tone, was the *tendency* of his works ; what a fool, he is here [2] reported to have pointed out, was Agamemnon for tearing his hair in grief, as if baldness would not merely add another to his misfortunes !

And borne along by this flood of mime-literature, comes in not merely the doctrine, but the rhetoric, of the schools ; and that gives new life to the native tendency of the *satura* towards dialogue. For Rhetoric, too, is an integral feature of the Sicilian tradition in Greek and Roman literature. It begins with the Syracusans Corax and Tisias, but it is their later fellow-citizen Gorgias who is the main agent in transplanting it to the fertile soil of Athens. There, of the pupils of Socrates, Plato as we saw took up the mime from the hands of another Syracusan, and a contemporary of Gorgias, Sophron ; Antisthenes, however, the founder of the Cynic school (and so in a sense of its greater offspring the Stoic), was a pupil of Gorgias himself. It is probably from the last two, mainly, though others such as Prodicus doubtless contributed, that the sophistic exploitation of heroic or poetic legend descends to the Cynic and Stoic pamphleteers. Besides (of course) criticising poets, Antisthenes wrote dialogues ; and though the two works which have come down to us as his are generally (but not by Blass) considered spurious, they represent the sort of thing that was soon to become common and to last long— argumentatious speeches, one by Ajax and one by Odysseus, on the award of the arms of Achilles. This, too, was thrown

---

[1] Acron on *Epist.*, II. ii. 60.
[2] Cicero, *Tusc. Disp.*, III. 26, 62.

into the hotch-potch of Latin satire ; compare, for example,
Horace, *Sat.*, II. iii. 187-207.

So far, then, from being " totally " Roman, as Quintilian
said,[1] satire was rather nearer to being totally Greek. Yet
that, again, it was not, and the difference is just all the difference. The native institution of *satura* provided the matrix ;
the impregnating forces were Greek. In more literal terms,
the matter of Roman satire, the " copy " of that ancient form
of journalism, was almost entirely Greek ; entirely one may say
in Ennius, in Lucilius one must except the autobiographical
stuff, which such as it was can hardly have required any originality worth considering ; but even in Lucilius one must not
except the filth ; despite the far-distant Fescennine ancestry,[2]
it is probably not (for the most part) native filth ; as Ennius
took it from Sotades, Lucilius probably got some more of it
from Bion, for it was a feature of the Hellenistic period, a part
of its general literary shamelessness ; it was an element in the
mime. But whereas in the Greek world the City as a moral
organism had long ceased to be, in the Roman the *satura* still
preserved, through continued ups and downs, the trace of a
social function, and this was to be its saving grace. The Greek
writings in this kind seem to have been generally pervaded by a
flippant spirit ; the Romans are all, in their various degrees
and ways, earnest, and the more Roman the more so. Lucilius
the Campanian is vehement in contrast to Ennius the Messa-
pian ; Horace the Roman citizen is, even in his satires only,
wise and deep by comparison with Lucilius. The matter, of
course, is Romanised up to a point ; more so than by Plautus
in his handling of the Greek New Comedy, not more so, on the
whole (despite Quintilian), than generally in Latin epic, or
didactic, or lyric ; names, anecdotal illustrations, local colour,
are often taken from (if we had the originals we might rather
say " transposed into ") Roman life, and this is so throughout
from Lucilius to Juvenal. But in the main the Roman element
lies in the use to which the material is put ; lies in the tone.
Roman satire is certainly coarse ; but at the same time, however
strange it may appear to us, serious and ethical.

---

[1] See, however, above, Ch. II., p. 53 n.
[2] Lucilius num in saturis suis fescenninorum hic illic imitatus sit
licentiam, nos divinare non iam possumus.—Marx, *Luc. Carm. Rel.*, xvi.

In saying so I am, of course, referring principally to the
extant remains, which are preponderatingly in the Lucilian
tradition. As Lucilius was a good deal more Roman than
Ennius, so did the *sermo* he founded remain [1] perhaps rather
more national than the *satura* as written by the direct successors
of Ennius in this branch. For both types now continued.
The Ennian type was revived by Varro with a fresh draught
from the same Greek waters. Bion having been exploited
(according to my account) by Lucilius, the similar exploitation
of his fellow-cynic and perhaps contemporary Menippus of
Gadara (*Gadareno de grege porcus*) was an obvious next step ;
and this was what Varro did in his *Menippean satires*.[2] The
general similarity, in fundamentals, between the two types of
Roman satire, appears once more from an examination of the
remains of Varro. The cynicism, the coarse " horse sense,"
connect him chiefly with Lucilius ; but the standpoint of the
abnormis sapiens, nature's philosopher, who at the same time
derides existing philosophic systems but inculcates a " philosophic " indifference to the blows of fortune and the attractions
of luxury ; the alternation of levity with earnestness ; the
praise, supported by zestful description,[3] of the simple life ;
the infusion of Greek material with Roman colour and Roman

---

[1] I become less sure of this, and inclined to think that the true
reason for the copious preservation of the Lucilian school of satire and
the almost complete loss of the Ennian is simply that the style of the
former was so very much purer and more literary.

[2] Another model of Varro was Heracleides, also a contemporary of
Menippus ; he was an Academic, and wrote serious dialogues. I note
this as one more connection between Roman satire and Plato ; who,
after all, with his general attitude of antagonism to the *schools* and
the *pedants*, and his general advocacy of *the ascetic life*, all through
the medium of dialogue, is for practical purposes (*i.e.*, discounting
Epicharmus) the founder of this whole class of literature.

It is also worth noting here, in more connections than one, that
Varro was very fond of the form which I have elsewhere called " dialogue with a setting," *i.e.*, the form of the piece is really a dialogue but
it begins as a narrative in the writer's own person ; just as, for example,
the *Pilgrim's Progress* begins as a dream recounted by the author. This
trick, too, was invented by Plato. It is a useful link (for classificatory
purposes) between the narrative-satire and the dramatic-satire.

[3] *E.g.*, Varro's *Manius*.

tone [1]—all these are features of the Varronian *satura* which it shares not less with that of Horace [2] than with that of Lucilius. In one respect, indeed, Varro is the half-way house between them ; he provides a transition from the political polemic of Lucilius to the moral censure of Horace.

Meanwhile the satire of invective, on the other hand, the " discourse," also continued to be practised ; we hear from Horace of one Varro Atacinus " and certain others," whose productions were evidently negligible ; so that it is practically from Lucilius that Horace takes it up.

From Lucilius Horace not only takes the " form," such as it is, but a good deal of raw material also, which he duly recasts—not to say transfigures—in accordance with his own purposes. The extent to which he did so we cannot tell, owing to the fragmentary nature of Lucilius' remains, but a considerable number of parallels demonstrably not accidental have been often enough pointed out. [3] Even, however, if Horace's immeasurable superiority as a versifier and stylist did not in themselves constitute an originality which renders that sort of indebtedness about as comparatively unimportant as it is comparatively uninteresting—even if that were not so, it would still be no part of our business here to examine these parallels ; we are here simply concerned with the question, what Horace as a literary artist did with the *satura*, or, if the other way of looking at it be preferred, what the *satura* did for him ; how he advanced by and through his experience of it. We shall see this most satisfactorily in the actual course of considering his satires, however summarily, one by one.

---

[1] " The whole intellectual contents are pervaded by Roman idiosyncrasy."—Mommsen on Varro.

[2] Here, for example, is a fragment of Varro which at once recalls Horace :—

> Non fit thesauris, non auro pectus solutum ;
> Non demunt animis curas ac relligiones
> Persarum montes, non atria divitis Crassi.

[3] See, *e.g.*, Tyrrell, *Latin Poetry*. The most recent work on the subject is Fiske, *Lucilius and Horace* (University of Wisconsin, 1920).

THE FIRST BOOK

The earliest satire of this book, the seventh, has already been considered. The next in chronological order is the second, about which it is not necessary to say much here. The real emphasis of the piece is undoubtedly in the second half, to which the first is introductory. The lesson enforced, and the ground on which it is enforced, are given succinctly in the lines :—

> quare, ne poeniteat te,
> desine matronas sectarier, unde laboris
> plus haurire mali est quam ex re decerpere fructus.

Various examples, mostly gravitating towards this topic, of the characteristically Horatian principle that " fools, in avoiding one vice, run into its opposite," lead up to the tirade against adultery. Horace being an ancient and a Roman, and as yet very crude, without the faintest consciousness of cynicism recommends fornication (within limits, it appears) as the natural and right alternative. So he himself had been advised by his own father, of whose admonition as reported at *Sat.*, I. iv. 113-4 this whole piece is simply an extension. So, we learn from this piece itself, had Cato indoctrinated the youth of his day—Cato, the embodiment of the old Roman virtues. For this reason more than for the frequent foulness of its language, the piece is so alien to modern taste, particularly in this country, that it becomes necessary to emphasise the fact that it unquestionably *purports* to convey advice which is individually and socially salutary ; it gives itself out for moral. The influence of Epicureanism is traceable in several places. It seems to us a strange mixture, this alternation of coarseness and corruption with ethical and philosophic proselytism, the speech of an unembittered Swift in the tones of an unreligious Chadband. But it is the diatribe right enough.[1] Parts of Epictetus are morally not much better.

There is only one other satire in this book which shows no evidence of acquaintance with Maecenas, the fourth, so it is natural to take it for the next written, and it has other signs

[1] For the striking parallel between this satire and one of the newly-recovered fragments of the Cynic " meliambist " Cercidas (flor. 230 B.C.) see Powell and Barber, *New Chapters in Greek Literature*, p. 8.

of being early ; it appears (71-4) that he does not as yet contemplate publishing his writings at all, and not even reciting them except privately. This is then the first of his three pieces which deal principally with the function of satire as he understands it. His main point here is that it is not malevolent. The piece was evidently occasioned by complaints that had been made of his previous work on the ground that it was offensive in its allusions to persons. As we have seen, the seventh and the second are probably the only satires of this book yet written ; and it is apparent from his reference to it (iv. 92 = ii. 27) that the latter had been the main trouble. That reference is characteristic of the whole piece in the way in which it deliberately clouds the issue. He attempts to make light of his offence by quoting as representative a comparatively trivial line. In the same way he conceals for some time the real subject of the pamphlet, and only gradually reveals that he is on his own defence. He begins by bluntly stating that Aristophanes and his fellow-comedians assumed complete liberty of social criticism, that even in Rome Lucilius had done so, and then he hastily attacks Lucilius for quite a different reason—his slovenly prolixity. Later, when his *apologia* does begin, he starts on a totally irrelevant tack ; he has spoken of the old comedians casually enough as poets, and he has said of the disapprovers of satire " they all *hate* poets " ; well in the first place, he now protests, I don't consider myself a poet. Even if this were not immediately shown to be a dust-raising diversion by his at once proceeding to question the right of *comedians also* to be called poets—since to prove that neither of two blacks is blue does not make them both white—it is stultified for logical purposes by his (evidently, I think, quite careless and unconscious) inclusion of himself in the " multa poetarum manus " of the last three lines. But he must come to the point. " You are quite wrong to think of me as a sort of informer [1] even ; what I jot down on *my*

---

[1] Such were the Sulcius and Caprius of 65-6, according to the received view, based on the schol. But I wonder if they were not rather satiric poets. 70-1 looks like a plain antithesis (I can't accept Gow's explanation) and cf. *libellos* 71 with *libellis* 67. In *acer* " keen-scented " (*canis acer, e.g.*, Epod., xii. 6), in *rauci* which I take to = " barking," and in *ambulat* (they grin like a dog and run about the city) I suspect

' libelli ' (71 ; cf. 139 with 66) is never made public."—Well, you are a backbiter in private.—" That I simply deny. I happen to know how it is done ; by the hypocritical testimonial which is really slander. There is nothing in my writings *like that*. My nailing-up of individual offenders is done for my own self-improvement, that I may have them before my mind as awful warnings; that was how my own father taught me morals. And look at the result, my only vices are very mild and harmless ones—such as the writing of satires ! " We note in 136-7 the Horatian parallel to " there but for the grace of God go I." The way in which he effects a sudden surprise return to his real subject just before the end of the piece is clever. But it is not a particularly interesting piece. It is worth noting that he does make some claim for satire—the right to be outspoken without being taken too seriously. In actual fact, of course, he subsequently moderated his tone.

Closely connected with the fourth in subject (though not, according to my view, by its main purpose) and probably in date also,[1] is the preceding. If this piece is really, in effect, a sermon against the uncharitableness of society,[2] with an implied contrast of the disinterested moral seriousness of the satirist,[3] then it is an amplification of 93-103 of the satire just considered, and indeed nothing could be more natural as the second step in his own self-defence than to follow up the returned charge in just this way. But I cannot feel that such is what is primarily in Horace's thoughts. To me the piece reads simply like an attack on Stoicism, no whit the less characteristic in that it is a flank attack, and does not give away its purpose at the beginning.

The transition occurs at 76-9. The appeal for charity leads to the observation that of all offences, the trivial ought most of all to be overlooked. " Stultis " in 77 determines this at once to be aimed at the Stoics, and at 96 the objective begins to be openly declared. The Stoic view was—to borrow

---

he is suggesting the same comparison of the satirist to a dog as the arch-foe of robbers (*latronibus*, 67) which he makes in Epod. vi. ; and, perhaps, cf. my remark on Epod. iv. 19.

[1] L. Müller even thinks it the earlier, assigning iii. to 40 or possibly 39, iv. to 39.

[2] So *e.g.*, Palmer, Sellar.   [3] So Wickham.

the language of the " Shorter Catechism "—that all sins are equally heinous. The remainder of the satire is a protest against this doctrine, and other Stoic tenets with which it was associated. The distinction between right and wrong, maintains Horace, is *not* in the order of the Universe, it has no transcendental basis ; it is a convention established by society for the purpose of self-protection.

If the piece is a plea for charity in judgment, then the second half of it goes off at a tangent, and as Wickham has to admit " the connexion of 1-19 with the rest " is " not made perfectly clear." Anti-Stoicism, on the other hand, is the one thing that gives unity to the whole satire. Horace objects to the Stoic's intransigence, to the purely visionary character of his belief ; he is sincere enough, but his idea of himself will not work when brought into contact with the facts of life, and to that extent he is like Tigellius—with whom the poem began. At 137-41 Horace gathers up the thread of his previous remarks about forbearance, and inserts it in its proper subordinate relation to the more important theme. It is remarkable with what iteration, in the latter half, he protests that there are different degrees of sin. His exceptional insistence here shows that already Stoicism is at least a matter of great concern to him. The piece as a whole evinces a distinctly Epicurean standpoint, under the influence of Lucretius, and yet after all it is not so much an " attack " on Stoicism as a complaint against it, made not without bitterness. In point of fact, the Stoic religion has now an evident fascination for him, a fascination which he resists, it is haunting his meditations like a " hound of heaven." In the second book we shall find him " almost persuaded " ; in *Odes*, I. he tells of his conversion ; in the *Epistles* we certainly find him much more of a Stoic than of anything else.

Such is the unity of the piece, but it is not a very conscious or deliberate unity. We may note, however, that he has now got the length of addressing a satire, with tolerable consistency, to a single individual, in this case Maecenas.[1]

Palmer thought i. the last written, but I incline much more to L. Müller's date—early in 37. It has quite distinct signs

---

[1] Not mentioned till 64, but *tibi* in 33 probably denotes him.

of immaturity ; 23-6 smacks of the novice in satire-writing, since to an older hand *ça va sans dire*,[1] and its Lucretian echo [2] connects it with the satire which we have just considered—and also with our next ; 108 is a poor device, and so is the sudden and lame conclusion, 120-1. But to say that the piece lacks unity of subject is completely to misconceive its purport ; and in point of fact it has usually been misunderstood. Horace is writing in one of those ages when men were not happy, did not relish their daily work. He begins by remarking the fact and asking what is the cause of it. Question them why they toil so incessantly, and they will tell you that it is in order to earn the means of subsistence, like the ant. The satirist denies the parallel, and in so doing discovers the cause of the general discontent. Go to the ant, thou over-active one ; consider her ways, and be wise ; when she has amassed enough, she rests. What makes men miserable is not anything inherent in the order of things, but their own insatiable lust for money. They are not conscious that that is their real motive. In fact Horace's method here as the self-constituted physician of his age is some-what similar to that of modern psychotherapy ; he makes the patient face the subconscious desire which is causing all the morbid spiritual friction. It is because he has thus diagnosed the malady of the times as competitive capitalism, that he then devotes so much space to a series of arguments against avarice. With his instinct for the concrete and the graphic he not only singles out an imaginary representative of this vice and from time to time conducts the argument in a sort of crude dialogue, but he portrays his opponent with all the telling accompaniments of the miser of popular tradition, as one who keeps an underground hoard of gold and silver, or gloats over his money-bags. In these days it would all be put in the technical terms of economics ; to the modern reader the miser is a stereotyped figure as almost totally obsolete in fiction as in fact ; with the result that he is apt to miss the applicability to contemporary society of the main points in

---

[1] X. 14-15 is quite another matter ; he is there defending his pro-fession of satirist ; it is relevant there. Apart from that, I can't believe a man would express himself as in i. 24-6 who had previously written x. 14-15.

[2] Cf. also 119.

this satire. And in others of Horace's works ; for this is only the earliest appearance in his writings of what is on the whole his favourite doctrine ; taking now an Epicurean now a Stoic colouring, but always fundamentally one and the same ; the doctrine that it is never external but only internal well-being that can make men happy. Our age of industrialism may find his misers tedious, but *mutato nomine de te fabula narratur*. It is not Silas Marners that he is thinking of. *Sit finis quaerendi, cumque habeas plus, pauperiem metuas minus*. There is perhaps a certain youthful aridity in the manner in which the doctrine is expressed here ; in the *Odes* and *Epistles* it is deepened considerably. To the last it retains its significance for the age of the automobile ; *strenua nos exercet inertia, navibus atque quadrigis petimus bene vivere*.

In the fifth piece he returns to the plain narrative form ; it is simply a diary in verse. Considering the occasion,[1] and still more the persons—Maecenas and Virgil, who mean so much to us ; Varius, who meant so much, apparently, to his own age—or set ; and others with interesting associations—it would, one must think, have been impossible to write an account that should be for posterity quite uninteresting ; but Horace has surely come as near to that as he or anybody could. Hogg can perpetuate the disgusting fare he had when in the very company of Shelley, but even he is fairly communicative on less ephemeral matters. The water was bad ; so it is in various parts of Italy to this day. The bargemen cursed ; what bargeman cannot ? At Feronia we had a wash ; well, that is perhaps significant ; it is the sole entry of its kind, and the journey occupied a fortnight. Maecenas joined us, and I put ointment on my bleary eyes. The bread was good here (not so the water) but gritty there. The water was bad again. The road was bad. Virgil went to sleep ; no wonder. There was, it is true, a local miracle on view at Egnatia ; where once more, by the way, the water was bad. Of the encounter, on the other hand, the encounter of wit, humour, subtlety, and refinement between Sarmentus and Messius, we hear enough to satisfy anybody, and are assured that the company enjoyed it. The water must have been good there. The scholiast tells us

[1] See p. 93.

that this piece was written in imitation of an account of a journey in Lucilius, and even if a Mexican-sounding extract [1] or so were not still extant we should have no difficulty in believing him. " The strictures on Lucilius in the preceding satire," says Gow, " probably suggested to Horace the propriety of writing a piece which should challenge comparison " ; and so far as that particular sort of " propriety " is concerned, it must have succeeded. The most charitable explanation is doubtless also the right one. Even if he had here recorded any remarks of Maecenas these would probably not have amounted to anything more diplomatically significant than " What's the time ? " [2]—his object being, as Wickham suggests, to show the ease and freedom and entirely non-political character of the intimacy.

Of the remainder, the eighth is obviously a comparatively early one.[3] The purpose, as in the fifth Epode, is to expose Canidia as a sorceress ; and here again this is done indirectly and dramatically. The form is narrative as in vii., v., and ix., but spoken in character. Maecenas had recently bought property on the Esquiline hill and was now building a house and laying out a garden ; the site had formerly been used as a paupers' burial-ground. The piece is put into the mouth of a rough wooden statue of Priapus which had been duly placed there, not so much for ornament as for use ; for Priapus, though the god of gardens, served also, in the utilitarian spirit of Roman religion, as a scarecrow.[4] Gow is, so far as I know, the only editor whose insight has detected in the narrative an aetiological mythus. This particular avatar of the divinity had a large crack in the rear ; and the satire " humourously explains that the crack was caused by the uncontrollable emotion of Priapus at beholding the horrible sorceries of Canidia and Sagana." Both the bones—for the graveyard is in the same scandalous condition as that in *Hamlet*—and the funereal plants, make the place unrivalled as a happy hunting-ground for witches, who explore it by moonlight to collect specifics. Of their nefarious proceedings on this occasion the statue is at

---

[1] Hinc *catapeiratera* puer deorsum dedit, unctum plumbi *pauxillum* raudus linique *mataxam*.

[2] Cf. *Sat.*, II. vi. 44.

[3] It is alluded to in several passages of *Epode* XVII.

[4] Wickham.

first, like Tam o' Shanter in a similar locality, a silent spectator. On the occurrence of the climax above referred to, the witches, of course, disappear in panic ; this is regular, but Horace's witches are not in themselves supernatural, and the miraculous and instantaneous element at Alloway produces a far more forcible effect :—

> Till first ae caper, syne anither,
> Tam tint [1] his reason a' thegither,
> And roars out : " Weel done, Cutty [2]-Sark ! " [3]
> And in an instant all was dark.

On such occasions the knowing artist will always be careful that after the catastrophe something is left behind from the material to the spiritual world, or vice versa. The tail of Tom's mare becomes the carlin's trophy ; Canidia and Sagana in flight involuntarily " coost their duddies " and jettisoned false teeth and a wig respectively, articles fortunately no longer thus incriminating.

The interest of the sixth satire is mainly autobiographical, and in that connection its matter has already been considered. The poet's intimacy with Maecenas had exposed him to malevolent gossip ; his object here is to defend himself, his patron, and the relation between them. At the same time he manages to preach some of his favourite lessons, denouncing ambition and extolling the simple life. Apart from the general circumstances which prompted him to write it, this satire has further, it is probable,[4] a particular occasion. The last line [5] gains in point if we understand that his patron had been urging him to become candidate for office. At or about thirty he would be of a suitable age for the quæstorship ; the satire then will belong to 36-5 B.C. If this occasion is not quite unequivocally indicated, the reason probably is that, as in the fourth satire, he

---

[1] = lost.   [2] = inadequate.   [3] = chemise.

[4] So P. J. Willens, followed by Gow.

[5] And others, *e.g.*, 7-22. On that difficult passage I entirely accept Gow's view ; he seems to me to have cleared it up wonderfully. I may also, perhaps, here point out, as supporting those who hold the *Appius* of line 20 to be the censor of 50 B.C., that when Horace wrote this, his was the last preceding censorship ; there was none between that and the quasi-censorship of Augustus himself in 28 B.C. Cf. Shuckburgh, *Augustus*, 137.

is still writing with his eyes focussed on Maecenas' coterie and not on posterity. The addressee is Maecenas, and it is noteworthy that the piece remains conscious of this fact, thus marking an advance upon other such in the first book.

The gem of the collection is, of course, the ninth ; a late one, since the writer is obviously well established in his patron's circle. Wickham is doubtless right in his diagnosis of its ultimate subject, and so of its connection with one of the main themes of the book. We are to be given a strong impression of the high ideals of Maecenas and his literary coterie, the absence from it of anything in the nature of jealousy or jobbery. But this is expressed the more effectively by being expressed indirectly and dramatically. Availing himself of the immemorial tendency of the *satura* in this direction, Horace casts his eulogy in the form of reported dialogue.[1] The result is something like a scene from a comedy of manners. It is thus in form approximate to those of the second book, as in point and finish of expression it equals any of them ; in liveliness it stands alone. The poet is buttonholed in his morning walk by a stranger, who proves to be an " æsthete " [2]—type abhorred by Horace—thirsting for admission to the most coveted but the most exclusive of literary social circles. The fun lies chiefly in the gross and blatant barefacedness of the intruder, in the irony of Horace's answers or asides (Lamb with the Comptroller of Stamps is farcical by comparison, mere horse-play), and in the increasing horror of a situation in which each successive attempt of the poet to free himself by withering —politely withering—his captor is foiled by the latter's impenetrable crust of egotism. For in his way the cadger is as invulnerable as the Stoic of the famous image,

> fortis, et in se ipso totus, teres atque rotundus,
> externi ne quid valeat per leve morari,

and upon him the point even of Horace's rapier *semper manca ruit.*[3] A good deal of all this is indicated in highly idiomatic

---

[1] Not, of course, that we have any reason to suppose the episode did not happen, perhaps very much as Horace tells it.

[2] 23-5.

[3] See *Sat.,* II. vii. 86-8. For an actual instance of still greater pertinacity and even thicker skin see Coulson Kernahan's *Swinburne as I Knew Him,* pp. 57-60.

Latin, and even then the points are often very delicate, rather hinted at than pressed ; so that if some translators, in their efforts to be faithful to everything, end by evolving a kind of language which nobody could ever have spoken either in a street or out of it, one may well be shy of blaming them. The effects probably cannot be represented without some sacrifice either of literalness to the text or else of English idiom, perhaps even of both.

> *Stranger* (seizing Horace's hand). Oh, how do you do, my very dear sir ?
>
> *Horace*, Very nicely as I am, thank you. As for you, sir, I wish you God speed. (*Proceeds. So also stranger. Then Horace stops.*) Can I oblige you with anything ?
>
> *Stranger.* Sir, with your acquaintance. Er—I am a poet, you know.
>
> *Horace.* Oh indeed ; then I shall be all the more pleased some day to—er—meet you.[1] (*Proceeds. So also stranger.*)

" But I am afraid," said Browning to a leech of this sort at a social gathering, " that I am monopolising you." " Have you not some relative," asked Horace, " upon whom you ought now to be paying a call,[2] somebody who would—ahem—be glad to see you ? " Later it appears that someone would be glad to see him, the plaintiff in a suit now due to commence, in which he is the defendant. (Was it for forcible entry ?) For once the fellow is almost nonplussed, and reflects aloud—this is a good touch of the ridiculous—" Which had I better renounce, now ? You, or my case ? " In the inimitable reply, " *Me —please !* " the disguise of irony as politeness reaches its climax ; for when the topic of Maecenas is introduced by the unsnubbable one, Horace bridles and becomes icy.[3] They run into Fuscus

---

[1] *Eris*, not *es*, and emphatic.

[2] Surely such is the point of 26-7, otherwise variously and sometimes perversely explained.

[3] 44 *paucorum . . . sanae* is said by Horace and implies " I see what you're after and I may as well tell you it's no good." The other understands it as a reply = " I don't get on so well with M. as some others do." Then at 45 I cannot agree with any of the existing interpretations. After *dexterius* I understand *hoc homine* from 47 ; after

Aristius, one of the poet's bosom friends, who, aware of the reputation of the third party, takes in the whole situation at a glance, but heartlessly enjoys it and refuses the distracted prisoner a single loophole. On his departure things look their blackest, when suddenly the plaintiff spies his man. One of the most effective tricks in the whole bag of the dramatic writer is to make someone say, either with deliberate ruthlessness (as Paulina in *A Winter's Tale*) or with sudden violence (as Emilia in *Othello*) the home-truth which every reader has been thirsting to hear told. After all Horace's strained formalities, the single phrase, shouted unexpectedly from a new quarter, " *Quo tu, turpissime ?* " gives at once the relief demanded and sums up the situation. That is the master-stroke ; but the immediate speeding-up of the conclusion in the last two lines is also very good.

All who share Horace's terror, less even of intruders as such than of talkers and bores (ix., 13, 33-4), will easily understand his impatience with the redundant and meandering manner of the voluminous Lucilius, whom he had called *garrulus* in iv., 12. His criticisms of the father of " sermo," more particularly the charge of slovenliness in versification, had it appears called forth indignant protests from a certain school of contemporary litterati. To them, or to an imaginary sort of a *bête noire* compounded of them (20-30, 52), the tenth satire addresses itself. The last line shows it to be the latest written, and we shall see that it reflects some modification of his theories of satire since he wrote the fourth. On the subject of Lucilius however his attitude is not changed but stiffened. The chief interest of the piece in relation to the basic ideas of this present study is, that we here see Horace as the practical poet breaking a lance with the dilettanti. We are hardly to imagine these

usus read a comma ; the bore prattles on (cf. 13, etc.) " Nobody can use a good introduction to better advantage than your humble servant ; I could improve your position considerably if you would only present me ; and, of course, you can trust me never to take an unfair advantage over yourself." *Nemo . . . usus* is thus explained by the following two lines—a habit very frequent in Horace. This, I think, not only gives the simplest sense here, but adds point to *quae tua virtus, expugnabis* (54), now seen to be an allusion to 45 (cf. *Epist.*, I. xvii, 41 in light of whole context) and therefore a clear hit ; the bore is met with his own argument.

opponents of his as grey-bearded "admirers of the old writers";[1]
such a school indeed there was, with its distinguished *doyen*
Varro, now aged eighty ; but these are far less *bona-fide* cham-
pions of the ancients than shallow partisans of the modern
and the fashionable, not so much jealous for the reputation of
Lucilius as jealous of Horace's. They may profess to admire
the hearty old knight, but they do not even understand the
desiderata in his kind of writing, and they are quite unacquainted
with his models, whose humane humour would indeed not suit
their mincing taste. Hermogenes Tigellius Bunthorne and
Demetrius the All-Right, they are the æsthetic oracles of their
day (17, 90-91). This satire represents at once the advertisement (81-90), and the preface, of a modern book. Horace
was not exactly a Wordsworth, but between Wordsworth's
reformatory principles and those of the Augustan court poets
there is much in common, and the essence of this piece is a protest against the current affectation [2] in diction and style, seen
for instance in the exotic theme (36) and the outré epithet (37).
The poet proclaims what he stands for, the virile as opposed
to the effeminate, the national as against the Alexandrine or
the Hellenising ; purity of vocabulary and compactness of
expression. The romantics of his age, with their eye (as ever)
on mere detail, enthused over the grotesquerie of foreign words
in Lucilius—whom I have elsewhere [3] compared to the romantic,
Browning. The point of Horace's reply to that (25-36) lies in
its implication, which is clear enough ; poetry is no mere
" fine " art for society ladies, but an art as serious, as national,
as practical, and even in its way as indispensable, as oratory ;
suppose yourself counsel for the defence in a great criminal
cause, with the prosecution using all the Latin at their command, and then see what would be left of your fancy tricks !
National poetry is, for us Romans, an immediate need ; the

---

[1] A phrase used by Sellar (57) in this connection.

[2] The force of Agrippa's dictum about *nova cacozelia* lies, I take it,
in its being a paradox ; affectation was just what Virgil and the rest
of them were out against ; but to the great field-marshal, *vir rusticitati
propior quam deliciis* (Pliny, *N.H.*, 35, 26), most poetry probably seemed
affectation as poetry, " and yours is the latest kind—' affecting to seem
unaffected.' "

[3] Below, pp. 189-90.

little we have, an Ennius or a Lucilius, is not up to the standards of this age ; of Greek there is ample ; and Latin verse on a Greek subject is a mere academic exercise.

All very well, but is satire poetry ? *Is* it " like oratory ? " In the fourth piece it apparently was not the former ; now Horace has discovered that it has affinities with both. It must not confine itself to the mirth-provoking or the ironical ; it must sometimes be serious (or rather perhaps indignant) ; [1] it must perform at times the function *of the orator and the poet* (12). It counts, that is, as poetry, not indeed according to modern but to ancient notions thereof, which included declamation.

These principles of satire (7-14), excellent as they are, represent, as I have just said, a discovery which Horace is just now making. To exemplify them from the book we have now considered would require an effort not to be justified by the results ; for so far from being the lines on which he has been writing satire, these are the fruits of his experiment. Throughout no small part of this book he has been learning by experience how *not* to write satire. On the other hand, they would make a more or less precisely appropriate motto, word by word, for the second book ; he has no sooner seen the trick than he puts it into execution.

THE SECOND BOOK

The order in which these pieces were written seems to be that in which they are arranged (it was like Horace to do so in one only of his publications) with the exception that the first must be transferred to the end ; [2] for a preface is naturally written last. But as Horace is no longer a mere proficient, it will henceforth be pointless, for our purposes, to follow the chronological order of separate poems.

Taking number one to be, as just said, a preface, we may note that the seven pieces which constitute the body of this book have a unity both of theme and form and style which puts them in strong contrast with those of the first. They are all ultimately tracts in advocacy of the simple life as the only

---

[1] *Tristis*, 11.
[2] *Caesaris invicti*, 11 ; and see Gow, Introd., p. xx.

really moral one ; they are all either dialogues (iii., iv., v., vii., viii., and incidentally i.) or marked by a tendency to pass into dialogue (ii.[1], vi.) ; and they are wonderfully uniform in maintaining the terseness and pungency of style, and the economy and distinctness of outline, which in the former book are perhaps only to be found in combination in the ninth, a satire that would, indeed, not show up unworthily if it had been transferred hither, though of no other member of the first book, unless conceivably the sixth, could this be said.

One result of all this is that I have less to say of them individually. My purpose in these chapters is not to save idlers the trouble, or hustlers the time, required for reading Horace, but to attempt to explain difficulties and to point out aspects of his work which seem to me to have been comparatively ignored. Now apart from the second (and we have here no concern with textual problems as such) and the eighth, where the reader is apt to be a little put out by apparent anomalies of Roman etiquette, these satires are perfectly easy to understand, and it is one of their virtues. The situations are within the grasp of anybody, the points are tellingly made. There are subtleties, there are allusions, but these have been practically all long since explained.

The first is naturally taken in connection with the last of the preceding collection. Some five years have now elapsed since that was published, and the jealous criticisms have, not unnaturally, shown that they were not to be silenced by it. Two other themes are also common to both pieces. A somewhat pointed (16, 29-34, 62-75) repetition, but without the previous reservations, of the tribute to Lucilius which the old outcry had extorted from him, shows that that copious journalist was still a popular idol. And the question of the function of satire is once more touched on. Besides its public and detective value, it now further appears as the poet's instinctive weapon of self-defence ; *nemo me impune lacessit* is the purport of lines 39-46 ; all of which is doubtless directed at the literary enemies afore-mentioned. Horace's egotism has, indeed, its unpleasing side, and in this satire we see it at its worst. The mood is self-conscious in the extreme ; he not only plumes

---

[1] See Gow, whom (with some reservations) I follow on this satire.

himself upon having enjoyed the favours of the great, but makes his supposed interlocutor overcome at last by this crowning argument ; he proclaims that his works have been admired by Augustus ; and the climax of the piece is the contrast between the wickedness of those he attacks and the blamelessness of himself.[1] Neither is there any humour in all this posture of resentful self-esteem (the humours of the piece lie elsewhere, in points of detail) nor, when he has bidden a general defiance to all detractors, does he improve the effect by then hurriedly taking cover behind his patrons. However, the piece distinctly makes promise of more (60) and better (16-18) things, which in the light of the sequel we can take as a half-conscious anticipation of the *Odes*.[2] Elsewhere his promises are to the opposite effect, that the present is his last appearance.

With this exception the book is spirited and entertaining. In these seven poems the chief excellence—the quality that has made them live—is, as so often in Latin literature, right on the surface ; it consists in the style ; it is in the parts rather than in the wholes. In the matter of form or subject the poems are, indeed, not without interest, both from the standpoint of literary history, as will be indicated presently, and even to some extent in themselves. Thus in the fifth, seventh, and one might add the eighth, individual passages for the most part derive their force or piquancy primarily from the situation and the character who speaks. Primarily, but not principally ; for even in those three, most of the good passages if separated from their context will lose incomparably less than they retain. And in general, the immediate passage is what counts ; you are led from jest to declamation, from maxim to elenchus, from description to narrative ; *unus et alter adsuitur pannus ;* not without the most skilful stitching, and, when the whole is viewed, not without some sort of a design, of course ; but it remains the symmetry of a well-executed patch-work quilt, never the " symmetry "—the vital unity creating its own

---

[1] *Integer* (85) is very different in effect from its echo in *Odes*, I. xxii. while in the Epistles he sees himself with a more Pauline consciousness of imperfection (cf. p. 264), and so even in this book, though less seriously, iii. 300-end, vi. generally.

[2] 16-18 is fulfilled by *Odes*, III. iii.

symmetry—of a tiger.[1] Satire at the best is an artificial, not
a natural, form. But one must be fair ; the style of this
second collection of satires has *bite*. It gets that, the supreme
quality of style, by means of (i.) crispness of sound, ring,
resonance ; (ii.) terseness, compactness, economy of words ;
(iii.) " colour," or the selection—in a decent proportion—of
other-than-ordinary words, now of allusive words, now of
queer words, now of proper names ; for the reader's appetite
must be maintained by an occasional judicious stimulant :

> tostis marcentem *squillis* recreabis et *Afra*
> potorem *coclea*.

That may not be the sort of thing men murmur to themselves
in the hour of danger ; but it has style, and therefore proves
more vital than the most exemplary sentiments which have not ;
and justly, since genuine moral feeling will make its own " bite "
on all occasions whether of fact or fiction, and the styleless
moralist is a hypocrite who would have other people good.
(iv.) Fourthly, the point is generally just sufficiently draped by
the expression, the reader's pace is just enough retarded, that
the acid of the language may have *time* to bite, that the sound
may sink in. That is how it is all done ; but even in verse
it is not always easy, and in prose it is, of course, impossible.

Along with this general stiffening of style which distinguishes
the second book from its predecessor, goes also a firming-up
of form. Each piece has a much more distinct unity of subject.
This is, of course, partly due to the writer's suddenly-acquired
mastery of technique in general. But there is demonstrably
another factor. Either he is here developing much more fully
certain tendencies latent in Latin satire (so far as it was Latin)
from its birth, or, what I take to be much more probable, he is
instinctively turning to such effusions of Lucilius as were most
purely Greek in subject and outline, and all but confining
himself to the exploitation of those.[2] And it is of course

---

[1] Tiger, tiger, burning bright
In the forests of the night,
What immortal hand or eye
Could frame thy fearful symmetry ?
—WILLIAM BLAKE.

[2] At first I thought he was turning rather less to Lucilius at all,
more to original Greek sources. And that view might seem to be sup-

quite possible, it is I suppose more than likely, that he is at the same time utilising some Greek materials directly.[1] For the important and interesting fact remains that the six characteristic satires of this book are all [2] of one type, a type not found in the first book at all ; and that it is a peculiar type of treatise which can be traced back, whether through Lucilius or not, to the Greek literature of what I call the Great Sophistic tradition ; of which tradition it formed one regular vehicle ; that it can be traced back in fact to Epicharmus, the patriarch of the debased Greek literature as Homer was of the classic.[3] Its marks are these : it is a dialogue between two persons, one of whom is some sort of a pundit—either a cook or a philosopher, a professor or a wizard ; and this professional person instructs the other in the rudiments of some particular " way of life," δίαιτα, whether within the actual sphere of " dietetics " or the closely connected one (as all primitive and even some modern thought recognises) of morals. Hence its wide vogue ; it deals with the eternal question, what shall we do to be saved ?—saved from our misery or our flatulence or from the sin that is the cause of both. In ages of cheap popular culture it provides the plebeian with the two things his soul most dearly loves, the two commodities he regards as indispensable, his

ported by iii. 11-12, where we get a glimpse of him packing Greek authors to take to his Sabine farm as raw material for his writings. But Archilochus of course is for the Epodes, and Eupolis and Menander can have supplied no more than touches here and there. Plato is much nearer the class of writing in question ; and the beginning of viii. is very like that of a Platonic dialogue ; the piece is a *Symposium* of sorts, not without its philosophising (65-74) ; still, this is a far cry. (Some think it is " Plato comicus " who is referred to.) On the other hand, ii. is demonstrably Lucilian in theme, and a Lucilian origin for viii., probably vii., and parts of iii. and v., is hardly to be doubted ; cf. Tyrrell, *Lectures in Latin Poetry*, 176-9, who sums up (180) " certain pieces of the two poets had a common basis and frame " ; well, that frame is a Greek invention.

[1] *E.g.*, for Stoic doctrines ; or perhaps Menippus for the situation in viii.—though he may have taken that too from Lucilius ; cf. preceding note.

[2] viii. is a partial exception ; it is not didactic, at least not directly, though it certainly has a " moral." But its topic, feasting, marks it as " sophistic."

[3] Cf. Plato, *Theaet.*, 152, E.

patent physic and his patent metaphysic. The aristocrat—I
speak, of course, of the ideal or complete aristocrat as he has
emerged at intervals from the welter of history, appearing
generally as a good democrat—the aristocrat knows not the
need of either ; he has his sports, and is not miserable ; his
arts, and is never costive.   He is for prowess and morality, " to
shoot straight and to speak true." He gives you song and drama.
But he never lasts long ; and after him come centuries when
men's two desires are, to overeat with impunity, and to *know*
what is likely to happen to them, what sort of a universe they
are let in for.   For them arises the type of didactic mnemonic
above described.   In the hands of poets it is, of course, apt to
be treated with more or less of playfulness.   In form it remains
a sort of catechism, sacred or profane ; in either case it preserves the tradition of an oracular pomposity, a style, of course,
equally serviceable for purposes of impressiveness or ridicule.

In his own examples of it, Horace is most serious in numbers
ii. and vii. of this book, ironical in v. and still more so in iv. ;
but he prefers, and hardly ever quite neglects, to alternate the
" rhetorical and poetical " with the diverting and " urbane "
according to his principle of *Sat.*, I. x.; and of this combination
the long third piece is the most representative.

Number two is a sermon [1] on plain living.   It is put into
the mouth of Ofellus, a self-taught " philosopher " of the type
of the poet's own father ; [2] but though Horace affects to be a
reporter merely, the doctrines are evidently congenial to him.
The logical beginning is at line 16.   Even in your luxurious
lives it will sometimes happen from one *contretemps* or another
that you are forced to appease a real hunger with a simple
meal.   You enjoyed it, of course ; sensation is in yourself
and not in matter.   That experience ought to teach you to
lead an active life on plain fare and so always enjoy your meals.
But no ; even within the sphere of diet you are a materialist ;
misled by mere appearance, with an eye only to the inessential,
you prefer dishes not according as they are wholesome but
according as they are rare or fashionable.   The simple life is

[1] I follow Gow to the extent (*inter alia*) of regarding it as in parts
a dialogue.

[2] *E.g.*, cf. his habit of pointing to living persons as warning examples,
55, 67-8.

then further defined in the light of the opposite extreme, meanness.[1] After this Ofellus enumerates the blessings which come in its train ; and the lesson is driven home when Horace, now speaking in his own person, tells us how the worthy man lived up to his principles, and of the noble words he uttered on the subject of his own misfortune. It is the old story, the Gospel of the pagan world ; vice is not merely sin, but folly ; and greed is a vice.

The implication of the fourth is the same, but its method is the opposite. It preaches the epicure's life, ironically. All the post-Socratic schools voiced what was ultimately the same doctrine ; they merely gave it a different complexion. It is always " *the* Gospel," now " according to " Chrysippus, now " according to " Epicurus. So here we must not be surprised to find the missionary of a supposed new " way of life " advertising his doctrines as the latest thing in the true. philosophic tradition ; they are to go one better than Pythagoras and Socrates and Plato (3). The *Sapiens* is the regular name for the ideal man of the schools ; but *sapere* is not only " to be wise," it means " to have a nice taste." We now hear the whole theory and practice of—not *sapientia* but *sapores* (36) ; we learn what will be eaten and drunk by the man that hath understanding (*sapiens*, 44). In the same spirit of parody is the whole deliverance of the apostle-gourmet couched in a mock-heroic vein. Immediately after the line

> ipsa memor praecepta canam, celabitur auctor

the comic surprise [2] of " eggs " begins the fun. To serve up a large fish cramped on a small dish is sin. An error in table-appointments is a crime. The whole piece is in the regular old didactic proverbial oracular manner.

The third and seventh are connected by the fact that the homilist in both is in process of becoming a convert to Stoicism. Each has for its text one of the paradoxes that were

---

[1] The proverb in 64 is given a punning application which, such as it is, has not, I think, been pointed out ; *canis* (cf. 56) represents meanness and foul feeding, *lupus* (cf. 31, 36) the fastidious diet of the epicure. " What am I to do ?—since it evidently *is* a case of ' between *lupus* and *canis* ' ! "

[2] Cf. *Sat.*, II. v. 10—*turdus*.

characteristic of the school; that every man but the philosopher is, properly considered, insane (iii.) ; or otherwise, that he is, in the true sense of the term, a slave (vii.).   In each case the speaker is appropriate to the text.   Damasippus, an art-connoisseur,[1] had developed that practice into a mania, squandered his fortune, and was on the point of suicide when a Stoic preacher cured him, proving to him that he was at least no madder than the world in general.   Davus is actually a slave in station, but has learned from a Stoic's house-porter to realise that there is no true slavery but that of sin.   The recipient of the sermon is in both cases Horace himself.   In spite of a certain amount of irony—Damasippus appears at first as a rather ludicrous figure, and the ultimate source of Davus' illumination is the once-ridiculed Crispinus—it is quite clear that the writer is himself to a very considerable extent in sympathy with the doctrines here put into the mouths of his supposed mentors.   When Damasippus proceeds to drive his lessons home, Horace represents himself as forced in the end to beg for mercy ; and when, in the other piece, we are shown the poet flying out into a rage with his slave, it is to imply that the shafts from that quarter were still more effective. And anyhow, the doctrines are all along expressed in such a form as brings them into line with Horace's invariable anti-materialistic crusading.   In fact, his attitude to Stocism has changed entirely since the preceding book.   Then it irritated him ; now it attracts him.

The third is the longest of the satires, but its structure is comparatively simple.   The bulk of the piece is a tirade against the folly of the world, under four main heads, avarice, ambition, " luxury " (including the Elizabethan sense of that term), and superstition.   The real excellence is in the style, according to the qualities thereof indicated a few pages back ; it is terse and forcible, and the points are driven in by a series of smart hammer-strokes, each of which hits the nail on the head.   A special feature of this piece is the number of " inset " dialogues, where the main merit lies in the skill which has fitted them to the exigencies of the hexameter without the least loss of

---

[1] Horace does not see the plastic arts as moral agents like poetry, but as among the worldly things which the wise man does not " care too much about " (*nil admirari*) ; cf. *e.g.*, *Sat.*, II. vii. 95-101.

sparkle and vitality ; or rather with all the more thereof. Particularly good is the little scene between the sick miser and his medical attendant :

> " ni tua custodis, avidus iam haec auferet heres."
> " men vivo ? " " ut vivas igitur, vigila ; hoc age."
>   " quid vis ? "
> " deficient inopem venae te, ni cibus atque
>   ingesta [1] accedit stomacho fultura ruenti.
>   tu cessas ? agedum, sume hoc ptisanarium oryzae."
> " quanti emptae ? " " parvo." " quanti ergo ? "
>   " octussibus." " eheu !
>   quid refert, morbo an furtis pereamque rapinis ? "

Staccato effects are frequent :

> exclusit ; revocat ; redeam ? non ! si obsecret !

There is a particularly admirable example—never yet, I think, remarked—of the playful adaptation of sound to sense, when a father is solemnly and impressively imposing an oath on his two sons :

> praeterea ne vos titillet gloria, iure-
> iurando obstring*am am*bo : uter aedilis fueritve
> vestrum praetor, is intestabilis et sacer esto.

It is a good story, and really comic as comparatively few Roman comic stories are, that the actor Fufius, performing the part of Iliona, a daughter of Priam and a wife and mother, who in a tragedy of Pacuvius was represented as having a vision of her murdered son in sleep, one day came on the stage so drunk that he went to sleep in actual fact. " When he was *sleeping off* Iliona," as the Latin succinctly puts it, the ghost of Deiphilus duly entered and began: " *Mater, te appello*," but on his receiving no response from the helpless lady the Roman audience quickly apprehended the situation and in a moment the whole theatre was thundering: " Mater ! te appello ! " (" Wake up, Mother ! ")

" No man does wrong deliberately "—the famous paradox of Socrates it is which forms the real theme both of this satire and of the seventh. Wrongdoers—and that means everybody but the philosopher—do what they do not mean to do ; there-fore they are, properly speaking, possessed. Or otherwise

---

[1] *Ingesta*, Markland ; *ingens*, MSS.

they are slaves ; they execute the behests of the tyrant appetite, not their own wishes. Such is the thesis expounded by
Davus. The occasion is once more the Saturnalia, and Horace's
servant is represented as availing himself of the immemorial
licence associated with that festival, by which slaves had entire
liberty of speech in addressing their masters. But this situation is not maintained very faithfully beyond its actual externals.[1] The reason is that although Horace is ready enough to
have a sly dig at himself here and there, he is more concerned
to make the lesson general. Indeed his main object in representing himself as the supposed recipient of it is to make it
less offensive, and for that purpose it is enough that only some
out of the various thrusts should appear to go home (*e.g.*, 28-9,
29-42, 111-15). Some twenty-five lines which begin the declamation reported by Davus from his fellow-slave are directed
against adultery, and at their conclusion Horace is heard
protesting that this particular tirade does not apply to him.
That " *non sum moechus* " is meant to be understood as literally true, seems probable from the serious tone of passages
where Horace speaking in his own person inveighs against this
vice or rather crime ; as, for instance, *Sat.*, I. ii. ; *Odes*, III. vi.
And his whole moral code and standpoint is just the sort which
is generally found to take a particularly strong line about
adultery. At all events, this passage, though very properly
the first to disappear in editions where expurgation is necessary,
contains what I must admit strikes me as the most effective
(because it is at once the most pointed and the most powerful)
piece of sophistical declamation in the whole two books of
satires. The adulterer, to gain admission, disguises himself as
a slave. " *Disguise ?* "

> tu cum projectis insignibus, anulo equestri
> Romanoque habitu, prodis ex iudice Dama
> turpis, odoratum caput obscurante lacerna,
> non es quod simulas ? metuens iuduceris atque
> altercante libidinibus tremis ossa pavore.
> quid refert, uri virgis, ferroque necari
> auctoratus eas, an turpi clausus in arca,
> quo te demisit peccati conscia erilis,
> contractum genibus tangas caput]?

[1] It *is* maintained to *that* extent, *e.g.*, 36 (what the slave overhears),
43, 96-100 ; but it has been remarked that there is no attempt to make
the slave's part realistic in *style*.

" Quivering with lust and fear together " is surely a physio-logical and psychological impossibility, but none the worse on that account as a striking and vivid phrase.

The fifth alone takes characters and situation from heroic legend. The seeker after illumination is Ulysses, the purveyor thereof Teiresias ; the occasion that of the heroic wanderer's famous visit to the underworld. Once more we are present at an exposition ; but here as in iv. Horace is in ironic vein ; the whole is mock-heroic ; the wizard initiates his pupil into the mysteries of legacy-hunting. The effect is, therefore, that of a satire upon the votaries of that ignoble art, and the piece falls into line with the writer's general campaign against the idolatry of money. The great sophistic dialogue-form took its settings from mythology, and this practice is, I suspect, to be traced right back to Epicharmus, who in such pieces as *The Marriage of Hebe* recast heroic situations in terms of everyday life. Of one grave charge Horace is almost certainly to be acquitted, that of having been the first to breathe upon the name (or the motives anyhow) of Penelope ; this joke he took over from Lucilius,[1] and we can hardly be wrong in attributing its invention to some funny fellow of the Hellen-istic age. *Obsequio grassare* [2] is a good phrase ; and there are others.

Plato's *Symposium* is the most elevated example of a copious class of ancient mime-satire, the semi-dramatic (in divers degrees) dialogue of highly-educated persons at dinner, on literary and philosophical topics. The most convenient label is perhaps that supplied by the title of a late (*circ.* 230 A.D.) example, the *Sophists at Dinner* of Athenæus. Bear in mind the general relation outlined earlier in this chapter between " Dialogue " and " Diatribe," and it will not be surprising that this class of dialogue also has its diatribe-like counterpart, humorous, homely, or grotesque. The education and refine-ment are here matters of pretension and not of fact. Obvious examples are the Cena Trimalchionis and the eighth satire of Horace's second book. In both the joke is against the host. Nasidienus is a *nouveau riche* who wants to give dinners in

---

[1] Cf. Tyrrell, *Latin Poetry*, p. 179.
[2] " Stalk him with little services."

the grand style but is much too much of a fool [1] to be able to carry through the affair successfully. He had evidently already made himself notorious as a host among Horace's friends—the satire seems to represent an actual occasion, and with the real names—for the absurd over-elaboration of his appointments and over-ingenuity of his *cuisine*, as well as for the conscious pride with which, either himself or through his *claqueur* Nomentanus, he drew attention to these points, in ludicrous unconsciousness of the breach of form. The piece has sometimes been at least partially misinterpreted. The key lies in the fact that Nasidienus takes dining as a thoroughly serious business (cf. iv.), the most serious, in fact, in life. Vibidius and Balatro are young bloods who are resolved to make a " rag " of the whole thing. And, of course, even apart from them, luck itself is against him ; there is an accident ; the host is reduced to tears ; his confidant consoles him by reminding him, in all good faith, of the disappointment that Fortune ever reserves for the most cherished of human dreams ; Balatro, " with his tongue in his cheek " (*suspendens omnia naso*) seconds ironically in the same vein ; the grossness of Nasidienus is blind even to sarcasms as withering as Balatro's, and he actually thanks the kind gentleman for his sympathy. It is just the grossness of this type, who evidently appeared then as now among the epi-phenomena of a world-war, that the satirist here aims at holding up to ridicule. And it is on the ridiculous aspect that he dwells, rather than on the gross directly, as a Juvenal would. *Ridiculum acri fortius ;* Horace aims at exposing, where Juvenal is declamatory.

The one remaining satire, the sixth, is not of the type characteristic of this book ; like the first, it is a reversion to the type of Book I., to the rambling discourse in his own person. Yet even so, with a difference ; it has more shape, proceeds more smoothly and intelligibly ; and it is more interesting, there is more smartness and sparkle in the style, more humanity in the matter. He contrasts the responsi-

---

[1] " There *is* that joke," as the Oxford (but it should really have been a Cambridge) don, who had classified all jokes in thirty-one types, is reported to have said whenever one was afterwards made in his presence ; there is that joke, and it may now be seen *passim* in post-war numbers of *Punch*.

bilities and worries which dog him whenever he resides in Rome, with the simple pleasures of his life in his Sabine farm. The point is summed up, and the satire concluded, by the famous fable of the town mouse and the country mouse, which as told by Horace becomes a little masterpiece of narrative verse, at once more artful and more skilful by far than might appear The passage is, if one may say so without fatuity, very Latin in style and very Roman in colour ; it is delightful to hear a mouse called *pater ipse domus*. Every description is unpretentiously but deftly graphic—

> tangentis male singula dente superbo

—or of the rich man's house,

> rubro ubi cocco
> tincta super lectos canderet vestis eburnos

—and the hush of night (or is it the stealth of the adventurers ?) is subtly suggested by a very slight but sufficiently abnormal assonance,

> iamque tenebat
> nox med*ium* caeli spat*ium*, cum ponit uterque . . .

After the catastrophe and the hairbreadth escape, the " rustic," proved right, contents himself with the irony " I really don't *need* this kind of life," and the piece ends on the appropriate note, " vetch." *Bos, sus, mus*, these are homely animals, and Roman poetry dwells fondly on their names [1]; the Roman imagination lights up at the mention of them, even when not for slaughter. It is significant of Horace's change of outlook that the mouse against whom the moral points is a pronounced Epicurean.

Form in literature is not the merely adventitious elegance it is often treated as ; it is as much the essence of a poem as it is of a work of any of the other arts. Nor is form proper the product of a cold sense of proportion (the " three unities " and such false " form " generally is what that produces) but of spiritual intensity. As the loquacious man is always shallow,

---

[1] Cf. Ch. VIII., p. 279, n. 1.

so surely and naturally does earnestness in its effort at expression tend towards the terse.

> di bene fecerunt, inopis me quodque pusilli
> finxerunt animi.

It is just in this point that Lucilius and Horace differ most. In his *Satires*, indeed, Horace's work is neither deep in thought nor firm in form as compared with its other two phases ; but even within the *Satires* it does make progress in both directions ; and the fact I wish to emphasise is that it makes them together. When the post-Actium reconstruction begins in good earnest, Horace discards both his early modes, the epode and the satire, simply because in themselves they were not good enough ; they were not capable, however handled, of being the vehicles of his message, so much had it by then become intensified. In the meantime, his invigoration and redemption of the Lucilian " discourse," in versification and diction from the very outset, in style and structure from the end of his first collection, and his gradual emancipation from the Lucilian grossness and shamelessness, are but two aspects of what is essentially the same advance. He ended by giving the *sermo* what artistic and moral vertebracy it was capable of taking. Many may think that that was not much. Earnestness has at any rate given him style ; we are now to see it, as it increases, lead him from style to form, true form, which was impossible to " the medley." In the *Odes* he still is, certainly, to some degree, " moralistic," but he is to a very much greater degree " moral " ; the form is worthy of the matter, the medium of the message ; the action is far more direct ; the æsthetic and the ethical factors are working in perfect harmony instead of merely doing their best independently.

But the writings of an ancient like Horace cannot perhaps altogether be understood by the modern reader until he has in some sort of way placed them according to *modern* literary categories, or at least shown them up in their true bearings both by contrast with some current forms of writing and comparison with others. An interesting paper on " Roman Satura and English Satire " was contributed by the late Mr. R. J. E. Tiddy to *English Literature and the Classics* (Oxford, 1912).

But, accepting as I do more fully (perhaps [1]) the wider conception of *satura* indicated in Nettleship's well-known essay, and convinced as I am of its connection with the older Greek sophistic or "mime" literature, upon which I take it to be based both in form and content, I cannot think that what we call " satire " is its true affinity. " Satura " or " mime " is not a category that we use much nowadays ; but for all that, it should be a very useful category. The reason why we do not use it is somewhat similar to the reason why the original Greeks did not call themselves Hellenes, nor the Greeks of history call themselves Greeks, nor the early inhabitants of Italy call themselves Italian ; a people is apt to be named from outside. Lyric, Drama, and the Epic—these are the true forms, these explain themselves ; they are the only things worth writing. Mime or Satura is what is not one of these three. Of course it is *about* something ; we have seen that it tends particularly towards certain subjects. But that is nothing to the point ; it is words, not action ; it is " about it and about." It is addressed only to the intelligence. It has not, in itself, though an occasional artist here and there may foist into it one or another of these things, either form, or function, or occasion. Take away from modern literature its epic, drama, lyric ; what you take away is small indeed compared with what is left over, and increasingly so as you approach our times. " Satura " is the form taken by native literatures other than the Greek ; it was the only native Roman form ; it is practically the only one that flourishes among ourselves to-day. *Si exemplum quaeris, circumspice.*

The novel—that is *satura ;* its Roman archetype is the *Satyricon* of Petronius, the last development of the pre-Lucilian miscellany. Long, rambling, colloquial, realistic, mostly about low life, tending to pornography or (failing that) to sentimentality ; these are the main characteristics. Horace, of course, is a satirist of the other lineage ; but I. v. is an obvious cousin. And anyhow, there is so much in common between the two types of *satura* that modern instances even of the novel may

---

[1] Mr. Tiddy speaks of the Ennian type as being, despite affinities, a " very different " thing (p. 203) ; but he offers interesting analogies to it in *Piers Plowman* and (as the special equivalent of Varronian satire) Cowper's *Task*.

supply illustrations of Horatian features. Gastronomy, for
instance. I doubt if it would be possible to find in modern
literature a more all-round analogue to the *satura* of Ennius
and Varro and Petronius, or a more remarkable example of the
way in which the various features even of this apparent miscellany and hotch-potch tend to repeat themselves (and often
quite apart from actual imitation), than the novels of Peacock.[1]
There you have the true deipnosophy, the zestful disputation
on *cuisine*, the learning and antiquarian spirit and light ironical
satire against progress, the series of mild adventures, all of
which are characteristic of one or more of the three Roman
writers just mentioned ; and you have its peculiar atmosphere,
neither quite serious nor quite devoid of seriousness, almost
never really comic but almost always slightly amusing.

Popular Science—Science at all, in so far as it masquerades
in literary get-up—there goes another enormous class of modern
books into the same category, where they will find plenty of
congenial company among the older contents ; and " Christian
Science " will fraternise not only with the Stoic ethic but with
a metaphysic as elastic as its own. I must repeat that I refer
only to scientific *treatises* and only from the literary standpoint ;
that once granted, it is quite simple ; such works come under
the class " didactic." I could hope that it were not necessary
to add here that this paragraph is perfectly consistent with
the utmost possible respect for all Science *as such ;* but Science
neither *is* literature nor can supply its place, and that is what
our age seems almost to have become unable to understand.

Literary theory and literary criticism ; that, too, is *satura ;*
and so far from boggling at the obvious inference, I will use it
to support my point ; the alternation of the satirical with the
moralistic, the general medley, the voluminousness, the awkwardness of expression—here they reappear, not through imitation, nor from choice at all, but because this, too, is really
satura, and these things haunt the writer in that kind.

Finally, here are a few parallels, taken quite at random as
beseems the subject :—Milton's prose pamphlets are *satura ;*
they are, ostensibly at least, moral in purpose ; profess to be

[1] Other instances in this kind—to take a couple at random—are
Rabelais, and the *Noctes Ambrosianae.*

written for the general good of the community, which end is found to involve polemical controversy and the rhetorical castigation of individuals. They exhibit the same peculiar blend of vigorous colloquial vocabulary with a formal and at times highly artificial style. Like Horace's, they are in passages autobiographical. In Milton's case, indeed, all these similarities are probably to be explained as unconscious imitation, Milton having, of course, known his Horace well ; in particular, his use of autobiographical digression—his way of adducing his past life in his present defence—is derived, I doubt not, from that source.

Landor's *Imaginary Conversations* are *satura*. Their Roman equivalent was Varro's *Loghistorici*, in which distinguished figures from past history conversed with one another on topics of inexhaustible importance such as the writing of history and the training of children. His model here was—of course—a Greek, Heracleides, an Academic philosopher of about 300 B.C. ; and *he*, needless to say, was following in the footsteps of that school's founder. So that when Landor shows up Plato and Lucian in conversation, to the obvious disadvantage of the former, he is turning the edge of the tendencious dialogue against its own inventor. This particular variety was long a favourite with philosophic and sophistic writers. Cicero's *Cato Major* and *Laelius* are examples of the same kind ; another is Lucian's *Dialogues of the Dead*, in which he was indebted to the cynic Menippus.

And much of Robert Browning is *satura*. He, indeed, presents in a number of ways a curious parallel to Lucilius. Rich, highly educated, energetic ; *in* society though never quite *of* it ; of generally liberal views, certainly for their time ; with no occupation, and by temperament as well as circumstances of a very copious, almost incessant, output—that much I suppose would readily be granted of both of them. To me they seem to have in common a good deal more. Neither of them literary artists, they strove to make up for their poverty and barrenness by the usual resort of throwing in anything and everything they could think of ; both thus tending to the grotesque and the macaronic. Both delight in pursuing the most trivial side-scent.

ut periisse velis, quem visere nolueris cum
debueris. hoc *nolueris* et *debueris* te
si minus delectat quod τεχνίον Isocratium est
ληρῶδες que simul totum et συμμειρακιῶδες,
non operam perdo.

In both the thought is as a rule fundamentally commonplace, and could not fail to appear so even to most of their
admirers if stripped of its verbiage and affectation and expressed accurately. As a versifier no less than as a composer,
Browning was, like Lucilius, a thorough and born sloven. I
shall, I know, make many people very angry by having said so ;
just as many were made angry when it was said of Lucilius.
The mere coarseness of Browning's versification is still regarded as originality by those who have never yet learned to
conceive of verse as something other than prose which scans
(or at other times can be forced to scan, with the indispensable
aid of a capital at the commencement of each line).

But Browning also serves our purpose here in providing a
modern analogue to the Horatian satire. We see from his
case what a vogue among the semi-cultured middle-class can
be attained by that sort of piece—short poems with a semi-
dramatic tendency, some monologues, some dialogues, some
narrative, some epistles—all preaching. We see in particular a
close parallel to the special type of satire I have drawn attention to as characteristic of Horace's second book ; one of the
most admired of Browning's shorter works is *Bishop Blougram's
Apology*—a dialogue between two personified " viewpoints " ;
a purely argumentative one, on an abstract issue, but disguised
with a superficial actuality to make it popular ; one speaker
presented as in the main authoritative, the other as on the whole
an *Adikos Logos*, the latter puppet being duly vanquished at
last—at very long last—by having a position [1] forced upon
him which any real Gigadibs would almost certainly not have
accepted. The form is substantially the same phenomenon,
despite some obvious differences in the tone conveyed to it.

[1] Oh, men spin clouds of fuzz where matters end,
But you who reach where the first thread begins,
You'll soon cut that !—which means you can, but won't,
Through certain instincts, blind, unreasoned out,
You dare not set aside, you can't tell why,
But there they are, and so you let them rule.

Abortive drama with a thesis ; that is what mime and *satura* really are ; that is the Platonic dialogue, the Euripidean literary-marionette-play, the Horatian satire. The thesis is the inevitable accompaniment of the abortion ; there are two factors, for the simple reason that the thing having miscarried is no longer one. Drama is action ; mime is argument in the form of mock-drama. The most obvious modern instance is the plays of Mr. G. B. Shaw, each of which has a " tendency." Drama is poetical and religious and imaginative and organic ; mime is prosaic and sceptical and realistic and ramshackle. Drama is the expression of an age of faith, mime of an age of science.

CHAPTER VII

COMPOSITION : "THE ODES"

ego apis Matinae
more modoque
grata carpentis thyma per laborem
plurimum circa nemus uvidique
Tiburis ripas operosa parvus
carmina fingo.

—Odes, IV. ii. 27-32.

ἐστὶ περὶ τὴν ἐργασίαν τῶν μελιττῶν πολλὴ ποικιλία.

—Aristotle, *Hist. Animal.*, 9, 40, 5.

THE Latin *satura*, whether we believe in its derivation from *lanx satura* (= hotch-potch) or no, had been before Horace, and was destined to become after him, a formless miscellany. The extent to which he succeeded in imposing form upon it has been indicated in the preceding chapter. As a good cook likes much variety of ingredients to harmonise into one concoction, so is a good poet all the more stimulated by the task of fusing a plurality of themes. When Horace turned from satire to lyric, he passed from a Roman tradition of slovenly discursiveness to a Greek one of extreme art and elaborate finish. But it is important to realise that multiplicity of subject, at least, was a feature no less characteristic of the latter than of the former. The difference is that here Horace had the example of artists before him, there he had not. Having plenty of originality himself, he was not paralysed by having to follow in the steps of great masters, but inspired by their success to make great advances in actual art upon his own previous work, and in many ways even upon theirs.

That some degree of complexity was felt by the Greek

lyrists themselves to be proper to an ode as such is partly
indicated by the use of the metaphor "wreath" as applied
thereto. An ode has to be *woven ;* if Pindar calls that "a
light matter," he must mean that it is so only for a Pindar ;
to "weld gold and ivory white in one, and therewith the lily stolen
from beneath the ocean dew " [1] is hardly given to everybody.
The hymns that he "plaits" are "variegated" (πλέκων
ποικίλον ὕμνον, *Ol.,* VI. 87). Horace indeed, in the ode from which
a passage has been taken as motto for the present chapter,
deprecates comparison between Pindar's methods and his own.
Pindar is a swan, himself a bee. But for one thing, the operation of bees is full of ποικιλία, as Aristotle observed ; and for
another, Pindar too compares his work to that of the industrious insect, when he says (*Pyth.,* X. 53) that the perfect
triumphal ode " flits like a bee from theme to theme." Fundamentally, their art is the same, in so far at least as its object
is to effect a synthesis out of diverse topics.

The lyric poet *par excellence* is thus, in classical tradition,
a sort of conjurer whose performance consists in skilfully keeping a large number of balls in play together—if a baser metaphor
may be substituted for the sake of convenience. When Horace
sits down to compose an ode, he knows that first and foremost
it must be *literary.* True, both he and Pindar believe in new
songs ; " praise old wine indeed," wrote the Theban, " but
the flowers of song must be fresh " ; *carmina non prius audita*
says Horace in the advertisement to *Odes,* III. But no ancient
poet " scraps " literary tradition in the way the present-day
singers do ; these have a horror—perhaps rather a terror—of
conventions ; the ancient poets utilise them. For the conspicuously *literary* surface of classical poetry there are several
reasons ; servility is not one, nor is lack of originality ; perhaps
the two most important as affecting Horace were, first, that as
" priest " of the Muses he must give a semblance of traditional
formality to his *carmina* or chants—that, however original the
phrases are (*notum si callida verbum reddiderit iunctura novum*),
they must have a sort of time-honoured *sound* about them—and
second that, within the limited compass of a lyric, it is quite
impossible for him or anybody to attain the big or deep or

---

[1] *Nem.,* VII. 77-9.

subtle effects he aims at, unless he avails himself of the possibility of suggesting by association. The poem must not *be*
an imitation ; because, for only one reason, there are many
other balls to be got into play ; but it must, in a detail here
or there, waken and play upon imaginative reminiscences of
half-remembered older poetry ; and it must, in its general
effect, disarm the natural sceptical attitude to all new poetry
by sounding like the real thing. This literary vesture is really
little more than the stalking horse under cover of which the
poet " shoots " (that metaphor is Pindar's) his new effects ;
but for all that, it is—at least it was for the ancient poet—the
first condition of his work.

DELIBERATELY " LITERARY " QUALITY OF THE *ODES*—HORACE'S RELATION TO HIS GREEK PREDECESSORS

It is not properly any demerit in the *Aeneid*, though it has
sometimes been thought so, that it reproduces many features
of the Homeric poems. On the contrary, it is to no small
extent a virtue, since to create a Latin analogue to Homer was
just Virgil's chief aim. Similarly, although Horace's purpose
in the *Odes* may be denoted in various ways, it is, primarily,
just what he himself said it was, to parallel in Latin the achievement of the Greek lyric poets,[1] and especially of Alcæus.[2]

Exactly to what extent the *Odes* as we have them are
modelled on the Greek Lyric in general, it is not possible to
say, because of the scantiness and irregular distribution of the
Greek remains. Of course we can point to a number of places
in which it is clear that the Latin poet has translated or paraphrased passages (which happen to be extant) from Alcæus,
Pindar, Anacreon, Archilochus, Simonides, Bacchylides. These
are well known and have often been quoted. But, apart from
the probability that there were more than we can know of,
such echoes are after all but a minor part of Horace's debt
to the inventors of the classic lyric ; and there is some ground
for thinking that they decreased in number as his work advanced. What would be more profitable, if it had been possible,
would be to see to what extent and in what ways the more

---

[1] *Odes*, I. i. 35-6.
[2] *Ibid.*, III. xxx. 10-14 ; *Epist.*, I. xix. 32-3, II. ii. 99.

formative elements of his lyric poetry, such as style, tone, structure, were imitated from the Greeks. Here we can, indeed, remark at once a general indebtedness to Alcæus, and also a general indebtedness, variously estimated by different critics, to Pindar ; also to Anacreon, who was, however, not an originator as those were. As regards style and tone, moreover, we can go somewhat further than this ; we may well fancy, for instance, that we see in one place a touch of the tenderness of Simonides, of the gravity of Stesichorus in another. But as regards structure, we are in a difficulty ; for apart from Pindar and Bacchylides, we have no Greek lyric poem which we can regard with certainty as complete, except Sappho's (complete and perfect) *Ode* to Aphrodite. However, on the subject of Horace's debt to Alcæus and to Pindar something more detailed remains to be said. Also, in the course of a very brief review of the development of Greek lyric, we may observe the first appearance of this or that feature which remained to be preserved by Horace, some such features becoming so general that the Latin poet himself may not have known to which individual Greek lyrist he was indebted. In the matter (for example) of earnest admonition in epistolary odes addressed to individuals, it might be rash to say whether he was under the influence of Alcæus exhorting his squire, or Sappho writing to her former pupils.

The rise and growth of Greek Lyric as a literary form, in the seventh and sixth centuries B.C., constituted a sort of " Romantic Reaction." In style and spirit as well as in metre poets rebelled against the hitherto universal tyranny of epic convention, much as our own Romantics rebelled against the eighteenth century. Similarly, on the more positive side, poetry set itself to exploit new themes and to express itself in a more spirited and spontaneous manner. Accordingly, whereas Epic had been impersonal, Lyric is personal ; Archilochus, Alcæus, Sappho, sang of their own animosities, delights, or loves. And—hardly less important, if at all, for literary history—Lyric is *thoughtful*, whereas Epic had been *picturesque*. Not only are the elegists, Callinus or Mimnermus or Solon or Theognis, sententious ; the lyrists proper, Alcæus, Sappho, Stesichorus, Simonides, Pindar, moralise according to their several degrees and ways. So much for content. In style, among other differences, they all react against epic smoothness and fluency and lucidity in favour of dramatic and abrupt effects and a certain oracularity. All of these three main characteristics are admirably preserved in Horace. He is very " personal," not merely in the obvious instances, but to some extent throughout ; even in the political odes he does not forget that he is Horace the poet-laureate, and often remembers, even in those, that he is Horace, the man, with preferences, *e.g.*, for the simple life. He is very moral ; he loves, that is to say, *the poetry of thought*, aims at achieving sublimity by giving noble sentiments a noble expression. And he studies a terse manner, sings with fine " attack," enunciates his themes boldly.

Some of these were more remarkable innovations than they might appear now that they are familiar. It probably required some courage, certainly some originality, to fit one's own ordinary everyday name into the metre and the time-honoured sanctity of Song. We may remember the consequences when Pheidias did the same sort of thing in sculpture. So far as our remains can tell us, Alcman seems to be the first to have done so.[1] It soon became an effective card to play, just occasionally, in the game of lyric. Sappho does it, and so does Horace just once, in a passage where he addresses himself, with a paternal geniality very much in Alcman's manner, to the maidens of his choir.[2]

The real originator of this romantic movement was—there can be little doubt—Archilochus. The soldier who runs away in battle is a coward, and there, for the epic audience, the matter ends. Archilochus, writing of war from personal experience, dislikes heroics ; the passage [3] in which he congratulates himself on having escaped capture at the expense of his shield is characteristic of his general nonchalance and paradoxicality ; and it gives the successive cue, through Alcæus and Anacreon, to Horace, *Odes*, II. vii. 10. The *Epodes*, then,

[1] Alcm., 25 and 33.
[2] *Odes*, IV. vi. 44 ; and for other Alcmanic features of the same poem see Smyth, *Greek Melic Poets*, on Alcm., iv. 39. That Horace knew Alcman's poetry seems probable ; cf. *Odes*, III. iv. 1-2, with Alcm., 45 ; *Odes*, I. xxx. 2, with Alcm., 21 (and see Bergk's note).
[3] Archil. *Fr.* 6.

in the composition of which Horace imitated the general *verve* of Greek lyric at the source, were thus a profitable rehearsal for the *Odes*.   Another link is the parallel between *Odes*, I. xxxiv. 12 *foll.*, with Archilochus, 56.

But Archilochus is, of course, only " semi-lyrical."   The purest expression of the Archilochian spirit in lyric proper is in the work of Alcæus.   And Horace was no doubt right in representing Alcæus as his main model.   It is not merely that the parallel passages are here more in number and closer in detail than in regard to the other Greek creditors.   The affinity rests on deeper grounds.   All the chief types of Horatian ode can be paralleled in Alcæus ; hymns to gods, political poems, admonitions to friends, songs of light love, wine and revelry. In particular, one of these types, the political song or στασιωτικόν was Alcæus' own invention ; Horace's national poems, however different, are a direct development from that ; and in so far as these represent the most important element in the *Odes*, in so far has Alcæus a very special claim to be Horace's pioneer and model.   But the Alcæan spirit goes further than that, and further does Horace follow it.   The truest affinity between the two is the affinity of general poetic temperament.   Each sings joyously of his own freedom of spirit ; and it is the same kind of freedom, the inner freedom of the poetic life, attained through the service of the Muse.   That the poet as such is endowed with a certain peculiar immunity is one of Horace's favourite ideas ; and the germ of it is in Alcæus.   Horace rides a freelance in the spiritual world, Alcæus had been a freelance literally.   This affinity was quite clearly felt by Horace himself.   When, in I. xxxii., addressing his lyre, he speaks of it as " first played on by the Lesbian citizen," he adds this picture of Alcæus :—

> qui ferox bello tamen inter arma,
> sive iactatam religarat udo
>   litore navim,
> Liberum et Musas Veneremque et illi
> semper haerentem puerum canebat
> et Lycum nigris oculis nigroque
>   crine decorum.

It is in precisely the same spirit that he depicts himself :—

> pone me pigris ubi nulla campis
> arbor aestiva recreatur aura,
> quod latus mundi nebulae malusque
> Juppiter urguet ;
> pone sub curru nimium propinqui
> solis in terra domibus negata :
> dulce ridentem Lalagen amabo,
> dulce loquentem.[1]

Over and above all the multiplicity of the *Odes* there is un-doubtedly intended to be a prevailing harmony and unity of spirit ; often though they are placed, and deliberately, as foils to one another, they are meant to voice one view of life, one poetic character ; and it is for this reason that Alcæus is taken for their one arch-patron, that he is the precedent not for this and that type only but for the variety of the whole. Or, as Sellar wrote : [2] " By claiming Alcæus as his prototype he seems to imply that he regarded his lyre as equally tuned to the lighter pleasures and to the sterner and more dignified interests of life."

But there is another side to all this. Alcæus, if one goes direct from his reputation to his remains, is a disappointing poet.

> ἦρος ἀνθεμόεντος ἐπάιον ἐρχομένοιο

is a line of perfect loveliness, but it represents a level that its author very seldom reaches, if indeed ever again. For one does not, in sober verity, *hear* spring approaching ; and Alcæus habitually writes of what is—splendid, no doubt, or vivid, but always actual. He has grace, but no charm ; and energy, but not power. His catalogue of his armoury is typical; desirable objects enumerated with satisfaction ; splendour without wonder. Alcæus deals with fine themes, but in exact language. Horace, in fact, cannot have got his *style* from Alcæus, for Alcæus can almost be said to have no style. And, though an Opposition may become a Government and its

---

[1] I. xxii. 17-24, but see the ode generally ; cf. also III. iv. 21-36, esp. 25-8. Poetry confers a saving grace on the cause or the individual with which it is associated, that is the idea of III. iv.

[2] Sellar, *Horace*, etc., p. 136.

policy then appear in much more glowing colours, it still remains
a far cry from a " faction-song " to a national ode.

The evolution of the Greek lyric proceeded. Stesichorus is
the next landmark, and a very important one. He started a
new school, which continues to the end of the lyric period ;
in his train are Simonides and Pindar. Briefly, he swung the
pendulum back from Archilochus. He reached towards epic,
towards the heroic generally ; he made lyric epical. Up to his
time, the lyric, whether it were the direct utterance of an
individual poet or composed for a choir, had been personal ;
the choirs of Alcman and Sappho had had playful personalities
written for them. With Stesichorus it became impersonal.
That a lyric might be in the grand style and yet still be a lyric,
that was the discovery of Stesichorus. To his poems Horace,
who mentions him [1] (*Stesichorique graves Camenae*, *Odes*, IV.
ix. 9) may well have owed a direct debt in various ways ; [2]
unfortunately his remains are exceptionally scanty even for
lyric. But of the indirect debt there can be no question,
nor of its importance. The whole side of Horace that contrasts him with Alcæus, in whom it is conspicuously absent—his
national idealism, his moral earnestness, his elevation of style,
his sense of the sublimity of heroism as in the Regulus ode—is
ultimately traceable, as a constituent of lyric, to Stesichorus.

Greek lyric thereafter is in its main stream no longer naive
lyric, but grand lyric. Ibycus alone wrote separate poems of
either type, the Dorian and the Aeolian ; to that extent he
may be regarded as a precursor of Horace. [3] The later Ionian
blend of Alcæus and Alcman, the elderly amorist Anacreon, is
in one sphere much more Horace's model than Alcæus was ;
in the sphere, that is, of light unimpassioned graceful love-
poems or wine-poems. Horace in one place warns his Muse
that she is in danger of taking upon herself an alien function,
that of the " Cean dirge " ; and in passages where he laments,
with such poignancy as rhetoric can command, the devastation
wrought on men and things by the Civil Wars, he may well be

---

[1] And again *Epod.*, xvii. 42-4.

[2] *E.g.*, the " palinode," I. xvi.

[3] There are also parallels : *Ibyc.* 1, *Odes*, II. ix. ; *Ibyc.* 2, *Odes*, IV. i,
init.

under some influence from Simonides of Ceos.[1] That poet must
in any case be mentioned here, were it only that by his invention
of the *epinikion* or ode of victory, with its inset of heroic myth,
he is the link between Stesichorus and Pindar. But apart
from that Simonides was the originator in lyric of certain
features that remain prominent in Horace. Living at the time
of the renewal of the national athletic festivals, and then
through the Persian wars, he was the first to make the Greek
lyric national. He, before Pindar, made it his object in the
epinikion to link the glory of the present with the wonder of the
past. He commemorated contemporaries—another innovation
—along with the old heroes ; even so does Horace place Augustus, drinking nectar with his purple mouth, beside Pollux
and Hercules. As Smyth observes,[2] he is the first poet who is
also a critic, who is interested in the theory of his art ; and
here is at least a further point of affinity with Horace.

Finally, there is Pindar. As already remarked, Horace
himself deprecates comparison with the swan of Dirce. But
often in the *Odes* does Horace in light irony deprecate the
attempt to achieve something which he has as a matter of
fact himself achieved a moment before, even if then only for a
moment. I have already implied,[3] and I hope to show still
further presently, that I think Horace is to a considerable
extent the disciple of Pindar, both in regard to style (which
in these two poets presents a special blend of magniloquence,
allusiveness, and oracularity) and in respect of composition
proper, that is to say, in the structure or perhaps rather *conduct*
of an ode, the abrupt commencement with something the
exact relevance of which to the true theme does not appear
till further on, the sudden transition the point of which is
similarly left to explain itself, the allusively-introduced story
whose present significance is left to the context and the reader
between them. It was from Pindar that Horace learned how
to manipulate, and where to dispose, the various ingredients
which his first instinct selected for the material of each ode ;
it was from Pindar that he learned to be elliptical. Or if it

---

[1] That Horace read Simonides is attested by his having appropriated
a gnome or two ; Sim., 65, *Odes*, III. ii. 14 ; Sim., 66, *Odes*, III. ii. 25.

[2] *Greek Melic Poets*, p. 306.

[3] Ch. III., pp. 73, 76 foll. ; Ch. VII., p. 193.

was not from Pindar, then we are the victims of the caprice of textual tradition, for surely there are no other [1] extant Greek lyrics that are at all comparable to Horace's longer or more close-packed odes for unity in complexity.

The history of Greek lyric—and the statement could be much more amply substantiated in a fuller account than I have here found space for—is a series of syntheses made by a succession of creative artists. Horace in lyric is the direct successor to the Greeks, and made, as it seems to me, the crowning synthesis of all. First was Epic, then Simple Lyric; then came Stesichorus to make a synthesis of these two and produce Heroic or Ornate Lyric. Ornate Lyric culminated in Pindar. Then came Horace and effected the synthesis of Simple Lyric with Ornate Lyric. In the metres of Alcæus and Sappho he wrote with the art of Pindar.[2] His work is like the Aeolians' in limitation of length, in compactness of rhythm, in precision and directness and lucidity; but it is like the Theban's in loftiness of theme and tone, in richness of style combined with economy of language, and in elaborate poetic artistry. The *Odes* of Horace were thus the consummation of the Ancient Lyric. They are now that and something more; of a very large proportion of it they are the sole surviving representative.

But, of course, all this is not to imply that Horace as a lyrist is not in the highest degree original. Rather the contrary; for to make a true synthesis, one which has artistic individuality, demands creative originality in the poet. Apart from the skill by which he makes the Latin language move freely in rhythms it had never known before, there is the splendid sonority, a quality comparatively absent from the work of his Greek predecessors, owing to the degree in which Greek lyric had in its inceptions been dependent on a musical setting. The Horatian lyric makes its own music. Such passages as he deliberately transferred he sufficiently transformed in the process; and his actual poetic art, however much he learned its basic principles from Pindar, is in the result quite his own, as may be seen, for example, in his skilful foiling

---

[1] Not Stesichorus, though he did invent the Ornate lyric; for Stesichorus, we learn from Quintilian (X. i. 62), was redundant and diffuse.

[2] *Magna modis tenuare parvis,* as he himself puts it in the last line of one of the most Pindaric of his odes (III. iii.).

of the grave with the gay and *vice versa*, a resource unknown to the Greek singers. His practice in this respect is really the exact lyrical analogue to his principle of satire :—

> et sermone opus est modo tristi, saepe iocoso,
> defendente vicem modo rhetoris atque poetae,
> interdum urbani, *parcentis viribus atque*
> *extenuantis eas consulto.*[1]

Pindar by comparison " sows with the sack."

OTHER CONSTITUENTS OF THE HORATIAN ODE

Horace rarely or never seems to paraphrase a Greek lyric *en bloc*. One reason is that, while he regards it as desirable that each ode should commend itself to the conscious or unconscious reader by a subtle suggestion or general aroma of Alcæus or Anacreon or another, that is only one of several desiderata. Every normal ode, for example, has to have an occasion, a contemporary occasion, actual or imaginary ; the weather, a feast, an anniversary, an act of worship, and so on. And every normal ode must have an addressee, whether god, or mortal, or more rarely an inanimate object. Another almost inevitable element is the moral one. Then there is the mythical element, which varies in bulk from a story more or less fully told or indicated, to a passing allusion. There is the national element ; not merely the Roman colouring, but the Roman tone. And very often there is the personal element ; the poet inserts something about himself. This last may at times be identical with one or other of the foregoing (*e.g.*, the occasion), but not necessarily, and it is a distinct constituent.

Bearing in view the general lines already laid down for the interpretation of the *Odes* of Horace, partly in Chapter III. (pp. 68-81) and further in IV. (pp. 113-14), as well as in the preceding pages of the present Chapter, we may now briefly examine the majority of the collection, passing over several that have already been sufficiently considered in one context or another. It will be convenient to examine first the longer odes, or those to which the poet evidently wished to give special prominence ; partly because the notion is still often

---

[1] *Sat.*, I. x. 11-14.

entertained in one form or another, that Horace's *Odes* do not really mean anything much, that he was a specialist in metrical effects or a dallier with conventional poetic dainties, and these particular odes refute the notion; and further, because we may here see Horace's poetic method *in extenso*, and so be perhaps more prepared with clues for other pieces in which he has applied it more sketchily or elliptically or idly—that is to say, for his more compressed or more casual poems.

The More Elaborate or Complex Odes—Horace and Pindar

Recently, in his *Sappho und Simonides* (1913), Wilamowitz-Moellendorff has published an essay on *Horace and the Greek Lyric Poets*, in which he takes the view that Horace never got the length—or rather deliberately renounced the idea—of writing a Pindaric ode. The *Carmen Saeculare* was " a Pindaric commission," resulting, however, in an ode which still [1] " held to the Sapphic form." IV. ii. (*Pindarum quisquis*) is, he thinks, the result of the renunciation; I. xii. (*Quem virum aut heroa*) is one of the latest in the first three books, and had gone the length of challenging comparison by beginning with a Pindaric tag; IV. vi., a processional, takes its " myth " from a processional of Pindar's, part of which has been recently discovered; [2] in IV. ix. the admonitory element is Pindaric.[3] Only in IV. iv. (*Qualem ministrum*) has Horace attained to composing as greatly as Pindar, but even there [4] " what he composes is his own, and is Roman." So Wilamowitz.

It seems to me, however, that it is only if Pindar's *metrical* complexity is in question, that we are justified in saying that Horace never wrote a Pindaric ode; it is true he never wrote in triads, nor does he care to rival Pindar in length. But Pindar did not only write long poems; the twelfth Olympian seems to me very characteristic; the occasion (a victory for which the winner, once a Cretan, could not have been eligible had he

---

[1] Metrically, yes; in length, style, tone, structure, etc., **anything but** !

[2] See Pæan VI. in Sandys's *Pindar* (Loeb), 75-86.

[3] No doubt; but why only there ?

[4] No doubt; but that qualification was inevitable.

not through exile become a Sicilian) kept to the end ; the moral drawn from it (you never know your luck, so it is best to have faith) made to precede it, and given the value of independent statement as an eternal truth ; and then the whole disguised at the beginning as an invocation to the Goddess Fortune. That is surely quite like Horace's method ; I am not thinking of I. xxxv. alone. Horace's way of inverting or otherwise disguising the order in which the main thoughts had first suggested themselves ; his habit, at a pause or juncture, of passing on, not direct to his next point but to something introductory thereto ; these devices, to ensure that each utterance shall get the benefit of arresting and apparently independent statement, are among the most fundamental features of his art, and these he surely learned from Pindar. The only difference of any real importance that I can see is that Pindar—

> monte decurrens velut amnis, imbres
> quem super notas aluere ripas—

Pindar is like a stream in spate, he is apt to be turbid ; *cum flueret lutulentus, erat quod tollere velles;*[1] Horace by comparison is rather like his own Liris—

> quieta
> mordet aqua taciturnus amnis.

At all events, I agree with Wickham, Gow, and others in seeing a distinctively Pindaric structure, often combined with an equally Pindaric style, in such odes as III. iii., iv., v., xi., xxvii.; IV. iv. ; while, as Gow well puts it, " the Pindaric tendency . . . to wander into mythology may be noticed too in many of the shorter pieces," examples of which he gives in *Odes*, I. vii., xviii. ; II. iv., xiii. ; III. xvii. ; IV. vi.

III. iii. and iv. have been already dealt with (Ch. IV., pp. 106-7 and 111-12). The latter, it should be added here, is a fine example of the unity which Horace can achieve out of complexity. The harmonising idea of the whole ode is, the saving power (the saving *grace*) of poetry. Poetry is on the side of the angels (*i.q.* the gods) ; and they are on the side of poetry. For its sake, they keep the poet under their special care (9-36). So if poetry is on *your* side, you are safe ; and

---

[1] Horace, of course, says this not of Pindar but of Lucilius.

Augustus' régime has poetry on its side ; we poets fight for him, as Apollo and Athena (cf. Bacchus in II. xix. 21-8) fought for Jove against the giants. It is intellectual power *versus* brute force ; *that* is how we poets are powerful.

Shakespeare in the first of his sonnets urges the young man whom he addresses to marry and have children, and in the eleventh poem of this book Horace gives similar advice to a young girl. The ode, like many, is directed *at* rather than *to* the admonished person ; it begins with an invocation, partly of Mercury, the god of gentle persuasion through music, but principally of the poet's lyre, once as a tortoise entirely absorbed in its single animal vitality, now a thing acceptable, hearkened to, and revered. The lyre is besought to utter such strains as may prevail with Lyde, who still throws up her heels like the filly in the meadow, and bolts at the thought of matrimony. A filly in some story-book of my infancy was, I remember, told fables by its mother, but when the worthy mare began to wind up with the moral, it would always canter away. Lest Lyde should do likewise, not only is the moral conveyed to her wrapped up in the fable itself, but the fable which is the kernel of the whole poem and represents the lyre's own answer to the singer's initial request, introduces itself quite innocently as a mere development ; a development of what is artfully designed to be intrinsically much more attractive to the ear of idle female youth, namely, the enumeration (still made to the instrument itself and in ostensible disregard of Lyde) of the lyre's own wonderful exploits. This choice of an *apparently* accidental starting-point for his main myth is, of course, a device derived from Pindar, but employed here with, I think, distinctly more point and charm. Wickham complains that " the application of the story is not very close." Tyrrell declares that it is " entirely irrelevant " ; [1] and no wonder, when he so far misunderstands the situation as to imagine that the poet himself is the supposed suitor ! With such an idea, it is strange that he should have missed so obvious an opportunity of being amusing (as he certainly sometimes is) at Horace's expense ; for surely it should be remarkable that

---

[1] Though two lines lower down he has discovered that it has " very little " reference to Lyde.

Hypermnestra is held up by the lover as an example to the reluctant object of his addresses, on the somewhat inadequate ground that she refrained from knifing her husband at the commencement of the wedding night, and amicably dismissed him at its close.

The story of the Danaids must have been, as Ritter argued, especially familiar to the Roman public about this time, as it formed the subject of a sculptural group in the portico of the famous temple of Apollo on the Palatine, consecrated by Augustus in 28 B.C. The significance in mythical tradition of the single one among so many sisters to become a mother and a national ancestress is not open to doubt; she stands for womanly desire of offspring.[1] Romantic attachment to the father is not suggested as a motive by the Aeschylean reference; neither does Horace attempt to influence Lyde through any such appeal. The myth is surely as appropriate as it need be considering the poet's purpose.[2] Not only is it natural that Horace, somewhere about his " eighth *lustrum*," should be moved by the sight of a lively healthy young woman of his acquaintance to hope that she might fulfil herself in matrimony, but it is obvious that Augustus with his schemes of marriage reform would be expected to look with favour on a poem of this tendency. And it must be remembered, as a consideration doubtless not forgotten by the poet here, that Hypermnestra's act was proved by the event to have been not only humane, but patriotic.[3]

" Sad stuff," wrote Landor in his pocket *Horace*, at the end of III. xxvii. This is the " ἀποπεμπτικόν," or valedictory address, to Galatea about to go on a voyage, and telling her the story of Europa. It is not perhaps one of Horace's very finest odes; though Mr. Mackail has put it in his hundred best lyrics of the Latin language. The poet has not succeeded in avoiding the strained sentiment, false pathos, and frigid rhetoric to which the ancients in general show so strange a tendency whenever they are dealing with that most difficult

---

[1] Aesch. *P.V.*, 865. Cf. also Mr. J. T. Sheppard's view of the conclusion of the Danaid trilogy, *Greek Tragedy*, p. 30.

[2] Gow rightly draws attention to the force of *virginum*, l. 26. But I cannot agree that Lyde was already a married woman.

[3] Cf. Sheppard, *loc. cit.*

of all myth-material, the animal-transformation-story. The character of Europa seems harsh and Euripidean ; her purely external conception of female honour (for between loss of reputation and loss of modesty she sees no distinction) *and* the bloodthirsty vehemence of her fury against her unknown kidnapper, form a combination that is particularly unpleasing. But the two stanzas in which her fabulous voyage is described are perfect in the simplicity, the charm and the directness of their imaginative pictorial effects. And the conclusion is delightful ; it is strange that Landor should have seen no grace or playfulness in the consolation given by Venus : " Don't cry ; you shall have a whole continent named after you." It is less strange that he should have been quite unaware of any climax, or of any connection between such climax and the occasion of the ode. On that point it seems to me that the commentators have gone wrong in pressing the analogy too closely. They suggest that Galatea is urged to turn for consolation to the wealth and greatness of some distinguished person who was to be the companion of her travel. If that were so, it is hardly likely that Horace could address to her the phrase " ubicunque mavis," she having then, of course, no choice ; nor again would " et memor nostri Galatea vivas " be very tactful in that case ; on the contrary it might be highly dangerous. Rather I believe that in these last three lines Horace means to comfort her (he is always an egoist in such matters) for her severance from *himself ;* in his feeling for her there appears no passion, but there is, as has been said by Wickham, some tenderness and kindliness ; " I am always your well-wisher," he would say, " do not forget me, but in your remembrance of me let there be no reproaches nor regrets "—and then the last stanza speaks quite clearly : " After all, our acquaintance has not been without good fortune for you ; your name shall be famous for ever—in my verse."

The Pindaric features of IV. iv.—the opening simile of the eagle, the archæological digression, awkward enough, of 18-22, the series of terse fine maxims, the conclusion in a noble prophetic speech [1]—are about as unmistakable as the general drift and single purpose of the poem.

---

[1] Wilamowitz compares the prophecy of Teiresias at the end of the 1st *Nemean* (*Sappho und Simonides*, p. 320).

I now turn to a more compressed and elliptical piece ; complex though not Pindaric. III. xiv. has fared roughly at the hands of critics. Peerlkamp and others have even denied that it is genuine. Wickham himself, who as usual shows the points well, calls it " not in Horace's best manner." Perhaps it is not, quite ; but, properly understood, it is very charming. As might be expected, the favourite subject of complaint, in one form or another, is just what constitutes the point ; Lehrs would delete the last three stanzas, Page finds their contrast with the preceding very harsh, Gow protests that the thoughts are jerky. But Tyrrell's is the naivest comment : " how sweetly," he remarks with irony, " how sweetly but uncharacteristically reasonable is the lover who bids his servant summon the charming Neaera in all haste ! adding, however, ' If there is any difficulty about her coming, never mind ; return without her,' ! " While others merely neglect to envisage the poem as a whole, by Tyrrell even the immediate context is ignored ; though four pages later he can quote it (deprived of half its significance) with approval ; such are the results of absorbing the text of Horace piecemeal. The poet has, as a matter of fact, but one purpose in this short ode. It is intended to convey a sensation of relief, ease, good humour, and gentle conviviality, as the direct result of the return of Augustus from a victorious campaign. If Horace had been " classic " in the vulgar sense, he would have hailed the conqueror with inflated epithets, and woven in elaborate allusions to the particulars of the war ; and then, if his work had survived, it would have been understood and explained by commentators. In a less happy moment that is the sort of thing he does ; [1] but here he is too festive to bother about local colour from Spain ; and the allusions, which are brief but pointed, are chosen rather with a view to the poem itself than to the occasion. He first imagines himself addressing the crowd [2] assembled to watch the triumph (voted but, in fact, refused) ; Cæsar, who

---

[1] *Odes*, IV. iv. 18-22.

[2] *Plebs* ; some editors say that that is here, for once, a synonym of *populus* in the strict sense ; but why should it be ? It is not inclusive, as 5-12 show.

was just now rumoured on the point of death,[1] is returning from yet another of his Herculean labours for humanity, the defeat of the Cantabrians ; it is a religious function ; with a momentary assumption of his priestly tone the poet enjoins silence. For his own part, he will spend the remainder of the day as a holiday ; secure in the reflection that the rule of Augustus means peace in Italy and order in Rome. Now is the time for every lazy sun-loving genial playful thing that may have survived the cataclysm to come forth and enjoy itself ; for a Horace, who though fiery enough " in the consulship of Plancus," had the discretion to withdraw from battle ; for a jar of the wine-god, who though not without his fiercer aspects (*Odes*, II. xix. 25-8 and generally), and tracing his nativity, in this case, to the very commencement of the long period of civil wars, has yet succeeded, simply by lying low, in escaping even the worst and widest depredations which Italy was to suffer during the ensuing sixty years. Thus does he subtly relegate these battles of long ago to the region of old unhappy far-off things, with a touch at once of romance and of Cæsarian propaganda ; this wine is mellower since the fratricidal eighties, and so are politics. Now too let Neaera come, if she is willing ; and if she is not, none shall force her ; the age of aggression and militarism is past ; [2] the times are milder now, and he feels he cannot more effectively suggest it than by winding up with a description of how he himself is growing milder. The last word is, as usual, quite deliberate, and on his contemporary public its effect would not be lost ; for even if some of them had forgotten that Plancus was consul in the actual year of Philippi, he had at least been notorious as a political turncoat, and his name stands here as the reminder of a time when men as well as wine-jars were often hard put to it to survive.

The only complaint that might be reasonably made against such a poem as this—though for my own part I should not make

---

[1] *Morte* is the emphatic word ; we had feared that the Spanish campaign of Cæsar was to end as fatally for him as did that final expedition of Heracles against Eurytus. Editors misinterpret the allusion.

[2] Wooing the *demi-monde* was regarded as a sort of war ; the metaphor is too common in Latin poetry to need illustration ; *militat omnis amans*.

14

it—is that, as often happens with the post-mature work of a constructive artist (Beethoven's is a good example), it runs a little too much to bone; the connections are left to be supplied by the hearer; the inherent richness of the combination is suggested rather than expressed. Why not express it, then? Because to a reader already sympathetic, through familiarity, with his author's harmonies, the instinctive response of supplying them gives a peculiar pleasure. Much more, even of the general appreciation of poetry than is commonly supposed, depends on some degree of such unconscious self-training in literary associations. But to the typical Romantic, with his eye ever on surface qualities to the neglect of structure, and his *penchant* for meandering descriptions and high colouring, one can easily understand that a poem so full of subtlety and so free from padding of any sort as this is must stand a poor chance as against even a piece like the second epode, which with all its skill in descriptive versifying belongs in fact to a much humbler poetic category.

Hymns and Prayers

Although, as already remarked, Horace was probably under a special debt to Pindar for his " sacerdotal " style of language and his oracular manner with its rhetorical [1] transitions of mood, in respect of the *form* of his odes the debt was rather to the Greek lyric in general,[2] and especially to the Aeolian school. As they were his models for length and metre, we should expect that he copied their forms also; and what we know of their forms supports this view. They evidently dealt largely in the Hymn, the Prayer, and the Exhortation general or personal; and it has been indicated in my third chapter that the *Odes* of Horace fall into these three formal categories. (To " prove " this rule there are, as a matter of fact, a very few exceptions.) I propose, however, to examine here selected examples only; I will take those on which such a classification seems to me to

[1] *I.e.*, as of an impassioned speaker; a good example is III. vi. 44-5.
[2] Our knowledge of the forms of Greek lyric comes, in default of integral remains, almost entirely from the Alexandrian classification preserved in Proclus's *Chrestomathy*; see Smyth, *Greek Melic Poets*, Introd. xxv. The classificatory arrangement by books in the *Anth. Pal.* is also not without its illustrative value for Horace's *Odes*.

throw some light. Others can be more profitably studied in other connections ; for that reason I have just now dealt with several *apropos* of their more or less Pindaric complexity, and will afterwards discuss others in the light of this or that *special* feature of Horatian technique.

To begin with, this "sacerdotal" view in general explains several regular features of the *Odes* which strikingly differentiate them from the average modern notion of a lyric poem. It explains why almost all of them are *addressed* to someone, God or man ; and why the advice contained in the latter sort is usually in reference, as with oracles, to some definite occasion. It justifies the scholiast and some old editors in refusing to take I. xv. as a detached exercise in lyric narrative ; it supports Dr. Leaf in his recent contention [1] that the language of I. xiv. (as pure an "oracle" as any poem of Horace's) demanded a fuller and more satisfying explanation than had ever previously been given of it. It accounts for the frequency of references to, and directions for, sacrifice, and helps us to understand why descriptions of the victim are so curiously detailed.[2] It also explains some special features. It may often serve to excuse them ; but not always.

The first category will naturally be *Hymns*. Our old friend III. xiii. (*O fons Bandusiae*) is, of course, a hymn to what is at one and the same time a fountain and a deity, like Arethusa ; it is written as if on the eve of the *Fontanalia*, a festival in honour of fountains in general, the existence of which is attested by Varro. It might be expected that the gross breach of poetic taste I have already [3] complained of is, not indeed justified, but at least accounted for, by the ritual concerned. But it is not ! "On that day they throw wreaths into springs and wreath wells" is all that Varro says ; [4] there is no mention of any victim. We are therefore, I think, justified in considering Horace's gratuitous insertion of it an offence, not

---

[1] *J. Phil.*, XXXIV. 68, pp. 283 foll.

[2] One of the Roman elements in the *Odes ;* the votary could not hope for an answer to his prayer unless every detail of the rite were performed exactly according to prescription. It is a mannerism of Horace's to end an ode with a reference to a sacrificial victim ; *e.g.*, I. xix. ; II. xvii. ; III. xxii. ; IV. ii.

[3] Ch. I. *init.*   [4] *L.L.*, vi. 22.

merely by modern standards, but by those of his own day,[1] crude as the Roman writers often are on the subject of animal slaughter. And, as a matter of fact, Horace is here sinning not only against his age but against himself; for has he not elsewhere told us that the Muse delighteth in *un*polluted fountains ?—*O quae fontibus integris gaudes* (I. xxvi. 6).

III. xxi. is a hymn to a wine-jar, and again I say " hymn " advisedly, not merely because a wine-jar contains Bacchus and is in so far divine, but because this poem both in form and style is modelled (consciously I believe) after the regular type of ancient hymn, and because I do not find that anyone seems quite to realise this, though to me at any rate it is at least half the point of the piece. " Gentle wine-jar, my twin, whether it be jest or melancholy that you are storing for us, or brawls and mad loves, or easy sleep, no matter for what attribute was gathered the Massic that you preserve—you are worthy to be carried forth [2] on a day of gladness. Descend, *etc.*" Now this enumeration of the various phenomena of intoxication has puzzled people, and it has been suggested that " the point seems to lie in the expression of its potency, ˹it must have some great effect, whatever that be.' " Not at all. You begin according to the immemorial tradition of hymns, by giving your God his choice of the particular attribute by which it pleases him to be addressed ; attribute or name, it is the same thing, and so the poet sums up " quocunque . . . nomine." I am willing to admit that that phrase means " in what capacity," literally " under what head," " on what account," that in fact *nomen* is used in its technical commercial sense ; but I am sure Horace chose the word because he was thinking of the variant names of deities, and of such formulæ as that of Catullus, xxiv., 21, *sis quocunque placet tibi sancta nomine.* This is *why* the commercial metaphor appears in a decidedly strained sense here, a sense which cannot be exactly paralleled ; so that there is no need to adopt the variant *numine. Descende* (7) means, of course, " come down from the storeroom," the

---

[1] I have to admit, however, that there is evidence of animal sacrifice to fountains. The ritual of the Fratres Arvales prescribes two sheep for the generic deity Fons ; and Ovid, *Fasti*, III. 300, represents Numa as sacrificing a sheep to a fountain.

[2] As statues of gods often were at their festivals.

ancient "cellar" being at the *top* of the house ; but it is also a deliberate parody of such phrases as *Descende caelo* in III. iv. 1. In the last half of the poem the various powers and provinces of the particular divinity are explicitly set forth after the orthodox fashion.[1]

The next category is *Prayers*, but I am not concerned to enforce any great distinction between prayers and hymns ; praise of a deity is seldom found unaccompanied by a request for him to do something ; and many of Horace's odes contain elements of both. Prayer pure and simple is I. xxxi., and it may be taken as a good example of the Horatian prayer-poem in one respect, showing as it does to anyone who remembers what Roman official religion was, that there was indeed room enough in Roman life for this *poetical* class of "prayer," and that it was very far from being a gratuitous secular duplicate of the official sort. "There is no trace in the Roman religion," wrote Warde Fowler, "of prayer for other than material blessings." *Quid dedicatum poscit Apollinem vates ?* What does the *poetic* "seer" petition from his frankly literary and imaginary god ? "Not"—a series of material blessings ; but sufficient health and sanity to make the best of the little he has got, and a continuance of honour and of a delight in poetry into his old age.[2] How many modern prayers can show so high an ideal ?

The poem which follows is an invocation to his lyre, into which is subtly woven, under the appearance of a digression on Alcæus, a prayer that his poetry may be as spirited, and may show as wide a range of theme from the political to the playful, as that of the Lesbian adventurer.

As in these two instances, Horace's prayers are often personal in form ; but, of course, there is always a general significance underlying the personal disguise, there is always some propaganda, social or poetic or other. III. xviii., for instance, has in view the Augustan campaign for advertising the delights of country life. But, as usual, half out of poetic artfulness and half from natural egotism, Horace puts it in the form of a

---

[1] *E.g.*, Verg., *Aen.*, VIII. 287 foll., esp. 293-300.

[2] Frui paratis et, valido mihi, Latoe, dones apprecor, integra cum mente nec turpem senectam degere, nec cithara carentem. The correction *apprecor* is due to Prof. Housman. *Proc. Camb. Philol. Soc.*

propitiatory address to the god who, he has already told us in I. xvii., often visits his own farm. This is Faunus, one of the true old Italian deities, by this time identified with the Greek Pan and so endowed with that divinity's literary associations (I. xvii. 2) and prestige. Faunus to Horace is one of those genial deities, like Mercury and Bacchus, who protect their kindred mortal spirits the poets.[1] The first two stanzas are prayer, of the orthodox poetic structure and construction ; the last two hymn, praising the joys of the *Faunalia*, on the eve of which, as we see from the analogy of others of the *Odes*, we are to suppose the poem written. The pleasing picture of the festival here given is doubtless true in most particulars ; in Horatian style and metre it makes an exquisite vignette ; but that the Sabine wolves and lambs had an acute enough sense of the Roman calendar to recognise the Nones of December and keep one day's fraternisation, the sceptical archæologist will deny. In point of fact, the whole passage takes on from this line an atmosphere of the Golden Age. We see that the millennium formerly sighed for has now arrived, and that its realisation is due, through the revival of old-time cults, to the rule of Augustus ; *quod erat demonstrandum.* A similar picture of rural peace and happiness is associated with Faunus in the other ode which begins with him ; I. xvii. and III. xviii. lose none of their charm if read together.

One of our old puzzles, III. xxii., has a similar personal reference, and is so far to be taken literally ; the poetic farmer dedicates a pine-tree on his estate, overlooking the farmhouse, to Diana.[2] The poem belongs to a special class of Greek lyric or epigram, the ἀναθηματικόν or dedicatory piece ; such are ostensibly inscriptions attached to the object. II. xxvi. is another ἀναθηματικόν, but of that more anon. In regard to the present poem, the question naturally arises, Why to Diana ? All the more so, as the special and prominent mention of her aspect as goddess of childbirth makes the reader inclined to exclaim *caelebs quid agit ?* The editors do not help us.[3] Probably it was because Diana was regarded as in a special degree

---

[1] II. xvii. 28, 29 ; III. viii. 7 ; I. xvii. 13 in light of 1-12 ; *etc.*

[2] Cf. *Sat.*, II. vi. 14, where he represents himself as praying to Mercury, *pingue pecus domino facias.*

[3] Orelli raises the question but does not answer it.

the patroness of farmers, the deity who brought prosperity to crops.[1] Horace leaves this unsaid, as obvious from the context, but stresses a different aspect of her fertilising capacity ; and we may remember that Warde Fowler has recently remarked on the desire of Augustus, evident in the *Carmen Saeculare*, to *associate* the ideas of fertility of man, beast, and crop, with religion and morality ; [2] *i.e.*, to make his religious revival the common foundation of agricultural reconstruction and marriage reform.   Why a *boar*, it has been asked, as goddesses usually receive female victims.   It may be that Horace, still retaining an eye for the more practical aspects of successful pig-breeding, did not wish to make the ritual retard the efficacy of the prayer.   " Meditating his sidelong thrust " is to be explained as indicating the age of the victim, according to the convention (cf. III. xiii. 4-5).

The *Carmen Saeculare* is, of course, a hymn-and-prayer in a fuller sense than any other ode of Horace ; it is a real one, not only literary ; the poet is here performing the function of priest in sober earnest.   It is an interesting and important document to students of Roman history and in particular religious history.   But its literary merit is not much ; the first two stanzas are fairly pleasing.   It is, however, hardly fair to judge it at all from a purely literary point of view ; unless we admit its undoubtedly ritualistic suggestiveness as being, in the case of this ode alone, part of the effect aimed at. Such structure as it can be said to have at all seems to have been conditioned, not by poetic considerations, but by the circumstances of its performance.[3]

The ancients [4] recognised a class of hymn called εὐκτικόν in which—so far at least as it is distinctive—the poet asks a god to confer some special favour on a particular friend of his own.

---

[1] Cat., xxxiv. 17-20. tu cursu, dea, menstruo | metiens iter annuum | rustica agricolae bonis | tecta frugibus exples; and cf. Hor. *Od.*, IV. vi. 38-40.   But as the Goddess of Groves she would have a special interest in trees, and Prop. II. xix. 19 speaks of dedicating the horns of animals killed in the chase to Diana *on a pine tree.*

[2] *Religious Experience of the Roman People*, 443 ; *Roman Essays and Interpretations*, 115.

[3] See Warde Fowler, *The Carm. Saec. and its Performance*, in *Roman Essays and Interpretations*.

[4] It is post-Alexandrian ; see Smyth, *Greek Melic Poets*, cxxxiv.

This, on the whole, seems the most satisfactory formal category for I. xxvi. (*Musis amicus*); and perhaps also for I. xxxv. (*O Diva, gratum*, but see 29 foll.) and IV. i., a prayer to Venus of which the material part is in the interest of young Paulus Maximus.

Two particular classes of ancient hymn there are which manifestly exercised a strong formal influence on several of the *Odes*; these are technically known as the κλητικόν and the ἀποπεμπτικόν. The terms are perhaps late; we have them from Menander,[1] a rhetorician probably of the third century A.D. But the types themselves are authenticated beyond question by numerous ancient examples, which present a certain degree of conventional uniformity. For definition and characteristics I cannot do better than quote from Smyth's *Greek Melic Poets* (Introd. p. xxxii.) :—

Kletic or invocatory hymns, which summon the god to leave his present abiding-place. It was a favourite device of the poets to describe the rivers, meadows, shrines, and dancing places where the god might be tarrying and whence he was expected to come at the call of his petitioner. So common was this feature that it degenerated into a mannerism, which is imitated by Aristophanes in *Nubes*, 270 ff. In case a prayer followed upon the invocation, the element of description was abridged. Examples of kletic hymns are: Alkm., 21, Κύπρον ἱμερτὰν λιποῖσα καὶ Πάφον περιρρυτάν (of Aphrodite); Alkm., ii. Sa. i., v. 6, ἤ σε Κύπρος καὶ Πάφος ἤ Πάνορμος (scil. ἔχει, of Aphr.); Aristoph., *Ranae*, 875 ff.; *Lysistr.*, 1296 ff. (Aisch., *Eum.*, 287 *ff.*). Echoes in Theokr., I. 123, 15. 100; Kallim., I. 4; Catull., 36; Hor., I. 30. 2., cf. A 38.

The valedictory (ἀποπεμπτικοί) hymns dealt with the supposed or actual absence of the god and contained a prayer for his return. The country, city, and people which he is quitting, the place of his future sojourn—any spot that fancy could paint as the domicile of the god—became the object of a description even more elaborate than that of the kletic class. Bacchylides is reported to have excelled in the composition of valedictory hymns.

A pure and simple " kletic " hymn is I. xxx., *O Venus, regina Cnidi Paphique*, which, short as it is, is not merely perfect but charming. It is characteristic of Horace that the charm is very largely one of literary associations. The last line is just *Mercuriusque*, yet it is a line upon which it would be impossible to improve ; not merely because of all that the name means to

[1] Walz, *Rhet. Gr.*, 9. 135 ff.

Horace and to the reader familiar with him,[1] but because of the unexpected simplicity and, as it were, metrical convincingness, of the climax.

Of ἀποπεμπτικά proper—addressed to a god, that is— there are no examples, but the form of one is clearly embedded, like a fossil in rock, in IV. i., and extends from the 7th to the 28th line ; there we see the conventional expatiation on the place which the deity is desired to visit.

But the Horatian hymn or prayer need not necessarily be addressed to a standard god. We have seen it addressed to a wine-jar ; and there is no reason why it should not be addressed to any divinised thing or person. In the fourth book, xiv. and xv. are hymns of praise to Augustus, while v. is a " kletic " hymn to the same divinity.

The influence of the hymn-form, however, extends further than this. It extends to two other classes of ode, addressed to personal friends of the writer ; in which, although the addressees are not in any degree (as in the three poems to Augustus just mentioned) regarded as divine, certain features are reproduced of the κλητικόν and the ἀποπεμπτικόν respectively. The majority of Horace's odes to friends belong to the category of exhortations ; those which do not, and also as a matter of fact some which do, will be found to conform to one or other of these two classes, the *invitation* and the *valedictory address*.

INVITATIONS AND " SEND-OFF " POEMS

I do not mean to imply that within these poems there can be traced a modelling of the structure upon the sacred κλητικά and ἀποπεμπτικά ; I mean that the existence of these two sacred forms is responsible for the prevalence—in itself remarkable and demanding explanation—of the two secular types derived from them. Apart from that, an occasional touch, indeed, of " atavism " or playful parody is the most that could be expected. In sacred κλητικά it was regular to name the deity's present whereabouts, which you were asking him to leave ; *sperne dilectam Cypron*. Presumably if you did not do so, you ran the risk of failing to catch his attention at all ; the formality corresponded, in fact, to " ringing him up." If

[1] Cf. p. 220.

he had many residences, you tried them all in turn, adding, either for safety's sake, or to show off your powers of ornament, a more or less detailed description.   Horace in his secular invitations does just once reproduce it ; there is, to my mind, a playful semi-deification in his manner of inviting or " invoking " Maecenas, in III. xxix. 5-12 : " Don't always be gazing at moist Tibur or the upland field of Aesula or the ridge of the parricide Telegonus (= Tusculum) or the smoke the wealth the roar of Rome ; come down from your palace in the clouds."

But consistently with his pursuit of variety, Horace composes each invitation on a structure of its own, often, according to his general practice, disguising for some time at least the fact that it is an invitation at all.   Thus the most pleasing of his invitation odes (I. xvii.) begins (1-14) as if it were going to be a poem of the type (to be considered presently) in which he says in effect, " I am a poet and therefore the favourite of Heaven."   III. viii. and (if the text is sound [1]) I. xx. are invitations to Maecenas to dine with him.   In Greek society the return from a long and distant absence was made the occasion of a special welcoming dinner given to the wanderer by his friends ; this was technically known as an ἀγλαΐα, and poems were often composed for it.[2]   The spirited II. vii. is clearly an exercise in this kind ; it welcomes an old friend and battle-comrade, Pompeius, returning to Rome under the amnesty which followed Actium, and rings with a genuine and warm-hearted affection that is less common in the writer than in Catullus.   In IV. xii. the poet invites one Vergilius not only to dine with him, but to supply one of the accessories of the feast ; this young man was evidently on the make both politically and financially, but nothing is now known of him. The piece is mildly playful, and the reference to the youth's absorption in money-making is the bluntness of pleasantry, not of rebuke.   Horace's tact has been spoken of, but it was

---

[1] Horace likes abrupt beginnings, but this is so elliptical as to be obscure, and blunt to the point of rudeness. I suspect Vollmer is right with his " *Vile potavi* " ; it then becomes a simple life poem, and by occasion congratulatory.

[2] J. M. Edmonds on Sappho, *Charaxus-Ode* in *Class. Rev.*, 1920, p. 5. He refers to Theocr. vii. 52 foll. *Odes*, I. xxxvi. (not an invitation) is on the occasion of an ἀγλαΐα.

not the sort—different perhaps in kind—that could extend
to the other sex. The modern reader of the preceding ode,
IV. xi., may be allowed to smile three times. He will smile
at the nature of the inducement offered to the lady ; she is to
banquet with her Horace because it is the birthday of his
dearest friend ; they will drink—to the health of a Prime
Minister. He will smile, even though he should feel that there
is something pathetic in the picture, at the wistful egotism
which innocently proclaims a friend's nativity as something
only less sacred than one's own. And he will smile at the reassurance given to Phyllis that she is positively the last.

Only the thirst for paradox that could identify the " Virgil "
of IV. xii. with the great poet, could fail to identify with him
the Virgil of I. iii.—" animae dimidium meae." Other apo-
(or pro-) pemptic odes to mortals are I. vii., a masked variety,
as we have seen ; I. xxix. to Iccius about to follow the wars
—the scholar turned soldier ; and I. xxxv. which, disguised
at first as a hymn to Fortune, is revealed at the conclusion
as a send-off to Augustus. III. xxvii. combines farewell good-
wishes to Galatea with a promise, full of true priestly bene-
volence, that he will work the omens ; this poem has been
discussed above.[1]

CHARACTER SKETCHES

The ancient hymn, in fulfilling its purpose of praising the
deity addressed, habitually reminded him of his various attributes and exploits. These were often enumerated exhaust-
ively and indiscriminately enough ; in other instances the
writer is evidently mainly concerned to seize an excuse for
straightforward narrative. Horace always writes with a clear
conception of the character of the god, and thus several of
the odes are in effect vignette character-sketches. II. xix. is
technically a *dithyramb* or hymn to Bacchus ; but however
Greek the mould and the materials, its coherence and vitality
constitute it an essentially original work. I cordially agree
with Wickham : " There is no reason to believe that it is a
reproduction of any single original. The art of its composition, the climax through which the celebration of Bacchus'

[1] pp. 206-7.

triumph rises, and the studiedly quiet conclusion after the
abrupt bursts of the beginning, as though the strained mind
had found relief and the ' turbida laetitia ' run itself clear,
are Horatian rather than Greek." The opening stanza con-
jures up at once a delightful and truly pagan picture ; it is not
for nothing that its last word is a graphic epithet.

> Bacchum in remotis carmina rupibus
> Vidi docentem, credite posteri,
> Nymphasque discentis et auris
> Capripedum satyrorum acutas.

From the final stanza we see that even the grim creatures
of Tartarus yield to the charm of this divinity, who in the
patronage of poetry as in other respects is a kindred spirit
with the gentle Mercury ; which kinship will appear from a
comparison of the two odes in their respective honour, and
especially in regard to the conclusion of each. I. x. has been
regarded, after a common fashion, as a merely conventional
tribute to an Olympian ; Landor branded it as " very puerile."
It seems to me another of Horace's most pleasing poems. He
felt *himself*, as he has told us elsewhere,[1] to be a *Mercurialis vir*,
and in Mercury he has here drawn for us a being after his own
heart ; civilised, refined, literary, health-loving, songful, sportive, but at the same time kindly ; a well-wisher, as we have
seen that Horace was, to all who must go forth to brave great
perils ; altogether what we should now call an attractive personality, and one not without its use and function. Mercury
is the herald, the mediator, the neutral who provides safe
conduct ; nobody can be *really* angry with him, because he
himself is never angry ; his charm is irresistible ; his geniality
is privileged ; he is, as we can see from his connection with
another ode (III. xi.) the embodiment of the persuasive, paci-
fying and harmonising power of song—that very power or
privilege which Horace exercises for the correction of his erring
friends. We miss the point of this delicate and graceful poem
if we fail to realise that it becomes more serious in the last
two stanzas. Again, it is not for nothing that the last word [2]
is what it is ; the end is something of a climax ; Mercury is

---

[1] II. xvii. 29-30.   [2] *imis.*

welcome even among the powers of Hades, whom all other sky-gods hate.

This type of ode is extended to a mortal in II. viii., which is addressed to Barine, represented as a famous beauty. The piece belongs to this category because it contains nothing admonitory, but simply sings the praises of the " divinity " addressed ; the last stanza with its " te . . . te " is in the regular hymnodic style. It is to be noted that all these poems have just that obvious unity of theme which is conspicuously *not* a feature of the characteristic Horatian ode.

INJUNCTIONS OR EXHORTATIONS

A number of odes are best classified as " Sacrificial " or " Festal " ; that is, they purport to be written immediately before a more or less sacred festivity, and give directions for its proper celebration, not infrequently delivered with a staccato vivacity, wherever the tone is light. III. xiv. (already considered) begins sacerdotal and ends festal ; the difference is not much for the ancient, nor perhaps for the Italian of any age, but it has offended the modern Northerner. Purely typical odes of this category are I. xix. (*Mater saeva Cupidinum*), and xxxvi. (*Et ture et fidibus*) on the return of Numida ; III. xxviii. (*Festo quid potius die*). To it also belong such pieces as I. xxxvii. (*Nunc est bibendum*), III. viii. (*Martiis caelebs quid agam Kalendis*). Some of these poems read strangely to the average modern, but if read together would probably soon seem much less strange ; they hardly need much light apart from what they throw on one another. It is probably our own utter unfamiliarity with this sort of thing either in our life or literature that makes a poem like III. xix. (*Quantum distet ab Inacho*) such a stumbling-block. It falls naturally and easily into the present category ; something more will be said of it presently.

But the great majority of " Injunction " odes are in a moral strain. Of these a minority, but an important minority, are addressed to the whole civil community ; in them the poet speaks more in his official vein, with here and there even a " sacerdotal " touch—*vetabo, qui Cereris sacrum vulgarit arcanae, sub isdem sit trabibus*, etc. Such are the famous first six odes of

Book III., with the exception of the fourth, which is a hymn to Calliope and the Muses.

But as already observed, by far the larger number of the admonitory odes are addressed to particular individuals. The second book especially abounds in this type, with the result that it has a character of its own, as numerous critics have noted. Many of these odes present similarities of structure, while as for the doctrine, it would hardly be too much to say that it is always the same, at least in principle. In the result, however, they are sufficiently various. II. ii. is matter-of-fact and keeps severely to the illustration of its single point; iii. is grave, wistful, and poetical; iv. is playful and mock-heroic. Horace thought of holiday-making what we say of Charity, that it is often best when it is done at home, and that is the lesson of the sixth ode of this book, as of *Odes*, I. vii. 1-13, and *Epist.*, I. xi. ix. and xi. I have already dealt with; x. is to Licinius Murena, and if we can judge from the fate that was so very soon to overtake him, we may take it that the point the poet mainly wishes to drive home is that with which he concludes, *contrahes vento nimium secundo turgida vela ;* but in order to prevent this warning from appearing too pointed and so failing of its effect, he tones it down by throwing in a decent sprinkling of injunctions against the opposite error. xvi. and xviii. are in the characteristic anti-materialist strain, the former poetical, the latter rhetorical, both effective ; xvii. is to rally Mæcenas from an attack of hypochondria.

In some odes the admonition is not directed to the person addressed ; the poem formally apostrophises one person, but is for the benefit of another ; thus I. v. is *to* Pyrrha, but *at* her too-credulous latest lover ; similarly I. viii. ; xi. of the same book warns a *demi-mondaine* against believing in astrology ; women of that type have been addicted to superstition in all ages ; the advice is well-meant, it is the same as he gives to his best friend.[1] The exhortations to drink (I. xi. 6) or love (I. xxiii.) are quite genuine, no less genuine than any advice of Horace's, and often result, as in the last-mentioned ode, in genuine poetry. It is as much an axiom of Horace's poetic repertory as of Augustus's social scheme, that all women

---

[1] III. xxix. 29-32, 41-3.

cannot be—are not by nature—Roman matrons ; [1] and this
vein, even if it had not been congenial to himself, was a considerable part of the legacy of Greek lyric. In xxiv. we see
that even an elegy has become in Horace's hands an admonitory address against over-indulgence in grief. xxvi. is another
of those poems that somewhat mystify the modern reader ;
it is probably best explained as purporting to inspirit Aelius
Lamia, who is anxious about the political situation. Horace
does this, not merely by holding up his own light-heartedness
in that respect as an example, but by hinting that that light-
heartedness itself is attributable to his being " a friend of the
Muses " ; so if he wishes to infect Lamia with the same feeling,
it is *via* the Muses that he can best do so ; in plain language
by sending Lamia a poem, so that he shall read it and be made
happy by the Muses. To that end Horace prays [2] to the Muse
to " weave a chaplet " for Lamia, a chaplet meaning (as often
in Pindar) a poem, to wit this very ode, which the poet thus
prays her to inspire. The ode is to be a song sung " with a
new lyre and the quill of Lesbos " ; that is to say, it is to be
Horace's first experiment in Alcaics. The 33rd of this book
is another " rallying " poem. The 38th is a simple-life sermon
in a nutshell, in the form of instructions to his " boy " who is
laying the table for dinner.

The warning (III. x.) to the haughty Lyce that he will not
sue to her indefinitely is put in the form of a serenade, technically known to the Greeks as παρακλαυσίθυρον ; but that
the piece is meant to throw its emphasis on the warning which
forms its climax, is indicated by IV. xiii., where we find that
the tables are turned and it is Lyce who has now become an
unsuccessful suitor to the young men who are unmoved by
her faded charms and ridicule her useless arts. The latter
poem is Horace's *Belle Heaulmière*, and with all its pagan
vindictiveness remains a fine and powerful poem. The main
differences between it and its French affinity are two, and they
are characteristic. First, Horace selects, Villon makes a
catalogue, with the result that the romantic's poem is much

---

[1] That is Horace's quite simple argument on the point ; *non te
Penelopen difficilem procis Tyrrhenus genuit parens*—III. x. 11-12.

[2] The ode is a εὐκτικόν, see above, p. 26.

longer. Secondly, the ode has movement, progress, it proceeds
from a dramatic and allusive opening to a sudden climax ; the
Complaint is crooning and monotonous.

IV. x., similar to III. x., is hardly a success.   III. xv. sounds
a warning in the opposite direction.

Change of Mood, Antithesis, and Subtlety in Endings

Towards the end of Chapter IV. it was pointed out how
Horace in his odes often makes abrupt modulations from one
mood into an opposite or different one ; and also that he is
fond of presenting a single main antithesis of mood or subject
as the basis of a single poem, that he often deliberately concludes in the opposite vein to that in which he began.   This
brings us to the further subject of his technique in the matter
of endings, which is unquestionably careful and subtle.   All
these features of his art may most conveniently be discussed
together.

The " test case " of I. iv. has already been considered.[1]   A
composition of similar elements is IV. vii. ; the modulation at
line 7 is less bold than that at line 13 of the other poem, but
the effect is really a good deal finer, for this poem is more
poetically written and more harmoniously conceived.   It
seems to me quite one of the supremely beautiful among the
Odes, though Wilamowitz in 1913, with his eye on the imperial
commissions of Book IV. and the *Carmen Saeculare*, pronounced it insignificant.   Comparisons between the arts make
some people sick ; otherwise I should record that the one thing
the slumbrous final couplet of this ode recalls to me whenever
I read it is the end of Schumann's *Traumerei*.   The same
lesson here drawn from spring—to drink deep of life—is also
drawn by Horace from winter ; witness epode xiii., in a manner
I. xi., and particularly I. ix. (*Vides ut alta*).   That the ode
which begins with a picture of snow-capped Soracte should
end with an account of out-door pursuits that must be, at
the best, highly inappropriate to such a season, is so characteristic of Horace's practice that we must regard it as in-

---

[1] Ch. III., p. 78.

tentional;[1] and in point of fact the third stanza itself implies a transition from winter to spring; the advice thereafter becomes general.

Similarly, we are not to complain of III. vii. (*quid fles Asterie*) that the poet in first consoling a young wife for her husband's absence and bidding her dry her tears, then finally hinting to her not to lend a too ready ear to the handsome young athlete who lives next door, has forgotten what he is about. The beginning is ironical. But it is not obviously so? No; it is not *meant* to be seen to be so, until the end of the poem is reached; that is the joke. For the rest, it is a melodious, clever, and graceful piece.

II. xvii. (*Cur me querelis exanimas tuis*) is similar to two poems already considered,[2] ix. and xi. of the same book. It begins with assurance of tender affection, such as will be congenial to Mæcenas in his present valetudinarianism; but doleful dumps are just what it is meant to drive away, so it ends in a couple of thanksgivings. II. xii., also to Mæcenas, is a characteristic example of change of theme; the first three stanzas treat of wars mythical and historical; the poet, it is true, is saying that he will have none of them, but that is simply his excuse for the detail which brings out his antithesis; the last four stanzas celebrate the Prime Minister's domestic felicity. Was the ode perhaps written for the express purpose of confirming that felicity? History or gossip tells us of many a rift within this particular household lute. III. xix. (*Quantum distet ab Inacho*), which has been regarded as a puzzling ode, may perhaps appear, in the light of this category, to be normal enough.

The very pleasing little poem III. xii. (*Miserarum est*) on the stock subject[3] of the love-sick maiden's difficulty in pursuing her household drudgery, begins in a picture of herself and ends in the very opposite picture, the out-door sports of the more fortunate young man. This habit of ending a poem by a

---

[1] One reason for the change of mood or theme, here and elsewhere, is probably the desire to give an *appearance* of spontaneity in his poems; he often makes them read almost like a yard or two cut out at random from the continuum of his casual thought. He does not want the form to be obvious; but it is there.   [2] See p. 79.

[3] See Smyth (*Greek Melic Poets*, p. 247 *fin.*) on *Sappho*, 90.

15

more or less sudden modulation into a totally new key—by a new vision, it often amounts to—is a quite special instrument of the poetic repertory.[1] Matthew Arnold, for example, has employed it with fine effect, both in *Sohrab and Rustum* and *The Scholar Gipsy*. Horace uses it in several different ways. Sometimes—and this is really the purest use of the device— the object simply is to make the change for its own sake ; to pass, for example, from a painful subject to a peaceful one, to ensure a quiet ending. Of all odes of Horace the " Regulus " ode (III. v.), while one of the finest generally, has always appeared to me to have without exception the most wonderful and beautiful conclusion. In such cases the first necessity for the poet is to *attach* the final picture so naturally, to make its introduction so apparently relevant, that the reader does not foresee the trick that is about to be played on his emotions, and so is caught off his guard. Horace tells us that the de- meanour of Regulus on his departure from Rome to certain death was marked by just the same grave self-possession [2] as when on many a previous occasion he had left, on the con- clusion of business, for a visit to the country—" to the Venafran fields or to Spartan-built Tarentum " is the literal translation. This does not only indicate his heroic fortitude, though it does that and vividly ; the illustration itself is in tone with the true situation ; we feel, as we are surely meant to feel, that the *longa negotia* of life are over, the stress of the final contest has ceased with the decision which he had himself advised, and although he has the ordeal of martyrdom before him, his soul is at rest, he is going to his long home. This last epithet is conventional, as if it were effortless ; not pointed, because what is desired is not point but quietness.[3]

[1] The general object is, perhaps, to give a kind of *resonance* to the conclusion, by making it " vibrate in the memory " ; otherwise it might end too pat.

[2] Not light-heartedness, save the mark ! " He went back to torture and death with as light a heart as if he were going for a holiday " is the paraphrase of one editor. For " Tarentum " substitute " Margate " and this language becomes reasonable enough. There is a great deal in names. To those who (like Tyrrell, compare next note) can see nothing in " Lacedaemonium Tarentum " I suggest this sort of *reductio ad absurdum* method.

[3] Yet Tyrrell (" Style in English Literature," *Nineteenth Century*, Jan., 1913) wrote " the last lines are a blot, a mark of the absence of

Other odes which in their various different ways end "off" are :—I. xvii., which, being generally concerned with pleasing objects, winds up with a reminder of a distressing situation by way of foil. ; II. i., to be considered later ; also I. iv., xxxiii. ; II. v., xiv., xvi. ; III. xiv., xx. ; IV. ii.

Rather different are those cases in which there is some special point in the sudden turn. III. xxvi. begins as a general farewell to love. Horace's farewells to love have just about as much finality in them as the " positively last appearance " of some celebrated actor. " I have served through my campaigns," he says, in a metaphor familiar to Latin poetry in this connection, " and now I hang up and consecrate my armour in the shrine of Venus—my lute, my torches, my crowbars, and my [1] bow-and-arrows." (Such were the instruments of ancient courtship ; compare Theocritus, II., 128.) Then comes the dedicatory prayer : " O goddess who dost hold blessed Cyprus and Memphis that knows not of Sithonian snows, O queen "—and then we expect something like " now at last let me have peace hereafter " ; but no—" O queen, raise high thy whip and give proud Chloe just one single lash ! "

A similar turn is given to the conclusion of III. ix. (*Donec gratus eram tibi*), and of IV. i. (*Intermissa, Venus, diu*).

Of some other odes it may simply be said that the poet makes them end in a picture the reverse of that with which they are chiefly concerned. Thus I. xiii., a poem of jealousy, ends with a reference to the enviable lot of those who are happily mated ; I. xviii., a recommendation to temperance, with the evils which result from excessive drinking ; and II. xiv., on mortality, with the revels of your heir.

On the other hand, Horace often, and just as purposefully,

---

distinction," and said of the final line that it " is surely the most bathetic in Horace." These things are not, I believe, to be explained only by obtuseness, nor even by obtuseness plus prejudice, but by the modern habit of cultivating an admiration for fifth-rate poetry, which results in not knowing what effects are even to be *expected* in good poetry.

[1] Editors object that this is an unsuitable weapon against closed doors. But cf. *sagittas Sat.*, II. vii. 116, where it is almost as unexpected, inside a room. Perhaps a loose use, = offensive weapon. (Recently Mr. G. P. Bidder, in an interesting article, *J. Phil.*, No. 69, pp. 113-127, explains *arcus* here as " bow-drills.")

employs the very opposite type of ending, the climax. Examples are I. x., xxx.; II. x., xviii. (the final instance of the fundamental equality of the poor man with the rich); III. viii., xxvii.; IV. xiii. The finest of all, however, is the last stanza of III. vi.; even more effective, if not more original, than the often and rightly praised terseness of the last three lines which anathematise four generations, even more effective, in my opinion, than the last line with its pair of words fitted with such a terrible convincingness to the metre, is the *suddenness* with which the " rhetorical question " breaks in upon the description of the better times that were—*damnosa quid non imminuit dies?* [1]

OTHER CATEGORIES

One class of odes, not very large, seems to suggest special consideration, although in fact all the members of it can be ranged under the main classes originally laid down. In several odes Horace's theme is simply himself as poet, and such odes have three *leit-motiven:* "I am a poet; poetry is a mighty power; the poet is under the special protection of Heaven." His famous and, indeed, finely triumphant envoi to the first three books—III. xxx. (*Exegi monumentum*)—is in this vein. The finale to the second book is, to say the least, a less felicitous exercise in the same style; where, after listening to the only too Ovidian details of his metamorphosis into a swan, we receive the strikingly superfluous assurance (21) that " nothing is here for tears "; what is less obvious being rather that several things are not just possibly here for laughter; on the whole it seems, however, that they are not. This, again, is the single or at least principal subject of I. i., xxii.; of II. xiii. and IV., ix., each of which has, however, an accretion of the " admonitory " type; also of IV. iii. and viii. II. xiii. is more interesting than the most of these; here, instead of openly glorying in his great profession, he indicates his affinity

---

[1] Page says: " Harshly thrown forward at the commencement of the stanza, the word *damnosa*, as Plüss remarks, ' sounds like a sigh.' " Well, every man to his opinion; I should have thought it sounded more like something else. But there may be different grades of sigh; we have all heard of a profane silence.

to Alcæus and Sappho after a subtler and archer fashion ; a tree once came crashing down within an ace of him, with the result that he very nearly found himself—an immortal !

III. ix. is in form abnormal, a lyrical dialogue. I. xxviii. has by some been regarded as a dialogue, but I think it has now been made abundantly clear that this will not work, and that it is a dramatic monologue put into the mouth of a drowned voyager ; his body has been cast ashore close by the tomb of the famous philosopher and scientist Archytas, whose shade he first apostrophises, and later addresses himself, in request for burial, to a passing sailor. It is, of course, " admonitory " to this passer-by, and indirectly to the reader ; learned or ignorant, all are mortal. These two odes, however, along with III. xii., in which Neobule (addressing herself) is the speaker, can be regarded as forming one small anomalous class, to the extent that they are " in character " ; in all other odes Horace writes in his own person.

HORACE'S εἰρωνεία. DEPRECATING BUT DOING

No account of Horace's art in composition properly so-called, could be quite complete without at least a passing reference to the way in which he acquits himself of that part of his official task which consists in celebrating victories. On a first reading of the *Odes*, or to a superficial critic, it might well appear that, except for those comparatively few passages where he openly enlarges upon the facts of the case in the obvious way,[1] his general attitude to this particular duty is to get through it as perfunctorily, and get quit of it as quickly, as may be possible. The truth, however, is rather that he is aware from the first how much any tedious expatiation must run the risk of defeating its own end ; and it is because he is determined that such events shall stand out clearly as unquestionable realities that he almost always celebrates them not by description but by allusion. In the matter of Roman exploits, he cares almost wholly for the fact, for the poeticising of it practically not at all. Like orthodox modern educational theorists, he realises that the information which the knowing teacher slips in as if incidentally will take a quicker and firmer

[1] *E.g.*, IV. iv. 17-28 ; or xiv. practically *in toto*.

hold of the pupil's mind than that which is emphasised or placed in a position where it is too readily expected. Yet such allusions in Horace are generally more deft or arch than they appear to be ; the apparent unconcern is deceptive. In I. vi. (*Scriberis Vario*), for example, he is ostensibly protesting that exploits so Homeric as those of Agrippa require a Homer to do justice to them ; but in point of fact he is writing their panegyric. Similarly II. xii. and IV. ii. In III. xxv. again, " the glory of Cæsar is only mentioned as the subject of the coming burst of song ; but the place of honour given to it is in effect the celebration which is promised." [1]

But the ode in which this device is employed with the greatest skill, and also with the finest result, is the first of the second book ; altogether, perhaps, about as good an example as could be chosen of Horace's poetic mastery, of the inspired art by which he conducts an ode through a whole series of evolutions, all subordinated to a single ultimate effect. The structure of the poem is thus :—

First movement, lines 1-8. Simple statement of the occasion, *You, my friend Pollio, are engaged in writing a history of the great world-war that is just over.*

Second movement, 9-16. As the first two stanzas were about the book, these are about its author.—*A series of compliments to Pollio.* (It becomes evident that this will be a book by a man of the highest distinction both in action and letters. The passage is chiefly marked by its pervading *dignity ;* a " maeostoso " movement.)

Third movement, 17-24. Still apropos of Pollio's forthcoming book, the poet suddenly lets his imagination take fire. —*Already I seem to hear you telling your story, and to thrill to the excitement as you conjure up the scenes of battle.* (And so without further parley he works this up into a fine spirited passage with plenty of sonority, what we should call in music a bravura passage ; the climax of that is the name of Cato, with all that it suggested to Roman ears.)

Fourth movement, 25-36. He has forgotten all about Pollio's book. He has remembered the civil wars, and who remembers them cannot forget what a tragedy they were, not

---

[1] Wickham.

primarily for this party or for that, but for Rome—for Italy—
for the world. *What a devastation! It is as if a Nemesis had
come upon us for the last of all our crimes against Africa, the
cruel death of—Jugurtha!* (Now this, it should here be noted by
the way, is to be a sustained *decrescendo* movement extending
over three whole stanzas ; in the first of these stanzas, he can
still allow himself to end on the emphasis of a rhetorical point.
But he resumes in a more tender strain.) *Where is there a
field that does not testify, by its graves, to that criminal strife ?*
(In the second stanza he can still allow himself to end with re-
verberating echoes—" auditumque Medis Hesperiae sonitum
ruinae." But he becomes more and more awed by the thought
of it all as he goes on.) *What strait, what river, but has been a
scene of carnage ? What sea has not been incarnadined with
the blood of Italy ? What region is there where a Roman has not
died ?*—And then, quite suddenly :—

Fifth movement, 37-40. That last *ora* (in *decoloravere*)
. . . *ora* . . . *cruore* had been the final distant thunders
and now " fled is that music ; do I wake or sleep ? " Horace
is speaking ; he is addressing his Muse. She is exceeding her
licence and encroaching upon the sphere of Simonides, the
memorial poem ; gently she must be diverted to the light
themes that are her proper province.

The effect of the unexpected change is to make the reader
feel that in the preceding part there has been pathos. But
Horace will not dwell on pathos ; he has led up to it inobtrusively, as if by accident ; having in the 36th line just touched
it upon the quick, he knows that that is enough. To achieve
this effect of pathos is the single purpose of this whole poem.
It is not Asinius Pollio that is going to make Romans feel the
tragedy of the Great War ; all that was pure camouflage ;
it is Horace, and he does it largely by pretending not to do it.
Any fool could—every fool would—return in the conclusion
to the subject of the projected history text-book. Once Horace
has soared away from it he never remembers it again.

Against that last stanza Landor wrote : " better without."
I do not agree.

If any reader here protests that all this has, however, left
him cold, I reply that that is just what I should expect it to
do. Analysis is an arid business. The way to feel the point

of this ode is to hear it read by a fit reader, if that has been possible since 1912. Dr. Verrall's *Studies in Horace* are not referred to in this book, his thesis being one which strikes me as untenable ; but I gratefully acknowledge here that it was his reading of this very ode, at the conclusion of a lecture on the poet in Trinity College, Cambridge, some seventeen years ago, which first exploded for me in an instant that conception of Horace as a complete bore which is the heritage of almost every public school boy ; and as my view of Horace dates its inception from that hour, I feel that in a sense the present work must owe a deeper debt to Verrall than to any other single source.

CHAPTER VIII

COMPROMISE : THE ARS POETICA AND EPISTLES

nil cupientium
nudus castra peto et transfuga divitum
partis linquere gestio.

AS I have already [1] shown, I agree with those who
would assign the *Epistula ad Pisones*, or *Ars Poetica*,
not to the last years of Horace's life, but to a date
between the publication of *Odes*, I.-III. (23 B.C.) and that of
the first book of *Epistles* (about 20 B.C.). In adopting that
view I was influenced solely by the incidental internal evidence
already adduced by such scholars as Francke, Michælis, and
Nettleship, not by any preconceptions of my own regarding
the poet's general development. But I am thankful the evidence points where it does, since it entirely suits my book.
As I have indicated in my fourth chapter, it seems to me that
when Horace had published his great collection of lyrics, the
obvious next step for him was to attempt drama. In Roman
literature there had been a strong dramatic tendency [2] and a
distinguished, if rather academic, dramatic tradition ; in
Horace himself there had declared itself a distinctly dramatic
vein. The Augustan age witnessed a revival of dramatic
writing ; and the Emperor, however little we may regret the
suicide of his *Ajax*, cannot have been blind to the enormous
possibilities of the theatre as an instrument of national reconstruction. *Spirat tragicum satis et feliciter audet*, says Horace
of his fellow countrymen, and it might have been natural
that he should have found opportunity for his own *curiosa
felicitas* in the tragic style. But it takes a great deal to make
drama. There may not perhaps be potential tragedians in

[1] Ch. IV., pp. 114-15.
[2] Cf. Teuffel and Schwabe, vol. i. § 3.

233

every age, but who shall say how many of them are not from time to time perverted or extinguished by a Society too barbarous to have even a place for them ? The Augustan was evidently one of those epochs, like our own Victorian, in which a series of attempts were made to achieve this crowning triumph of the poet, but all in vain. The external conditions which make serious drama possible for the born dramatist are perhaps so many that they cannot often occur together ; and yet they are perhaps simple enough ; but however it be, one thing at least does seem to be essential, and that is (to put it in its simplest form) Faith. In the Periclean and the Elizabethan ages there was Faith, whatever else there may have been alongside. θνήσκει δὲ πίστις, βλαστάνει δ' ἀπιστία.

Horace's was not a large enough character to make serious drama possible for him. It is not that he was not religious ; for him, as for many a Roman of his and of later times, Stoicism was a religion. It is that his religion was too merely intellectual. It is almost pathetic to read sophistry so admirably and so earnestly expressed as here :—

> scribendi recte sapere est et principium et fons ;
> rem tibi Socraticae poterunt ostendere chartae

(study Bacon if you would write Shakespeare !)

> verbaque provisam rem non invita sequentur.
> Qui didicit patriae quid debeat et quid amicis,
> quo sit amore parens, quo frater amandus et hospes,
> quod sit conscripti, quod iudicis officium, quae
> partes in bellum missi ducis, ille profecto
> reddere personae scit convenientia cuique.[1]

Literature had, as we have seen, begun under Roman influence to recover something of the social and moral function it had lost since Euripides and the "illumination." Beginning from the Hellenistic end of Greek literature, Roman poetry had worked back to purer models. There had been established the didactic form—Lucretius and the Georgics ; the lyric—Catullus and Horace's own fresh achievement ; and Virgil was now in the last stages of his creation of a national epic. By all the rights of the case there ought to have arisen a Roman counterpart to Aeschylus and Sophocles ; and Horace had

---

[1] *A.P.*, 309-16.

now just emerged from the lyric stage of the poet's evolution, which ought in a complete poet to be succeeded by the dramatic. The chief reason why he failed to do so—if it is not simply the temperament of the man—is that he was under the influence of Greek sophistry and in particular of the arch-sophist Socrates, the father of all the schools. What he, what Rome,[1] then failed to do, has not been done to this day. The secret of Greek tragedy has never yet been recovered. *Tantum philosophia potuit suadere malorum.*

The *Ars Poetica* was written at some time between 23-20 B.C. inclusive, and the first book of *Epistles* within just the same limits. If the former were to be regarded as a patchwork, it might be inferred to have been on the loom all the time, and to have been gradually composed in the intervals of the small masterpieces of the other work. But in this view of the *Ars Poetica* I cannot quite concur. Whether or no it was written before *all* the Epistles, I do not see any means of determining; but it certainly represents the prior stage in the poet's evolution. As the product of that impulse towards drama which I take to be the natural sequel of a poet's lyrical phase, the *Ars Poetica* is an abortion. Instead of writing drama he writes about it; is very desirous that it should be written— but by other and younger men; and shows them how, both generally and in the circumstances of the time. The *Epistles* proper, on the other hand, are finished products in another kind—the kind he adopted as a result of his renunciation. Thus the consideration of the *Ars Poetica* must take precedence.

ARS POETICA

This traditional title, which occurs first in Quintilian,[2] is (as has repeatedly been pointed out) misleading; it implies a complete and formal treatise, whereas the poem is not properly even a treatise at all; and the immense influence it has exercised is partly due to this misconception of its character.[3] At the same time, it is, of course, more than a discourse upon Drama. Like most or all of Horace's works, it is essentially

---

[1] Varius being a mere name to us.
[2] Quintilian, VIII. iii. 60, and *Epist. ad Tryph.*, 2.
[3] Cf. Dimsdale, *Lat. Lit.*, p. 303.

occasional ; it has a definite and practical purpose, it has
particular circumstances always in view, and it is impossible
to understand it clearly without reference to these. It is a
letter of advice from an acknowledged master to a young man
about to become a poet ; but not to any young man in any
age ; to a certain Gnæus Piso,[1] and in the thick of the Augustan
Revival.

The position, and by consequence the poem, may perhaps
be made clearer by reference to a rather partial modern parallel. It has already been remarked that Horace's preparations for a bout of poetry-writing almost suggest a University
student packing his box for the production of a dissertation
for a fellowship. It is the young Piso who has now reached
the stage when he feels a call upon him to produce some
" original research." In these days, unfortunately, pure
literature has become just about as much divorced from
learned industry, as culture and hard work have been cast
off by poets ; but just as a tutor or lecturer might have a long
talk with a promising graduate, giving him at once general
directions as to how he may become an expert in his subject,
and particular suggestions as to fields of research now most
requiring exploration, coupled with hints about the lines on
which he will best attack some special problem ; so does
Horace tell young Piso, not only about the poetical profession
in general, saying of it exactly what every wise and experienced
professional man says of that particular one which happens to
be his own, how arduous it is, how swarming with quacks who
expose it to the criticism of its enemies, how exalted and
honourable if properly understood and practised—so does
Horace, with such warnings and exhortations, grumblings and
moralisings, introduce, punctuate, and still more earnestly conclude the concrete and special advice which is the outcome
of this particular consultation—that what is now wanted in
Roman literature is drama ; drama more or less fit to be at
least mentioned in the same breath with the Greek productions. To that end he gives the pupil as much as occurs to him
of the best advice that he has extracted from his own 'experi-

---

[1] Including occasionally his father and younger brother who had
similar literary tastes.

ence and can apply to the new problem; the advice is naturally
for the most part practical, but reinforced with something of
theory. And besides indicating general lines on which to
approach the writing of drama, he even adds a hint on the
particular mode of drama that might then be profitably attempted as holding, for a Roman, possibilities of fresh development—the satyr-play.

Such is the explanation—and quite a simple one—of the
fact that has so often been regarded with surprise, the apparent
anomaly that the subject of drama bulks so largely in the poem,
and yet the poem is not primarily about drama but about
poetry. But as always in Horace, the " occasion " is made
the occasion of utterances which have a value beyond it ; and
the *Ars Poetica*—which I must say, looking at it irrespectively
of its historic vicissitudes, its periodic inflations and deprecia-
tions, I feel to be a very brilliant work—is studded thickly,
as no other essay on the subject can make the smallest claim
to be, with the most penetrating generalisations and practical
maxims about poetry, most trenchantly and felicitously expressed. As for its practical value, it has, of course, already
exercised an immense influence on the development of European literature ; but who is to say ? Gnæus Piso's abandoned
mantle has never been taken up yet ; Aeschylus and Sophocles
remain still without affinities ; or, to take a more special point,
even a modern analogue to satyr-drama (Greek gods and heroes
would make excellent material for light opera) is not quite
unthinkable. In plain language, the *Ars Poetica* is not obsolete,
since it has not yet had its chance.

He begins (and with characteristic abruptness) by inculcating unity ; not the pedant's unity of mere subject, but
the poet's unity of organic life. Even the imagination has its
laws. " But the poets are licensed to give us Centaurs and
Scyllas " (9-10).[1] Yes ; but a monster overdone, recklessly
conglomerated upon no principle,[2] is merely ridiculous (1-5).
Your visions, imaginations, conceptions (*species*, 8) must have

---

[1] As frequently in the following pages, I paraphrase freely, to bring
out the point as I see it ; a point missed, I fancy, by Bentley's complaint
that the monster of 1-5 is too monstrous.

[2] Cf. preceding note.

a consistency analogous to that of each of the natural species
(7-9, 12-13).

Throughout the poem the precepts are given in Horace's
invariably succinct and incisive fashion, without connecting
particles and even with a deliberate appearance of discontinuity. But here, as in the rest of Horace, that appearance
is often deceptive ; line 14 looks at first sight like a transition
to the subject of style ; the subject, however, is still the same.
" Thus, for example," he would say, " it often happens that
while you are (and very naturally) concentrating your attention on your *style*, which you want to continue as elevated as
it began, you unwittingly lead yourself into irrelevancies of
matter." [1] The proper unity of a poem, already illustrated
from nature, is now illustrated from art—from the applied
arts ; it is unity of *function* (21-2). But indeed, as our instance
(14-19) has just suggested, it is from a very natural tendency
to get our attention fixed on one of the several desiderata and
forget the others, that the lapses of us poets most frequently
proceed ; and then, in language which it would be as impossible
to improve as it is to translate, the chief examples are given :—

brevis esse laboro,

obscurus fio ;

(brief, effortless—you see ?—and lucid)

sectantem levia nervi
deficiunt animique ; professus grandia turget ;

and so on ; in point of fact, as we saw that a laudable endeavour to maintain the level of the style may yet result,
oddly enough, in what is virtually a patchwork, so on the
other hand may the equally laudable endeavour after variety,
if it be carried beyond the variety of Nature. The humblest
craftsman can make himself an expert in details ; it takes
what Goethe called the " architectonic " faculty to cast a
complete statue (32-37).

The subject, in fact—that is *the* primary consideration.
Whoever would avoid the aforesaid pitfalls, let him choose
a subject that happens to be accommodated to his own particular endowments. The poet who chooses his subject ably

---

[1] Wickham's note on 14 seems to me entirely wrong.

will find that his subject itself rewards him; a congenial theme at once means two great things—it suggests the appropriate *structure*, and it inspires a forcible and pointed *style*. There again is one of the diamonds of the *Ars Poetica*—hard, certainly very hard and very small, but more than justifying its existence by the sheer intensity of its glitter, unobtainable elsewhere.

> cui lecta potenter erit res,
> nec facundia deseret hunc nec lucidus ordo.

But for some, perhaps, this is but another of Horace's "commonplaces." I have already shown how the structure of many a Horatian ode is the direct outcome of its subject. As to style, we shall see in a moment. Horace at once takes up these two points in turn. As the ridiculous neighbours the sublime, so does one step from the tight-rope of epigram precipitate into the yawning gulf of platitude. On structure there are only three lines, but they take the breath away :—

> ordinis haec virtus erit et venus, aut ego fallor,
> ut iam nunc dicat iam nunc debentia dici,
> pleraque differat et praesens in tempus omittat.

" Aut ego fallor " !   Probably what he meant to say was that to concentrate on what is relevant is the best way to secure a good construction. But even that is hardly illuminating. It is to the subject of style that he warms. " Judgment, discrimination—these are requisites not only in construction but in the business of stringing together words " (*etiam*).[1] To use—for the most part—familiar words, but to make them sound as no one else has done, that is style ; and it is done— since the character of words (and, one may perhaps add chords and colours) is influenced, to an infinite variety of effects, by the context—it is done by original phrasing.

True, we may here put in, the *cliché* is the great canker of literature ; yet hardly less is the original, in a sense, but affected and self-conscious phrase ; what about your own objection to " Rheni luteum caput " ? How shall a man achieve the golden mean ? Horace's answer has already

---

[1] Transposing 45 and 46.

been given us ; *nec facundia deseret hunc*—it is your theme (provided you choose it well) that will itself provide you with the original phrase. And he has given us examples too. *Strenua nos exercet inertia*—how otherwise than by a penetrating scrutiny of the godless fuss and fruitless activity of an age of materialism could such a perfect phrase be coined ? Or, again, Petronius, perceiving that herein lies the specific difference between Horace and all other poets, that he alone was able to push to the point of genius his infinite capacity for taking pains, and he alone could produce by a sort of deliberate spiritual incubation language that glowed with as full a vitality as others had achieved by inspiration only, expressed this discovery in the phrase *curiosa felicitas*, a phrase that, like the great majority of such, will bite into the minds of many who are as yet not quite conscious of its point. Yes, when you have coined such phrases, then you have indeed spoken *egregie*, in striking wise.

This policy of intensifying familiar words, of raising them to a higher power, is a distinct feature of Augustan poetry. Its chief exponent is Virgil, as was recognised in contemporary criticism, when Agrippa playfully observed that the poet had been " suborned " by his patron to invent a new kind of affectation consisting neither in turgidity nor barrenness, but based on words in general use, and all the more subtle on that account. Literature always requires some alternation of systole and diastole to maintain its existence, and in the matter of diction it often happens that one age lives by expansion and the next by contraction. The authors of the Republican period had not only allowed themselves the widest licence in the use of words of their own tongue, but had never hesitated to admit Greek words, occasionally even to the extent of writing sheer " macaronic," an affectation which, it is clear from *Sat.*, I. x. 20-30, had its admirers even in Horace's own day. The Augustans succeeded in superseding the earlier literature by reacting towards " retrenchment and reform." But here as elsewhere Horace is careful, on the other hand, to distinguish his standpoint equally from that of the pedants (of his day or of any) by asserting (60-72) the principle of " flux " in language and insisting on the poet's right, and indeed he would imply almost duty, of admitting—within decent limits—new words, provided, he adds, they be of Greek derivation.[1] Or provided, as he goes on to imply, let us hope, alternatively—provided they have received the sanction of general contemporary use. The name of Horace has in modern times become so persistently associated with the idea of poetic conventionalism, and his method and practice, truly classic as they are, have been so often confused with the *pseudo*-classic method and practice of the eighteenth century, that it is important to point out how explicitly the poet here protests against the academic tyranny of a stereotyped poetic diction, and how sanely he states the case for a judicious *modernity* of vocabulary.

> licuit *semperque licebit*
> Signatum praesente nota producere nomen.

" Producere," for poetry makes the speech of later generations at least as much as poetry is made from the speech of elder ones, and the eagle must not catch up at haphazard a verbal Ganymede who for better or worse is to become a regular inmate of Olympus. And again, in language which it would be impossible to better :

> usus,
> quem penes arbitrium est et ius et norma loquendi.

After " proper diction " comes naturally " proper style." At 73 Horace takes up this subject ; as usual, the transition is quite abrupt, but (again as usual) the logical connection is given us in time, at 86-88. He is no poet who does not know the various existing forms (*vices* [2]) and the tone (*color*)

---

[1] The condition seems a strange one, and, in fact, the passage is not absolutely clear. 48-9 with its reference to " abstruse subjects " appears to point to such uses as, *e.g.*, Lucretius' of *homoeomereia ;* yet that is the Republican, not the Augustan, way of using Greek words. In 53-9 Horace defends both Virgil's and his own occasional recourse to a Greek term ; and Macrobius, I. xxiv. 7, is independent evidence that Virgil was criticised on this score ; examples are from Virgil, *dius, daedala, trieterica, choreas, hyalus ;* from Horace, *ephippia, trigo, apotheca, mazonomus, amystis, balanus, barbitos ;* but then, it is difficult to see why such words should be spoken of as *nova fictaque nuper ;* perhaps some of them had passed into general use in Roman society within the preceding century or so.

[2] Literary " phases " (cf. *Odes*, IV. vii. 3 ; Ovid, *Met.*, xv. 238) ; *i.e.*, Horace instinctively regards the several Greek forms as having

appropriate to each. Therefore Horace surveys rapidly the main Greek forms in their historic succession, with an eye to what naturally dictates the tone, namely, their respective subjects. It is a mistake to affix to 73-85 the label " metre " ; the label should be " metre in relation to style." At 89, still on the same main subject, he proceeds to consider style *in the drama,* and that carries him to 118 ; but once he has embarked on the drama, he goes off entirely on this tangent ; true, he will have things to say again about style in general and about poetry in general, but that is rather because these subjects reappear in his path than because he returns to them ; at 89 begins the second of the three main divisions of the poem, and it is concerned entirely with the Drama.

In drama, too, as has been hinted of the older forms, epic, elegiac, iambic, and lyric, style is partly dependent upon subject (89-91) ; in drama, still more important, it is greatly dependent upon character. Accordingly we first consider style as it is (or should be) conditioned by character (93-118) ; we next proceed to characterisation as a problem in itself.

If it is a case of one of the famous persons of tragedy, an Orestes or a Medea, you must accept the conception which already exists. In point of fact, you must not portray Achilles as a dastard or Odysseus as a fool, or there will be no illusion of reality, so actual are these figures in their traditional rôles. But you may prefer to break new ground, which means, of course, not to invent an entirely new story, but to exploit some Greek myth that has hitherto escaped dramatic handling by a Roman writer. You may attempt to " create a new character "—in a somewhat similar sense to that in which a modern actor is said to " create " a part, *i.e.,* to reinterpret it [1] ; that is to say, you would *vivify* some hitherto comparatively colourless figure, let us suggest Deiphobus. Then he must be consistent. It is a difficult task, this imposing your own conception on what is common property (128, *difficile est*

been originally successive phases in a continuous literary evolution ; cf. my Chap. II.

[1] Cf. Sidney Lee, *Shakespeare's Life and Work,* p. 139: "Burbage . . . made his reputation by creating the leading parts in Shakespeare's greatest tragedies. Hamlet, Othello, and Lear . . . ," etc.

proprie communia dicere[1]),—on what, therefore, another writer might have treated very differently.[2] But you may attempt it (131), provided you really *will* be bold.

You must not, in this case, be content with an obvious and commonplace treatment of your theme (whatever it may be) ; you must not, of course, merely translate your originals (whatever they may be, whether a Holinshed or even a Homer) ; and not only that, but even in the matter of general narrative outline you must not follow them too closely, or you will almost certainly sooner or later find yourself admitting features which are as a matter of fact irreconcilable with the general conception of the play, the conception with which you started. Other pitfalls, too, await the dramatiser of epic raw-material ; [3] the temptation, for instance, to which the epic poets themselves —the ruck of them, at least—are seen to have succumbed ; the temptation to think that immensity of subject secures dignity, whereas it actually tends rather to produce turgidity and bathos. How much better—for in structural technique the dramatist may learn a lesson or two from epic itself—how much better is Homer's own method. He does not (150) throw in everything he can think of ; so neither must you transfer all that you find in the literary tradition of your particular theme ; you must, like Homer, select, you must

[1] *Dicere* = narrate (here, dramatise) an episode in the history of a certain character, as in *dices laborantes in uno Penelopen vitreamque Circen*—*Odes*, I. xvii. 19-20. On *communia* (" unclaimed," so Nettleship, following Acron) see Mr. R. L. Dunbabin, *Class. Rev.*, Feb. 1922, p. 21 (though I do not agree that Horace is here thinking at all of *Roman* poets *composing* epic ; cf. next note).

[2] Here Horace adds, for the particular reassurance of his addressee, " and indeed a man is safer employed in simply turning parts of the Iliad from narrative into stage dialogue, as *you* are now doing, than if he were to attempt to evolve a new tragedy out of some of Homer's less exploited characters "—*e.g.*, again, Deiphobus.

[3] I cannot see that there is any digression here (so *e.g.*, Wilkins, and similarly Nettleship). At 136 Horace ceases to deal with Greek epic as raw material, but proceeds to deal with it as a model of method, for the Roman tragic dramatist. This way of illustrating dramatic principles by epic references is certainly confusing ; further, it implies confusion in the writer's own mind ; but it is one of the disconcerting features which our poem shares with its predecessor, Aristotle's *Poetics*, cf. esp. Ch. 8 of that work, also 1453 A 30-5.

arrange ; in the features that are your own invention you must, like him, preserve consistency with the general outline of your subject. In particular, the dramatist is no mere chronicler ; indeed, even in epic it is only the inferior writers who so regard their function (cf. 137) ; Homer does not ; he begins at some point in the middle of a continuous series of legendary events, where action is already in full swing. And in that matter, too, the dramatist will do well to take a leaf out of Homer's book. All this is surely no less sound advice than it is sound criticism.

One more point in regard to characterisation ; if you want your play to " grip," you must observe a fair amount of realism in the matter of ages ; you must not forget that a man is inevitably either young, or middle-aged, or old, and so on ; in each of your personages, you must definitely relate the character in some degree to the age you have assigned him, or, of course, *vice versa* (153-178).

Then follow miscellaneous precepts : Certain classes of episode are more suitable for being reported, certain others for transaction on the stage ; a tragedy should have five acts ; the *deus ex machina* must be used sparingly ; the number of actors should not be more than three ; the rôle of chorus should form an integral part of the dramatic action, their lyrical passages should not be otiose and (it is implied) the style of these ought to be elevated, moral, and oracular. Throughout this passage (179-219) Horace is evidently thinking [1] of Greek tragedy as a model for Roman ; and if here and there we find details which it is difficult or impossible to square with Greek tragedy of the classic period or with Aristotle's *Poetics*, the explanation is to be sought in the probability that Porphyrion's account of Horace's authority for the *Ars Poetica* is right, and that he derived neither these nor even the other and more congruous precepts from the fountain-head, but from the Alexandrine critic Neoptolemus of Parium. The most obvious and also most interesting discrepancy consists

[1] Although he renders himself liable to mis-statements (*e.g.*, 215) through tending to speak of it in Roman terms. Thus 210 (*genius*) gives Roman colour to what is evidently (206-9) meant for a Greek picture. The only deliberate contemporary reference is at 202, and that is only in order to point a contrast.

in his recommendation of an apparently already recognised, though not universally observed, five-act convention, of which Aristotle evidently has never heard. As this convention was to acquire so great a vogue from the Renaissance, it would be interesting to trace it back to its own origin, but unfortunately its history previously to the present passage is a subject of conjecture only. Briefly, however, it seems to have arisen, as might in any case be inferred from Horace's own language just below at 194, from a division of Greek tragedies according to their ἐπεισόδια or portions between one chorus-song and the next. Although in the extant tragedies the number of these varies indifferently from four to eight,[1] there seems reason to believe that soon after Aristotle's time it tended to become fixed at five. Legrand has shown that the five-act division of the plays of Terence. which dates back as far as the time of Varro, was almost certainly based on a similar division obtaining among the plays which supplied Terence's model, those of the " New " Greek comedy ; and the " New," again, as Leo had shown, was very considerably under the influence of Greek tragedy in its final phase which began with Euripides ; and " probably the new parts of that technique " (*viz.*, the technique of tragedy) " were not the last to be adopted " by Menander and his fellows.[2] (Although the " New," unlike the " Middle " and " Old " Comedy had apparently no chorus as an integral part of any play, it is certain that the action was stopped at intervals to make way for a choral interlude, somewhat as a present-day theatrical performance is punctuated by musical *entr'actes* which have no connection with it.) Such an observance in post-Euripidean Greek tragedy would very naturally have become a rule by the time of Horace's Alexandrian authority, or by him been formulated into one.

As the performance of a tragic trilogy was followed at Athens by that of a satyr-play, Horace naturally now passes to the consideration of this latter type, which, he implies, is not without its possibilities as a Latin form. There is no evidence that satyr-plays ever were attempted in Latin either

---

[1] Including προλόγος and ἔξοδος.

[2] Legrand, *The New Greek Comedy*, English trans., p. 372. On the whole subject, cf. *ibid.* 368-80.

before or after Horace.[1] But that does not in the least require
us to think that he is here " merely beating the air," as was
inferred by Nettleship, who preferred to suppose that a passage
in Diomedes pointed to the existence of such a form. So far
as Latin literature is concerned, Horace in his advice to young
Piso has in view, not its actual past, but its potential future.
It seems to me that he is recommending Latin satyr-drama to
his pupil as a form which he himself might well have attempted
if he could have cared to give himself the trouble ; the first-
person which he employs from 234 to 244 is, of course, general
in effect, but it is none the less remarkable that he should have
chosen to use just this figure of speech here, and the whole
passage demonstrates that he had given quite a considerable
amount of thought to the technique, not so much of Greek
satyr-plays, as of the Latin ones which he here imagines himself as writing ; note the future tense throughout, 225-240.
Moreover, it is very natural that the idea should have particularly attracted Horace ; for as I have occasionally remarked,
Horace shows from the first in his *Epodes*, and retains throughout his work, a special fondness for, and felicity in, the mock-
heroic ; and satyr-drama was " tragedy at play." [2] The
playful-heroic is the quality of diction which he emphasises
(225-239, 245) as desirable for this prospective satyr-drama.
It is clear, too, that he is not in this place merely reproducing
his Alexandrian authority ; the pleasing figure (232) which he
applies to his ideal satyr-play is entirely and characteristically
Roman, and in his warning against what he regards as the
sentimental-erotic (*teneris* 246) the opponent [3] of Catullus and
Propertius voices a personal antipathy.   240-43 deal with
structure ; [4] 244-50 with tone.

[1] I regard Porphyrion's note on 221 as merely a desperate attempt
to support his own gross misunderstanding of the whole passage 220-4,
which he imagined to refer to *Latin* writers. Diomedes's " Graeca
satyrica " is *not* a hyphenated title of a Latin form ; if it had been, he
would not in this one instance only, have prefixed the epithet " Latina "
to the " Atellana " he contrasts therewith ; see the whole context,
most of which is quoted by Nettleship, *Essays in Lat. Lit.*, p. 180.

[2] παίζουσα τραγῳδία, Demetrius of Phaleron called it.

[3] To speak more strictly, the *presumed* opponent.

[4] *Ex noto fictum* = giving original treatment to a pre-existing myth-
subject, and is similar to *proprie communia dicere*, 128, and *veris falsa
remiscet*, 151.

As to metre (251-74), Horace continues, the most important piece of advice I have to give you two young people is this : Do not follow the example of the old Latin poets. The time-honoured idolatry of Plautus' metric is as absurd as that of his wit ; both are crude to the last degree. In metre study the Greek models, not the Latin ; and study them perpetually. They will teach you not only what to avoid, but what positive effects to aim at. As to the negative side—the rules that you find in the Greek tragedians, observe strictly ; take no advantage of the deplorably low standard of Roman taste in this matter ; let not even the authority that invests the name of Accius and Ennius tempt you to pass a spondee where a Greek would not have admitted it. Ennius was either indifferent to, or still worse ignorant of, the principles of tragic verse, and the so-called " nobility " of Accius' lines is merely lumpishness. Spondees must *never* occur in the second or fourth foot ; the admission of the spondee at all was doubtless (and here Horace theorises in the *a priori* manner which marks his handling of literary origins) a comparatively [1] late development in the evolution of the verse ; its basis is pure iambic, and that is why it is called not " spondaic " but " iambic " trimeter.[2]

---

[1] " Comparatively," for *non ita pridem* " not so very long ago " " only the other day " is *not* to be understood literally ; it could evidently be used (probably colloquially) to refer to a period that was actually a long way back ; cf. *Sat.*, II. ii. 46, of Gallonius whose date is more than a century earlier. Both passages have given rise to unnecessary assumptions.

[2] It will be noticed that I have explained this passage by paraphrasing it backwards. This method of study again and again gives the clue to the connection of thought in Horace's mind. Prevalent interpretations of these lines are, it seems to me, seriously mistaken at several points ; *e.g.* (i) *vos exemplaria Graeca nocturna versate manu, versate diurna* is repeatedly quoted as if it referred to the Greek poets in general as artistic models and not solely to the Greek tragedians in respect of metre ; (ii) editors mistranslate 251-4 in a way which results both in ignoring *etiam* and in attributing to Horace such nonsense as the statement that the iambic trimeter is called a trimeter despite the fact that the number of its feet is six, for the reason that the iambic is so swift a foot that it takes a couple of them to count as one ! Were there then no other feet that were habitually grouped in dipodies ? I paraphrase : " The foot ‿ —, a swift foot, is named *iambus ;* and it is from that name (*unde*) that it (the foot, personified as far as 262 *premit*) bade trimeters *too* (*etiam*) receive the additional name (*adcrescere nomen*) of

275-308 forms a final paragraph to this central section of
the poem. Horace reminds his pupils that the Drama, both
on its tragic and comic sides, is a Greek invention. Our poets,
he goes on to suggest, were quite right in endeavouring, after
their inevitable period of imitation and apprenticeship, to
make the Latin drama national by extending its application
to Roman subjects. There is a future for Roman poetry—a
potential future. But in a literary field with so distinguished
a tradition, the nation of soldiers can never hope to parallel
the achievements of the nation of artists unless our Roman
poets will submit to taking endless trouble over their general
technique. At present, unfortunately, the cry is all the other
way. Well, as that cuts *me* out from a poetical career (for
I prefer health and decency to a cheap and affected Bohemian-
ism even at the price of remaining undistinguished), I will fall
back upon the next best, and do what I can to be the cause of
true poetry in others. Thus does he introduce his concluding
section of general advice. It is interesting to see, and it also
appears elsewhere in Horace, that there was in his day a " cult
of genius " similar to that now in fashion. What is of importance, however, is the distinct attempt to stimulate a new and
a far better school of serious national drama (cf. 288). It is
simply the inveterate preconception that the *Ars Poetica* is an
essay, like the academic effusions of a Boileau or a Pope, that
has prevented readers from recognising the drift of these repeated personal exhortations (cf. 268 with 291 in their respective contexts) ; " there is a great task before you if you will
rise to it." And if we will only interpret 275-94 in the light
of other well-known passages in which Horace expounds his
theories about literature, we shall see that he indicates to his
pupils just *how* they are to rise to it ; we shall see what these
references to Greek origins really mean. " Do not, as our

'iambic ' trimeters, at a time when (*cum* with subjunctive, implying
connection, practically = ' since ') its six feet were all the same, *viz.*,
iambics. For it only admitted spondees later, to steady its pace somewhat, and even then with reservations." In other words : Do not
forget, says Horace, that " iambic " trimeters *were* originally strictly
true to their surviving name. I do not believe he intends any antithesis
here between the Latin numeral *senos* and the Greek verse-name (as
familiar as *hexametrus*) *trimetrus*. The reason why he at once says
pes citus in 252 is to prepare the way for *tardior* 255.

early school did, suppose that you can become the rivals or even the successors of the Greek writers by reproducing their *matter*. What you ought to imitate is their *principles*. And that means, particularly, two things : (i) in artistry and technique, learn all you can from them ; (ii) in theme, so far from reproducing their themes, emulate their noble example and be (*a*) *national*, (*b*) *original*." As he says elsehere,[1] unanswerably : " If the Greeks, too, had hated originality in literature, what ' classics ' would there be now ? " All this quite sufficiently accounts for what has very naturally caused perplexity to many of his modern readers and editors, his habit of apparently confusing features from Greek and Latin literature in his semi-historical and semi-theoretical summaries, as, for example, at 202-219 ; he is thinking of the Greek past, but has the Latin future in view. For he also means, unless I am much mistaken, to insist on a principle which I have for my own part already tried to thump out at the conclusion of my second chapter ; the principle that poetic or pure literature irrespective of languages is one art, and that the continuity and affinity of the same forms in different " literatures " is of far more importance than the undoubted fact that a sublime tragedy and a wretched pamphlet may happen to have been written in the same tongue. The drama, he would here say, the drama as an art is one, its evolution is one, and if Rome is to carry on that evolution she must add her own improvements and developments.

The future he hoped for Roman poetry never materialised. But this was not because the succeeding poets remained, like the old ones, impatient of the *limae labor et mora*. Technique both of verse and of style is as careful and professional after the Augustan age as it had been amateur and slovenly before it. It was, alas, just the *ingenium* that failed. Horace's diagnosis here is wrong. The real malady was one from which he himself suffered. The great Roman National Drama which the *Ars Poetica* seeks to stimulate was never achieved, and the reason is the same as that which caused Horace himself to shrink from attempting a Roman National Drama and to write the *Ars Poetica* instead. It was the Philosophic

---

[1] *Epist.*, II. i. 90-91.

Fallacy; the intellectualist conception of Morals. Instead of a Roman National Drama there appeared, in due course, the plays of Seneca. In Seneca we have, not Roman tragedy, but, on the contrary, Roman Euripides; he is a writer of sentiments, a rhetorician, a sophist, but without moral *feeling*.[1] If anyone does not believe in this affinity of the *Ars Poetica* with Senecan tragedy, or has not hitherto given it a thought, let him read the first fourteen lines of the following and final section of the poem. We persist in regarding poems as isolated phenomena; or we study, indeed, their purely literary connections, but not their spiritual kinships; the *Ars Poetica* got in time its dramatic progeny, and through their influence on the Elizabethan drama its effects were operative centuries later.

" The first essential for a (dramatic) writer is a knowledge of Moral Philosophy. That you will acquire from the literature of the Socratic tradition." (That *is*, from Plato to the Stoics, whether Horace was here thinking of the Stoics or not; and he himself used the works of the later schools much more than Plato's; and the following lines suggest Stoicism.) " τὸ καθῆκον—what Duty is, in the various relations of life—learn that, and then you will have a standard by which to make each character (father, son, etc.) talk. In the second place, exploit the life of your own time for realistic touches.[2] The right sort of *sentiments* [3] and the right sort of *psychology* will go far towards making your play a success, even if it has no other merits whatever." Such, in a paraphrase, is the gist of 309-322. Sophistry plus " Realism "; yes, it is a popular combination, from the days of Euripides to the days of Shaw. But if language is to be an instrument of thought and the same word is not to mean two opposite things, you cannot call it drama and apply that term to Aeschylus and Sophocles and Shakespeare. Their method is far other. For true tragedy, it is not realistic " imitation " but creative imagination that is required, and not moral philosophy but moral feeling.

---

[1] Why does not somebody attribute to Bacon the plays of Seneca ? The *a priori* case is very strong; incomparably more so than with Shakespeare.

[2] Cf. 153 foll., where he bids Piso note from life what he, Horace, thereupon proceeds to expound from philosophic literature.

[3] *Locis, i.e., loci communes.*

Be that as it may, the interesting point is to notice that the recipe for drama given in 309-11 did once get the length of a practical demonstration ; the prickly self-contained cactus of Stoicism did produce its one dramatic flower ; in the single case of Seneca the *sapiens* wrote tragedies.[1] And whatever we may think of the flower itself, it at least preserved the germ of literary drama as a species across the dark ages until modern times. To vary the metaphor, Elizabethan tragedy is, of course, an incomparably finer variety and its fruit by contrast sweet and sustaining, but it was grafted on the old crude bitter stock.

We have seen that a series of disconnected injunctions was a feature of the most primitive poetry known, and we have seen [2] that Horace can follow the *Works and Days* in concluding a long poem in that manner. 309-476 is to the bulk of the *Ars Poetica* as a sort of appendix ; for the most part, connection is not here to be sought for between the paragraphs, which, however, vary from 5 to 70 lines. For all that, neither is its matter less interesting nor its style less trenchant than in the body of the poem.

323-32. The Greeks were idealists ; the Romans are materialists, their very education makes them so.

333-46. The aim of some poets is to teach only, of others only to delight ; both have their " public " ; but the only poetry that has a universal appeal and that can hope to endure through the ages is the poetry that *combines both* aims.[3]

347-60. If the work *as a whole* is a fine one, especially if it is *on the right lines*, an occasional flaw, an oversight here or there, practically does not matter ; any critic who is not a mere pedant will more or less discount altogether such blemishes as are not either, (i.) radical, or (ii.) pervading. Especially, of course, in a work which is by its nature long. Conversely :—

361-5 distinguishes beauty of *form*, " architectonic " merit, from beauties of detail, with a clearly implied preference for the former. [As we should, in fact, expect ; either this passage amounts to nothing in particular, or it is *form* that " you

---

[1] *E.g.*, the choruses are simply diatribes on Stoic commonplaces, the *loci philosophumeni ;* there, in fact, you have plays which fulfil the desideratum *speciosa locis.*

[2] Pp. 40-1.   [3] Cf. Ch. II., p. 55.

can see when you stand some way off," form that loves the light and does not shrink even from the most searching criticism, form that *decies repetita placebit.*]

But—and now comes a passage which, if the *Ars Poetica* is to be considered seriously at all as a didactic treatise or a practical art, is surely one of the most remarkable in the poem ; which is, in any case, remarkable as coming from Horace, and still more so as forming the crowning injunction of the *Koran* of classic principle in poetry. " But," says our author (between line 365 and line 366, yet quite unmistakably) " even architectonic excellence is not enough. Even all these principles that I have just been showing you are not enough. You may observe them all, you may produce a work which is at once well constructed and well versed, and yet not achieve a place in the roll of poets. Why ? Because the proof of the pudding is in the eating ; the *efficient* part of a work of art is its actual material surface ; and the surface—the workmanship—must have "—and now we come to the lesson driven home in 366-90—" must have *Distinction.*" " With things," he goes on, " that are not absolutely essential to the ordinary course of life, like champagne [1] and pineapples, it is a case of either first-rate or not at all. And poetry is one of these. ' Mediocrity ' in poetry—that is what neither gods nor men nor booksellers will tolerate." Now it is surely very interesting to find the great exponent of the doctrine of the golden mean insisting that it does *not* apply to poetry. (Not but what the famous stanza holds *literally* true here also.

> Aure021m quisquis mediocritatem
> Diligit, tutus caret obsoleti
> Sordibus tecti, caret invidenda
> Sobrius aula.

Yes, he will escape destitution, but he will also miss " the envied hall "—the hall of Fame.) And it is surely a surprise, at any rate for the reader who comes to his Horace with the current preconception, to find in the end of the classic handbook for poets this virtual admission of the comparative helplessness, the almost wholly negative value, of all the rules that

---

[1] I choose distant but illuminating parallels to the dinner-accessories of 374-6.

it has just been enunciating. But this necessity for distinction of style, for an individuality of spirit expressing itself right on the material surface, above and beyond even the highest purely artistic merits, is, I should have thought, the very last discovery to be made by those (whether critics or poets) who have thought deeply about the nature of the art, and explored and probed and sounded every means by which success in it might conceivably be attainable ; and it remains remarkable that Horace, who after all has his limitations, should have made that discovery. For indeed it obviously is the last discovery ; it leaves the fundamental problem once more where it was (and where it always will be) ; for this " distinction " no recipe can be given, no hint even. Originality in writing always means creation in some degree and no man can tell you how to create, you can only do it by creating. Horace, naturally, does not attempt to give any such recipe. But he does proceed to give the best he can, two purely negative but so far distinctly helpful counsels. (i) Never write when you do not feel the strong inward prompting of having something to say ; for, he adds, and adds it *more suo* beforehand, poetry being an attractive pursuit is perpetually being attempted by gentlemen of means and integrity.[1] (ii) Do not rush into publication ; if one has written, as *you* doubtless would, under that strong inward prompting, the product will seem to have the desired " distinction " while you still re-read it under the influence of your own afflatus ; but that is no test at all ; the only true criteria are, the opinion of sound critics, and your own opinion a long time afterwards when—to anticipate the choice and illuminating language of a later writer who was as stupid a critic as he was a master of transparent prose [2]—the

[1] There is the usual Horatian " elliptical antithesis " between 385 and 383-4. An example is Browning, who often wrote because his wealth and leisure got on his conscience.

[2] Quintilian has at least two reminiscences of *A.P.*, 388, and as I shall get into trouble for my view of him, or better still because they both deserve to be more known, I give myself the pleasure of transcribing them, italicising what seems to me most admirable. (i) *Dedicatory Epistle :* Usus deinde Horati consilio, qui in arte poetica suadet, ne praecipitetur editio nonumque prematur in annum, dabam iis [sc. libris, " this book of mine "] otium, ut *refrigerato inventionis amore* diligentius repetitos *tanquam lector* perpenderem. (ii) X. iv. 2 : Nec dubium est

zest of creation has cooled down again and you can regard your own work from an almost totally detached standpoint.

All of which seems to me to be not more remarkable than true ; with one exception. If *animis natum inventumque poema iuvandis* is meant to be a statement like Juvenal's theory of the origin of boars, *animal propter convivia natum*, partial and rhetorical and by the boars themselves at any rate frankly questionable, then I have no quarrel with it. If it is meant to be an assertion of the fundamentally *æsthetic* basis of the appeal of poetry, on the understanding that even the moral appeal is not to a system of ethical judgments but to a moral *sense*, then I applaud it. But if it is meant, and to this 369-76 quite clearly points, as a denial that poetry has any serious and, in fact, indispensable function in society at all, then I am bound to conclude, and do conclude, that Horace is here, just for the moment, nodding ; for of course, *quandoque bonus dormitat Horatius ;* or if not nodding, smiling, possibly. This is no mere inference from my own (already enough dwelt on) personal preconception on the subject. It is proved by Horace himself, who at once proceeds (391-407) to expound a theory of poetry which demonstrably [1] represents his own confirmed belief, as amply indicated by his *general* theory and practice, and with which 377 is entirely irreconcilable. That 377 is false is also shown by the fact that the conclusion to which it leads him is at variance with the patent phenomena. *Do* " gods and men and bookstalls " (so much at variance on other points) agree in boycotting mediocre poetry ? No, they all— the publishers and the readers and the reviewers—delight in it ; not in all ages, possibly, but in most, for the reason that in most ages they get nothing better given them. The case is, in fact, precisely parallel with those which he for the nonce contrasts with it in 369-72 ; what is not first-rate in poetry *tamen in pretio est ;* and for the same reason, to wit, that poetry, so far from belonging to the same category as madrigals at a " gaudy," or *pâté de foie gras*, is one of the basic

---

optimum esse emendandi [" revising "] genus, si scripta in aliquod tempus reponantur ut ad ea post intervallum *velut nova atque aliena* redeamus *ne nobis scripta nostra tanquam recentes fetus blandiantur*.

[1] See Ch. III.

needs of social life. Horace knows it is ; but 391-407 is a passage I have already partly dealt with.[1]

There is really a not inconsiderable division at 390-1. From here to the end is a peroration, and its purport is : The poet's is a high vocation, properly understood ; he is, as shown by traditions, nothing less than the civiliser of his fellow-men. χαλεπὰ τὰ κάλα ; training, training, training, is the imperative preliminary ; otherwise—then follows a playful picture of the fate of the bad poet, and our author's frivolous moralising thereon provides a suitably or characteristically ironical conclusion.

On this peroration just a little remains to be said. In the first of its two paragraphs he refers summarily to the evolution of Greek poetry from prehistoric times (391-401) through epic and lyric (401-407, stopping at lyric, since the origin of Drama has already been touched on), in order to illustrate his view that the art of poetry is functional and that its function is religious, national, and social ; whether it be in succeeding phases civilising, martial, didactic, political, or festal. The second begins, characteristically, from a deliberately selected *point de départ* which seems to have misled some of the expositors ; Horace is *not* here concerned at all, really, with the old question whether poetry is the product of art or of inspiration. As he was to say elsewhere [2] of civic virtue, the *vis insita* requires *doctrina*, training, to bring it out to the full ; failing which it must inevitably degenerate. But *vis insita* is outside the teacher's sphere ; all he can say is, it must be there for the *doctrina* to operate on ; on *doctrina* in general he *can* give positive counsels, and he does. Poets, like kings, are a special mark for flatterers, and should be equally cautious in taking opinions. If you have the good luck to get a candid critic like my late lamented friend Quinctilius Varus, appreciate it. A ridiculous début [3] may prove thoroughly damaging, and leave a writer with no hopes of a following other than of the giddy-

---

[1] In Ch. III.   [2] *Odes*, IV. iv. 33-6.

[3] *Exceptumque sinistre*, 452, certainly refers to reception by the public ; this interpretation gives *semel* its proper force, and is proved by 453 foll. (= the " seria mala "). The other does not even make sense, and would surely not have occurred to anybody if it had not been suggested by the Scholiast.

minded. Such a poet, uncastigated and self-satisfied, with his
head in the air and his thoughts only on the sublime, is practically certain sooner or later to find himself in a pit of bathos
which his absorption had prevented him from seeing while it
yawned before his feet. And who is going to stir a finger to
help him out ? Who is to say that he did not do it deliberately ?—like Empedocles ; for he, too, was aiming at " immortality " when he jumped down the crater of Etna. No,
poets must be allowed to commit *felo de se* [1] if they want to.
It is useless to rescue him ; he will only do it again. After
all, a poet is something—don't you think ?—that is not quite
human.[2] It is a madness, a visitation ; one had best give him
a wide berth.[3]

This last of the poem's three divisions, from 309 to the
end, is really all concerned with general aims, with poetic
ideals. It is one of Horace's chief virtues as a literary critic,
that he cares most about fundamentals. His object here is
to put his young pupils on the right lines,[4] to make them
realise what is the aim *proper* to poetry, in an age and among
a people where " bad art " was everywhere acceptable. But
that an organic, a vital, coherency, a beauty neither less nor
more dependent on the adaptation (not ruthless subjugation)
of means to ends than is the beauty of the creations of Nature
herself, is the ideal pointed to by the school of criticism properly called Classic ; that that is its ideal, and not as often

---

[1] The real reference is, I take it, to artistic suicide. As I have
indicated, I see behind the *prima facie* meaning of 457-76 a metaphorical application to the subject with which Horace has been concerned ever since 416, the folly of ignoring candid criticism. Some
such significance seems demanded by the grotesque improbability of the
disaster instanced as a climax of the " seria mala " quite seriously
threatened in 451-2. And *sit ius liceatque perire poetis*, if made purely
as a literal claim, whether ironically or not, surely lacks point. It is the
only right that has always been accorded them.

[2] 469 fiet homo ; cf. inhumanae Camenae, *Epist.*, I. xviii. 47.

[3] 464-end (" deus . . . hirudo ") should be in inverted commas,
like " qui . . . nolit " 462-3 ; it is all supposed to be addressed to the
would-be rescuer. But, of course, it is *at* young Piso, or at least for his
benefit ; I have aimed at bringing this out and at representing the concluding irony.

[4] Cf. esp. 347-50 = mere flaws of execution differ *toto coelo* from radically perverse methods.

supposed a frigid formalism or geometrical regularity; this surely is apparent not from the concluding section only but from the whole treatise. And surely that ideal and the principles it involves have nowhere else received expression so appropriate.

EPISTLES I

The first book of Epistles is, after all, the consummation of Horace's poetical development. The only other portion of his work that can reasonably compete with it is the Odes; not in their entirety, where the comparison would be unfair to either side, but assuming a selection to have been made of all the best. As poetry, as pure and absolute poetry, that would, indeed, take precedence. The style is much more elevated; there is more richness, more romance, more colour —far more, certainly, of all these things; there is more brightness and more variety. In the finest of the lyrics the tone is that of one inspired; in the Epistles it is never so. Yet in the Odes, for all that, there is seldom or never absent a consciousness of performance; we watch deliberate ambition, with power behind it, realise itself; the poet has mounted his reciting platform and donned his traditional sacerdotal robes, and he is acquitting himself magnificently; but our predominant feeling is admiration, we have a sense of great achievement. We may feel, too, though this at least is probably largely prepossession, that the Odes are " inspired " also in the ironic sense; the performance has a genuinely honoured and revered certainly, but still an imperial, behest behind it. Horace's previous writings had been (when not mock-heroic) entirely in the " unofficial " vein; not for nothing had he been a disciple of Archilochus, the father of the free-lance style, for which style the satire had but provided him with a more characteristically Roman vehicle. After the Odes (as he supposed) were finished, he incontinently cast off his bardic robes. He returned to the hexameter, and he returned to the comparatively colloquial style; but he returned with a great difference. The Horatian epistle, as an art-form, is the joint offspring of the Horatian satire and the Horatian ode; nor is it easy to say which parent truly contributed the greater share. At last the " satire," which meant just anything, has become a *form*, doing so in the only manner possible, that is by ceasing to be satire ; at last the favourite Horatian type of ode, the earnest personal adjuration invented (probably) by Sappho, has lowered its tone sufficiently to be frankly and powerfully Latin. This is the formal, or perhaps we may be allowed to say the evolutionary, reason why the epistles— meaning naturally the first book, those of the second and the *Ars Poetica* being too extended properly to represent the type—why the epistles are the summit of their author's work. The other and more telling reason lies in the intimacy of their appeal. The Odes have more of many qualities ; more of almost everything, as has just been said. The Epistles have the advantage over them in no respect but one, yet that is a strong one. The Epistles have more depth.

It has sometimes been said that the epistle as a literary form is Horace's own invention. This is perhaps hardly true. Certainly, as just shown, he himself evolved his particular type of epistle ; and certainly it was he who first practised it as a regular and special form. But in this field he had, at least, antecedents. Cicero's letters have been mentioned in that connection, but they (and all such) [1] are really another matter ; not so much because they are prose, but because, though often and to a considerable degree " literary," they are not primarily so ; they remain essentially correspondence. What matters more is that a number of the *sermones* of Lucilius were in the form of letters ; and since the epistolary form as a vehicle of popular moralising appears again later (in prose) with Seneca, who was much influenced by the Greek " dia- tribe " of the Hellenistic age, it is not improbable that the form itself took rise in Alexandrian times. Certain of the compositions of the Cynic Menippus of Gadara purported to be letters. The formal letter of exhortation, however un- familiar to our own day, seems quite clearly to have been something of an institution in the Hellenistic world. It was a regular *genre* with the late Greek sophists of the Antonine period. But much earlier, it was extensively used by St. Paul. If our remains were less fragmentary we might even find that it had a continuous history going back to (for ex-

---

[1] *E.g.*, the Platonic letters, genuine and spurious.

ample) Sappho, whose poem to (or rather at) her brother Charaxus must undoubtedly be regarded as one of the ancestors, through the ode, of the Horatian letter ; and to Hesiod, whose *Works and Days* is the earliest extant didactic epistle, and as already observed [1] presents certain formal traits which even reappear in Horace. But there is a much closer parallel, and it is curious that it does not seem to have been noticed. Two poems of Theocritus, the sixteenth and the twenty-eighth, are the only things in ancient literature that can really be called to some extent anticipations of Horace's epistles. The former is a letter to Hiero, military governor, soon to be king, of Syracuse, gracefully conveying a broad hint that his patronage would be cordially welcomed, and deploring the universal money-worship of the times. Its detail not infrequently reminds one of Horace.

> δαιμόνιοι, τί δὲ κέρδος ὁ μυρίος ἔνδοθι χρυσός
> κείμενος.
>> quid iuvat immensum te argenti pondus et auri
>> furtim defossa timidum deponere terra ?

> δειλοῖς ἐν νεκύεσσι μακροὺς αἰῶνας ἔκειντο
> εἰ μὴ θεῖος ἀοιδός . . .
>> sed omnes illacrimabiles
>> urguentur ignotique longa
>> nocte, carent quia vate sacro.

> ἐκ Μοισᾶν ἀγαθὸν κλέος ἔρχεται ἀνθρώποισι,
> χρήματα δὲ ζώοντες ἀμαλδύνουσι θανόντων.
>> cedes, et exstructis in altum
>> divitiis potietur heres.

The other belongs to the type of *Epist.*, I. xiii., the " invoice " letter accompanying a gift ; in both these cases it is indirectly addressed. In the Theocritean piece compliments are conveyed with something of Horace's grace and urbanity. It is in a choriambic metre, the so-called second Asclepiad, and in the view of Mr. J. M. Edmonds, " was almost certainly modelled upon Sappho or Alcæus."

---

[1] Ch. II., pp. 40-1.

Horace himself, however, was not consciously following up any of these trails. In the final ode of his third book he had, he thought, taken his farewell of the somewhat over-arduous delights of lyric poetry. In the *Ars Poetica* he had then, according to the view already expressed, exonerated himself from what was obviously his next duty, the writing of drama. He now found himself reverting, as it were automatically, to the form of composition which had been his first choice, and in which he had quickly learned to feel himself in his proper element; the familiar hexameter. The epistles, that is to say, are *sermones*, "discourses," and to that extent in the same class with the satires; he applies the term to his satires in *Epist.*, I. iv. 1, II. ii. 60, to both in *Epist.*, II. i. 250, while in the fourth line of the same piece he uses it to denote an epistle. But they are *saturae* with a difference, and the difference is considerable, and it is due to the influence of the Odes. It is not, probably, that Horace deliberately applied to the satire the formal principles of the ode. Rather, as often happens in such matters, the habits of style he had contracted in the more laborious sphere of work reacted on him when he returned to the more artless. Consequently the fundamental formative constituents of the ode all reappear in the epistle. The addressee, to begin with; the satire, indeed, is apt to address itself to somebody, but it is also very liable to forget him for considerable passages; or he may be a mere "man of straw." The epistle never, perhaps, quite forgets its addressee, and some have all along an acute sense of his individuality. The occasion, again; that in the satire is a mere *point de départ*, in the epistle it is what Aristotle would call the "formal cause" of the poem; the moral—the element that Horace cares most about, and in the case of the epistles one may add, his readers too—is regularly in close connection with it. Further, the epistles are all, in their different degrees, carefully constructed, and the structure is largely similar to that seen in the Odes. The tone is generally earnest. The style is often elevated, and in places really becomes "poetry" in the modern strict sense of the term, which in the Satires it cannot be said to do. The moral element is, of course, the predominating one, and it is in this book that we see Horace most purely as a moralist.

The fifth is perhaps the one which remains throughout most like an ode [1] in theme and structure. The occasion is once more the eve of a festival, in this case Augustus' birthday, and the poem is an invitation to his friend the Torquatus of *Odes*, IV. vii. to take advantage of the opportunity of sleeping late to-morrow and dine to-night with the writer. It begins by the reminder that the poet can only offer a comparatively modest entertainment ; urges his friend to dismiss all business worries from his mind ; preaches the gospel of making the most of life's rare opportunities for enjoyment ; praises wine ; promises a neat and tasteful table and congenial company ; ends with a roguish touch ; and has one lapse into the sort of reference to armpits and smelly goats which the modern reader finds so pointlessly crude ; all these things being such as can be paralleled from the Odes by any reader. While the first book of Epistles—it has always been noted—is prevailingly stoical in tone, this piece is rather Epicurean, and the fact may be due to something in Torquatus' character which seemed to Horace to call for just this sort of medicine, since the ode addressed to him is also of an Epicurean tendency—or would be if it were less beautiful.

On the other hand, if a passage peculiarly recalling the manner of the Satires is desired, one may point perhaps to the second half (lines 53-108) of the first epistle. This piece serves, of course, as a dedication and preface of the book as a whole, and consequently there is a good deal in its general purport which recalls the first of the first book of Satires. But whereas there the general materialism of the age seemed to the satirist to be most representatively embodied in the figure of the miser, here his diagnosis goes much deeper. And as a result his remedy is different. Since the piece has sometimes been slightly mis-represented owing to a tendency to regard this mere pagan as never having made any spiritual progress and as maintaining throughout his life one and the same standpoint of (at the best) a sort of formal eclecticism, it may be worth while briefly to re-summarise it. Lines 10-27 give us at once a statement of his general state of mind at the period of the epistles. He now feels in himself the want, the supreme need rather, of what we

---

[1] Another that is very like an ode is xi ; cf. *Odes*, I. vii. all along.

should call a faith, of what the ancient calls a philosophy ; he is as yet only in the course of working out one for himself, and in so doing he finds himself tossed by the storm of life now to one port of doctrine, now to another ; [1] now to Stoicism, now to the Cyrenaic's opposite extreme. But that it is now in Stoicism that he sees the nearest approach to the true way of life, he already indicates by speaking of his Cyrenaic moods as a " relapse " ; and the book as a whole clearly bears this out. At all events, however, the first step in the attainment of wisdom is, he is well aware, the getting rid of folly. Such is his present preoccupation ; not so the world's, where the prime care is still the acquisition, not of sweetness and light, not of " culture " (*cultura*, 40) but of riches. Then follows a satire thereon. But the worship of money is merely a symptom, the most typical, of the universal materialism ; it is not only the rich man who suffers from that malady ; the poor is just as bad.[2] Materialism leads to no security ; there are a hundred ways of pursuing it, but they all converge to the same sick lion's den (70-80) ; however you change your tack on *that* course, you will never find it bring you to the happiness which is your ultimate aim (80-93). So far, Horace has stressed the contrast between himself and the world ; now he admits that, opposite as their ideals remain, he himself is, of an occasion, chief of sinners (97-101) ; the damning fact about materialism is that it is inconsistent and therefore self-contradictory, and Horace himself has not yet attained perfect consistency. Who, then, has ? ζῆν ὁμολογουμένως—the Stoic ; the very Stoic whose cast-iron uncompromisingness I have so often laughed at. At any rate when he isn't suffering from a cold in the head.

The characteristically playful conclusion (106-8) implies no more than in Horace it ever does. Just as there are wiseacres who solemnly assure us that the second epode is proved by its last four lines to be a satire on the fashionable affectation of praising a country life, so there are those who as early as line

[1] Quo me cunque rapit tempestas deferor hospes—15.

[2] 91-3. I cannot agree with Wickham's note, still less with the suggestion of Cruquius. It is Horace himself who exclaims *quid pauper ?* Cf. 24-5, *id quod Aeque pauperibus prodest, locupletibus aeque.* [Incidentally, cf. also 55 and 26.]

91 of this epistle begin taking about the ironical conclusion, thereby obscuring the fact that Horace is quite sincere in his confession of his frequent delinquencies and that, therefore, the general trend of the moralising is strongly towards Stoicism ; not excepting the light irony of the last words, the object of which (as elsewhere) is to prevent the effect of the good lesson from being defeated by over-seriousness. How far the character of Horace has mellowed since the first book of the satires may be gathered from a comparison of this epistle with such a piece as the third of that book ; we see that while unchanged in his censure of inconsistency [1] he is changed in the conclusion which he draws therefrom ; there it had led him direct to anti-Stoicism. It is also interesting to note the alteration in his attitude to himself, as between *Sat.*, I. iii. 29-34 and the corresponding lines (94-100) of this epistle ; in the former passage he had claimed the credit at least of possessing the qualities of his defects ; in the later he is much humbler—" I have even more serious faults than those."

The figures employed to illustrate his meaning are felicitous, particularly in 70-80 with its subtle transition from the beast of Aesop's fable (further appropriate because it is " sick ") to the many-headed monster of which he had very probably read in Plato's *Republic*. The idea in 42-52 is the same as that of the *quod petis hic est* of another epistle ; the athlete is imagined as having been miraculously offered an Olympic victory for nothing ; can one even conceive his not taking it ? Well, the same chance is yours ; " virtue " is not only as far more valuable a thing than the gold you are ever pursuing as is an Olympic victory in comparison with a local success, but its attainment will actually mean for you a cessation of all this struggling.

Further resemblances might easily be pointed out between the epistle as such and the satire. Dialogue is fairly common, so is inserted narrative as object lesson, in which capacity fable also reappears.[2] One is occasionally reminded of Juvenal in a special degree, as at vi. 17-64. The fifteenth is a satire on himself, the nineteenth a satire, once again but from a position of advantage now, on his literary enemies.

---

[1] Cf. *Sat.*, I. iii. 1-19 with *Epist.*, I. i. 82-100.

[2] *E.g.*, fable, x. 34-8 ; and vii provides dialogue 15-19, fable 29-33, narrative 46-95.

At the same time, a Horatian epistle is something different at once from a satire—than which its tone is more mellow—and from an ode, than which its personal element is more intimate. The eighth, for instance, like the first, shows us Horace feeling deeply about his own shortcomings in a way which is quite new to him. Not that that is its object. It is an exceedingly skilful, and must, one thinks, have been felt as a very effective, not to say moving, reproof. Characteristically it does not disclose itself as such until the end. It begins as a letter of congratulation to his young friend Celsus on receiving an appointment as secretary on the staff of Tiberius —the future emperor. Celsus seems to have belonged to the type—or to have been at the age—which sees all the good things that come to it in life or literature [1] as its own by right of merit, and conducts itself accordingly. The danger of a reproof, especially when addressed to a spirited nature, is that it may cause resentment, and have the opposite effect to what it intends. Here the writer's candour, in the modern sense, is softened by his " candour " in the old. His honest and honourable admission that he, too, sometimes, and now particularly, finds it " hard to be good," especially in the matter of behaviour towards others, puts the recipient off his guard, so that when the rebuke comes, which it does suddenly and quite unexpectedly in the very last line, his instinct of resentment finds itself already disarmed.

Another that is prevailingly serious in tone is the seventh, which is called by Sellar the gem of the whole collection, and of which it has been said that it " will always rank among the most valued of Horace's poems ; it shows the man in his most attractive aspect—simple, frank, affectionate, tactful, manly, and independent." [2] It is addressed to his patron to whom he excuses himself for having stayed in the country all August, thus breaking his promise to return in five days. In all periods of patronage a certain amount of attendance on the great man has been understood to be one of the regular duties of the dependent.

Your worst materialist is your ascetic on principle. To

---

[1] Cf. iii. 15-20.
[2] Sir T. Martin, (mis)quoted by Wilkins.

renounce matter altogether is to shirk it merely ; to prove yourself really superior to it you must be able to use it. Various forms of false " idealism " may be detected in this age as in that ; no one has seen through them more acutely than Horace, or so repeatedly used the best object-lessons he could think of to expose them. However he gravitates towards Stoicism, he never loses his admiration for the type of character who can turn to practical advantage, as opposed to mere sensual enjoyment, such material good fortune as comes in his way. We shall find this type represented for us in a later epistle by the Cyrenaic Aristippus. The test of true spiritual freedom is not only that a man can do without external goods, but that he can also do with them, for so long as he is dependent on either aspect of Fortune he has not independence. In a fine passage of the Odes, Horace had sung *si celeres quatit Pinnas, resigno quae dedit et mea Virtute me involvo*, but just before that he had said *laudo manentem*. Vulteius, in the story which forms the second half of this epistle, had got himself let in (rather against his will, indeed) for dependency, and in due course found that he had gained material well-being at the price of freedom. Similarly the fox in the fable. If I am challenged with that fable, says Horace, with an echo of the passage just referred to, *cuncta resigno*, I am ready to give up all again, to show that I *could* exist without it ; and that the mere parasite dare not do. No, I am not committed to dependence by having accepted clientship ; the right sort of patronage is an association honourable to both sides ; I have also my side of the bargain, which I do my best to perform as worthily as you (Maecenas) have yours (14-24) ; on the one hand, I do not sleep away what you give me, nor on the other hand am I going to impair my efficiency by partaking more than is good for me of the exciting life of the capital—not even to give a slight gratification to *you*.[1] That I could really accept such a challenge, you will realise if you reflect on my past conduct as your protégé ; you have yourself praised my modesty, and my gratitude you know.

The first half of the piece is, perhaps, the best long example

[1] This is how I incline to take lines 35-6, though I admit the ordinary interpretation may be the right one. *Somnum plebis* = the leisurely life, cf. 46, 50-1 ; 36 is explained by 44-5.

in hexameters of his characteristic mature style, terse and elliptical, not easy reading yet worth the trouble of thinking out, and marked by abrupt transitions where the connection with what has preceded can only be discovered by reading on for some distance.[1] The story of Philippus and Vulteius is told in his very best manner ; friendships have strange origins, and there is something curiously subtle and telling in the picture of the great advocate and politician going home tired, and being attracted by the worthy citizen whom he saw in the leisurely act of cleaning his nails. Volteius was then happy and clean-shaven ; the distraction wrought in him by his experience of patronage is effectively suggested by a clever touch ; at their last rencontre Philippus finds his client *scabrum intonsumque*. The story leads to the necessary ingredient of a moral.

Another of the graver epistles is the sixteenth. It begins by a description, purporting to be in answer to the inquiries of the correspondent, of his Sabine farm ; but the bulk of it is an exposition of the theme that the only true virtue is the virtue that has its roots in a man's inner character, and is irrespective of public opinion ; thus the piece is thoroughly Stoical in tone. The relation between these two subjects is not immediately apparent ; some deliberate relation, by all analogy, there undoubtedly is ; and I do not think it has been put better than by Wickham : " The retirement and simple pleasures in which he paints himself as finding health and contentment are a fitting introduction to the remainder of the letter in which he is to argue that happiness cannot be separated from goodness, and that they both are to be sought within us, not without us." That the connection is not too obvious is intentional, for, as the same editor observes, we are meant " to feel something of the easy inconsequence of a letter." Of the extent to which Horace has by now become converted to Stoicism, we have a striking indication at 55-6, which amounts to an admission of all that the Stoics really meant by their doctrine of the equal heinousness of all sins, the very doctrine Horace had so insistently attacked in the third of the first

---

[1] *E.g.*, the relevance of 14-24 is not seen until 25-8 is read ; 37-8 is not understood until 39 is reached. The best instance is perhaps *Epist.*, I. xvii. 39-42.

book of Satires. The end strikes a deep note rare in Horace. Even at the worst, the philosopher is still, if he cares to be, unconquerable ; because at the worst death will release him. It is remarkable how the shade of Socrates haunts all subsequent Greek philosophy ; here is the idea of the Phædo that philosophy is preparing for death ; and we are reminded of its concluding episode. The passage itself is an adaptation of a dialogue in Euripides' *Bacchæ* between a person who is " king " in the worldly sense and therefore supposes himself to have entire power over his interlocutor, in whom he sees nothing more than the fanatical protagonist of a certain religion, but who is, in fact, divine. It is the Stoic who is *truly* a king ; and it is the Stoic who knows that he has that in him which is divine.[1] *Non vultus instantis tyranni . . .*

The eleventh is, on the whole, my own favourite among the epistles. In the bare thoughts of which it is constituted there is perhaps nothing, or very little, that Horace has not also said elsewhere, and many times ; but in poetry it is the deed and not the thought that ultimately matters, and the deed is the expression. It is here that certain of these thoughts find their most felicitous expression :

> Caelum non animum mutant qui trans mare currunt—

and certain others their most poetical :

> scis Lebedus quid sit ; Gabiis desertior atque
> Fidenis vicus ; tamen illic vivere vellem,
> oblitusque meorum obliviscendus et illis
> Neptunum procul e terra spectare furentem.

" Furentem " is good ; to the man who has found peace it is the symbol of what he has escaped from, ever present to make his peace the more felt ; *suave mari magno.* Lines 17 to 21 of course, are not without a naive provinciality ; after all, some people's lots are cast in " Rhodes and Mytilene and Samos and Chios." But the sum-total of the efforts of an age of materialism and superstition, whether the Augustan or another not so far distant—the endless thoughtless mechanical competitive activity along conventional lines, that produces new inventions and new books by the million and yet in point

---

[1] Epictetus, *Diss.*, I. 14, 5.

of fact achieves literally nothing at all since its inventions bring human enlightenment not an inch further and its writings are too jerry-built to leave more to posterity than a mass of rubble—when was the output of such an age better summed up than in the words

strenua nos exercet inertia ; navibus atque
quadrigis petimus bene vivere.

It is only the Latin language that can say, and perhaps only Horace who could place in its most telling position, such a phrase as *quod petis hic est*. Not but what I confess to liking *est Ulubris* even a little better ; it would make a sublime motto.

The fifteenth is very good fun. It is a surprise, of course ; the effect will best be got by reading it immediately after the one just considered. There we had seen that peace of mind was to be had even at Ulubrae ; here we find the philosopher making the most minute inquiries about certain alternative fashionable watering-places ; and exercised not so much about the degree to which peace of mind is there procurable, but on such questions as, which of them has the larger bread-supply, which the better water. I must have this and I must have that—and all as if it were a matter of course, as if his correspondent would not be in the least surprised by his particularity. Climate, wines, game, fish, sea-urchins—you will, of course, tell me about everything. In the eleventh letter we had learned that

ratio et prudentia curas,
non locus effusi late maris arbiter aufert ;

now we are told that when the fine sea-view is duly reached, it is not to be philosophy that is requisitioned, but a very special quality of wine, " to drive away cares." And the whole letter, it should be noted, is artfully and archly concocted into an appearance of spontaneous volatility, so as to suggest that the writer is in high spirits ; it is garrulous and full of long parentheses ; [1] from the start down to the end of the twenty-fifth line is all one sentence ; then he suddenly takes breath, and with one of his inimitable transitions—one of the best—he starts off on a long rigmarole about a certain

[1] Besides 2-13 and 16-21 ought to be reckoned 28-31.

Maenius, a society spunger and diner-out, who blackmailed for dinners as others would for money. The abruptness at 26 keeps the reader wondering what the story is going to be used for. When he could not get a recherché meal he had a cheap and big one (the Soho style) ; tripe, or—for ancient gastronomical conventions were sometimes strangely at variance with ours—lamb. In good or bad fortune equally, he always tried to make the best of life. " And that is just the sort of person I am." Yes, after all, you know, despite the Stoic tendency of this book, I'm *really*—hush !—an Epicurean ! [1]

For indeed, if αὐτάρκεια—self-sufficiency or independence —is really the supreme ideal, as the Stoics will have it, then Aristippus the Cyrenaic was a more perfect Stoic than the Stoics themselves ; in the seventeenth letter we hear how he was in his element anywhere.

> omnis Aristippum decuit color et status et res,
> temptantem maiora, fere praesentibus aequum.

Culture is not only pleasanter than asceticism, it goes further. The other type, the Cynic—be it noted, we do not quarrel with the Stoics in this book even when our theme is the old one of satirising doctrinaire austerity [2]—is really a helpless dependent on his own rule of life.

> contra, quem duplici panno patientia velat,
> mirabor vitae via si conversa decebit.

Without his blanket—and without his dirt, it might be added —he is almost certain to catch cold. This letter purports to be addressed to a young man with social ambitions, who is about to serve his apprenticeship in the almost inevitable way even (as the next piece shows) for a youth of means and good family ; by attaching himself as protégé to the patronage of some distinguished and wealthy elder. But for my own part I feel almost certain that Scaeva is one of Horace's invented

---

[1] Mr. R. Hackforth points out to me the close parallel between lines 41-6 and Epicurus, *Epist.*, III. ap. Diog. Laert., X. 130 (see in Ritter and Preller, 472 b. med.). He thinks Horace here is " *sincerely* Epicurean " ; I think a comparison of the two passages will only emphasise the gaiety of the poet.

[2] Besides, the Stoics, unlike the Cynics, found room for the practical in their view of life, as Horace has by now realised, *Epist.*, I. i. 16-17.

names, and that it represents σκαιός, the gauche, boorish man.[1]
XVII. and XVIII. are companion pieces ; the ancient scholiasts
ran them into one, but they are really contrasted and comple-
mentary ; I have little doubt that the eighteenth was the
original one, and that the seventeenth was written to set it
off. This does not mean that " Scæva " is a mere lay figure ;
Horace may well have had some particular person in his thoughts,
but under the circumstances would naturally not care to name
him.

Lollius, to whom XVIII. is addressed, was demonstrably a
real person [2] and a young friend of the poet. He is called
liberrimus in the first line, which means that his manner towards
social superiors is always free-spirited and independent ; and
Horace, who intends in due course to read him a gentle lesson,
at once pays him the compliment of saying that the last thing
he may be expected to turn out [3] is an obsequious toady.
From various parts of the epistle we can gather quite a clear
idea of his personality ; refined, accomplished, manly, with
healthy outdoor tastes, but reserved and studious, he may
not, the older man fears, be quite worldly-wise enough ; he
may not entirely realise the obligations of his position ; he
will probably be too often thoughtful, taciturn, perhaps even
moody. It may at first surprise some to find Horace inculcating
worldly wisdom. But he always enforces just the sort of lesson
which he feels to be required by the particular case. Moreover,
it is clear from both these epistles [4] that Horace's own view is
that patronage is far from an unmixed blessing. If a man has
really high, if he has fastidious, principles, he had better keep

---

[1] A Stoic conception ; σκαιότηs was discussed by Chrysippus.

[2] 50-64. He is presumably to be identified with the Lollius addressed in the second epistle of this book, and was probably the son of
the hero of *Odes*, IV. ix.

[3] *Metues* in line 1 I take to be another instance of the peculiar
Horatian use of this verb = *nolle*, on which see Lucian Müller at *Odes*,
II. ii. 7, *pinna metuente solvi*. Müller, however, does not take it so here ;
on the other hand he does at *Odes*, III. xiv. 15 (reading *nunc* for *nec*),
where the context makes just all the difference and renders this impossible ; despite the fact that the same phrase *non metuam mori* at
Odes, III. ix. 11 is, I believe, an instance of this idiom—" and I will
dare even death itself for thee." Add *Sat.*, II. v. 65.

[4] XVIII. 86-7, 103, 107 ; XVII. 6-10.

out of it altogether if he can. But if for one good reason or another you elect to avail yourself of it, you must be prepared to make such sacrifice even of freedom of mind as it reasonably enough requires of you.

> dulcis inexpertis cultura potentis amici ;
> expertus metuit. tu, dum tua navis in alto est,
> hoc age, ne mutata retrosum te ferat aura. (86-8).

That is the sum of his general advice on the subject—accept the position and act up to it whole-heartedly and heartily—and at once he proceeds to the application of it to the special case of Lollius ; this is given in 89-95, of which 89-93 is tactful preparation, and then he suddenly addresses his man directly :

> deme supercilio nubem ; plerumque modestus
> occupat obscuri speciem, taciturnus acerbi.

There we have the crowning injunction of the piece, characteristically brief and sudden (though the ground had been prepared by the central portion, 40-66), and forming the conclusion of the main subject ; what follows is just general fatherly advice by way of softening the lesson. " And you will find time enough for your studies even so."

Lollius is *liber* and *modestus* and *taciturnus*. Scæva, I suspect, is none of these things ; what his mentor fears for him is that he may be too confident and loud, too rough, brusque, and tactless.[1] To him Horace begins with a veiled irony ; " Yes, I know, M. le Gauche, you have a fine eye to your own interests ; *of course* you know how to manage (*uti*) a great man." Still, there may be a few points that I can give you.` Then follow a couple of repartees by which Aristippus scored off the Cynic. Diogenes, of course, was arguing originally against patronage altogether, but that is not the significance of his standpoint here ; if it had been, Horace would never have asked Scæva, " With which do you agree ? " ; for Scæva is *ex hypothesi* (2, 11-12) committed by his own choice to a period of dependency. In the picture of the Cynic, Horace is talking *at* Scæva ; the Cynics gloried in being rude and they had a great deal of false pride. The implication clearly is that in

---

[1] It ought, perhaps, to be made clear that the contrast is *not* that drawn in XVIII. 9-20. Neither Lollius nor Scæva is of a servile type.

answer to Horace's question Scæva would have said " With Diogenes ! " if Horace had not anticipated him by answering it himself the other way. If you *must* go " on the make " and attach yourself to a patron, Aristippus is at any rate your best model : courteous and affable, he made himself agreeable everywhere. You have deliberately put yourself in the position of a subordinate ; you are tacitly asking for favours, and the best you can do is to be consistent and ask gracefully, *viz.*, in just the opposite manner to that described in 43-62, which is a brief lecture against being loud (*tacentes*, 43), and shameless (*pudenter*, 44) ; thus confirming our view of Scæva's character. As usual, he winds up with what is his main advice ; as usual, he prepares for it artfully by concealing his art. There is, doubtless, as both Sellar and Wickham observe, an undertone of irony which crops up in several parts of this epistle ; for example in 37-42, which with its picture of the *sapiens* as primarily and pre-eminently a man of enterprise would be rank heresy to the Stoic and is far from orthodox Horatianism.[1] Yet it is important not to exaggerate that aspect of it. With his dislike of rigid principles and his belief in adaptability and social sense, Horace is clearly in a certain degree of sympathy with the founder of the Cyrenaic school. It is not everybody who *can* acquit himself creditably and successfully as the companion of the great (35-6) ; it is not so easy as one would think ; it demands certain positive qualities of character, as, for example, tact. This is simply (though xv. is a better instance) one of the epistles heralded in his preface when he spoke of " relapsing into the precepts of Aristippus," and the half-playful eulogy of the bold and manly (38-41) and enterprising type is the best illustration of *mihi res, non me rebus subjungere* and its connection with the Cyrenaic teaching. But, of course, *hic est aut nusquam quod quaerimus* (39) is a direct contradiction of the more famous phrase which it recalls, *quod petis hic est ;* [2] and it only needs a reference to both contexts to see which is the authentic voice.

Horace will not have anybody embark on any line of life with a rash confidence ; count first the cost, and then if you

---

[1] The conception of *virtus* in 33-42 is nicely illustrated by *Sat.*, I. x. 54 (*quae tua virtus*) in its general context.

[2] XI. 29.

can face up to it do so by all means. We saw how the very last of all his counsels to a young poet was that even if it is good one's poetry will be a failure ; it must be better than good, it must be distinguished ; and that in the view of others, since to find it so oneself is, for poets, one of the most natural and commonest delusions. The same in effect, ultimately, is the last line of *Epist.*, I. i., which has sometimes been misunderstood : " the Stoics are really right after all—but it is difficult to live up to ! " In a similar spirit both these letters to young men about to attach themselves to patrons contain an emphatic warning that the life of the protégé is not a bed of roses. All this helps to explain the sixth letter, which is " the most enigmatical " (Sellar), but not, I venture to think, an enigma which does not admit of a fairly simple solution. It is probably a mistake to go through it in a careful attempt to " distinguish between irony and earnest meaning." The last two lines really contain the key ; " such," says Horace in effect, " is my way of tackling the problem of life ; if you know of a better method than this (*istis*), let me hear of it ; if not, try my way (*his* = *istis*)." What is the method referred to ? The testing of different principles in turn, to see which shows up best. Has this method been explained anywhere in the piece ? No ; but the whole piece up to the last two lines is an *example* of it, an object-lesson. Each principle is tested fairly, and pushed to its logical consequences ; in several cases this is at once seen to amount to a *reductio ad absurdum ;* but there is hardly more " irony " than there can be said to be in Euclid—though, of course, Horace omits the final steps (" which is impossible, therefore, *etc.*, q.e.d.") as unnecessary. The first doctrine to be considered is the " nil admirari " or ἀθαυμαστία (" quietism " is the modern term) which we know from Cicero [1] to have originated with the Cyrenaics. But the principle is stated, not categorically, but hypothetically ; that, indeed, is not obvious, nor is it meant to be—until line 29, which is, of course, the *logical* commencement, Horace according to his practice having begun by a plunge *in medias res*. After " vis recte vivere ; quis non ? si virtus hoc una potest dare," it is at once clear that the preceding as well as the following is experimental.[2]

---

[1] Tusc., *Disp.*, iii. 14.   [2] Cf. XVII. 6-12.

From much that has just been said above, it must be expected —and from what the poet says here it is evident—that the Cyrenaic doctrine turns out quite congenial to him. And as has often been remarked, their ἀθαυμαστία has a good deal in common with the ἀπαθεία of the Stoics. But for all that, a man cannot be both a Cyrenaic and a Stoic, and throughout these epistles Horace is everywhere well aware of it ; here, too, the standpoint of Aristippus and Epicurus (for—despite Cicero—the first thirty lines are still more in the Epicurean vein), though it is not exploded like the other hypotheses, is subtly but pointedly labelled as but a second-best. " Remember, however, that to be a *wholly* consistent quietist you must not be too much devoted even to Virtue itself " (15-16). But though such a view was once his own and is still intelligible to him, it is by this one corollary diametrically opposed to the next-mentioned :

> si virtus hoc una potest dare, fortis omissis
> *hoc age* deliciis.

That is all he says here about Stoicism ; it is the only principle he does not discuss ; the obvious implication being that it does not need discussion. It carries its credentials on its face.

In sum : Life, you and I are agreed, must be lived on a principle, of some kind (67-8). That means, consistently ; so before you embrace a principle, be very clear what it must involve. " The avoidance of *all* extremes ? " But that consists with the avoidance of extreme virtue. " Virtue ? " Yes ; that is consistent with—itself.

Of these longer and more predominantly moral epistles there remains yet one, the second. In regard to the distinctions which the second chapter of this book attempted to draw between the moralist's and the poet's method of making the world better, there is perhaps no work of Horace's which shows us more precisely where he stands—just how far he had got in the way of progress from the Socratic fallacy to the Poetic faith. We have seen that he failed to achieve drama, and we have seen why ; because he believed in reason as opposed to instinct, in the understanding as against the emotions. But he was not, on the other hand, either an academic or a sectarian ; far from it. By this period he has indeed become, as we have seen, a Stoic in all but name ; but that makes just all the difference. The chief reason why he still refused to " sign their basis " (*Epist.*, I. i. 14) was, we may be sure, his deep-rooted *disbelief* in all abstract formulæ. He believes in teaching by means of concrete and living images and to that extent is on the side of the poets. And what is interesting about this epistle, and also important, is that in the "immemorial antagonism between Philosophy and Poetry," he states quite distinctly that he *does* side with the latter. " Homer teaches morality at once better and more intelligibly than the Stoics and Academics " (3-4).[1] This assertion he at once proceeds to make good ; the *Iliad* is of a deterrent purpose, as being a continuous tragedy of passion ; the *Odyssey* is an incitement to virtue, with one hero successively set off against this or that corrupt society. True, this is to regard each as something more a parable [2] than a poem ; true, the language of the interpretation itself smells of the schools ; the princes and nations of the *Iliad* " have not learned wisdom," Ulysses is a " sage," proof against the worst that fortune can do to him, adamant to the wiles of appetite. But down the centuries from Xenophanes to Mr. J. T. Sheppard many and various are the things that have been said about the Homeric poems, and in his attempt to indicate their main significance Horace has come a great deal nearer to the truth than most. So far as the Trojan War is concerned, is it not remarkable that the most creative, and one of the least (strictly) philosophical of all poets, has seen it in precisely the same way ? It would be impossible to get from any other source so good a motto for *Troilus and Cressida* as

> seditione, dolis, scelere atque libidine et ira
> Iliacos intra muros peccatur et extra.

[1] The writings of Mrs. Eddy (which I take to be the nearest modern parallel to Stoicism, *New Statesman*, 30th June, 1917, "A Stoic Moralist") undoubtedly do embody, and convey also, a genuine spiritual experience of a certain degree ; but all that is sound in them is implicit in Shakespeare, and incomparably more besides. There are many people to whom that statement would sound anything but obvious, and doubtless some who would contradict it. The importance of *Epist.*, I. ii. 1-4 is that it is the sort of thing that needs reassertion age after age, as it needed it in the world of Horace's day.

[2] Cf. his treatment of a scene in Euripides' *Bacchae*, xvi. 73-9.

And the ethical interpretation which Horace gives to the cup of Circe can hardly have been quite absent from the mind of the writer himself of the remarkable lines :

οἱ δὲ συῶν μὲν ἔχον κεφαλὰς φωνήν τε τρίχας τε
καὶ δέμας, αὐτὰρ νοῦς ἦν ἔμπεδος ὡς τὸ πάρος περ.

At the same time, it cannot be denied that all this, though it is not Philosophy, is Sophistic ; it is even to a large extent Stoicism. To begin with, the allegorisation of Homer was itself, as is amply attested,[1] a favourite Stoic practice from the foundation of the school until Horace's own day ; Chrysippus in particular, despite the contrast drawn by Horace at line 4, had himself contributed to it,[2] though after a different and much more Procrustean fashion. But even the more human and ethical method which Horace here employs had also been practised by the Stoics ; and when we add that they applied it to the *Odyssey* to just the same effect, interpreting Ulysses as an embodiment of their ideal of the virtuous man, and Circe as sensuality, and that these ideas are all found in an extant treatise by a Stoic of Horace's own time, Heraclitus's *Homeric Allegories*, the inference becomes inevitable that either Horace derived them from Heraclitus or both from a common source ; [3] at all events they were then in vogue. It looks, in brief, as if the Stoics got this sort of thing from the Cynics,[4] and the Cynics from the original sophists. Thus the great companion saint of Ulysses in the Stoic canon, Hercules,[5] had been treated as the hero of a " Pilgrim's Progress " by the Cynic founder Antisthenes, in a dialogue named from him ; [6] and that dialogue was clearly indebted for its presentation of the muscular Christian of antiquity to the moral apologue of *The Choice of Herakles* composed by the sophist Prodicus and pre-

[1] Zeller, *Stoics, Epicureans and Sceptics*, pp. 354-69.

[2] *Ibid.*, p. 356 n. 1, E. V. Arnold, *Roman Stoicism*, § 254, Cic., *N.D.*, ii. 24.63. Less remote from Horace's is the method of Crates ; Athenæus, 489 c. foll.

[3] Heraclitus wrote in Greek, but his source was the Roman Varro.

[4] Arnold, *Roman Stoicism*, § 325.

[5] " Ulixen et Herculem . . . Stoici nostri sapientes pronuntiaverunt, invictos laboribus, contemptores voluptatis et victores omnium terrarum," Sen., *Dial.*, ii. 2, 1.

[6] See Gomperz, *Greek Thinkers*, ii. p. 151.

served for us in Xenophon's *Memorabilia*. Again, we see from the last-mentioned work [1] that the reading of ethical symbolism into the Circe legend goes back to the Arch-Sophist himself. The similar treatment of a passage from Euripides' *Bacchae* at the end of the sixteenth epistle is probably also to be attributed to a Stoic origin,[2] since the Stoics were also particularly addicted to rationalising not only that god but the numerous legends relating to him.[3] And there are other signs of a Stoical mood in this epistle, for example the idea of a probation in virtue (προκοπή), a state not of perfection but of grace, as indicated at 40-4, 70-71.

The difference, the practical difference, is that out of this stuff Horace has produced poetry, and to that extent made it not only more permanent but more operative. On the other hand, it is a far cry indeed from this way of handling legend to that of Aeschylus and Sophocles, which is also primarily moral, but on very different—in some ways almost opposite—lines.

Poems such as those we have just been considering are " letters " only in an extended sense. But several in this book, while no less literary, have in different ways far more of the appearance of letters as employed in ordinary life. Some were obviously written, and doubtless sent, in connection with a particular occasion. The thirteenth is, in effect, a letter to Augustus (though he is not the actual addressee) [4] " covering " certain enclosures, to wit the first three books of the *Odes*, which would be sent as soon as they were published.[5] Nominally it is to the bearer, one Vinius Asina (or Asellus), who is adjured not to thrust them upon the emperor until he is entirely ready to receive them ; the inevitable admonition to him " not to be an ass " is excused by the subtler references to his cognomen, the hint that the light lyrics will not " gall "

---

[1] Xen., *Mem.*, I. 3, 7. [2] Cf. above, p. 267.

[3] Zeller, *op. cit.*, pp. 364-5.

[4] Was it on receipt of this that it occurred to the emperor that he would like to have an epistle addressed to him, and that in the circumstances the suggestion must proceed from himself ?

[5] I take it that Augustus was in Rome, and the presentation copy is supposed to be despatched from the author's country house. See Wickham, p. 242 *fin.*

him, the final caution not to stumble, and smash what it is implied is delicate ware. The shortest (IX.) is an extremely clever letter of introduction, commending the Septimius of *Odes*, II. vi. to the young prince Tiberius. Two others are somewhat similar in purpose. The twelfth addressed to Iccius the student of philosophy and man of action in one (*Odes*, I. xxix.), now Agrippa's estate-agent in Sicily, inobtrusively commends to his good offices the writer's other friend Grosphus, whom we know from *Odes*, II. xvi. to have had property in that island ; in a " p.s." (*tamen*, 25) he gives the news from Rome, victories both East and West, a fine harvest, the Golden Age returned—all this, of course, with a clear eye to publication. The bloodless pacification of Armenia by Tiberius and the restoration by the Parthians of the standards captured at Carrhae were much exploited by Augustus for propagandist purposes. With the future emperor on that expedition had been several young friends of Horace's, and the third epistle is mainly concerned to reconcile two of them with one another, though this topic according to Horace's manner is introduced incidentally and at the end. The piece gives us a very interesting glimpse into the literary activities of fashion or officialdom encouraged under the Augustan régime—national epic, ambitious ode, rhetorical tragedy. The Florus to whom it was addressed was evidently credited with real literary ability by Horace himself, who refers to his genius as neither scanty nor over-exuberant ; and that 21-5 is not empty compliment is confirmed by the dedication to the same friend of *Epist.*, II. ii., a high honour. Here, too, the poet goes on to recommend philosophy to him. The Celsus of viii. here appears as one whose besetting sin was plagiarism. The crow stripped of her stolen plumes " moves laughter " somewhat less than does the unconscious " young female fox " of Servius's unwary memory who clothed herself in feathers still less her own—a *vulpecula*, one may plead in her favour, obviously of that authentic grain-eating variety known to Horace himself, as witness vii., 29-31. Here, too, do we hear of Titius, who had the courage to imitate Pindar ; " soon to be famous " apparently ; and now you will search even the map in vain ; there is not so much as a sea named after him. This epistle, like some letters in real life, is full of questions ; the first twenty-one lines consist of nothing else. " Quid Titius ? " " Quid mihi Celsus agit ? " " Ipse quid audes ? " *Mais où sont les neiges d'antan ?* I note another poem of Horace ending with a votive heifer. The following ends in a pig,[1] purely secular, however. It is similar in a sufficient number of respects to make us think that Horace placed it here as a companion poem. For this one also leads the reader to reflect on the vagaries of Fame. It happens to be to a poet who has survived, no less a poet than Tibullus ; and it is not without surprise that we find the suggestion that he may be now writing elegies superior even to those of Cassius Parmensis ! " There was ever more in him to be praised than to be pardoned," Ben Jonson took care to " tell posterity " about Shakespeare. *Non tu corpus eras sine pectore.* Horace's *bêtise* is, of course, venial and natural and very mild by comparison, but Nemesis afterwards got in her little fling at him to pay him in kind. " Of our lyric poets," opined Quintilian, " Horatius is practically the only one worth reading ; for he does rise sometimes, and he has always charm and elegance ; he shows a wide range in his tropes, moreover, and is the master of a happy audacity of phrase. One might, indeed, couple with his the name of our late lamented Cæsius Bassus. But then there are living geniuses incomparably greater than Cæsius." The philosophy to which Florus had been exhorted was of a Stoical[2] complexion ; the elegist, Horace feels, is more in need of a mild dose of Epicureanism. He tends (*Odes*, I. xxxiii.) to take life somewhat too sadly ; and we note that Horace tells us he was rich, a statement confirmed by Tibullus's own description of himself as a poor man.

The tenth is at least like a real letter in beginning with the conventional greeting and ending with the writer's present address. Horace writes from the country to his dear friend Fuscus in town ; for such is their respective choice of habitat, the one and only point on which they do not agree. The chief point made in the poem—what could be more natural than

---

[1] Pig makes an effective climax ; Virg., *Aen.*, viii. 83. Similarly *ibid.*, 43 ; *Georg.*, iii. 255 ; Ovid, *Met.*, viii. 359 ; far superior, and with really fine effect, Hom., *Od.*, xix. 439, perhaps the prototype; cf. iv. 457. And so too in its way does cow ; *Aen.*, v. 481.

[2] *Patriae*, iii. 29.

nature ?—is less of a truism than, to the modern reader, would at first appear. Once more, as so frequently in these Epistles, in a Stoic vein, the poet starts from the assumption that our ideal is to live " consistently with nature," that is, κατὰ φύσιν, " nature " being the nature " of things," of the universe, not, as in the common modern sense of the word, natural scenery, the country—a sense which it does not bear either in Greek or Latin. But it is just this identification which Horace is here concerned to establish, and in the twenty-fourth line, considered with its context, he practically does it. You town-lovers may decry the country, but your own acts belie you ; even between the columns of your palaces you plant trees—the eye desires some of nature's columns, as Wickham happily interprets ; in point of fact, says Horace,

naturam expelles furca, tamen usque recurret.

The writer of these lines would undoubtedly have been charmed with a modern fable which provides a still more literal illustration of this text—the most literal I know—even to *perrumpet* of the next line—Alphonse Daudet's fascinating little tale of *Woods-town*. But a plantation or a fine view can never do for your soul what the country itself does ; [1] for you are still under the spell of the happiness offered you by the χρηματιστικὸς βίος, the competitive life, and that is a no less specious fake (26-9). Money, though a good servant, is a bad master (47-8) ; the former relation is apt to slip into the latter in a manner imperceptible to the man himself—for this is the lesson conveyed with such admirable indirectness in Horace's use of the old fable about the horse and stag—and once that has happened you have let a rider mount your back whom you will never be able to shake off. So would I wish not only my friends to live, but myself ; I really mean it all. And I do my best to act up to it ; I am writing now from the neighbourhood of the old crumbling temple of Vacuna ; it, at least, remains entirely unconcerned to keep pace with the age.

" Naturam expelles furca, tamen usque recurret " is a sentiment frequently heard on the lips of gardeners, and in fact of field-labourers generally, who as a profession hold less

[1] Such I take to be the latent connection between 25-6 ; cf. Lucr., ii. 23-33.

to the Stoical view that nature is moral than to the modern one that she is red in tooth and claw. In the fourteenth letter Horace affects to discuss the question whether he or his chief farm-hand (he had eight altogether) is the more efficient at coping with the rankness of nature ; which, therefore, is in the better condition and more to the credit of its possessor—his soul, or his property. The theme is rather, however, the same as that of the tenth, but treated in a coarser tone, such as seemed to the writer more appropriate in addressing a slave, who though now perforce a countryman, sighs for the restaurants and brothels of the city he had seen in a former post, and prefers the surprise fare of regular daily rations to dishes with whose contents he has already had only too much to do. We hear at second-hand the grumbles of the overseer, and get a glimpse of the poet pursuing the simple life with conscientious thoroughness, at work in his own fields " moving stones and clods "—a somewhat slow and certainly laborious method of ploughing which, we hear without surprise, evoked an occasional smile from the non-poetising farmers who were his neighbours. Exchange their regular spheres of operation, and for intensive " culture " one would almost be disposed to back the bailiff. The existence of this piece gives Tyrrell a stone to throw even against the Epistles, upon which he has nothing else to say, since it appears that Lucilius had already applied the rare word *mediastinus* to a *vilicus*,[1] that *inhospita tesqua* is undoubtedly a quotation from him, that he said (and to say it, I allow, is something of a feat), *stat sentibus pectus ;* and that, therefore, " there is not a remarkable expression in the letter, which has not its origin in Lucilius."

That even in his own life-time Horace had to run the gauntlet of just this sort of criticism, appears from the nineteenth epistle, which draws a distinction, neglected by pedants in all ages and even by critics in not a few, between the spirit and the matter of literary works ; it is in respect of the former that he here indicates the claim of his lyrical work, odes and epodes, to originality. At first sight, indeed, it looks in one place at least (23-5), as if he said exactly the opposite ; for he explicitly states that in the case of Archilochus he reproduced (along

---

[1] Tyrrell himself, by the way, does not seem to make use of this.

with the metres) the " spirit," and not the " matter." [1] But, in the first place, to introduce a new spirit in Latin literature was by general consent to derive it from the Greek. And in the second place—and much more important—even to *reproduce* the true spirit of a living thing, a hero or a poem, requires, under any circumstances and in any age, original force ; and Horace knows this and states it in a characteristically subtle but characteristically concrete and unequivocal manner. His claim to be a pioneer, in lines 21 and following, is obviously to be interpreted in the light of the passage which leads up to it ; no contrast could be more clearly deliberate than that which he draws between himself and his imitators ; and the passage about his imitators comes first, because (as is often the case with his opening topic) they are *not* the subject of the poem— the subject is, the poet's answer to a question [2] which it is supposed Maecenas has just asked him—and still more, in order that by showing just in what consists their servility and folly, he may preparatorily illuminate the statement he is about to make of what precisely constitutes his own originality and enterprise. [3] And he ridicules his imitators not for merely reproducing the spirit of Horace, but for *failing* to do so ; what they reproduced was evidently his " res," his subjects. [4]

[1] In his satires, on the other hand, where he is to a large extent reproducing the " res " of Lucilius but entirely reforming the metre, he repeatedly disclaims any such originality.

[2] Lines 35-6 :—

scire velis mea cur ingratus opuscula lector
laudet ametque domi, premat extra limen iniquus.

[3] That is, we have here *in extenso* the familiar Horatian idiom of elliptical double antithesis.

[4] I do not for a moment suppose that line 11 is to be taken literally, as the commentators seem to think. It is but another instance of a figure common in Latin poetry, by which an author is said to do what he represents in his writings as being done ; *e.g.*, *Sat.*, I. x. 36, II. v. 41. I think we are justified in inferring that there were now younger poets who were imitating Horace's Bacchanalian lyrics, and doubtless going one better, as they always do. But πολλοί τοι ναρθηκοφόροι, βάκχοι δέ τε παῦροι. Even their revelling is conscientious and their drunkenness unconvincing ; their morning Muses reek, but the smell of wine is less enduring than that of last night's lamp-oil.

He says to them in effect *cucullus non facit monachum*. But what best sums up the point I here wish to make—and Horace's —is the single word *repraesentare*, an excellent word in all its various uses which are really but one in sense ; a word of the kind that is only too rare in Latin ; and it means not to " represent " but to make (rather, " duly " to make) *praesens*, as in *praesens divus* (*Odes*, III. v. 2), to make incarnate, to produce as a visible *fait accompli* [1] ; it even means to pay. A man may have the external or accidental characteristics of a Cato, but —*virtutemne repraesentet moresque Catonis ?* Before we can say that of him, he must make himself virtually a Cato redivivus ; and to achieve that takes—a Cato. Even so, to reproduce the spirit of a great poet, to constitute yourself the affinity, in another language, of an Alcæus, proves you also a great poet ; a lesser man than Alcæus would burst in the mere attempt (15-16). This, I am bound to say, interests me even less as a statement of Horace about his own achievement than as the statement of a truth, and of a little recognised one.

Two types of men have never recognised it, as we gather from this epistle they did not in Horace's own day ; two very different, almost opposite, types ; the plebeian and the pedant. The masses are for lickerish delights merely, the " reviewer " [2] has an eye only for words, diction, style, the surface qualities. Neither has any sense of the *animi*, the vital energy ; to appreciate that you must have yourself some " spirited " ideal of life, some sort of a *Bushido*, you must recognise moral obligations whether national or philosophic ; in ancient parlance, you must belong to the class of the free-born and so inherit their traditions ; you must in any case be one of nature's gentlemen. I Horace in my Odes brought into Latin poetry a spirit like that of the Aeolian aristocrat and patriot, and for the first time ; *virginibus puerisque canto* I sang then, and I repeat here that it is by the gentle, by true Romans, that I would have my poems read. I definitely do not want to appeal to the popular

---

[1] Prof. Slater compares *Cic. Phil.*, ii. § 118, *si repraesentari morte mea libertas reipublicae potest.*

[2] The *grammatici* are " those who expound and criticize poetry and can make or mar the fortunes of a young poet " (Wickham). It includes professors of literature, cf. *A.P.*, 78.

taste,[1] and academic criticism I despise.[2] We can thus see quite clearly why he " ignores " [3] the Sapphics of Catullus in *Odes*, III. xxx. 13 ; for Horace, Catullus in this connection simply does not count ; his spirit, so far from resembling that of Sappho and Alcæus, is deplorable ; he is erotic, he is decadent, he is for æsthetes and intellectuals ; for a Demetrius to enthuse over (*Sat.*, I. x. 19 and schol.), for him and the " beautiful " Hermogenes Tigellius [4] to commend to their following of blue-stockings (*Sat.*, I. x. 90-1).

Of this epistle Wilkins says that " the epistolary form is more completely than elsewhere in this book a mere form." I do not agree. It has a distinct occasion ; it is, as I have said, an answer to Maecenas' question. " My dear Maecenas, you ask " . . . he would have written, had he not as ever preferred to avoid the obvious and prepare the ground by throwing in first 1-34. 35 is the single pivot ; from there to the end all obviously hangs together, while the backward connection is through the plain antithesis between the classes he does not appeal to (37-40) and the class he does (34). The piece is most carefully and deliberately constructed, and is as I have tried to indicate a good example of Horace's elliptical manner ; to be fully appreciated each passage is intended to be seen in the light of the whole. Maecenas' question, there is every reason to suppose, was really asked ; even if not, it is quite clear that the occasion of the poem is the adverse criticism with which the publication of *Odes*, I.-III. had been pretty generally (36) met, in spite of their wide circulation ; a not uncommon occurrence. Here is the middle phase between that reflected in such satires as I. iv. (78-80 and generally), I. x. (78-80 and generally), II. i. (1-4 and generally), and the ode IV. iii. ; first he had critics ; here he still has, but he

---

[1] *Epist.*, I. xix. 37-8 ; cf. *Odes*, III. i. 1, *Sat.*, I. iv. 72, x. 73 ; the concession in *Epist.*, II. i. 63, it is clear from the context, does not mean much.

[2] *Epist.*, I. xix. 39-40 ; cf. *Sat.*, I. x. 74-6, and to some extent *Epist.*, II. i. 51 and thereabout.

[3] *E.g.*, Wight Duff, *Lity. Hist. Rome*, p. 520.

[4] Who is, for Horace, as Wickham excellently puts it on *Sat.*, I. iv. 72, " the representative of the foppish and effeminate taste of the day in music and poetry."

has also imitators; finally the voice of detraction has been silenced.

For this present book he anticipates a good sale on its first appearance; later, when it is no longer the newest literary sensation, adverse criticism and then a slump; in due course a circulation in the provinces; ultimately, use as a school-book; finally, establishment as a classic. All this is prefigured in the last letter, which is addressed to the book itself, and takes the form of an *envoi*. Employing a figure more congenial to Augustan than to Victorian taste,[1] the poet affects to regard his young charge as a *verna* or home-born and indulgently treated slave, determined in spite of a good upbringing and in the face of all warnings to exchange his hitherto cloistered existence for the life of the *demi-monde*. Well, " see the world " if you must; but your fate from that day is settled. He then proceeds to outline in prospect the career thus indicated in a series of extraordinary clever and subtle *double-entendres* whose pointedness might surely excuse them even to a puritanical taste. Whether it was a case of *odium peccantis* or not, certain it is that *non desipit augur;* all Horace here prognosticates· has been fulfilled. When you have become passé, he says, you will either " run away " to Utica or be packed off " in bonds " (tied up, that is, with other books) to Ilerda. Here is a forecast of the Spanish and the African schools of later Latin literature; it was in just these centres that the tradition of Roman letters was to take strongest root. *Balba* in line 18 is to be understood literally; it is not merely that old men drivel, or gibber; it is that in its latter days the speech of this book will itself lisp or stammer on the lips of boys who have tried unsuccessfully to learn it for repetition.[2] Similarly throughout the last ten lines the joke lies in the fact that they are in themselves their own fulfilment.

And the book still charms, despite its past.

---

[1] See *e.g.*, Sellar, 97 *fin.* Wickham complains of the way in which commentators have " pressed " the metaphor into " tasteless detail "; on the contrary I am afraid the truth is that there is more than they have seen; *pumice mundus* is undoubtedly meant to have the same double meaning as *prostes;* see Ovid, *Ars. Am.*, I. 506, Martial, XIV. ccv. 1, Juv., viii. 16, and cf. Aristoph., *Frogs*, 516, etc.

[2] Cf. *Epist.*, II. i. 126.

The Second Book of Epistles

The two epistles of this book have already been partially dealt with in other connections ; [1] and though their interest is considerable, it lies first in the matter and then in the style, little if at all in the structure ; for all these reasons, there does not remain much to be said about them here. Both of some length, and concerned, the one almost entirely, the other considerably, with literary criticism, they naturally associate themselves, not with the first book of Epistles, but with the *Ars Poetica*. Some editors, indeed, have followed Cruquius in placing the last-mentioned poem as the third epistle of this second book, an arrangement for which, however, there is no ancient authority.

The letter to Florus, written probably [2] soon after the publication of the first book, is not, indeed, without resemblances to those of that collection ; particularly in the fact that the last third-part of the poem (145-216) consists of a long series of moral counsels, expressed with characteristic force and point. Much as he has had to say about the art of literature —especially interesting is the detailed account (109-25) of the true poet's principles of composition and self-criticism, a passage in which he practically depicts " the ideal of the classical school of Latin poetry " [3]—Horace nevertheless represents himself as having by now attained to the realisation that there is a still greater art, the art of life :—

> ac non verba sequi fidibus modulanda Latinis,
> sed verae numerosque modosque ediscere vitae.

The letter to the emperor, the last extant work of Horace, takes the form of a general defence of the principles of the Augustan school of poetry. Since the eighteenth century the term " classical " has been subject to so much perverse misunderstanding that it is necessary to draw attention to correct explanations of it, all the more so as they may be authoritative ; and this epistle is one of the oldest and best. We may here note briefly a few points. Horace is standing, not for poetry according to rules, but for poetry, or at least poetic criticism

[1] Ch. III., pp. 58-9, 64-7 ; IV., pp. 123, 126.
[2] See Wickham's general introduction to the Literary Epistles.
[3] Wickham.

and appreciation, according to principles ; his opponents, the partisans of the Republican school of Latin literature, have, as he cleverly shows, no principles at all, but simply prejudices, and chiefly that immemorial prejudice, not necessarily of dons, but of the donnish type of mind in all ages, according to which the greatest virtue a poet can have is to have been dead a long time. " Ut critici dicunt "—it is the academic school of criticism or rather dogmatism that he is out against ; more particularly, perhaps, Varro, the veteran scholar and voluminous satirist, the *doyen* of the old-fashioned formlessness and verbosity. In place of principles, they have their absurd rules of thumb ; for example—in Greek literature, the best period is the first, therefore it must be so in Latin also. Against this mechanical argument Horace appeals, as we have often seen him do, to the world of nature, as offering the only true sort of analogy with the world of art ; and ironically suggests that all growths there too are of exactly similar process :

nil intra est oleam, nil extra est in nuce duri !

—*and*, by consequence of course, there is no hope for the Roman arts of attaining to any greater excellence than they have already reached. Yes, the hope of *bettering* the past triumphs is the difference that makes so bridgeless a gulf between pedant and poet. Horace hints to his enemy the unbearable thought. He also hints at just that reversal distinguishing the development of Latin literature from that of Greek, which has already been emphasised in the present work.[1]

We see, then, that the standpoint *vulgarly* known as classical is that which Horace is *opposing ;* and more explicit proof soon follows. Horace, too, in his turn, appeals to the Greeks ; but he uses the appeal to antiquity in the right way. In language which ought never to be forgotten he tells his generation that the great classics were in their own day great innovators :

quod si tam Graecis novitas invisa fuisset
quam nobis, quid nunc esset vetus ?

That is unanswerable.[2]

[1] P. 149.
[2] Cf. in this connection the passages of the *Ars Poetica* referred to above, p. 241.

Greek literature, he now explains more fully, had the opposite development to that of Latin, and the reason is in the national character of either people. The Greek temperament, left free to express itself by the cessation of wars—he is thinking chiefly of the Periclean age—took instantly to the arts ; later its creative impulse flagged. The Roman's natural bent was in the opposite direction—" business," if one may so sum up 103-7 ; he was slow to turn to poetry—to true poetry—but, at a late stage,[1] he did.

In due course Horace does give his tribute to the *ingenium* of the old school ; but it is a judicious, not an indiscriminate one. The early Roman adapters of Greek tragedy found themselves, he tells us, in a congenial field,[2] because the Roman has a natural turn for the rhetorical and the elevated (*natura sublimis et acer* [3]). The Roman, he continues, has inspiration, and he has boldness ; but he sweeps along too fast, he rides too rough-shod. We had already seen Horace say something very similar about Lucilius, *Sat.*, I. iv. 8-13 ; and in the matter of Roman tragedy, he is here in very close accord with the later standard opinion as recorded by Quintilian, X. i. 97 : " Tragoediae scriptores Accius atque Pacuvius clarissimi *gravitate sententiarum, verborum pondere*, et *auctoritate personarum ;* ceterum *nitor* (' polish ') et *summa in excolendis operibus manus* (' finish ') magis videri potest *temporibus* quam ipsis defuisse." How well Horace here diagnoses the Republican poetry may perhaps be seen by reference to the single instance of Lucretius, " natura sublimis et acer," if anyone ever was, but apt to be rough in style, and certainly formless in bulk.

Of the remainder of this epistle, the most important and much the most interesting passage is the account (177-207) of the difficulties, general or peculiar to the writer's own age, which stand in the way of a serious and ambitious dramatist ; followed as it is by Horace's admission (208-15) that he could not face the worst of them. All this passage is of the greatest

---

[1] Cf. 161, *serus enim Graecis admovit acumina chartis*, where it was recently proposed to read *servus* (= Livius Andronicus)—too cleverly. (*Mnemosyne*.)

[2] I cannot agree with Wickham that 165 is at all ironical ; *placuit sibi* = he felt that he was getting on well.

[3] Cf. *acri, Sat.*, I. x. 14, which = (*ibid.* 12) *rhetoris atque poetae*.

significance in view of the substantially similar condition to which the English theatre has sunk to-day. The trouble, as Horace sees it, may be most conveniently summed up in that excellent Platonic word θεατροκρατία. The stage is in the power, not of the nation, nor of the public proper, but of the vulgar (*plebecula*, 186), who have by now, as a matter of fact, infected even the better type of playgoer with the prevailing taste ; the taste, to wit, for elaborate and pointless spectacle. Then follows a list of characteristic items in such pageantry, many of them, it must be admitted—such as giraffes [1] and white elephants—much more beautiful and interesting than what is nowadays usually exhibited upon the stage. Horace also complains of the noise made by a Roman audience, effectually drowning the actor's voice. It is amusing to notice how ancient is the convention of clapping the hands in sign of approval. Picture some modern beauty appearing for the third act in a new creation, and here you are :—

> divitiaeque peregrinae, quibus oblitus actor
> cum stetit in scaena, concurrit dextera laevae.
> dixit adhuc aliquid ? nil sane. quid placet ergo ?
> lana Tarentino violas imitata veneno.

The explicit statement which here follows that these are the reasons why Horace has himself " refused "—*recusem* (Or. Obl.) 208—to attempt dramatic work, brings us back to the subject with which the present chapter started. In the end of this last work of his period of " compromise," he defines and defends his position.

The long view of literature—that is what makes this epistle interesting ; the view which sees in it development, vital processes, evolution. It is not common in criticism, ancient or modern. It seems to me, not indeed capable of proof—far from it, but the only view that makes criticism worth while. Even with it, the thing is menial work compared to writing ; without it—who is there who cannot criticise ?

---

[1] Horace views the giraffe, I regret to say, like the old countryman at the Zoo ; " them things don't exist." *Diversum confusa genus*—it is a monstrosity, like that of *Ars Po.*, 1-4 ; it may be magnificent, but " it is not art."

EPILOGUE

> Poet he, that would have been
> A Christian poet if he could ;
> One that felt far more, I ween,
> Than he ever understood.
> —HARTLEY COLERIDGE, *Bandusian Spring.*

STILL, after all, the proof of the pudding is in the eating. In the course of this book I have been dealing with poems mainly in regard to their form or structure ; but the master reveals himself just as much in the surface-work. Moreover ·it is, in the first instance, the surface that tells. The beauty of an animal body is attained through the skeleton, but it is the body and not the skeleton that the creator meant to be seen. The poet must not forget that form itself, though in a sense the most important element of all, is only a means to an end. Its purpose is to exhibit the details in just that mutual relation which will give each of them the heightened value that he desires them to have ; but it is through the details alone that the whole harmony has to make itself felt.

No one knew this better than Horace, who has stated it once for all with a perfect combination of simplicity and precision.

Non satis est pulchra esse poemata ; dulcia sunto.[1]

And it is for that reason that towards the conclusion of the same work, after he has given all the practical advice he can, he caps it and supersedes it by reminding his young pupil that, most important of all, the poem once finished must not merely be faultless, it must be fine. Men can live—that much is,

---

[1] *Ars Po.*, 99.

indeed, a gross fallacy, if an almost universal one ; but it makes no practical difference ; so long as men *think* they can live without poetry, so long must it remain an absolute necessity for a poem to have that in it which positively commands attention ; which arrests ; and that quality, obviously, it must have upon its surface. Materially it consists of a number of words and nothing else ; that quality therefore must lie in the actual language.

I have not, indeed, hitherto ignored this aspect of the matter, but what I have said about it is not much. Nor shall I say much now ; the details of this subject are outside the scope of the present essay.[1] But certain aspects of it may be briefly indicated. So great is the poet's purely metrical skill that some critics have thought the Odes justified on that score alone. It certainly constitutes a very great part—one might call it the most prominent part—of their claim to originality.[2] On their prosodic technique, all the important things have, it is probable, been already said. But their effect of sonority is largely achieved through alliteration ; and in this respect there may still be room for further study of the practice, not of Horace only, but of the Latin poets.[3] In particular, the effects attained by complex alliteration upon different sounds

[1] For Horace's art in the *arrangement* of words (in relation to their significance) I commend the reader to Prof. H. Darnley Naylor's *Horace, Odes and Epodes.*

[2] Cf. Sir A. Quiller-Couch, *Studies in Literature*, I. 70 : " If you examine Horace's work—what he did (which I shall ever preach to you as the first business of criticism)—one thing, quite ludicrously missed by a good half of his translators and imitators, leaps forthwith to the eye. *He chose the most tantalisingly difficult foreign metres and with consummate skill tamed them to the Latin tongue.* Once grasp this—once grasp that the secret of the odes cannot at any rate be dissociated from their metrical cunning—once perceive that in an Alcaic, major Sapphic, fourth Asclepiad, fifth Archilochian, Horace is weaving his graceful way through measures intricate as any minuet, gavotte, saraband—and you will start by laughing out of court all easy renderings (say) in flat-footed octosyllables such as—etc."

[3] On this subject I find myself in entire agreement with Verrall ; see *Companion to Latin Studies*, §§ 901-27, but esp. 903-20. Since the above was written, a systematic treatise on this very subject has appeared, W. J. Evans' *Alliteratio Latina ;* only too systematic ; but his collection of examples is most remarkable.

together—what sometimes almost takes the form of playing at assonance with syllables—could be illustrated copiously from the Odes.

> Cres*cen*tem sequi*tur cura* pec*un*iam.

("These be his c's, his n's, and his t's.")

> Caesa*r* His*pana repetit Penates*.
> sp*erne* pu*er n*eque tu choreas.
> *ter* pede *ter*ram (appropriate to sense ; see
> *Odes*, III. xviii. 16).

His use of polysyllables is often very clever, and especially, it seems to me, in the metre known as the Greater Asclepiad. Here is how he represents in three consecutive choriambic words the buffetings of a storm on a rocky shore :—

> quae nunc *oppositis debilitat pumicibus* mare (I. xi. 5).

And here is a very clever line :—

> mordaces aliter diffugiunt sollicitudines (I. xviii. 4).

In his Satires and Epistles, again, he shows great invention and variety in his treatment of the hexameter ; *e.g.* :—[1]

> . . . qui stupet in titulis et imaginibus. quid oportet . . .
> (*Sat.*, I. vi. 17).
> . . . incutiunt urbis desiderium, video, et quod . . .
> (*Epist.*, I. xiv. 22).
> . . . possis. adde virilia quod speciosius arma . . .
> (*Epist.*, I. xviii. 52).

No poet, on the other hand, can excel him when he has occasion to aim at just that straightforward, terse, inevitable type of line which makes itself, as it is designed to do, unforgettable.

> oderunt peccare boni virtutis amore.

---

[1] The device (for pointing the antithesis) in the following lines is perhaps remarkable :—

> multos saepe vir*os* null*is* maior*ibus* ort*os*
> et vixisse prob*os* amp*lis* et honor*ibus* auc*tos*
> (*Sat.*, I. vi. 10-11).

What concerns us here and now, however, is the broader question of our final verdict on Horace as a moral poet. I have tried to show that this is less a question of his actual ethical views than of the " morale " of his utterances, their spiritedness or general idealism of tone. Yet obviously his formal opinions on moral points must count for something in the ultimate effect. It may seem to some mere paradox to apply the term moral poet to one whose view of life has so much in it that modern sentiment considers either heathenishly coarse or even positively immoral ; while to call him " priestly " may appear preposterous or possibly irreverent. Others, more formidable opponents, may point to the failure of Augustus, despite all this " reconstructive " poetry, to save Rome from moral decadence and ultimate collapse, and feel that some sort of explanation is required. And, in fact, it is.

Horace's ethic was certainly in some points very different from the Christian ethic, but it does not follow that on those points the Roman poet is either cynical or indifferent, or indeed anything but, so far as his intentions go, moral. The relations of the sexes are the obvious ground of cleavage. Though he is aware of different moods, Horace's view of life is fundamentally one, a moral one, and its morality is essentially male. The inevitable result is, a double code for women, and a double code for men's relations to them. Two types of women are recognised and (in very different ways) accepted : the free woman, the Roman virgin or matron ; the slave-woman, or courtesan. It is here, as it seems to me, that the modern reader, Ferrero for example, is apt to err through the application to Horace's writings of the modern view. I cannot feel that the erotic odes are wholly to be explained (though they are partly) as reflections of contemporary social life, literary exercises in the Romanisation of Greek light poetry, purely external to the writer himself. If they do, to some extent, " mark in literature the moral change proceeding in society," [1] it was a moral change which both Augustus and Horace favoured ; or rather, it was not so much a moral change as a reaction to the old Roman manly but crudely masculine

---

[1] Ferrero, *Greatness and Decline of Rome*, iv., p. 207 (English tr.) and cf. thereabout generally.

morality, against the *fin-de-siècle* sentiment of the new-fashioned poetry of such writers as Catullus and Propertius. That I believe to be the main ground of Horace's antagonism to those two poets.

There are and have always been two separate types of sexual morality ; the male, which goes by the standard of the good (or at least supposed good) of the community—public appearance, legality, and so on ; the female, which judges by the individual relation. A true code would consider both, and make the necessary adjustment ; but human history is not the place in which to search for it. That of Augustus was naturally the former. But however absolute the claims of public decency, facts, he would argue, cannot be ignored ; superfluous vitality must have its scope ; and the solution is found in the maintenance of two entirely separate classes of women, and the rigorous enforcement, for men and women alike, of the separation. This is also the old Roman view ; marriage is one thing and love another ; they are as opposite as duty and pleasure. It was Cato who had degraded a senator for kissing his wife in his daughter's presence ; and what sort of principles form the inevitable obverse to that kind of Puritanism may be seen from the tradition preserved in Horace that this paragon of Roman virtue, this *censor morum*, recommended fornication to young men.

When Ferrero explains " the moral change proceeding in society " by saying that " love had been the expression of a citizen's duty to perpetuate his race through the family " he overlooks the fact that although that had been—and still was, Horace emphatically declared—a citizen's duty, it neither was nor ever had been " love " to a Roman. Marriage was duty, and love pleasure ; but Catullus took love seriously, so is Propertius doing ; in the meantime, on the other side, too, the old Roman double-barrelled morality is breaking down, marriage is being taken lightly. The demarcation must be restored. The wantonness of youth cannot be prevented, and the political purpose, if one may call it so, of Horace's erotic odes is to direct it into a (supposed) socially harmless channel ; while at the same time he gives this suggestion not a coarse form but an attractive one. The object is to effect a working reconciliation between the old Roman and the new Greek views ; the clock could not be put back. Consistently, Horace regards his own light loves as proving, not disproving, the purity and blamelessness of his life (*Odes*, I. xxii.). He is characteristic of his age in being quite unaware that the existence of a socially disfranchised and parasitic class of women reacts injuriously both upon the individual and ultimately upon the nation.

That phenomenon is not only associated with prejudices of sex, it is associated with prejudices of class and caste. The other fatal factor in ancient society, the existence of an immense slave class, is another limitation which Horace, despite his Stoicism, did not wholly or consistently rise above. He may, half in irony, put high moral doctrine into the mouth of a slave, but his moral gospel, as it is addressed only to men, is addressed exclusively to free men, almost exclusively to men of private means, members of the governing aristocracy. Even his insistence on spiritual freedom is partly Cæsarian-propagandist, a counter to the old Republican ideal of political freedom.

And apart from these defects on the social side, the Horatian ethic also suffers, in its purely individual aspect, from the limitation common to all ancient ethic after Socrates—egotism. Before Socrates there was no scientific ethic, only the old aristocratic ideal ; you are, by the fortune of birth, a fine man —an aristocrat, or an Athenian, or something of the sort ; and fine men do fine things, are proud, sporting, chivalrous, give freely of their native energy without counting costs. Socrates introduced the democratic ethic, which is utilitarian ; it is not vulgar—you are not encouraged to save your skin or money— but it is ego-centric, you seek first and foremost to save your soul. That is the guiding principle of the post-Aristotelian schools, and so of Horace's Stoicism. It is a lofty ideal compared to some, and it is significant of the enlightenment of the Augustan régime to reflect that a poet of Horace's persuasion, a pro-Stoic and a "simple-lifer," would have belonged, under the post-Augustan emperors, to the opposition.[1] But being fundamentally egotistic, it does not survive the practical test of life, and it appears in the end as a form of

[1] Cf., *e.g.*, Horace on the Scythians (*Odes*, III. xxiv.) with Tacitus on the Germans.

pessimism. A man may have gained his own soul by this principle, but he has gradually lost the whole world in doing so ; and "what profit is that" to anybody ? It is remarkable how much the idea of being at peace, not with the universe or with other men (though these ideas occur) but with himself, enters into Horace's conception of the ultimate happiness possible to an individual. *Quid te tibi reddat amicum, Epist.*, I. xviii. 101 ; *mihi me reddentis agelli, Epist.*, I. xiv. 1. And the pessimism culminates in a feeling which, as Ferrero [1] has well remarked, haunts Horace's more serious writings ; " at the extreme limit of this moral vacuum "—say rather,ʻreligious vacuum—'' comes the fear of death.''

There is, moreover, the particular failure in Horace's own active life which I have already emphasised. Augustan reconstruction would, I believe, have had a far deeper and more lasting influence if the emperor could have achieved, what was then impossible, the overthrow of the Sophistic apologue and the establishment of a national drama ; a thing which was not to take place in European history until the rise of the English drama, founded as that was, not upon a philosophical, but a religious basis. In the meantime, the really enduring and vital factor in the Augustan moral system was the poetry, not of Horace, but of Virgil ; it was in his imaginative mysticism that Christianity, through the Middle Ages, found its one Pagan affinity.

The Augustan reconstruction, then, despite a large measure of temporary success, ultimately failed ; and Horace in various ways shared in the moral limitations of his age. But poetry is a mode of action ; it is what the poet does that matters, not what he thinks ; and the deeds of individual men, in whatever sphere, are often better than their own views, sometimes almost unrecognisably so. The tone of Horace's writing, its *morale*, is prevailingly noble ; not because he can, and often does, utter exalted moral sentiments, for that is within the compass of any reflective or moralising person ; but because he can, and often does, give them life, the life of spirited and ringing language ; that is action, and a form of action that is

---

[1] *Greatness and Decline of Rome*, iv. p. 210. He sees it as the result of " uncertainty." I see it rather as the result of too much certainty on the negative side.

within the capacity of very few. That manliness may not be an all-sufficing ideal, does not prevent it from being an ideal ; and perhaps there is no poet who excels Horace at infusing into manly sentiments a manly tone, thus making them into positive stimulants. His range, of course, is far from being confined to that. It may be there that he is most spirited :—

> gens quae cremato fortis ab Ilio [1]
> iactata Tuscis aequoribus sacra
> natosque maturosque patres
> pertulit Ausonias ad urbis,
> duris ut ilex tonsa bipennibus
> nigrae feraci frondis in Algido,
> per damna, per caedes, ab ipso
> ducit opes animumque ferro.

It may be in the fifth and sixth odes of the third book that he gets his nearest approach to passion. But his favourite incitement is not to action, it is to endurance, resignation, fortitude. And it must not be forgotten that that lesson, as preached by him, has also its soothing, even its attractive, side. He can help us not merely to bear, but to smile ; he can convey to us the delights of temperate enjoyment, and better, the more lasting delights of simple piety :—

> parvos coronantem marino
> rore deos fragilique myrto.

It is he, finally, who has given to the quintessence of the old Pagan individualist gospel its most triumphant, its truly sublime, expression. *Veni vidi vici* was, after all, what Rosalind calls it, but a thrasonical brag ; there is a still finer, a more victorious, perfect indicative first personal singular, and it is in the great ode to Maecenas—a sustained triumph of poetical skill—that it is used to finest effect.

> ille potens sui
> laetusque deget, cui licet in diem
> dixisse : " vixi ! cras vel atra
> nube polum Pater occupato
> vel sole puro ; non tamen irritum,
> quodcunque retro est, efficiet neque
> diffinget infectumque reddet,
> quod fugiens semel hora vexit."

[1] What a line ! Who does not thrill to it ?

That word is the poem's climax indeed, but it is followed up by a great phrase in a fine setting—" Fortune " is the topic—

> laudo manentem ; si celeris quatit
> pennas, resigno quae dedit et *mea*
> *virtute me involvo* probamque
> pauperiem sine dote quaero.

As he presently escapes from material shipwreck in his two-oared skiff, we may reflect, if we are curious-minded, that in modern times the captain would have shot him if he had tried to squeeze in before Lalage ; but we must recognise that, though it comes to us from an unchivalrous and fundamentally still barbaric age, to take refuge from calamity by cloaking oneself in one's own virtue represents a high ideal, and an ideal that Christianity itself can only better by transcending, not by ignoring. The Pagan gospel is an indispensable pre-liminary ; without independence there can be no such thing as love. Many a Christian poet, on the other hand, has been inferior to Horace in positive religious value, less actively conducive to his readers' spiritual salvation.

And he is certainly a great artist ; the purest Roman literature can show us, Virgil having more of genius and in-equality. Horace has indeed, as I have remarked already, a strictly limited array of themes ; though all are good ones. He has even, if my analysis of his form is not most grossly out—he has even, in by far the greater portion of his maturest and most characteristic work, but one single type of poem ! Yet not even by his own custom can his infinite variety be staled. It is what he does that tells, and he hardly ever does the same thing twice. His subjects he repeats innumerably, he almost never repeats himself. What the ancients cared about in poetry was two things ; the soul of the poem, and its body ; the structure, and the surface ; the composition, and the style. His treatment is always unique, his language al-ways individual. He takes over all the conventions that were available for him ; but he uses them for his own ends ; they are but a medium for his meaning. He cannot be translated ; metre and language are fused into his work ; the effect cannot be extricated from them. In Satire and Epistle, Juvenal himself is by comparison a mere slogger ; his sledge-hammer method dulls. The Odes, in addition to what has above been claimed for their sheer art, should get more credit for the material selected for them ; it is consistently so bright and beautiful ; the radiant Græco-Roman god-world, the magical Greek names—*Quid fles, Asterie ?* And if there were nothing else that could be claimed for them, they would still remain the only integral representative of the original Greek song. A " Roman copy " in sculpture means a debased copy ; but these we can well believe to be the equals in grace and charm of their exemplars. From Homer to Sophocles had been the great creative age of ancient literature ; from Euripides and Plato to the Alexandrians, the analytical and critical and fanciful. Horace alone of ancient poets is an original singer of the first order, and at the same time a student and critic ; a completely conscious artist, with a consistently thought-out and thoroughly applied theory of poetry.

Horace's poetry is good for this age ; but not sufficient. With a spiritual outlook, not truly possessed perhaps but at our command if sought, incomparably in advance of his, what we most need is poets that will express it in terms as durable, and with an art as large. At the universities adult men are still allowed to study him, on condition of imitating in Latin exercises, or of emending or explaining, his bare text ; but attempt to extend his work, and neither a university nor any other institution evolved by modern society would have a word to say to you. In default of a successor, Horace will, for those who care for moral poetry, still remain a formative and powerful influence ; nor is it likely, nor desirable, that even a successor should ever oust him from that niche ; a fate which could only overtake his work if history should continue for many centuries along the lines upon which it is now proceeding, and materialism and militarism should achieve in time a second eclipse of culture, a new Middle Age.

EXPLICIT

Non missura cutem nisi plena cruoris hirudo.

INDEX